The Gothic Other

The Gothic Other

*Racial and Social Constructions
in the Literary Imagination*

edited by
RUTH BIENSTOCK ANOLIK
and DOUGLAS L. HOWARD

McFarland & Company, Inc., Publishers
Jefferson, North Carolina, and London

Renée L. Bergland's essay "The Diseased State of the Public Mind" is from pages 49–68 of *The National Uncanny,* ©2000 by Renée Bergland, and are reprinted with the permission of the University Press of New England.

LIBRARY OF CONGRESS CATALOGUING-IN-PUBLICATION DATA

The Gothic other : racial and social constructions in the literary imagination / edited by Ruth Bienstock Anolik and Douglas L. Howard.
    p.   cm.
    Includes bibliographical references and index.

    ISBN-13: 978-0-7864-1858-9
    (softcover : 50# alkaline paper) ∞

    1. English literature — History and criticism.   2. Gothic revival (Literature) — Great Britain.   3. American literature — History and criticism.   4. Gothic revival (Literature) — United States.   5. Difference (Psychology) in literature.   6. Horror tales — History and criticism.   7. Social classes in literature.   8. Race in literature.   9. Fear in literature.   I. Anolik, Ruth Bienstock, 1952–   II. Howard, Douglas L., 1966–
    PR408.G68G68   2004
    820.9'11 — dc22   2004008618

British Library cataloguing data are available

Manufactured in the United States of America

Cover images: foreground ©2004 Clipart; background ©2004 PhotoSpin.

McFarland & Company, Inc., Publishers
 Box 611, Jefferson, North Carolina 28640
  www.mcfarlandpub.com

To Bob, Jonathan, Rachel, and Sarah,
for all the uncooked meals, with love and thanks
— RBA

To Jennifer and my family, for all of their love and support
— DLH

Acknowledgments

Ruth Bienstock Anolik thanks June Bienstock for her unswerving support; Barbie Zelizer, whose guidance helped to sustain the trajectory of this project; Barri Gold for her thoughtful comments; Carol Bernstein, Sandra Berwind, Susan Dean and Peter Briggs, of the English Department of Bryn Mawr College, for their careful reading and kind corrections; Bill di Canzio for his interpretative skills; Dale Kinney, dean of the Graduate School of Arts and Sciences at Bryn Mawr College, for allowing the time necessary to complete this project. And thanks to Douglas Howard, an indefatigable co-editor, and to our patient and talented writers.

Douglas L. Howard would like to thank all of the contributors: Renée Bergland, Joseph Bodziock, Gavin Budge, Stephanie Burley, Soledad Caballero, Eugenia DeLamotte, Katherine Henry, Karen Kingsbury, Daphne Lamothe, Erik Marshall, Steven Schneider, John Stone, and Sherry Truffin for their inspired work that made this collection possible, and for their professionalism and patience through this entire process. He would also like to thank Ruth Bienstock Anolik for envisioning this project and for all of her hard work in bringing these readings out into the light.

Table of Contents

Introduction:
The Dark Unknown

RUTH BIENSTOCK ANOLIK

The Gothic is marked by an anxious encounter with otherness, with the dark and mysterious unknown. From its early manifestations in the turbulent eighteenth century, this seemingly escapist mode has provided a useful ground upon which to safely confront very real fears and horrors. In fact, as Butler suggests in "The Woman at the Window,"[1] the very qualities that appear to identify the Gothic mode as irrelevant escapism allow for confrontation with real fears, establishing through artifice the distance that Burke,[2] writing of the Sublime, prescribes for a meaningful response to overwhelming phenomena.

Traditionally, the Gothic represents the fearful unknown as the inhuman Other: the supernatural or monstrous manifestation, inhabiting mysterious space, that symbolizes all that is irrational, uncontrollable and incomprehensible. However, with the advent of the Enlightenment and empirical science, as supernatural and religious mysteries were demystified, the sources of haunting dried up; conventional ghosts and monsters lost some of their frightening potency. Moreover, as the collection of essays *Frontier Gothic*[3] persuasively indicates, with the closing of the American frontier, and presumably all other geographic frontiers in the world, the locus of the unknown was colonized and denatured; ghosts were displaced from their habitations. In "The Legend of Sleepy Hollow" (1820), Washington Irving provides yet another, still viable, explanation for the denaturing of ghosts in the modern world: ghosts, and the stories that give them life, cannot endure in a fast-paced, ever-changing society.

1

> Local tales and superstitions thrive best in these sheltered, long settled retreats; but they are trampled under foot by the shifting throng that forms the population of most of our country places. Besides, there is no encouragement for ghosts in the generality of our villages, for they have scarce had time to take their first nap and turn themselves in their graves, before their surviving friends have traveled away from the neighborhood, so that when they turn out of a night to walk the rounds, they have no acquaintance left to call upon.[4]

Yet, as the writers of the introduction to *Frontier Gothic* suggest, the ghosts and monsters who are explained and displaced — as the result of science, change, and discovery — do not disappear; they relocate to new dark spaces, beyond the "frontiers in social, racial, and gender politics"[5] and consciousness.

The writers of the essays that compose *The Gothic Other* examine texts in which Gothic fear is relocated onto the figure of the racial and social Other, the Other who replaces the supernatural ghost or grotesque monster as the code for mystery and danger, becoming, ultimately, as horrifying, threatening and unknowable as the typical Gothic manifestation. The trope that lies at the center of this collection of essays — the racial or social construction of the Gothic Other — is, like the Gothic mode in which it appears, powerful and pervasive indeed. The range of essays reveals that writers from many canons and cultures are attracted to the always anxious and transgressive Gothic as a ready medium for expression of racial and social anxieties, and are drawn to the horrifying and monstrous figure of the Gothic Other as a ready code for the figuration of these anxieties.

The tendency to personalize the unknown Other has been noted by a number of critics. In her compelling essay "The Spectralization of the Other in *The Mysteries of Udolpho*,"[6] Castle makes a powerful case for the relocation of ghostliness onto material individuals, in response to Enlightenment dismantling of the supernatural and to Romantic valorization of the subjective self. Other critics note the racializing of this tendency, the projection of racial anxieties onto the figure of the Gothic Other. In his influential essay "Fenimore Cooper's White Novels," D. H. Lawrence identifies the figure of the displaced Native American as the ghost that haunts American culture.[7] More recently books by Bellin[8] (who takes his title from Lawrence's essay) and Bergland[9] (one of the contributors to this collection) consider the haunting of the American literary imagination by the figure of the Native American. These writers work within the critical tradition established by Toni Morrison, who stakes out the territory in "Romancing the Shadow,"[10] identifying the dark Gothicism of American literature with the African American presence in American culture. (An example of Morrison's vast influence and inspiration is the recently published *Romancing the Shadow*,[11] devoted to essays that develop the insights on Poe and race that support Morrison's essay.) Nor are studies of the construction of the Gothic Other as racial Other limited to American literature. Malchow,[12] arguing that the fear of the racial and cultural Other is buried in the whole genre of English Gothic horror, reads Dracula and Frankenstein's monster as codifying the racial Other. Schmitt,[13] in an Anglicization of Morrison's argument, suggests that English notions of national identity are derived by opposition to the horrifyingly un–English figures who inhabit Gothic novels; the Gothic heroine, besieged by depraved foreigners, becomes the code for a similarly threatened England.

While the close focus adopted by these critics is useful in affording the reader a profound understanding of each argument, and a sense of how a discrete body of texts, a specific canon, constructs a specific racial group as the dangerous Gothic Other, larger contexts may be neglected when a tight focus upon a single canon is too carefully sustained. This limitation is indicated by a comment of Arnold Krupat (who himself focuses on Native American literature) on Toni Morrison's work: "despite her admirable desire to map a new geographical 'space for discovery, intellectual adventure, and close exploration' ... she does not find a place within that space for the literature of 'the indigenous American'"[14]

The purpose of *The Gothic Other* is to find common ground within the discursive space delineated by the earlier critics to contain the array of figures and literatures that inform a multicultural and multinational canon and to unfold a larger context of literary and critical texts within which the closely focused investigations of the Gothic Other as racial Other operate. The essays in this work also move beyond the work of earlier scholars in considering the demonization of the social Other (defined by differences in class, social status and religion). In bringing together a diverse group of critical texts, each focused upon a particular instance of Gothic othering, as it is deployed in a broad range of literary and filmic texts; this collection will work to contextualize and synthesize the interpretations of the writers of the earlier studies, outlining the larger framework within which they co-exist. It works to create a critical space within which various studies of the trope of the racially and socially constructed Gothic Other, including the essays in this collection, can converse.

In undertaking a mediating role, this collection presupposes the canonical paradigm that Lauter posits: a model of multiple canons, a system of comparative multicultural literatures.[15] As Lauter and Krupat[16] indicate in their studies of Native American literature, the model of multiple canons suggests that no single individual or group is able to possess the entire canon of literature. Thus, the canon, within a multicultural paradigm, is figured as yet another unknowable and mysterious Gothic space. And yet such texts and canons do have much to say to each other. *The Gothic Other: Racial and Social Constructions in the Literary Imagination* uncovers a critical common ground for such discussion to take place. The project of negotiation undertaken by this collection develops, then, the work of writers like Brogan[17] and Goldner[18] whose work begins to discover in the transgressive Gothic mode possibilities for textual negotiation.

One way to read this collection is as a negotiating text, a text that presents investigations of a recurring trope to effect translations between the canons of the comparative literatures of various countries and cultures. In doing so, the essays in this volume allow the reader to scrutinize the gaps that exist between distinct imaginative and critical texts and between the disparate canons, expanding the focus of speculation to the interplay between texts and canons, to discover in the repetition and transformations of a single powerful and influential Gothic trope the meanings and opportunities for interpretation that Hillis Miller argues is generated within the gaps in instances of repetition.[19]

One example of the benefits to be derived from such transgressive investigation is afforded by a comparative reading of Dracula, certainly one of the most powerful and haunting figures of the Gothic Other. The figure of the vampire operates as a critical Rorschach test: the meanings that critics discover in Dracula depend upon what they bring to their reading. And so, in their respective monographs, Halberstam[20] convincingly argues that the figure of the vampire (grotesque, afraid of light, thirsty for blood) may be read as an emblem for the Jew; Deane (citing a vast array of critics who read Dracula as a sign for the foreign degenerate Irish) makes a compelling case for reading Dracula as the absentee Irish landlord, dependent on a "supply of soil"[21]; and Valente[22] reads the figure of Dracula as positing a critique of the racial anxieties toward the Irish that it appears to provoke.[23] A number of writers in this collection also turn to the figure of the vampire as the expression of Gothic horror in the face of the unknown. Stephen Schneider reads the late twentieth-century filmic representation of a vampire-like African American seducer as a code for racial anxieties. Gavin Budge discovers class anxieties at the core of an influential, early nineteenth-century depiction of the vampire and, finally, Erik Marshall discovers, within a late twentieth-century filmic depiction of an American Dracula, a fantastic deconstruction of the category of the Other. The convergence within a single volume of complementary readings such as these reveals the abundant possibilities offered by the figure of the vampire, a figure of Gothic Otherness that is always available to overdetermined readings, readings that gain added richness when broadly contextualized.

The conversation between the writers in this collection is also evident in the convergent and divergent use that they make of some key critical thinkers. For example, in their quite different readings of the vampire figure, both Budge and Schneider turn to Sedgwick's observation of the homosexual panic to be found in the Gothic mode. (The use of the trope of the Gothic Other as a projection of sexual anxieties is a large topic worthy of further development.) Not surprisingly, in Part I of this collection a number of writers build upon Morrison's theories, expanding her observations to remark upon other instances of the demonization of the racial Other — Mulatto, Native American, Chinese, Indian — through the deployment of the trope that Morrison associates with the Africanist figure. Several writers of essays in Part I as well as a number of writers of the essays in Part II —(tracing the demonizationing of the religious Other) and Part III (focusing upon the figure of the demonized Other from another social and economic class)—connect the Morrisonian notion of the dark Other with the Freudian model of the uncanny. The writers of the essays in Part IV of this collection turn to Goddu to make meaning of the response of members of marginalized and demonized groups to the trope observed by Morrison. These essays consider instances of what Goddu calls "haunting back"[24]— in which members of a marginalized group resist demonization and instead figure members of the dominant oppressive group as inhumanly and frighteningly monstrous— members of a subordinate group "use the gothic to haunt back, re-working the gothic's conventions to intervene in discourse that would demonize them."[25]

The essays in this collection, written by an array of critically and geographically diverse writers, consider a broad range of print and filmic texts and also focus attention upon the question of the Gothic canon. The writers of these essays examine previously neglected texts or read canonical texts in a new way, revealing the affinity of a range of writers for Gothic strategies. The discussions in this collection indicate the pervasiveness of the Gothic mode, haunting texts not generally associated with this traditionally marginalized tradition. In exploring the unexpected manifestation of Gothic tropology in texts not conventionally located within the Gothic canon, these essays demonstrate the indebtedness of seemingly non–Gothic texts to the Gothic tradition and encourage questions about the resistance of the transgressive Gothic to conventional demarcations of canon. The Gothic canon, like the multicultural canons of multicultural literature is, then, aptly figured as unknown and unpossessable Gothic space; its borders are permeable and undefined. Certainly, one of the attractions of the Gothic mode to the marginalized writer — and many of the writers discussed in this collection are marginalized in some way — is its resistance to canonical sovereignty by any one group, an attraction articulated by Hawthorne in his Preface to *The House of the Seven Gables,* in which he imagines

> laying out a street that infringes upon nobody's private rights, and appropriating a lot of land which had no visible owner, and building a house, of materials long in use for constructing castles in the air.[26]

In this Hawthorne speaks for all writers who discover in the vast, unpossessable and previously disdained and disregarded Gothic mode, a space to exert narrative authority.

Although the essays in this collection are categorized by the figure that is constructed as the Gothic Other, the interplay between the essays invites the reader to organize and read the essays by other taxonomies as well. For example, a number of writers invite a Wildean interpretation of the Gothic; read together, their essays present a compelling case that the art of the Gothic influences the lives, or the perceived lives, of characters and writers who fall within its shadows. Other essays share a Foucauldian approach, identifying in the figure of the unknown and unknowable Other a source of frightening epistemologic power. In another unexpected interplay, the figure of Satan, the iconic supernatural Other, appears in a number of texts discussed, indicating common ground in seemingly disparate texts. Readings of the essay in this collection could also be organized by the culture, nationality, gender or sexual orientation of the writer; by the type of monstrosity deployed –for example, the figure of the vampire; by the medium of the text discussed — three of our essayists discover evidence of Gothic Othering in film; or by other arrangements that suggest themselves. We hope that each reader will discover new meanings within the interstices of the essays in this collection.

Part I of this collection, "Demonizing the Racial Other, Humanizing the Self," comprises essays that consider texts in which the racial Other is figured as the Gothic Other. This figuring has a long and infamous history within the Gothic tradition, from the early constructions of the darkly Italian villains in the English Gothic of Walpole and Radcliffe, through the swarthy Bertha Rochester of Brontë's *Jane Eyre* and beyond, finding trans–Atlantic expression in American Gothic literature, in Brown's darkly disruptive Carwin (in *Wieland*) and his successors.

Eugenia DeLamotte, in "White Terror, Black Dreams: Gothic Con-

structions of Race in the Nineteenth Century," provides a valuable introduction to "Demonizing the Racial Other, Humanizing the Self" and a
helpful entry into the entire volume as well. DeLamotte, whose earlier
ground breaking study *The Perils of the Night*[27] identifies the relationship
of the Gothic to social structures, contextualizes the construction of the
racialized Other in both British and American Gothic literature. Noting
the "uncanny" parallel between "the history of racial formation" and the
formation of the Gothic genre, DeLamotte focuses on Radcliffe's *The Italian* and Dacre's *Zofloya* to trace the development of the trope of the racialized Other. In Pauline Hopkins's *Of One Blood; or, The Hidden Self*,
DeLamotte discovers an example of opposition to this trope, in Hopkins's
"concern to contest the color line as the central mystified metaphor of
Anglo Gothic." Drawing on Morrison's concept of the "African persona,"
DeLamotte discovers that "behind the fears of the dark, racialized others
on which the Gothic construction of whiteness hinges is the unspeakable
Other of that construction: the fear that there is no such thing as whiteness or even race," the fear that the black Other constructed by the Gothic
text is not essentially different from the white subject that is also a construction of the text.[28]

In "Slavery and Civic Recovery: Gothic Interventions in Whitman
and Weld," Katherine Henry examines the figuring of the slave and of
slavery in Whitman's temperance novel, *Franklin Evans*, and in Weld's
anti-slavery pamphlet, "American Slavery As It Is." Henry argues that
Whitman represents the Creole slave, wife of the white eponymous alcoholic, as the repressed Other of the Gothic imagination, who must die so
that her husband can be free of his disease. Surprisingly, Henry locates a
similar representation in Weld's anti-slavery pamphlet, in which the slave
appears as the owner's demonic Other and slavery is defined as a disease
of white selfhood that must be cured by and for the whites.

In "*Cane*: Jean Toomer's Gothic Black Modernism," Daphne
Lamothe, like Henry, considers the image of interracial union in a
quasi–Gothic narrative. Lamothe argues that Toomer struggles with the
boundaries constructed through racism that define interracial union, and
its product, as a source of transgressive Gothic horror. Lamothe traces
Toomer's anxious response to the categorizations of racism and argues
that Toomer discovers in the figure of the mulatto a means to synthesize
the vexing racial categories.

As in Henry's discussion of Whitman's novel, and Lamothe's discussion of Toomer, Steven Jay Schneider examines the motif of the mixed couple as the emblem of encountering the Other.[29] In "Mixed Blood Couples:
Monsters and Miscegenation in U.S. Horror Cinema," Schneider focuses

on the Gothic icon of the hero-villain as it manifests in the protagonist of the "race horror" film of the late twentieth century.[30] Schneider examines the dynamic of interracial coupling in a number of race horror films and discovers that the roles of monster and victim are ambiguous, shifting in meaning and open to multiple and even contradictory interpretations.

Other writers in this section supplement Morrison's questions regarding the "Africanist character" with the questions raised by figures that exemplify other racial and cultural differences. In her essay "Diseased States, Public Minds: Native American Ghosts in Early National Literature," Renée L. Bergland, responding to Lawrence, reads the Native American as the "national uncanny." She argues that the dominant discourses of American nationalism at the close of the eighteenth century presumed that the inevitable completion of Indian Removal would be accomplished through impenetrable national borders that would exclude all people of darkness. Bergland shows that Brown challenges this repressive national model in a novel peopled with white sleepwalkers and ghostly Indians who become indistinguishable in a region that is difficult to define.

In her essay "Yellow Peril, Dark Hero: Fu Manchu and the 'Gothic Bedevilment' of Racist Intent," Karen Kingsbury reads within the character of Fu-Manchu — who inhabits Sax Rohmer's popular early twentieth-century texts — Yellow Peril fears "deepened with dark undertones of occult and conspiratorial mythology and anti-immigrant suspicions flavored with the seductive flair of Oriental Gothicism."

Douglas L. Howard's essay "A Return to the Caves: E.M. Forster's Gothic Passage" focuses on Western misinterpretation of Indian mystery in *A Passage to India*. In demonstrating that the modern Englishwoman, Adela, dismisses supernatural explanations and substitutes the Indian, Aziz, as the encoded dangerous Other in the Marabar caves, Howard delineates the movement of the Gothic imagination from unenlightened representations of the supernatural Other to equally benighted representations of the racial Other as a source of danger, sexual and otherwise. Howard argues that the reader, too, is implicated in the search for meaning within the gaps and silences of Forster's novel, the motifs that link this modern text to the Gothic canon.

The writers of the essays that compose Part II, "Demonizing the Religious Other, Humanizing the Self," explore another aspect of the traditionally unknowable dark Italian (and Catholic) villains of Walpole and Radcliffe, a characteristic that also surfaces in the figure of the dangerously mysterious Wandering Jew who appears in a number of Gothic novels, including Lewis's *The Monk* and Maturin's *Melmoth the Wanderer*: the quality of dangerous religious Otherness.

In "Gothic Routes, or the Thrills of Ethnography: Frances Calderon de la Barca's *Life in Mexico*," Soledad Caballero demonstrates the continuing power of the anti–Catholic tropes that inform the Gothic mode from its earliest moments. Caballero argues that Frances Calderon de la Barca's observations of Catholic life in Mexico were directly influenced by the dark representations of the Catholic Church in the works of major Gothic writers: Radcliffe and Lewis. In her essay, Caballero makes some troubling connections between the project of the Gothic and the project of ethnography.

In "The Infamous Svengali: George Du Maurier's Satanic Jew," Ruth Bienstock Anolik focuses on the figure of Svengali who, like Dracula and Frankenstein's monster, is a figure of Gothic Otherness that breaks out of the confines of the text that engenders him (Du Maurier's *Trilby*) to haunt the popular imagination. Anolik argues that as the dehumanized and demonized Other troubles the realism of Du Maurier's text, so do the Gothic tropes deployed in the cause of racism vex the movement of history.

The essays in Part III, "Dark Master, Dark Slave: Class Hatred and Class Fear," highlight moments in which class hatred and class fear is displaced onto the figure of the Gothic Other. In her essay "The Death of Zofloya, or The Moor as Epistemological Limit," Stephanie Burley locates an early instance of demonization of the servant that is present most famously in James's "The Turn of the Screw."[31] Burley's essay discovers epistemological fears within Dacre's text and identifies the Gothic danger emanating from the figure of the Moorish slave as the danger of powerful knowledge, appropriated by a racial and social subordinate.

The other two essays in this section that consider the Gothic monster as emblem of unbridled social power tap into the pervasive and enduring representation of the dangerous Gothic patriarch beginning with Walpole's Manfred (lord of the Castle of Otranto), who is figured as an uncontrollable source of sexual and social danger. Gavin Budge fixes upon the figure of the vampire to discover the coded representation of aristocracy, a social category that is figured as a morally degenerate drain on society. In "'The Vampyre': Romantic Metaphysics and the Aristocratic Other," Budge argues that Polidori's narrative figures the aristocratic Other in terms of decadent vampirism. Within the ambivalence of the aristocratic figure — Lord Ruthven is at once repulsively evil and fascinatingly attractive, threatening to supplant the "natural" moral intuitions of Aubrey and of the reader with artificial values — Budge suggests that the horror in the story consists of the breakdown of the distinction between middle-class and aristocratic values. In "'Screaming While School Was in Session': The

Construction of Monstrosity in Stephen King's Schoolhouse Gothic," Sherry R. Truffin also locates the Gothic Other as the possessor of social power, in this case the schoolteacher. Truffin argues that King revises and updates the Gothic, inventing the "schoolhouse gothic," that reconfigures the familiar forms and institutions of power so that they continue to horrify the modern reader. In considering moments in which the subject of the patriarchy, the powerful white male, is shown as demonic from the perspective of the powerless, Budge and Truffin anticipate the focus of the essays in the following section.

The essays of Part IV, "When the Self Is the Other: Humanizing the Other, Demonizing the Oppressor," highlight moments in which the Other, who is conventionally demonized, inverts the roles and represents the Subject at the centers of power as the demonized Other. As noted above, examples of this strategy may be noted in the essays of Budge and Truffin.

Joseph Bodziock's essay, "The Cage of Obscene Birds: The Myth of the Southern Garden in Frederick Douglass's *My Bondage and My Freedom*," delineates an instance of what Goddu calls "haunting back." Bodziock argues that Douglass deploys Gothic tropes that would resonant with his intended audience; Douglass, however, subverts the trope of the Dark Other, figuring slaveholders as the white demons who inhabit the ruined garden of the South.

John Stone's essay, "Gothic in the Himalayas: Powell and Pressburger's *Black Narcissus*," turns to film for its text. Stone examines the consequence of Western misinterpretations of India, and argues that the film traces the resistance by India and the Indians to the Western tendency to Gothicize the Other. The conventional paradigm is inverted as the nuns, armed with expectations of discovering the Gothic Other in India, become Othered themselves through madness and displacement. (The conventional paradigm is also paradoxically sustained in that, as Caballero indicates in her essay, nuns, like all Catholics, are traditionally represented as the dark Other of the Gothic. This is another example of the critical conversations to be found in this collection: Stone and Caballero both turn to Sedgwick's discussion of the image of the veil to argue their perceptions of the figure of the veiled nun in the texts they consider.)

In Part V, "When the Other Is the Self: Deconstructing the Categories," this collection comes full circle. The collection comes with DeLamotte's argument that the essential fear of the Gothic is that there are actually no categories of Otherness. Many of the essays in this collection examine writers who engage in the hard work of demonizing the Other to ensure that the boundaries between the self and the racial and social Other are excessively visible, all in the cause of self-definition. These writers are driven by what Henry identifies as "the anxiety not of difference but of sameness." Other writers in this collection work to problematize the boundaries in various ways: Lamothe discovers in Toomer an attempt to make a tentative move toward synthesis; the writers considered in Part IV interrogate the barriers by inverting the paradigm to show the Other as Subject and to assert that from that perspective the hegemonic Subject is the actual demonic Other. In the final essay of this collection, "Defanging Dracula: The Disappearing Other in Coppola's *Bram Stoker's Dracula*," Erik Marshall discovers a Gothic text that celebrates and yearns for the deconstruction of the category of the Other. He locates the old anxiety of sameness reconfigured as the postmodern fantasy of the Gothic: the hopeful expectation that the Other *is* the same as the self. In his essay, Marshall identifies Coppola's cinematic version of Dracula as a revision that effaces the category of the Other, so powerfully deployed in so many texts. Marshall argues that Coppola recasts Dracula as a sexual liberator in repressed Victorian England and reframes the relationship of Dracula and Lucy as a supernatural love story. In this transformation, Coppola represents a postmodern fantasy of transcendence, imaginatively suggesting that the deconstruction of the category of the horrifying Other may be effected through the union of the self with the Other.

Notes

1. Marilyn Butler, "The Woman at the Window: Ann Radcliffe in the Novels of Mary Wollstonecraft and Jane Austen," in *Gender and Literary Voice*, ed. Janet Todd (New York: Holmes and Meier, 1980).

2. Edmund Burke, *A Philosophical Enquiry into the Origin of Our Ideas of the Sublime and Beautiful* (New York: Columbia University Press, 1958).

3. David Mogen, Scott P. Sanders, and Joanne B. Karpinski. *Frontier Gothic: Terror and Wonder at the Frontier in American Literature* (Rutherford: Fairleigh Dickinson University Press, 1993).

4. Washington Irving, "The Legend of Sleepy Hollow," in *The Norton Anthology of American Literature*, 2nd edition (New York: Norton, 1985).

5. David Mogen, Scott P. Sanders, and Joanne B. Karpinski, introduction to *Frontier Gothic: Terror and Wonder at the Frontier in American Literature* (Rutherford: Fairleigh Dickinson University Press, 1993), 26.

6. Terry Castle, "The Spectralization of the Other in *The Mysteries of Udolpho*," in *The Female Thermometer: Eighteenth Century Culture and the Invention of the Uncanny* (New York: Oxford University Press, 1995).

7. D. H. Lawrence, "Fenimore Cooper's White Novels," in *Studies in Classic American Literature* (New York: Viking Press, 1964). This is a particularly apt observation; typically, the Gothic ghost returns after being murdered and displaced.

8. Joshua David Bellin, *The Demon of the Continent: Indians and the Shaping of American Literature* (Philadelphia: University of Pennsylvania Press, 2001).

9. Renée Bergland, *The National Uncanny: Indian Ghosts and American Subjects* (Hanover: University Press of New England, 2000).

10. Toni Morrison, "Romancing the Shadow," in *Playing in the Dark: Whiteness and the Literary Imagination* (New York: Vintage, 1993).

11. J. Gerald Kennedy and Lilian Weissberg, *Romancing the Shadow: Poe and Race* (Oxford: Oxford University Press, 2001).

12. H. L. Malchow, *Gothic Images of Race in Nineteenth-Century Britain* (Stanford: Stanford University Press, 1996).

13. Cannon Schmitt, *Alien Nation: Nineteenth-Century Gothic Fictions and English Nationality* (Philadelphia: University of Pennsylvania Press, 1997).

14. Arnold Krupat, "Review: Red Matters," *College English* 63 (May): 655–661, 657.

15. Paul Lauter, *Canons and Contexts* (New York: Oxford University Press, 1991).

16. Arnold Krupat, *The Voice in the Margin: Native American Literature and the Canon* (Berkeley: University of California Press, 1989).

17. Kathleen Brogan, "American Stories of Cultural Haunting: Tales of Heirs and Ethnographers," *College English* 57 (1995): 149–165; *Cultural Haunting: Ghosts and Ethnicity in Recent American Literature* (Charlottesville: University Press of Virginia, 1998). Brogan demonstrates that a variety of multicultural writers deploy the figure of the Gothic ghost to recover the suppressed collective past.

18. Ellen Goldner, "Other(ed) Ghosts: Gothicism and the Bonds of Reason in Melville, Chesnutt, and Morrison," *MELUS* 24 (1999): 59–83. Goldner, writing on Melville, Chesnutt and Morrison argues that writers with different "subject position[s] with respect to both the dominant discourse and the historical moment" (66) reveal the Gothicism of slavery, a system that constructs the racial Other as the Other.

19. J. Hillis Miller, *Fiction and Repetition: Seven English Novels* (Cambridge: Harvard University Press, 1982).

20. Judith Halberstam, *Skin Shows: Gothic Horror and the Technology of Monsters* (Durham: Duke University Press, 1995).

21. Seamus Deane, *Strange Country: Modernity and Nationhood in Irish Writing since 1790* (New York: Oxford University Press, 1997), 89.

22. Joseph Valente, *Dracula's Crypt: Bram Stoker, Irishness, and the Question of Blood* (Urbana: University of Illinois Press, 2001).

23. The flexibility of the figure of the vampire, its ability to evolve to meet changing anxieties is evident in Katia Yurguis's "The Dark Gift: Vampires in the AIDS Era," published in *Discoveries*, a student publication of Cornell University.

24. Teresa Goddu, "Haunting Back: Harriet Jacobs, African American Narrative, and the Gothic," in *Gothic America: Narrative, History, and Nation* (New York: Columbia University Press, 1997).

25. Teresa Goddu, "Vampire Gothic," *American Literary History* 11 (1999): 125–141.

26. Nathaniel Hawthorne, *The House of the Seven Gables* (New York: Penguin, 1981), 3.

27. Eugenia C. DeLamotte, *The Perils of the Night: A Feminist Study of Nineteenth-Century Gothic* (New York: Oxford University Press, 1990).

28. This insight anticipates Marshall's conclusions in the final section of this collection: "When the Other Is the Self: Deconstructing the Categories."

29. The relationship between the produce of miscegenation and the Gothic are the focus of Edward's recent study: *Gothic Passages: Racial Ambiguity and the American Gothic* (Iowa City: University of Iowa Press, 2003). Edward's text connects the work of writers like Poe, Melville, Howells and Chesnutt to the concerns of this collection.

30. For a discussion of a related trope, the figure of African American as supernatural angel, see "Black Angel" by Krin Gabbard in *The Chronicle of Higher Education*, June 6, 2003, B15–B16.

31. Wharton's story "Mr. Jones," an interesting companion-piece to James's story, also locates fears of the serving class onto the figure of the servant as demonic ghost. For another discussion of the monstrous figuring of the lower classes, see "The Reading Monster," in

which Patrick Brantlinger traces the association between the figure of the mob and the Gothic monster (*The Reading Lesson: The Threat of Mass Literacy in Nineteenth-Century British Fiction.* Bloomington: Indiana University Press, 1998).

Works Cited

Bellin, Joshua David. *The Demon of the Continent: Indians and the Shaping of American Literature.* Philadelphia: University of Pennsylvania Press, 2001.

Bergland, Renée. *The National Uncanny: Indian Ghosts and American Subjects.* Hanover: University Press of New England, 2000.

Brantlinger, Patrick. *The Reading Lesson: The Threat of Mass Literacy in Nineteenth-Century British Fiction.* Bloomington: Indiana University Press, 1998.

Brogan, Kathleen. "American Stories of Cultural Haunting: Tales of Heirs and Ethnographers." *College English* 57 (1995): 149–65.

_____. *Cultural Haunting: Ghosts and Ethnicity in Recent American Literature.* Charlottesville: University Press of Virginia, 1998.

Burke, Edmund. *A Philosophical Enquiry into the Origin of Our Ideas of the Sublime and Beautiful.* New York: Columbia University Press, 1958.

Butler, Marilyn. "The Woman at the Window: Ann Radcliffe in the Novels of Mary Wollstonecraft and Jane Austen." In *Gender and Literary Voice.* Edited by Janet Todd. New York: Holmes and Meier, 1980.

Castle, Terry. "The Spectralization of the Other in *The Mysteries of Udolpho.*" In *The Female Thermometer: Eighteenth Century Culture and the Invention of the Uncanny.* New York: Oxford University Press, 1995.

Deane, Seamus. *Strange Country: Modernity and Nationhood in Irish Writing since 1790.* New York: Oxford University Press, 1997.

DeLamotte, Eugenia C. *The Perils of the Night: A Feminist Study of Nineteenth-Century Gothic.* New York: Oxford University Press, 1990.

Edwards, Justin D. *Gothic Passages: Racial Ambiguity and the American Gothic.* Iowa City: University of Iowa Press, 2003.

Gabbard, Krin. "Black Angel." *The Chronicle of Higher Education.* June 6, 2003, B15–B16.

Goddu, Teresa A. *Gothic American: Narrative, History, and Nation.* New York: Columbia University Press, 1997.

_____. "Vampire Gothic." *American Literary History.* 11(1999): 125–141.

Goldner, Ellen. "Other(ed) Ghosts: Gothicism and the Bonds of Reason in Melville, Chesnutt, and Morrison." *MELUS* 24 (1999): 59–83.

Halberstam, Judith. *Skin Shows: Gothic Horror and the Technology of Monsters.* Durham: Duke University Press, 1995.

Hawthorne, Nathaniel. *The House of the Seven Gables.* New York: Penguin, 1981.

Irving, Washington. "The Legend of Sleepy Hollow." In *The Norton Anthology of American Literature.* 2nd edition. New York: Norton, 1985. Vol. I, 728–753.

Kennedy, J. Gerald, and Lilian Weissberg, *Romancing the Shadow: Poe and Race.* Oxford: Oxford University Press, 2001.

Krupat, Arnold. "Review: Red Matters." *College English* 63 (2001): 655–661.

_____. *The Voice in the Margin: Native American Literature and the Canon.* Berkeley: University of California Press, 1989.

Lauter, Paul. *Canons and Contexts.* New York: Oxford University Press, 1991.

Lawrence, D. H. "Fenimore Cooper's White Novels." In *Studies in Classic American Literature.* New York: Viking Press, 1964.

Malchow, H. L. *Gothic Images of Race in Nineteenth-Century Britain.* Stanford: Stanford University Press, 1996.

Miller, J. Hillis. *Fiction and Repetition: Seven English Novels.* Cambridge: Harvard University Press, 1982.

Mogen, David, Scott P. Sanders, and Joanne B. Karpinski. *Frontier Gothic: Terror and Wonder at the Frontier in American Literature.* Rutherford: Fairleigh Dickinson University Press, 1993.

Morrison, Toni. "Romancing the Shadow." In *Playing in the Dark: Whiteness and the Literary Imagination.* New York: Vintage, 1993.

Mowl, Tim. *Horace Walpole: The Great Outsider.* London: Murray, 1996.

Schmitt, Cannon. *Alien Nation: Nineteenth-Century Gothic Fictions and English Nationality.* Philadelphia: University Of Pennsylvania Press, 1997.

Valente, Joseph. *Dracula's Crypt: Bram Stoker, Irishness, and the Question of Blood.* Urbana: University of Illinois Press, 2001.

Yurguis, Katia. "The Dark Gift: Vampires in the AIDS Era." *Discoveries* (Fall 2002): 9–21.

Part I

Demonizing the Racial Other, Humanizing the Self

1

White Terror, Black Dreams: Gothic Constructions of Race in the Nineteenth Century

Eugenia DeLamotte

"But it is not really difference the oppressor
fears so much as similarity."
— Cherríe Moraga

In over half a century of critical attention to the Gothic, one of the most salient aspects of that genre has been consistently ignored: its long obsession with race. From its rise in the late eighteenth century, through its development over the course of the nineteenth, to its flowering in such works as *Heart of Darkness* and *Absalom, Absalom!* and its continued popularity today, the formation of the genre I will term "Anglo-Gothic" has paralleled uncannily the history of racial formation. Beginning with two historical points of reference — Ann Radcliffe's construction of the reader as a normative center of racial consciousness in *The Italian*, and Charlotte Dacre's narrative enactment in *Zofloya* of the process whereby a biologically racial Other is constituted and demonized — this essay uses Toni Morrison's concept of the "Africanist persona" as a basis for understanding the relationship between these two formations. As their linked history reveals, behind the fears of dark, racialized others on which the Gothic construction of whiteness hinges is the unspeakable Other of that construction: the fear that there is no such thing as whiteness, or even race.

The impetus behind this essay, then, is a perception that the Gothic should be retheorized in light of Morrison's call for attention to "the way black people ignite critical moments of discovery or change or emphasis in literature not written by them." Her term "Africanist persona" refers to "symbolic figurations of blackness"—"the denotative and connotative blackness that African peoples have come to signify, as well as the entire range of views, assumptions, readings, and misreadings that accompany Eurocentric learning about these people." Morrison's argument centers specifically around "the process of organizing American coherence through a distancing Africanism." The present essay looks more broadly at both British and American literature and at the construction of the persona, more generally, of a racialized Other rather than an exclusively Africanist Other. It also looks more narrowly only at Gothic fiction, although Morrison's location of the Africanist persona at the very core of Euro-American literature strikes an interestingly resonant chord with Leslie Fiedler's classic location of the Gothic at its core. Despite this both broader and narrower context, my argument begins from Morrison's basic premise: that "the subject of the dream is the dreamer. The fabrication of an Africanist persona is reflexive; an extraordinary meditation on the self...."[1]

With this premise in mind, what should be a salient fact about the Gothic becomes immediately obvious: the rise and flowering of the Gothic novel in Britain and the U.S. between 1765 and 1850 coincides with the emergence and codification of modern conceptions of "race" as a biological division of humans into separate groups characterized by distinctive, non-overlapping physical, moral, intellectual, and emotional attributes. The idea that race exists biologically has long been discredited by scientists, and recent advances in genetic biology have produced a strong scientific consensus that evolutionary history has not led to the formation of races in the human species.[2] Nonetheless, the idea that race is a biological given continues to have as strong a hold on the popular imagination as does the Gothic itself. Those facts are perhaps related. A brief review of the history of racial formation from the late eighteenth century to 1900 suggests it is no coincidence that the rise and proliferation of this predominantly European and Euro-American genre, focused on anxieties about boundaries and obsessively concerned with marking off a dark mysterious Otherness from some normative coherent self, coincides historically with the rise of conceptions of "race" as a question of essential, biological dividing lines between a normative "white" self and dark, mysterious Others.

In recent years this history has been documented by a range of historians, literary critics, sociologists, scientists, and historians of science, beginning with Thomas Gossett's classic study *Race: The History of an Idea in America* (1963/1997), and including Stephen Jay Gould's *The Mismea-*

sure of Man (1981/1996), Reginald Horsman's *Race and Manifest Destiny* (1981), Kwame Anthony Appiah's "Race" (1990), Ronald Takaki's *Iron Cages: Race and Culture in Nineteenth-Century America* (1979, revised 2000), Alexander Saxton's *The Rise and Fall of the White Republic* (1990), Michael Omi and Howard Winant's *Racial Formation in the United States* (1994), Theodore Allen's *The Invention of the White Race* (1997), Valerie Babb's *Whiteness Visible: The Meaning of Whiteness in American Literature and Culture* (1998), and most recently Joseph Graves's *The Emperor's New Clothes: Biological Theories of Race at the Millennium* (2001). All these works illuminate, from different vantage points, a shift in views of race that began in the late seventeenth and early eighteenth centuries, took on new urgency in the late eighteenth century and by the end of the nineteenth century had transformed every field of intellectual discourse — anthropology, biology, history, literary study, linguistics.[3]

While eighteenth-century speculations on race included many interpretations of racial characteristics as environmental and therefore mutable, over the course of the next century theories of the essential and irremediable inferiority of "lesser" races were consolidated, with the term "Anglo-Saxon" coming into increasing use after the mid nineteenth century to describe the superiority of a particular version of Caucasians (a term that emerged in racial discourse in 1775), as distinguished from Slavs or the Latin race, for example (Gossett 310–12 and ff.). Significantly, a new eighteenth-century admiration for "Goths"—famously part of the political, cultural, and architectural background of Walpole's prototypical "Gothic Story" of 1764 — represented a midpoint in this move toward an exaltation of the Anglo-Saxon. Thomas Percy's *Reliques of Ancient English Poetry*, sometimes cited in connection with early Gothic romance, is part of this context, as is late eighteenth-century medievalism in general.[4]

This historical background allows us to see Gothic texts themselves as documents in the history of racial formation, documents that might give us a better sense of what the construction of whiteness involved, and in particular, of the white terrors it worked both to express and produce. Changes in characterizations of Gothic villainy are particularly significant in this regard, because they coincide strikingly with the rise of the increasingly biological conception of race that had already coalesced, by 1850, in the widespread acceptance of race as a scientific given that organizes humanity hierarchically.[5] From *The Italian* in 1797 to *Zofloya* in 1806 to *Jane Eyre* and *Wuthering Heights* in the late 1840s to *The Woman in White* in 1860, representations of Gothic villainy progress from religious and national categories of otherness metonymically associated with black as a color designating evil, through a category of otherness that conflates enslaved, sexualized dark people with the damning allure of the Prince of Darkness himself, and finally toward conceptions of a dark, sexual, bestial, *racial* Other that reflect the triumph of biological racism.

Consider, at the beginning of this historical sequence, the energy devoted in popular Gothics of the 1790s and early 1800s to constructing a normative reader in contradistinction to a defining Other, and the bodily forms that Other was beginning to assume. A case in point is the opening of *The Italian:* "About the year 1764, some English travelers in Italy, during one of their excursions in the environs of Naples, happened to stop before the portico of the *Santa Maria del Pianto,* a church belonging to a very ancient convent of the order of the *Black Penitents....*" Through these travelers' normative English gaze, the reader sees, "Within the shade of the portico, a person ... of a tall thin figure ... sallow complexion, and harsh features, and ... an eye, which ... seemed expressive of uncommon ferocity." The travelers enter the church into which this stranger, the lower part of his face mu°ed by a cloak, has "glided," whereupon Radcliffe devotes a paragraph to the fact that, unlike most churches in Italy, this one has that "simplicity and grandeur" appreciated by "persons of taste." Implicitly, this exception proves the rule that English Protestants in general are more likely than Catholic Italians to engage authentically in "the sublime elevation of devotion." The national distinctions are underlined when the mysterious man is identified as an assassin, and Italian churches as refuges for assassins. A friar explains earnestly to the English tourists (it is Radcliffe's Italian joke, not his), "Why, my friend ... if we were to shew no mercy to such unfortunate persons, assassinations are so frequent, that our cities would be half depopulated."[6]

In terms of emerging racial theory, what is significant in this passage is the effort directed toward constructing the reader in terms of a normative racial/national self that is emphatically not at home in Italy. Appiah points out that because political geography did not map coherently onto categories of nationality, eighteenth-century theorists of the nation "were obliged to draw a distinction between the nation as a natural entity and the state as the product of culture," leading, under the nineteenth-century influence of biological and anthropological conceptions of "human nature," to the increasing identification of nation itself "as a biological unit" (282). The development of nationalist theory was thus integrally connected with emerging biological theories of race, and thus played a critical mediating role in the production of biological racial theory from the late eighteenth century throughout the nineteenth — a role we can see clearly in *The Italian.*[7] Nation is the salient category in the opening narrative frame, which places otherness geographically, with reference to religion, coloring, temperament, taste, sensibility, and a moral nature implicitly associated with those factors. This conception of national otherness informs the novel so powerfully that, from the moment we meet Schedoni, we know who "The" Italian, out of a whole cast of Italians, must be. The narrative procedures that identify Schedoni as "the" national type are conjoined, by a method relevant to the emergence of biological racism, with those that associate him metonymically with shade, shadows, darkness, and blackness.

The importance of this metonymy to the racial project of the novel explains the apparently gratuitous narrative convolution whereby the Black Penitents dominate the opening chapter. Schedoni is not a Black Penitent, but his confession was made to them; the man we see in the shadow at the beginning is not Schedoni but an assassin protected by the Black Penitents, and his appearance provides the frame for the story of the assassin Schedoni, who belongs to yet another order. Why these contortions should be necessary can be answered in terms of the necessity for shoring up Schedoni's status as a national type, while at the same time elaborating the thrilling, stupendous, spectacular individuality that might cause his crimes, and his moral nature, to be read as unique and atypical. The oblique opening view of Schedoni through the Black Penitents allows the very individuality of his crimes to bleed out into the surrounding culture, revealing their generalizably Italian character. The name "Black Penitents" suggests the necessity, in Italy, for a whole religious order devoted to penitence for "black" deeds. Further, it implicates the penitence itself as mysterious and sinister: "black penitence"—penitence undreamed of by English travelers, of the kind that caused Emily St. Aubert to faint when she drew aside the black veil of Udolpho.

Radcliffe's Black Penitents are not black, but their presence at the opening of her work announces its obsession with blackness and darkness as markers for evil. Black hair, eyes, and eyebrows, black cowls, black veils, and "swarthy" complexions signify something frightening, suspect, evil, and distinctively other than the implied reader, and the anxiety they produce suggests a racial project of some urgency. Thus, while the emphasis here is not on what modern readers, heirs of later nineteenth-century racial thought, think of as "racial," in *The Italian* what is villainously Latin and what is villainously black are located metonymically in relation to each other, in ways that predict the history of the Gothic over the next century.

The Gothic reader meets a version of the Black Penitents many years later in Melville's "Benito Cereno," in mid nineteenth century—precisely the time when the metonymic association of blackness with evil in the context of national and religious otherness has merged ideologically with a biological conception of otherness.[8] In the distance, the ship *San Dominick* looks like a whitewashed monastery after a thunderstorm in the Pyrenees and the "dark moving figures" aboard it look like "Black Friars pacing the cloisters."[9] Up close, they are black *people*— African slaves. Radcliffe's Black Penitents are other in terms of their dress, religion and nationality. Melville's "Black Friars" are other *bodily,* and their deviance from the readerly norm has been established in an opening line quite similar to Radcliffe's: "In the year 1799, Captain Amasa Delano, of Duxbury in Massachusetts ... lay at anchor ... in the harbor of St. Maria..." (Melville 141). "About the year 1764, some English travelers in Italy ... happened to stop before the portico of the *Santa Maria....*" As the name St. Maria suggests, Radcliffe's Latin Others are in Melville's story, too, to complicate his always complicated uses of the Gothic, and, throughout the novella, the reader must hesitate between ascribing villainy to the mysterious Africans or to the mysterious Southern Europeans, in this case Spaniards. It is the secure place of both constructions in dominant racial ideology by 1856 that allows for the metonymic generation, between them, of the field of ambiguities within which the obtuse observing consciousness of Captain Delano, identified explicitly as American and *white,* must struggle to constitute itself as normative. Indeed, all of the work's ambiguities are generated within an ideological field that allows the question to be posed as to whether an aristocratic Catholic, Latin background might signify greater or lesser evil than black skin.

One of the more intriguing landmarks in the racial formation of the Gothic between Radcliffe and Melville is Charlotte Dacre's *Zofloya* of 1806, in which ideas of race, like those in *The Italian,* reflect the transitional status of racial thought at the turn into the nineteenth century. In Dacre's novel, not merely black clothing, shadows, darkness, and shade, but dark *skin* emerges as a signifier for the evil Other, in the closer-than-metonymic relations between the villainy of the Italian protagonist and her alter ego, the Moor. These evil characters signify each other's evil in complex, mutually reinforcing ways; even so, the normative implied reader is constructed differently with regard to the two kinds of difference they represent. The first Other of the work is the dark, passionate Victoria with her raven tresses, large black eyes, and origins in Venice, whose inhabitants unite "the Spanish and Italian character in its most sublimated state of passion" and are "sanguinary and violent by nature, climate, habit, and education." (Such is the "character" of their "nation," Dacre says.)[10] Victoria's national character makes it only logical that she should conceive a desperate love for the brother of her husband, who is virtuously affianced to the beautiful, fairy-like, delicate, blond, alabaster Lilla, and it is at this conception that the Moor appears, first in her dreams and then in the flesh, as a projection of her evil desire. What is other about Zofloya is less straightforward. First, his Moorish darkness is at one level a projection of Victoria's dark Venetian soul, which conflates their national/racial/religious otherness from the beginning in complicated ways. Second, there are two Moors: the cultivated slave, really of noble birth, whom the author treats sympathetically, and then the Moor's bodily form as usurped by Satan. Unlike the real Zofloya, this one is a figure of obsessive desire, revulsion, and moral contempt, but the two Zofloyas are represented as identical until the final few pages, which hardly serve to undo the novel's long work of establishing what we thought was the "real" Moor's darkness as an index of evil. Third, the false Zofloya is himself transformed as the romance progresses, in accord with his role as a projection of Victoria's expandingly evil nature.

What Dacre emphasizes as "other" in Zofloya shifts with these shifts in characterizations of the Moor. Initially, for example, the most salient category of otherness is not race but class, as Zofloya's "menial" status is emphasized again and again, and Victoria's association with one of such lowly rank is repeatedly represented as transgressive. Because her self-subjection to this social inferior is actually enthrallment to Satan, her monomaniacal loss of perspective on class is thus represented not only as destructive of the social order but as literally damning. Class continues to be emphasized throughout, but Zofloya's status as Other in terms of class increasingly gives way to an otherness represented in terms of color. Initially complexion is seen as an incidental, if aesthetically unfortunate, aspect of the real man Zofloya's appearance; he is beautiful despite it. When the Satanic Zofloya first appears in Victoria's dreams, his color also somewhat incidental; he emerges out of a "group of shadowy figures ... of a deadly paleness," which, like his dazzling white clothing, is perhaps contrasted implicitly with his complexion, but his darkness is not mentioned explicitly for some time (145). As the book goes on, however, Zofloya's color is increasingly salient, increasingly exoticized and eroticized, and increasingly an index both of his evil and Victoria's—her "blackest guilt," "the dark and ferocious passions of her soul," linked closely with "the dark abettor of her crimes" (192, 182). The real man Zofloya is described as physically attractive despite his complexion. The false Zofloya grows bigger, more terrifying, more sublime (we move from Venice to the Apennines to the Alps), more fascinating, more horrifyingly attractive, until he finally expands into grotesque ugliness, in a final revelation ("hideous to behold!") suggesting that, after all, the aesthetic status of the "real" Moor's dark skin has finally been clarified as a moral signifier.

In Morrison's terms, Zofloya, a symbolic figuration of blackness, ignites critical changes in Victoria and finally her most critical moment of discovery—that he is Satan, summoned by her dreams of evil, and that she herself is damned. The subject of the dream in *Zofloya* is quite literally the dreamer. As this very fact suggests, however, the demonizing of the dark racial Other in *Zofloya* is not without its ambiguities. In a profound sense it is not Zofloya-the-man but the *demonization* of the man that is Satanic—literally Satanic, since it is Satan who demonizes the Moor's body. On the other hand, the text overwhelmingly validates this demonization affectively, for the Gothic frisson depends on the premise of a monstrous dark Other, and on the racial logic implied in Satan's choice of a signifying body. Further, although Satan demonizes the Moor, the transformation of an attractive, accomplished, and well-liked Moor into a fascinating eroticized agent of damnation is also an outward projection of the internal transformation of the Venetian heroine, whose evil Italian qualities materialize in the person of the Moor, and who herself becomes not only increasingly evil but, as Adriana Craciun points out, concomitantly darker.[11] The result is an accelerating conflation of racial and national otherness. Finally, despite the possibly anti-slavery overtones of the minor part of the plot centering on the first Zofloya, the role of the second Zofloya makes the narrative look like this: All is well when the Moor is a slave. When the lines between slaves and masters are abrogated, he gets bigger, more devious, more frighteningly powerful, even masterful and domineering, escaping altogether the control of his former social superior, who is now in his power. Seen from this perspective, *Zofloya* articulates the classic nightmare-fantasy of the slaveholder.

Between Radcliffe's work and later Gothic—*Jane Eyre,* for example— *Zofloya* thus presents a complex intermediate category of dark evil that is both racialized and not racialized but is certainly nationalized. In its representations of racial difference through the two figures of the Moor, one a refined dark man and one a dark monster, *Zofloya* first rejects, then enacts, the demonizing of dark skin. This process is mediated by the less ambivalent, more forthright demonizing of the Venetian national "character," to which the figure of the Moor becomes increasingly assimilated and finally sexually united. At the level of narrative procedure, then, *Zofloya* enacts in miniature the history of the Gothic's conflicted and problematic involvement with issues of "race," conceptualized first as national or geographic and then as biological. That the racial ideology of *Zofloya* is so unstable makes sense in terms of the novel's historical position at a time of flux in conceptions of race more generally.[12] The schizophrenic splitting off of the "real" human Zofloya from the monstrous, superhuman Zofloya is a symptom of this flux, and a forecast of the schizophrenic psychology that would be necessary to sustain the contradictions of biological racism from its mid nineteenth-century triumph until today.

Thus, despite the unsettled, ambivalent, transitional status of race in *Zofloya*, it is actually only a small step from the moment when a dark, sexualized man, the projection of Victoria's evil desires, materializes between her parted bed curtains (a birth and a rape), to the moment when the dark, sexualized West Indian Bertha Mason usurps Jane Eyre's mirror and rends her wedding veil (likewise a self-projection and a rape),[13] or to the frightful apparition of Heathcliff's "black countenance" and "sharp cannibal teeth" at Isabella's window in *Wuthering Heights* (1847).[14] From there, the distance is not far to Walter Hartwright's encounter with "dark, dwarfish men" who "lurked murderously among the trees" in some tropical place in *The Woman in White*,[15] an episode whose exasperating gratuitousness in terms of plot suggests the extent to which the subject of Anglo Gothic had been clarified, by 1860, as whiteness. The extent to which the presence of racial otherness was an ideological requirement of the genre perhaps explains some strange anomalies in works that rely on the Gothic for their creation of atmosphere: not only the fact that Hartwright somehow cannot save the heroine from an Italian villain in England unless he first vanquishes dark people in the tropics, for example, but also the presence of Jim Crow in the House of the Seven Gables, or the horror of Injun Joe's hand, holding a candle, appearing from behind a rock when Tom Sawyer and Betsy are trapped in the cave. It explains, too, the necessity for the "accidental" walling-off of Joe's Native American otherness (which his disguise has revealed as interchangeable with "Spaniard" otherness) when the cave is sealed. The language in which this latter incident is described speaks tellingly to the question of racial boundaries and barriers, evoked in Tom's position beyond the frighteningly just-open door, sign of his half-sympathy and even half-identity with the outcast, but also the safety of the permanent barrier of death: "Injun Joe lay stretched upon the ground, dead, with his face close to the crack of the door.... Tom was touched, for he knew by his own experience how this wretch had suffered ... but nevertheless he felt an abounding sense of relief and security, now, which revealed to him ... how vast a weight of dread had been lying upon him since the day he lifted his voice against this bloody-minded outcast."[16]

In *Perils of the Night,* I argued that the major conventions of (Anglo) Gothic consist of barriers and boundaries (veils, cowls, precipices, secret doors, locked mysterious chests, massive gates, convent walls, bed curtains, and so on) between a stable, definable, unitary self and a terrifying *Other* that both challenges and ultimately establishes that very stability and definability.[17] To that argument should be added the critical fact that this terrifying metaphysical, suprapersonal general Other is embodied in the physical persons of particular racialized, nationalized, and/or sexualized "Others," whose inherent otherness is identified with an inherent evil. Thus, although in one sense the presence of these "Others" functions to interrogate the distinctions between a safely bounded, innocent and virtuous self and something "darker" that Anglo-Gothic always suspects to be less safely separate than "we" — always defined as white — may wish, the fact that the dark *persons* in the work are always already spooky and sinister, and that the implied reader is always already what would eventually be termed "Anglo Saxon," or is constructed as such early in the text, means that in interrogating the boundaries of a normative middle-class white "self" by means of racialized dark Others, the Gothic is not by any means interrogating — at least overtly — the idea of race *per se*. The reverse is in fact the case: the ideological work that representations of terrifying, deviant "Others" in these works perform is not to ask whether, after all, Anglo Saxons and Moors (or gypsies, or "savages," or "cannibals," or Africans or Native Americans or Spaniards) are really as different as rapidly coalescing racial conceptions would have it, but whether, after all, good characters might have within them a capacity for evil for which the physical persons of those who are biologically deviant by definition would logically be an excellent metaphor. The presumed biological stability and moral, intellectual, spiritual significance of the physical markers of difference between groups of people are exactly what allow for their role in raising this question of whether the normative Anglo Saxon self has internal moral or psychological boundaries that are as stable as those external, biological dividing lines.

This paradoxical status in the Gothic of race, which is nothing but a trope, as a dependable biological given that can therefore trope something other than human difference means that Anglo Gothic suspicions that the "Other" may really be the "self" operate not to interrogate the racial ideologies that structure the central metaphors of difference embodied in Gothic boundaries and barriers, but rather to help construct the racial ideologies that associate dark persons with deviance to begin with. Thus it is only logical that the century-long racial project which is Gothic romance should culminate in *Heart of Darkness*, with its circular entrapment in the exploration of an evil that is simultaneously typified *in* a colonizer's exploitation of dark other people and *by* those people themselves, whose literal dark otherness and deviance from a European norm tropes the colonizer's spiritual assimilation to some dark horror within himself.

The inescapable circularity of this story of the white man whose evil manifests itself in his oppression of people whose bodily darkness establishes them as the natural and logical metaphors for that evil points to the limits of Gothic insight into its great subject of what Pauline Hopkins would call in the subtitle of her most overtly Gothic work "the hidden self." For the Gothic suspicion that the dark evil Other is, after all, a projection of the darkness at the heart of whiteness must be played out, by definition, completely inside the bounds of an ideology that defines dark people as profoundly "other" to begin with. The line this suspicion threatens to abrogate is emphatically, then, *not* the line that is assumed in Gothic to divide Anglo-Saxon characters from darker peoples literally — that is, biologically. On the contrary, the natural, biological inviolability of racial differences is the given on which the metaphor of a threatened abrogation of the line between a mundane and daylit moral Anglo-Saxon self and some colossal dark evil oneiric Other is based in the first place. The result of this ideological commitment is that, amongst all those barriers and boundaries whose potential instability evokes such terror in Gothic, by the late nineteenth century the one unproblematized, emphatically stable boundary in that genre was the color line. That stability had been produced by a long history of Gothic representations in which the color line was conceived of not as a metaphor, but as a natural biological fact that could quite naturally be deployed as a metaphor for something else: the line between the good and evil sides of white characters in *Zofloya*, for example, or between Jane Eyre's virginity and her sexual desire, or between an everyday interior civilized world and the alluring, exteriorized, supernatural world of Heathcliff. The importance of that line, the anxiety to maintain it, is inherent in a literary racial project whose goal was the construction of whiteness.

Recognizing this fact should enable us to place more accurately a number of works that, in this context, appear explicitly to be problematizing their own Gothic conventions. This category includes works by Euro-American authors who summon up, through their Gothic arts, both the spectre of a fearful racial Other and the fear that spectre always implies: that there are no racial boundaries; that, in Morrison's terms, the so carefully organized American coherence of their free white identities may dissolve into some nebulous white mist of undefinition. Among such works would be Poe's *Pym*, in which careful, even neurotically maintained racial distinctions finally run up against some ultimate white veil that can never, within Poe's racial ideology, yield up its mysteries.[18] They would also include Faulkner's most Gothic work, *Absalom, Absalom!* in which racial differentiation fades out at the end into Shreve's vision of a bleached-out blackness overtaking the world so that "in a few thousand years," as he taunts the racially obsessed Quentin, "I who regard you will also have sprung from the loins of African kings."[19] Most interesting in this context, however, are those African American authors who use the Gothic to investigate the many kinds of anxiety attaching to racial boundaries, presenting African American dreams in the form of Gothic visions that expose and demystify the white terrors created by white terror of black Others. Such authors would include, among many others,[20] Victor Séjour, Richard Wright,[21] Paule Marshall,[22] and Pauline Hopkins. Hopkins is particularly important because of the position her oppositional Gothic romance, *Of One Blood, or, The Hidden Self,* has at the beginning of the twentieth century, when arguments of Anglo-Saxon superiority were being invoked to justify the domestic and global white terrors manifested in lynchings, race riots, and American imperialism.

The title of Hopkins's novel, whose Gothic scenes are set in the U.S. and Africa, suggests immediately her concern to contest the color line as the central mystified metaphor of Anglo-Gothic. The biblical allusion — "Of one blood have I made all races of men"— announces from the beginning her stance on the monogenist side of the controversy as to whether people of African origin did (polygenism) or did not (monogenism) constitute a separate species.[23] Whatever a particular Gothicist's position on this scientific question, Gothic fascination with radical, irreducible otherness lent itself to a kind of moral polygenism that placed characters like the swarthy Heathcliff, for example, almost outside the pale of what was human, despite any *literal* kinship they might have with Anglo Saxon characters (in Heathcliff's case, for example, the possibility that he is Earnshaw's son and Catherine's half-brother.) It is this moral polygenism that the revisionary Gothic conventions in *Of One Blood* work to undo.[24]

Among these conventions is Hopkins's brilliant counter-representation of the Africanist persona. All of the Gothic mysteries in her text center in some way around the mysteries of the body as signifier, beginning with the opening representation of the hero's phenotypically ambiguous appearance, and leading to his discovery of what the African American background he has been hiding really means: that he has within him "the shadow of Ethiopia's power" (558). On the same Gothic journey, his white racist friend also discovers that Ethiopians are the "primal race" of the whole human family, including him. But in the shadow of slavery, the recognition of "one blood" inevitably entails the unmasking of incest and fratricide. The heroine has married not one but both of her brothers; the apparently white man who tried to murder the hero is his brother, son of the same slave mother. The great Gothic insight of Hopkins's novel is that to mystify the "one blood" of all humanity is to make it a source of horror. By the time she wrote *Of One Blood,* the dominant metaphors of Gothic had been implicated in that mystification for over a century. Her oppositional Gothic, although it ends in tragedy, also holds out the hope that such mystification can end — that white terrors of an Africanist Other, which might horrifyingly erode a racially constructed self, will finally be exorcised by black dreams of a lost, originary African Other that turns out, in a redemptive construction of race, to *be* oneself.

Notes

1. Toni Morrison, *Playing in the Dark: Whiteness and the Literary Imagination* (New York: Vintage, 1992), viii, ix, 6–7, 8, 17.

2. Joseph Graves, *The Emperor's New Clothes: Biological Theories of Race at the Millennium* (New Brunswick, NJ, and London: Rutgers University Press, 2001), 9. See also Graves's definition of race (5) and his discussion of discrepancies between lay understandings of race and scientific rejection of the concept, especially throughout the Introduction and Part 4.

3. For a detailed account of the emergence of this consensus in each discipline, see Thomas F. Gossett, *Race: The History of an Idea in America.* New Edition (New York: Oxford University Press, 1997).

4. Reginald Horsman, *Race and Manifest Destiny: The Origins of American Racial Anglo-Saxonism* (Cambridge, MA, and London: Harvard University Press, 1981), 30–38.

5. See Anthony Appiah, "Race," in *Critical Terms for Literary Study,* ed. Frank Lentricchia and Thomas McLaughlin (Chicago and London: University of Chicago Press, 1990), 276.

6. Ann Radcliffe, *The Italian: or, The Confessional of the Black Penitents* (1797; London: Oxford University Press, 1968), 1–3.

7. See Horsman, chapter 2, and Appiah, 276 and 282–85.

8. While Appiah points out that it should "be clear that the racial theme never required a simple identification of one race with evil and another with good" (280), I would argue that this identification was a major part of the work the Gothic performed throughout the period Appiah is describing.

9. Herman Melville, "Benito Cereno," in *The Piazza Tales* (1856), in *Billy Budd and Other Tales,* ed. Willard Thorpe (New York: Signet, 1979), 143.

10. Charlotte Dacre, *Zofloya; or, The Moor: A Romance of the Fifteenth Century* (1806; Ontario: Broadview, 1997), 41.

11. Adriana Craciun, "Introduction" to *Zofloya* by Charlotte Dacre, 18. Craciun points to the increasing emphasis on Zofloya's and Victoria's darkness, and reads Victoria's darkening as "a sign of miscegenation." Miscegenation is of course one of the most taboo border-crossings between a dark "Other" and a "white" self constructed as normative.

12. A story about a Moor set in Venice in the Renaissance can hardly fail to evoke *Othello,* so that the treatment of racial difference here in an early Gothic work is especially interesting as an index of what has changed, and not changed, since the Renaissance in terms of racial theory. In this regard it is interesting to think about the conscious grounding of much late eighteenth and early nineteenth-century Gothic in the literature of the Renaissance, which — because it was the period of the Encounter — is the other great turning point in the history of modern racial formation.

13. Charlotte Brontë, *Jane Eyre* (1847; Harmondsworth: Penguin, 1982), 311.

14. Emily Brontë, *Wuthering Heights* (1847; Harmondsworth: Penguin, 1980), 212.

15. Wilkie Collins, *The Woman in White* (1860; Harmondsworth: Penguin, 2000).

16. Mark Twain, *The Adventures of Tom Sawyer* [online]. The INTERNET WIRETAP

First Electronic Edition of *The Adventures of Tom Sawyer*, 1993. Available from World Wide Web: (http://www.cs.cmu.edu/People/rgs/sawyr-table.html).

17. Eugenia C. DeLamotte, *Perils of the Night: A Feminist Study of Nineteenth-Century Gothic* (New York: Oxford, 1990).

18. See also Morrison on *Pym*, 51.

19. William Faulkner, *Absalom, Absalom!* (1936; New York: Modern Library, 1964), 378. On race in *Absalom, Absalom!* see Carole Anne Taylor, *The Tragedy and Comedy of Resistance: Reading Modernity through Black Women's Fiction* (Philadelphia: University of Pennsylvania Press, 2000).

20. See for example Kari J. Winter, *Subjects of Slavery, Agents of Change: Women and Power in Gothic Novels and Slave Narratives, 1790–1865* (Athens: University of Georgia Press, 1992).

21. As, for example, in Michel Fabre, "Black Cat and White Cat: Richard Wright's Debt to Edgar Allan Poe," *Poe Studies* 4.1 (June 1971): 17–19.

22. See, for example, my reading of Selina's dream of the beast in Marshall's *Brown Girl, Brownstones*. Eugenia C. DeLamotte, *Places of Silence, Journeys of Freedom: The Fiction of Paule Marshall* (Philadelphia: University of Pennsylvania Press, 1998), 36–38.

23. On this debate see Graves, Chapter 3.

24. Hopkins's Gothic is the subject of a longer analysis in my forthcoming article, "Collusions of the Mystery: Ideology and the Gothic in *Hagar's Daughter* (*Gothic Studies* 2005)

Works Cited

Allen, Theodore W. *The Invention of the White Race. Vol. 2. The Origin of Racial Oppression in Anglo-America*. London and New York: Verso, 1997.

Appiah, Anthony. "Race." In *Critical Terms for Literary Study* Edited by Frank Lentricchia, and Thomas McLaughlin. Chicago and London: University of Chicago Press, 1990.

Babb, Valerie Melissa. *Whiteness Visible: The Meaning of Whiteness in American Literature and Culture*. New York: New York University Press, 1998.

Brontë, Emily. *Wuthering Heights*. 1847. Harmondsworth: Penguin, 1980.

Brontë, Charlotte. *Jane Eyre*. 1847. Harmondsworth: Penguin, 1982.

Collins, Wilkie. *The Woman in White*. 1860. Harmondsworth: Penguin, 2000.

Conrad, Joseph. *Heart of Darkness*. 1901. New York: Signet, 1950.

Dacre, Charlotte. *Zofloya; or, The Moor: A Romance of the Fifteenth Century*. 1806. Edited and introduced by Adriana Craciun. Ontario: Broadview, 1997.

DeLamotte, Eugenia C. *Perils of the Night: A Feminist Study of Nineteenth-Century Gothic*. New York: Oxford University Press, 1990.

_____. *Places of Silence, Journeys of Freedom: The Fiction of Paule Marshall*. Philadelphia: University of Pennsylvania Press, 1998.

Fabre, Michel. "Black Cat and White Cat: Richard Wright's Debt to Edgar Allan Poe." *Poe Studies* 4.1 (June 1971): 17–19.

Faulkner, William. *Absalom, Absalom!* 1936. New York: Modern Library, 1964.

Gossett, Thomas F. *Race: The History of an Idea in America*. 1963. New Edition. New York: Oxford University Press, 1997.

Gould, Stephen Jay. *The Mismeasure of Man*. 1981. Revised Edition. New York : Norton, 1996.

Graves, Joseph. *The Emperor's New Clothes: Biological Theories of Race at the Millennium*. New Brunswick, NJ, and London: Rutgers University Press, 2001.

Hopkins, Pauline. *Of One Blood, or, The Hidden Self.* 1902–03. In *The Magazine Novels of Pauline Hopkins*. Edited by Hazel V. Carby. New York: Oxford University Press, 1988.

Horsman, Reginald. *Race and Manifest Destiny: The Origins of American Racial Anglo-Saxonism.* Cambridge, MA, and London: Harvard University Press, 1981.

Melville, Herman. "Benito Cereno." 1856. In *Billy Budd and Other Tales.* Edited by Willard Thorpe. New York: Signet, 1979.

Moraga, Cherríe. *Loving in the War Years.* Boston: South End Press, 1983.

Morrison, Toni. *Playing in the Dark: Whiteness and the Literary Imagination.* New York: Vintage, 1992.

Omi, Michael, and Howard Winant. *Racial Formation in the United States: From the 1960s to the 1990s.* Second Edition. New York: Routledge, 1994.

Radcliffe, Ann. *The Italian: or, The Confessional of the Black Penitents.* 1797. London: Oxford University Press, 1968.

Saxton, Alexander. *The Rise and Fall of the White Republic: Class Politics and Mass Culture in Nineteenth-Century America.* London: Verso, 1990.

Takaki, Ronald. *Iron Cages: Race and Culture in Nineteenth-Century America.* 1979. Revised Edition. New York and Oxford: Oxford University Press, 2000.

Taylor, Carole Anne. *The Tragedy and Comedy of Resistance: Reading Modernity through Black Women's Fiction.* Philadelphia: University of Pennsylvania Press, 2000.

Twain, Mark. *The Adventures of Tom Sawyer* [online]. The INTERNET WIRETAP First Electronic Edition of *The Adventures of Tom Sawyer,* 1993. Available from World Wide Web: <http://www.cs.cmu.edu/People/rgs/sawyr-table.html>.

Winter, Kari J. *Subjects of Slavery, Agents of Change: Women and Power in Gothic Novels and Slave Narratives, 1790–1865.* Athens: University of Georgia Press, 1992.

2

Slavery and Civic Recovery: Gothic Interventions in Whitman and Weld

KATHERINE HENRY

In his 1838 *Memoir on Slavery*, defending his claim that the philanthropic efforts of the abolitionists were misguided, William Harper of South Carolina wrote, "I have heard it expressed [that] the further you extend the circle of light, the wider is the horizon of darkness."[1] Although Harper doesn't identify the source of his figure, it is likely *An Essay Concerning Human Understanding*, in which Locke urges us to "[consider] the capacities of our understandings, [discover] the extent of our knowledge, [and find] the horizon ... which sets the bounds between the enlightened and dark part of things."[2] Harper's appropriation of Locke's figure of the "horizon" that separates light from darkness is significant because he revises it in two crucial respects. First, he envisions it specifically as the boundary between freedom and slavery — not simply the figurative "enslavement" of human ignorance, but also the American institution of race slavery. "When the greatest progress in civil liberty has been made," he explains, "the enlightened lover of liberty will know that there must remain much inequality, much injustice, much *Slavery*, which no human wisdom or virtue will ever be able wholly to prevent or redress."[3] Thus Harper turns Locke's argument for accepting an inevitable degree of human ignorance into an argument for accepting the institution of slavery and, in doing so, racializes Locke's metaphors of "light" and "darkness." In Harper's figure, the "circle of light" has become the compass of white American "civil liberty," both limited and produced by the existence of Negro slavery beyond its defining boundary.[4]

The second key revision that Harper makes to Locke's figure is to destabilize its circumference, imagining it as expanding rather than fixed. As Harper describes it, the circle's expansion means not simply a more inclusive region of "light," but also— as a necessary consequence — a more extensive and more threatening border of "darkness," one that we can imagine will prove increasingly difficult to police. Thus, to apply Harper's own analogy, we have a zone of civic liberty unsettled as to its own extent and, as a result, increasingly troubled by its own exclusions, creating precisely the conditions that, as Eve Kosofsky Sedgwick has argued, give rise to the Gothic.[5] This essay examines two popular American texts that, while unlike Harper's *Memoir* in their espousal of a progressive politics of reform, nevertheless make use of a similarly racialized boundary in their portrayal of a troubled realm of civic liberty. Using Gothic conventions, both Walt Whitman and Theodore Dwight Weld depict an unsettled white citizenry that has become haunted by its own exclusions. In the case of Whitman's 1842 temperance novel *Franklin Evans; or, The Inebriate,* Franklin's own "slavery to the bottle" gets represented in the character of the slave Margaret, while Weld envisions his 1839 antislavery pamphlet *American Slavery As It Is* as a courtroom, in which the testimony of white witnesses is tormented by the "shrieks" and "groans" of the brutalized slaves who must themselves remain on the outside.[6] Moreover, both texts engage in what I call "civic recovery"— the reconstitution or re-centering of a dysfunctional civic identity — redrawing the boundaries of American citizenship in a way that promises a return to stability. But in both cases those solutions eventually prove problematic, revealing a racist configuration at the heart of the developing liberal model of citizenship.

To represent this unsettled relation between the zone of civic liberty and its enslaved exterior as a relationship between a white citizen and a black slave is to invoke the paradigm of self and Other, and so I would like to begin by reviewing a few key theoretical accounts of that paradigm. In the Hegelian model, it is the situation of the Other outside the self that both initiates the dialectic and enables the moment of recognition that consolidates (and eventually calls into doubt) the self's masterful identity.[7] But critics of the Gothic have repeatedly noted that the Gothic Other is never situated unproblematically outside the self. As William Patrick Day has argued in his study of Gothic fantasy, "the Other resolves itself into a version of the self, a fragmentation and externalization of identity that destroys the self as fully and as surely as the overt attacks of its nemesis."[8] And in *Fantasy: The Literature of Subversion*, drawing on Tzvetan Todorov, Rosemary Jackson advances a strikingly similar thesis; in what she calls "fantasies of subjective dislocation," she argues, there is a "collapse of differences." "Other persons and objects are no longer distinctly other," Jackson explains; "the limit between subject and object is effaced, things slide into one another, in a metonymical action of replacement."[9] The anxiety registered by the slave's appearance as the citizen's Gothic Other, then, is the anxiety not of difference but of sameness, resulting not in "communication" but in severed "parallels and correspondences," to use Sedgwick's terms. It is the fear, perhaps, of the citizen's *own* enslavement, or the lurking suspicion that the slave's recognition of the citizen's mastery is not recognition at all, but rather some grotesque parody, a too-perfect figment of the citizen's own diseased imagination. If the moment of recognition in Hegel's paradigm functions to consolidate the self's identity, the uncanny distortion of that moment in the Gothic signals a crisis in civic identity. And, if the slave as Hegelian Other affords the necessary point outside to set in motion the dialectic, the slave as Gothic Other indicates a sort of civic paralysis—in the case of *Franklin Evans*, an overwhelming inability to act; in *American Slavery As It Is*, what Weld calls a "paralysis of heart" (*TDW* 171).[10]

Also useful here is Homi Bhabha's analysis of the function of the racially and culturally alien Other in colonialist discourse. The establishment of the imperial culture's authority, Bhabha argues, entails two mechanisms that are at cross purposes—imitation and identification:

> In the psychoanalytic sense, to "imitate" is to cling to the denial of the ego's limitations; to "identify" is to assimilate conflictually. It is from between them, where the letter of the law will not be assigned as a sign, that culture's double returns uncannily—neither the one nor the other, but the imposter—to mock and mimic, to lose the sense of the masterful self and its social sovereignty.[11]

Put in terms of master and slave, as imitator the slave affirms the master's fantasy of power but loses the capacity to construct his identity; as Other the slave's presence establishes the limits or "laws" that both define citizenship—distinguish it from what it is *not*—and compromise its mastery. As Bhabha's analysis suggests, it is in the conflicted space "in-between" these two mechanisms that the slave can appear as the citizen's uncanny double. For Bhabha, moreover, that space is manifested discursively as "nonsense": like the wordless cries of slaves that haunt the testimony of citizens in *American Slavery As It Is*, such "inscriptions of an uncertain colonial silence [mock] the social performance of language with their nonsense, [and ba°e] the communicable verities of culture with their refusal to translate" (Bhabha 124). "In these instances of social and discursive alienation," concludes Bhabha, "there is no recognition of master and slave, there is only the matter of the enslaved master, the unmastered slave" (131).

Underwriting the slave's appearance as Gothic Other, then, is the fear that citizenship will collapse into slavery, that the "horizon," to return to William Harper's figure, separating the realm of civic liberty from the "darkness" of enslavement — inside from outside — will expand to infinity, and that American civic identity will cease to be. Although Whitman's temperance novel and Weld's antislavery pamphlet use different mechanisms to recover a wholesome sense of civic identity, both texts imagine that recovery as the reconfiguration of the citizen's relationship to his enslaved Other, and both texts imagine the reformed citizen as white. Whitman uses what Bhabha calls "disavowal," the "splitting" that permits contradictory statements to occupy the same discursive space (131–33).[12] That splitting occurs on several levels, allowing the text to proclaim "the last slave of Appetite" free at the same time that the institution of slavery is growing ever more entrenched — indeed, I will argue, *because* the institution of slavery is growing ever more entrenched. It is, in the end, the suicide of the slave, Margaret, that restores Franklin to productive citizenship and sobriety, and replaces a destructive libertinism with a healthy civic liberty. If Whitman's text requires the insanity and eventual death of the Other, however, Weld's envisions civic recovery through the mechanism Margaret Morse calls "incorporation," which "involves introjecting or surrounding the other ... and ultimately, the mixing of two 'bodies' in a dialectic of inside and outside."[13] In Weld's vision of reform, a nation corrupted by slavery is permitted to heal by refiguring the anguished and excluded slave as its own brutalized heart, by internalizing the slave's suffering and assuming it as one's own. The figure itself is thus converted — turned inside out — from a zone of white civic liberty haunted by its exiled black slaves, to a reformed white civic body with a vulnerable black interior.

This essay examines the function of a racialized Gothic in projects of civic recovery.[14] In the readings that follow, I show that the appearance of the black slave as Gothic Other is both sign and symptom of a radical instability in American civic identity. By representing a white citizenry's internal pathology as racial difference, Whitman and Weld reveal just how ingrained race is as a category of civic discourse in the late 1830s: they envision the threat to liberty in terms of racial conflict and, ultimately, the reformed citizen as white.

Citizen Franklin

At the age of twenty-three, working as a journalist and printer in Manhattan, Walt Whitman published *Franklin Evans; or, The Inebriate* for seventy-five dollars cash down — a work he would later denounce as "damned rot."[15] The best selling and most profitable of any of Whitman's publications during his lifetime, *Franklin Evans* panders shamelessly to the popular taste for the sordid and the sensational. But what is perhaps more disturbing to twenty-first-century readers is what Eric Lott has called "the racialist-gothic subplot … in which the protagonist, after a drunken binge, finds himself married to a Creole woman, herself a figure for his profligacy."[16] By making a slave into a figure for the "demon of Intemperance" — the "demon" from whose clutches, the American Temperance Union's advertisement for the novel read, "Young Men" needed to be "rescue[d]" — Whitman not only promotes the racist association of mulatta women with licentious behavior, but also shifts the responsibility for a state of enslavement onto slavery's victims, imagining those who perpetrate and profit from slavery as the true sufferers in need of "rescue" (*WW* 17). Alongside the novel's complicity with racist and proslavery patterns of thought, moreover, is a pervasive anxiety over the state of civic liberty, manifested in Franklin's repeated falls into dependency. Indeed, temperance literature provided an ideal vehicle for registering concern over the Jacksonian era's extensions of the franchise to men who were previously excluded from citizenship by property requirements; the fear that debtors and wage-laborers would lack the capacity for disinterested public participation could be vividly expressed in the dependency and degeneracy of alcoholism. These two elements — racism and anxiety over the expanding compass of American civic liberty — come together in *Franklin Evans* with a disturbing conclusion: the institution of slavery turns out to be essential to Franklin's recovery, to his own "emancipation" from the tyranny of alcoholism and return to productive citizenship.

By the time we get to the "racialist-gothic subplot" of *Franklin Evans*, the title character has left his boyhood farm for New York City, where he is "thrown by circumstances into the vortex of dissipation": he gets a job and loses it, marries a virtuous wife who dies a few paragraphs later as "the innocent victim of [his] drunkenness," is swindled by his landlord and left destitute, falls in with a gang of thieves, is arrested and imprisoned, is saved by a benefactor from the Temperance Society, and signs the "Old Temperance Pledge" (*WW* 35, 99). But, despite having completed the usual sequence of events in the temperance plot, Whitman does not end his novel here. We discover that there is, in fact, a loophole in the "Old

Temperance Pledge" — that is, it forbids "the drinking of [only] the most ardent kind of liquors, and allow[s] people to get as much fuddled as they [choose] upon wines, and beer" (*WW* 136). And so the stage is set for Franklin to fall back into his old habits of intemperance. He leaves New York for Virginia, where he becomes friends with a planter, slaveholder, and wine connoisseur of French descent named Bourne, and the novel turns Gothic. One night, in a fit of "drunken rashness," Franklin marries one of Bourne's slaves, a "luscious and fascinating" Creole named Margaret (*WW* 148, 141). When he later develops a sober and "legitimate" love for a white widow, Margaret is overcome with jealousy; she stalks and eventually murders her rival, and the episode ends when she is found dead in her cell, a victim of suicide (*WW* 150).

The move from urban North to plantation South, as well as the shift from mere sordidness to Gothic sensationalism, evokes what Carroll Smith-Rosenberg has identified as "the Northern urban press's cultural war against the Virginia junto's political and intellectual domination of the new nation" — a campaign that involved representing "the slave South in exotic terms."[17] At stake was not only political and economic supremacy, but a vision of American citizenship: as Smith-Rosenberg writes, "the 'true American,' the new bourgeois press insisted time and time again, was not the Southern slaveholder but the Northern free producer; he was not Thomas Jefferson, but Benjamin Franklin" (247). The Franklinesque ideal of self-making, however, was not without its own set of anxieties — the concern, for example, that landless wage laborers would lack the means to make independent civic judgments — and *Franklin Evans* exploits both sides of the critique. The allusions to Benjamin Franklin are hard to ignore: besides Franklin's name, there are several scenes on Franklin Evans's arrival in New York, particularly when he is seeking the patronage of a more established citizen of the city, that clearly echo scenes from the *Autobiography*. Indeed, the project of temperance itself recalls the scheme for self-improvement that Franklin expounds in the *Autobiography*. But if Benjamin Franklin offers a model of discipline, of gaining control over one's desires and thereby living within one's means, Franklin Evans is the epitome of out-of-control extravagance. And if Benjamin Franklin escapes his "bond" of apprenticeship to find liberty in Philadelphia, Franklin Evans moves in the opposite direction, from freedom to the enslavement of alcohol addiction, "selling [himself]," as Whitman puts it, "for [his] term of life, to misery" (*WW* 106).

Nevertheless, the plantocracy of the South offers no more sanguine a model of civic liberty. Indeed, Whitman's portrayal of the Virginia planter Bourne seems drawn from precisely the "cultural war" that Smith-Rosenberg describes: "the planter," she writes, "appears a sybaritic and lethargic, effete and unproductive aristocrat who lives in luxury as others slave for him" (247). Bourne's father, we are told, left France at the end of the eighteenth century, not from any disapproval of the "revolutionizers," but rather "because of the liberty he might enjoy" on his slave plantation (*WW* 138). Although the narrator hastens to dispel the note of irony we might be tempted to hear, adding that Bourne's slaves are really very well cared for and much better off than the indigent masses of the Old World, Bourne's notion of "liberty" is much closer to libertinism than to the virtuous ideal of neoclassical republicanism. It is Bourne who provokes Franklin's relapse into drunkenness, and Bourne who promotes his marriage to Margaret. Moreover, Bourne's name — meaning frontier or limit — suggests his trans- gressive role in the novel: he could be said to represent the terrifying col- lapse that threatens from beyond the pale, where civic liberty falls into a destructive libertinism, and citizenship falls into slavery. That the novel turns Gothic when Franklin arrives at the plantation of Bourne, then, makes perfect sense, for the Gothic derives its "most characteristic ener- gies," as Eve Sedgwick has written, from its capacity to turn boundaries into sites of anxiety, to bring "what's inside, what's outside, and what sep- arates them" into a disruptive tension (13).

The basic paradigm for reading "what's outside" as a troubled man- ifestation of "what's inside" is the Freudian Uncanny, the frightening return of the familiar thing that had been repressed, and Freud provides an obvi- ous model for interpreting the Gothic chapters of *Franklin Evans*. The Vir- ginia slave plantation can be read as the terrain of Franklin's psyche, and the characters—most obviously the slave Margaret—referents for Franklin's own inner demons.[18] Margaret is clearly supposed to be a haunt- ing presence: she "peers" into a window, her eyes "two bright, small orbs, fixed, and yet rolling in fire"; she walks the grounds of the plantation at night "like some ghost condemned to wander on earth for the actions done there," and "start[s]" at "the first streak of light … in the east" (*WW* 162, 164). And it is not difficult to read her as a figure for Franklin's alcoholism: his feelings of fascination for her, his loss of self-control and abandon- ment to temptation and pleasure, followed the morning after by disgust and horror at what he has done, reenact precisely his earlier experiences of drunkenness. In New York, he "yield[s] to the fatal impulse" to drink and "[feels] no more repugnance"; in Virginia, he "strangely" disregards "every feeling of prudence and self-respect" to marry Margaret (*WW* 114, 144). In New York, he awakens after a five-day bender with "that inde- scribable feeling of horror; that detestable nausea"; in Virginia, he describes coming to his senses and recognizing his marriage thus: "And *when I* awoke! What disgust with myself filled my mind at view of the conduct I had been pursuing!" (*WW* 115, 146). And, making the connection between Margaret and the "fiend Intemperance" even more explicit, Franklin remarks, "how bitterly I repented of my drunken rashness—for the marriage deserved no other name" (*WW* 148). By marrying the "luscious and fascinating" Creole, in other words, Franklin remarries his old habits of intemperance. His alcoholism, which had been repressed in the signing of the Old Temperance Pledge, returns as his Other, personified in the haunting figure of the slave Margaret.

As Toni Morrison has maintained, a notable characteristic of white American writers has been to "transfer ... internal conflicts to a 'blank darkness,' to conveniently bound and violently silenced black bodies" (38). But I would like to ask what it means to use the explicitly racialized and rigidly conceived boundary between citizen and slave to represent the white self's internal pathologies. In particular, why, if the goal of temperance propaganda is to convert drunkards and (particularly) potential drunkards to a life of sobriety, would drunkenness be figured as race slavery — an institution in many ways designed to *prevent* slaves from ever becoming free?[19] There are, I would suggest, two key points to make about this problem. First, figures of enslavement — especially as they are deployed in propaganda, or inflected with the Gothic — are often concerned with representing things not as they are, but as we wish or fear them to be; they operate in the liminal regions of desire and terror, and are effective to the extent that audiences can be induced to imagine them as real.[20] The tension between the hopeful temperance story of the inebriate who is restored to productive citizenship, and the wish to strike fear into the hearts of young men who are tempted by the pleasures of drink, animate the very project of using race slavery as a figure for alcoholism. And second, the rigidity of the American system of race slavery can be made paradoxically to serve the cause of temperance when one's own enslavement is "transfer[red]," as Morrison writes, to the "conveniently bound and violently silenced black body" of the slave.

A closer look at how the slave Margaret functions in the narrative will illustrate this second point. After the death of the white widow Mrs. Conway, Franklin "shut[s himself] up in [his] room" and falls into what he describes as "a kind of morbid peculiarity" and, later, "a species of imaginative mania" (*WW* 166). For days, unaware that it was Margaret — or rather, his "drunken rashness"—that caused Mrs. Conway's death, he entertains visions of crowds and glorious empires and rousing temperance speeches. When the news of Margaret's role in the murder is brought to Franklin, he recalls, "I myself was as one petrified" (*WW* 174). He is unable to take any action, either in defense of Margaret or in the discovery of the truth; once again he "shut[s himself] up in [his] room" and waits for a resolution (WW 174). That resolution comes with Margaret's suicide. At last Franklin is released from his paralysis, and he returns to New York a reformed man. Margaret functions in the narrative, then, as the vehicle through which Franklin is restored to sobriety: she embodies his dependency, which can then self-destruct and initiate his recovery. By objectifying his alcoholism, Margaret allows Franklin to separate himself from his tendencies toward dissipation. And to mark that separation by racial difference is to render it absolute. Once Franklin's intemperance takes the form of a Negro slave, in other words, there is no longer any danger of relapse, because Franklin's whiteness makes it impossible for him to cross over a boundary delineated by race. Thus American race slavery actually turns out to suit Whitman's purposes better than alternative versions of Otherness in which the dividing line is more permeable, for it is precisely the *im*permeability of the boundary that makes Franklin's absolute recovery possible. The slave Margaret, in short, solves the problem of Franklin's propensity to relapse into alcoholism: she fixes a boundary that, before Franklin's journey to Virginia, was ever in danger of dissolving — the boundary between sobriety and drunkenness, between productive citizenship and enslavement to alcohol.

During his period of inactivity that follows Mrs. Conway's murder, Franklin experiences a series of oddly stylized "visions" that once again raise the issue of American citizenship. In a combination of Blakean allegory and patriotic hymn, Franklin wanders through the crowds of a "mighty nation" listening to eloquent speakers proclaim the end of intemperance. "Victory! Victory!" says one such orator. "The Last Slave of Appetite is free, and the people are regenerated!" (WW 167, 170). But Franklin's vision of an emancipated citizenry is in the end a troubling one for us, for it does not entail the end of the institution of slavery but, on the contrary, the liberation of a white citizenry *through* the institutionalized enslavement of its Other. The problem, in other words, is that citizens are always in danger of becoming slaves, that the boundary between citizenship and slavery is always at risk of dissolving. We can hear that danger clearly in George Washington's reaction to the 1774 passage of the so-called Intolerable Acts: "we must assert our Rights," he wrote to Bryan Fairfax, "or Submit to every Imposition that can be heap'd upon us; till custom and use, will make us as tame, & abject Slaves, as the Blacks we Rule over with such arbitrary Sway."[21] Similarly, two years later, issuing General Orders to the Continental Army, he wrote, "Remember officers and Soldiers, that you are Freemen, fighting for the blessings of Liberty —

that slavery will be your portion, and that of your posterity, if you do not acquit yourselves like men."[22] Citizens must be ever vigilant, in other words, lest they allow themselves to fall into slavery. Likewise, Franklin Evans's alcoholism appears incurable at the outset of the Virginia episode: the standard sentimental temperance narrative, even the signing of the Old Temperance Pledge, is powerless to arrest his repeated falls into dependency. In order to achieve true independence, in order to secure his liberty once and for all, his dependency must return as the repressed Other of Gothic convention, distinguished from him by race, and legitimately enslaved for life. *Franklin Evans* provides us with a striking example of how the institution of slavery works, as Toni Morrison suggests, to "create" freedom (38). Franklin's own figurative enslavement to the bottle cannot be extirpated until it returns in the form of a literal slave; his own emancipation, in other words, is contingent upon the existence of Negro slavery as an institution. In the republic of free citizens represented in Whitman's temperance novel, slavery is not an aberration; it is, on the contrary, what underwrites and enables that citizenship.[23]

The Antislavery Gothic

In 1838 — the same year that William Harper imagined American civic liberty as a "circle of light" surrounded by the dark "horizon" of slavery — Theodore Dwight Weld dispatched a circular to his many friends and acquaintances describing his idea for a new antislavery pamphlet and soliciting their input. Conceived as a trial, the pamphlet would offer irrefutable "evidence" of the cruelty of the American slave system, both through the signed "testimony" of reputable witnesses, and — still more powerfully — by republishing such items from Southern newspapers as advertisements for runaway slaves that identified them by their mutilations. The pamphlet, Weld anticipated, would "thrill the land with horror" at the "barbarous cruelties ... inflicted upon [American slaves]."[24] The following year *American Slavery As It Is* appeared, shortly to become the best selling antislavery pamphlet ever published in the United States, a collection of accounts that even today has not lost its power to horrify. Like *Franklin Evans*, *Slavery As It Is* imagines the corruption infecting American society as a kind of addiction — in this case a craving for arbitrary power, which Weld describes as a "fiery stimulant" that "is to the mind what alcohol is to the body" (*TDW* 116, 115). "The more absolute the power," he writes, "the stronger the desire for it; and the more it is desired, the more its exercise is enjoyed" (*TDW* 115). And, just as Whitman suggests that intemperance has incapacitated Franklin for productive citizenship, Weld argues that slaveholding has degraded American civic life. Although slaveholders are "no … worse than other men," he claims, "arbitrary power has poisoned their better nature" and "unfitted [them] for self control in their intercourse with each other" (*TDW* 185, 187). Weld goes so far as to accuse slaveholders of "convert[ing] the Congress of the United States into a very bear garden," settling disagreements by fights and brawls rather than civil debate (*TDW* 184). But the overwhelming evil in the universe Weld creates is the inhuman treatment of slaves, excruciatingly evident in account after account. To read *American Slavery As It Is* is to leave the "circle of light," and traverse the dark horizon of enslavement that shadows the history of American civic liberty.

Several critics have noted Weld's use of Gothic conventions in his pamphlet,[25] and I would like to begin by taking a closer look at the common American Gothic figure of the slave who returns to haunt the slaveholder—a figure that bears certain similarities to Margaret in *Franklin Evans*.[26] In *Slavery As It Is*, Sarah Grimké's "narrative and testimony" includes this detail about a gentleman "of one of the first families in Charleston":

> The girl on whom he had so often inflicted punishment, haunted his dying hours; and when at length the king of terrors approached, he shrieked in utter agony of spirit, "Oh, the blackness of darkness, the black imps, I can see them all around me—take them away!" and amid such exclamations he expired [*TDW* 23].

Like Margaret, the "black imps" in Grimké's account are clearly figures for the slaveholder's own unmanageable impulses, his own inner demons, whose intoxicating pleasures have turned inexorably into self-destruction. But unlike *Franklin Evans*, *Slavery As It Is* espouses an antislavery politics, and the differences are illuminating. Whereas *Franklin Evans* objectifies Franklin's intemperance so as to disavow it, this particular scene does not permit us to see the slaveholder's demons as separate from his own internal pathology. And so while *Franklin Evans* is complicit with a proslavery message — specifically, the message that productive citizenship can be achieved if only one's slaves can be brought under control — Grimké's account never pretends that the disease lies anywhere other than in the slaveholder's own sinful nature. It is a scene of justified punishment for what we know were the chillingly brutal and unjust punishments he had "so often inflicted" on his young female slaves.

Nevertheless, the passage is no more self-conscious than *Franklin Evans* in its use of a racialized master-slave binary to represent an internal, white pathology. To associate the slaveholder's inner demons explicitly with "the girl on whom he had so often inflicted punishment" is to conflate the victim with the impulse to victimize, and to imagine that impulse as itself a vulnerable and brutalized thing. In the slaveholder's damaged psyche *both* master and slave have their counterparts and, in the end, the slaveholder turns out to be a slave to his own barbarity. The reversal that such a figure enacts, turning slaveholder into victim and projecting the impulse to cruelty onto the slave — complicit as it seems to be with the racist thinking that was so often marshaled in defense of the institution of slavery — is at best a highly ambiguous strategy for empowering slaves. But Weld's antislavery vision in *Slavery As It Is* imagines not the empowerment of slaves, but rather the self-destruction of the slave system from the force of its own internal contradictions; it is an apocalyptic vision that is entirely consistent with Weld's adherence to a racialized version of the Gothic. Weld's overall strategy in the pamphlet is to allow Southern slaveholders to testify against themselves, using excerpts from the Southern press to "draw their condemnation out of their own mouths" (*TDW* 9). It is a vision not of attack from without, but of self-destruction from within. Moreover, since the "thousand witnesses" of the pamphlet's subtitle are all presumably white, Weld's governing fiction of the courtroom effectively abides by the South's own rules, barring the direct "testimony" of slaves. But although the slaves are not permitted to tell their own stories, their presence is nevertheless continually evoked through the repeated spectacles of their brutalization and their ever-present "shrieks" and "groans," what one witness calls "auricular and ocular evidence of the cruelty of slavery, of cruelties that mortal language can never describe" (*TDW* 25). The uncanny, wordless presence of the slaves — summoned through, yet not comprehended by, language — can be understood as the counterpart to the pages of white testimony, the Other through which the "cruelty of slavery" will make itself known. Indeed, it is itself a kind of testimony — "*nature's* testimony," as Weld describes it in his introduction, "uttered ... with a shriek ever since the monster was begotten" (*TDW* 7).

The strategy of making Southerners unwittingly testify against themselves, then, appears in Weld's introduction as the return of the repressed Other, the buried truth that will not stay buried, whose dark, ghostly presence will haunt the pages of Southern newspapers despite — or, rather, because of — all the citizens' denials. It anticipates precisely the language of one of the better known accounts in *Slavery As It Is*, the account of an atrocity committed one night by Lilburn Lewis, a nephew of Thomas Jefferson, who in front of an audience of slaves hacked off a teenaged slave's limbs with a broad axe, piece by piece, burned the body parts, and then concealed the remains in a wall (*TDW* 93). When questioned by his wife, who had heard "a strange pounding and dreadful screams," Lewis denied the atrocity, saying "that he had never enjoyed himself at a ball so well as he had enjoyed himself that night." But the matter, as the Rev. Dickey testifies, "*could not be hid*— much as the negroes seemed to hazard, they did *whisper the horrid deed*." The wall was dismantled and the remains found, but before Lewis could be brought to justice he died by his own hand, in a bizarre suicide pact gone awry.[27] The story brings together both of the elements I have been discussing: a racialized version of the Gothic — including the pervasive Gothic trope of physical entrapment — and an unwitting but inevitable confession of white cruelty that results in its self-destruction. The "negroes" who "*whisper the horrid deed*," like the irrepressible testimony of "*nature*," are the sinister forces of exposure that will result in slavery's undoing, the tortured souls whose ghastly truth "[*can*]*not be hid*."

The point that I wish to re-emphasize, however, is that racial conflict — the whispering of black slaves about white atrocities— is here manifest as internal, psychological conflict within the slaveholder himself, brought on by his misrepresentation of the scene of torture as an evening of pleasure, and ending in his own grisly suicide. The brutality on which the system of slavery depends requires that the slaveholder be untrue to him*self*, that he harden his heart against his own humanity, just as to deny the horrors of slavery is, as Weld maintains in the introduction, to "libel [one's] heart" with one's "lips" (*TDW* 7). The "spirit of slaveholding," according to Weld, is "the paralysis of heart, and death of sympathy"; it will "kill in the soul whatever it touches" (*TDW* 171). Violence to one's slaves *is*, in Weld's reckoning, violence to the vulnerable thing in oneself, to one's heart or one's soul. And the horror of slavery lies precisely in its failure to recognize that fact, its failure to "*recognise*," as Angelina Grimké puts it in her testimony, "*a human being in a slave*" (*TDW* 57).

The concept of recognition is key. If we read Grimké's phrase as a sort of mirror scene in which the slaveholder fails to recognize his own likeness gazing back at him through the eyes of his victim, then slaveholding is being figured as a disease of self — a compulsive self-"libeling" and self-brutalization, along with the inability to recognize one's slaves as bound up with oneself or, more precisely, one's victimized inner self as one's own. It is a diagnosis entirely consistent with the pamphlet's reliance on the Gothic that, as William Patrick Day has argued, enacts the fragmentation and destruction of identity through a dynamic of sadomasochism.[28] According to Day, "the hero, who seeks to dominate his world and acts out the role of sadist, is also inflicting pain and suffering on himself, as all of his actions lead to his own destruction" (19). Likewise, in story after story in *Slavery As It Is*, the more infuriated the slaveholder becomes at his slaves' insubordination, the more his sadistic violence spins out of control, and the more we can sense the sands shifting beneath the entire institution of slavery. Furthermore, because the Gothic Other is, as Day puts it, "a version of the self"—in Weld's rendering, the slaveholder's own unacknowledged tenderheartedness—violence to the Other necessarily entails violence to the self. Sadism, in other words, spirals inexorably into masochistic self-mutilation. And finally, Day maintains, "all attempts to reject the unwanted and feared half of the self turn into acknowledgments of the Other's existence and expressions of the desire to confront the Other" (78). As Gothic hero, then, the slaveholder not only actively participates in his own destruction and undoing, his violent efforts to establish mastery over his slaves turning inevitably against himself; his actions also end up affirming the very thing he would deny — his utter incapacity for productive citizenship, his terrified dependency on a race he deems inferior — in short, his own abject enslavement.

If the Gothic provided Weld with a model for imagining the disintegration of slaveholding citizenship, it also brought implications for the way his readers would approach the text — implications that have been usefully examined in terms of the interrelation of Gothic and sentimental strategies. As Marianne Noble has pointed out, although the spectacle of suffering is central to both Gothic and sentimental texts, the difference between the two modes is often conceived spatially, in terms of the reader's distance from the scene of suffering.[29] Citing Cathy Davidson's study of the rise of the American novel, Noble explains that "the reader of gothic fiction ... experiences terror along with the victim, while the reader of sentimental fiction is helplessly detached from it but forced to watch" (164).[30] Similarly, Terry Heller's taxonomy of "tales of terror" emphasizes what he calls "psychical or aesthetic distance," indicating the degree of separation between the reader and the work of art. "It seems to be in the nature of a tale of terror," claims Heller, "to threaten aesthetic distance," and in its extreme forms it can obliterate aesthetic distance entirely, inducing readers to interact with it as if it were reality.[31] Applying Sedgwick's schema of inside and outside, we might say that Gothic texts are most effective when we find ourselves trapped inside the world of the text, while sentimental texts most effectively elicit our tears when we are helplessly exiled from the scene of suffering, powerless to assuage it, and condemned to a sympathetic or vicarious experience that can never be sufficient. For Weld, it was precisely the distance of Northern readers from the horrors of slavery that was at issue — a distance he believed could be overcome in the "thrilling" testimony of his pamphlet. If only the defender of slavery could be induced to imagine *himself* enslaved, there would be no more need for antislavery arguments.[32] The Gothic also functions for Weld, then, as a means of enslaving his readers.

Nevertheless, as useful as the Gothic would appear to be, Weld ultimately prescribes a sentimental remedy for the civic contagion of slavery. Once slaveholding is defined as a "death of sympathy," a failure to recognize the slave's plight as one's own, readers of *Slavery As It Is* are left with no choice but to respond to the text sentimentally. In order to distance themselves from the "spirit of slavery," with its "paralysis of heart," and from the editors of Southern newspapers, who publish advertisements for runaway slaves "with iron indifference," the Northern readers must cultivate sympathy and tenderheartedness, and read with their own vulnerable inner selves on the line (*TDW* 152). If slavery entails a self-inflicted and self-enforced "paralysis" of sentiment, a denial of what "every man," as Weld writes in the introduction, "knows" in his "heart," then the antislavery cause must foster sentiment by contemplating the anguish of slaves, "remember[ing] those who are in bonds," as Sarah Grimké wrote to her friend Jane Smith, describing her work on *Slavery As It Is*, "as bound with them."[33] To internalize the bondage of slavery is to feel what the slaveholders have not permitted themselves to feel; it is to feel what slaveholders *cannot* permit themselves to feel without undermining the very foundation of the institution. Paradoxically, it is precisely the experience of feeling trapped within the text — something Weld appears to promote in his introduction — that inhibits the sentimental response since, as Davidson and others have argued, sentiment depends upon the reader's detachment from the scene of suffering. It is important, here, to distinguish between the effects of the Gothic and sentimental modes and the *desires* they produce: the Gothic effect is to entrap, producing the desire to escape, to externalize, to separate; the sentimental effect is to detach, thereby producing the desire to merge. Sentimental suffering is vicarious suffering; it is the desire to assume another creature's pain, and its primary fantasy is to imagine the suffering from which one is helplessly exiled as subsumed by and contained within the self.[34]

Slavery As It Is, then, by imagining slavery as a disease of white selfhood, also posits the remedy within white selves. But it does so in terms that are explicitly racialized: a white citizenry is reformed by internalizing and assuming black suffering as its own. Julie Ellison has examined some of the problems entailed in such a model in her reading of eighteenth-century British dramas of civic life, in which "representations of race are also representations of sentiment." Such dramas, she argues, "map out a zone of emotion that absorbs racial difference into subjectivity."[35]

Likewise, *Slavery As It Is* turns the torture of black slaves into the affective experience of the white reader, and imagines that process as the mechanism for healing the public life of the nation: it is, to apply Ellison's language, "affection experienced as public crisis, ... public crisis experienced as affection" (73). Such mechanisms, Saidiya V. Hartman has shown, are inherently problematic because they render actual black suffering secondary to vicarious white suffering:

> The effort to counteract the commonplace callousness to black suffering requires that the white body be positioned in the place of the black body in order to make this suffering visible and intelligible. Yet if this violence can become palpable and indignation can be fully aroused only through the masochistic fantasy, then it becomes clear that empathy is double-edged, for in making the other's suffering one's own, this suffering is occluded by the other's obliteration.[36]

As a cure for civic "callousness," then, *Slavery As It Is* induces tender-heartedness at the expense of critical insight: the experience of slaves is occluded by the reading public's affective response, and Weld's sentimental remedy for the civic corruption brought about by the slave system turns out to be no more politically inclusive than a racialized Gothic.

In her essay on the Gothic and social reform, Karen Halttunen reads one of Henry Ward Beecher's sermons in which moral reform is imagined as exorcising the feminized demons from the haunted house of prostitution.[37] Such configurations are problematic, as Halttunen points out, for their complicity with misogynistic representations of female sexuality, and also for their capacity to deflect the guilt from men onto women. Likewise, *Franklin Evans* imagines Franklin's reform as the exorcism of the "fiend Intemperance," and carries disturbing implications in its representation of that demon as a slave whose death precipitates Franklin's recovery: it too deflects guilt while reinforcing racist stereotypes. But Weld's application of the Gothic to the antislavery cause is more complicated, and more ambivalent in its politics. If Franklin Evans is restored to productive citizenship by learning to fear — rather than desire — his intemperance, thereby being absolved of his own complicity in his affliction, Weld's vision of reform hinges on acknowledging the tormented darkness within and recognizing it as one's own. And if *Franklin Evans* ultimately projects white guilt onto the slave and replaces it with fear, *Slavery As It Is* actively produces white guilt in ways that anticipate the so-called bleeding-heart liberalism of the twentieth century.[38] Indeed, we might say that Sarah Grimké's account of the Charleston gentleman's death agonies exposes the guilt that underlies his fear. Nevertheless, anguished and self-afflicted as it is, Weld's vision of a reformed citizenry is in the final analysis no less white than Whitman's. His courtroom is tormented by the cries of black slaves without permitting their testimony, imagining them not as participants in the cause of antislavery, but as haunting projections of a white citizenry's own dark interior; while his ostensibly inclusive alternative occludes black suffering by transforming it into the white reader's sentimental response.

Notes

1. William Harper, *Memoir on Slavery, Read Before the Society for the Advancement of Learning of South Carolina at Its Annual Meeting at Columbia, 1837*, in *The Ideology of Slavery: Proslavery Thought in the Antebellum South, 1830–1860*, ed. Drew Gilpin Faust (Baton Rouge: Louisiana State University Press, 1981), 78–135. The author received support for the writing of this essay from an Ohio State University Seed Grant, and acknowledges the gracious and competent assistance of the librarians and archivists at the William Clements Library, University of Michigan, in researching Theodore Dwight Weld. Nancy Jesser and Anne Bower each read an earlier draft of this essay, and my subsequent revisions owe much to their astute comments and suggestions.

2. John Locke, *An Essay Concerning Human Understanding*, Vol. 1, ed. Alexander Campbell Fraser (New York: Dover Publications, 1959), 31–32. See also Terry Castle's reading of Locke's figure of the horizon in *The Female Thermometer: Eighteenth-Century Culture and the Invention of the Uncanny* (New York: Oxford University Press, 1995), 7–9.

3. Harper, 85 (emphasis in original).

4. There is a vast literature, and much disagreement among scholars, on the role of slavery in the production of antebellum American citizenship. In *The Ideological Origins of the American Revolution*, Bernard Bailyn identified slavery as "a central concept in eighteenth-century political discourse," used not simply as hyperbole, but as a figure for "the condition of all who had lost the power of self-determination," and thus as "the absolute political evil." In Bailyn's analysis, then, it was "inevitable" that the institution of slavery come under attack, because it posed such a glaring contradiction to the values underlying American political discourse — an "anomaly," as Pauline Maier has called it. By contrast, Edmund S. Morgan and, more recently, Toni Morrison, have argued that, far from being an anomaly, slavery was the essential condition against which American citizenship came to be defined. According to Morgan, Negro slavery solved the problem of large numbers of landless, upwardly mobile white workers who would eventually be demanding the privileges of citizenship, providing instead a fixed class of laborers who, by definition, could never expect to attain citizenship, and fixing the boundary indelibly by race. Drawing on Orlando Patterson, Morrison argues that "the concept of freedom did not emerge in a vacuum": her analysis of literary representations of blackness leads her to conclude that "nothing highlighted freedom — if it did not in fact create it — like slavery." Bernard Bailyn, *The Ideological Origins of the American Revolution* (Cambridge, Massachusetts: Harvard University Press, 1967), 232–246; Pauline Maier, *American Scripture: Making the Declaration of Independence* (New York: Knopf, 1997), 147; Edmund S. Morgan, *American Slavery, American Freedom: The Ordeal of Colonial Virginia* (New York and London: Norton, 1975); Toni Morrison, *Playing in the Dark: Whiteness and the Literary Imagination* (Cambridge, Massachusetts: Harvard University Press, 1992), 38; and Orlando Patterson, *Slavery*

and Social Death: A Comparative Study (Cambridge, Massachusetts: Harvard University Press, 1982). For an analysis of the role of race in consolidating early American identity, which must distinguish itself from Europe without becoming associated with Europe's racial Other, see Jared Gardner, *Master Plots: Race and the Founding of an American Literature, 1787–1845* (Baltimore: Johns Hopkins University Press, 1998).

5. Eve Kosofsky Sedgwick, *The Coherence of Gothic Conventions* (New York: Methuen, 1980). Sedgwick identifies the "three main elements" of her spatial model of the Gothic as "what's inside, what's outside, and what separates them." "The self and whatever it is that is outside have a proper, natural, necessary connection to each other," she continues, "but one that the self is suddenly incapable of making. The inside life and the outside life have to continue separately, becoming counterparts rather than partners, the relationship between them one of parallels and correspondences rather than communication. This, though it may happen in an instant, is a fundamental reorganization, creating doubleness where singleness should be. And the lengths there are to go to reintegrate the sundered elements—finally, the impossibility of restoring them to their original oneness—are the most characteristic energies of the Gothic novel." Sedgwick, 13. See also Eugenia C. DeLamotte, *Perils of the Night: A Feminist Study of Nineteenth-Century Gothic* (New York: Oxford University Press, 1990), 25–28.

6. Walter Whitman, *Franklin Evans; or, The Inebriate: A Tale of the Times*, ed. Jean Downey (New Haven: College and University Press, 1967), hereafter cited parenthetically as WW; Theodore Dwight Weld, *American Slavery As It Is: Testimony of a Thousand Witnesses* (1839; Salem, New Hampshire: Ayer Company, Publishers, Inc., 1991), hereafter cited parenthetically as TDW.

7. See Hegel's analysis of "Lordship and Bondage," G. W. F. Hegel, *Phenomenology of Spirit*, trans. A. V. Miller (Oxford: Oxford University Press, 1977), 111–19.

8. William Patrick Day, *In the Circles of Fear and Desire: A Study of Gothic Fantasy* (Chicago: University of Chicago Press, 1985), 20.

9. Rosemary Jackson, *Fantasy: The Literature of Subversion* (London and New York: Methuen, 1981), 50.

10. Similarly, in her reading of Poe's *Narrative of Arthur Gordon Pym*, Toni Morrison describes the "figurations of impenetrable whiteness that surface in American literature whenever an Africanist presence is engaged." Such figurations, Morrison argues, carry a "strong suggestion of paralysis and incoherence; of impasse and non-sequitur." Morrison, 32–33.

11. Homi K. Bhabha, *The Location of Culture* (London and New York: Routledge, 1994), 137.

12. Bhabha is drawing on the Freudian mechanism of disavowal (*Verleugnung*).

13. Margaret Morse, "What Do Cyborgs Eat? Oral Logic in an Information Society," in *Culture on the Brink: Ideologies of Technology*, eds. Gretchen Bender and Timothy Druckrey (Seattle: Bay Press, 1999), 160.

14. My approach here generally follows Morrison in *Playing in the Dark*: "The slave population, it could be and was assumed, offered itself up as surrogate selves for meditation on problems of human freedom, its lure and its elusiveness. This black population was available for meditations on terror — the terror of European outcasts, their dread of failure, powerlessness, Nature without limits, natal loneliness, internal aggression, evil, sin, greed. In other words, this slave population was understood to have offered itself up for reflections on human freedom in terms other than the abstractions of human potential and the rights of man." As Morrison clearly demonstrates in her reading of *Sapphira and the Slave Girl*, the function of the Africanist persona is "reflexive"; it provides an opportunity for the troubled white subject to reflect on its own internal conflicts (Morrison, 37–38, 17).

15. See Jean Downey's introduction to *Franklin Evans* (Walter Whitman, *Franklin Evans*; or, *The Inebriate: A Tale of the Times*, ed. Jean Downey [New Haven: College and University Press, 1967]).

16. Eric Lott, *Love and Theft: Blackface Minstrelsy and the American Working Class* (New York: Oxford University Press, 1993), 78.

17. Carroll Smith-Rosenberg, "Black Gothic: The Shadowy Origins of the American Bourgeoisie," in *Possible Pasts: Becoming Colonial in Early America*, ed. Robert Blair St. George (Ithaca and London: Cornell University Press, 2000).

18. Sigmund Freud, "The 'Uncanny,'" in *The Standard Edition of the Complete Psychological Works of Sigmund Freud*, Vol. 17, ed. James Strachey (London: Hogarth Press, 1959).

19. It is significant, I would suggest, that Margaret must be emancipated by Bourne when Franklin marries her. But emancipation does not change her ineradicable racial characteristics, the "fire of her race" that, as Whitman writes, "burnt with all its brightness in her bosom, though smothered by the necessity of circumstances" (*WW* 141). Indeed, as Whitman explains, it is precisely the "remnant of the savage" still residing in her "heart" that provokes her murderous deed (*WW* 161).

20. For a useful discussion of the strategy of representation he calls "simulacral realism" (drawing on Jean Baudrillard), see Phillip Brian Harper, *Are We Not Men? Masculine Anxiety and the Problem of African American Identity* (New York and Oxford: Oxford University Press, 1996), 160.

21. From an August 24, 1774, letter. George Washington, Writings, ed. John Rhodehamel (New York: Library of America, 1997), 158.

22. Issued from Washington's headquarters at New York, August 23, 1776. Ibid., 239.

23. As Orlando Patterson writes, "The joint rise of slavery and cultivation of freedom was no accident. It was ... a sociohistorical necessity" (Orlando Patterson, *Slavery and Social Death: A Comparative Study* [Cambridge, Massachusetts: Harvard University Press, 1982], ix).

24. From a 28 November 1838 circular Weld sent out under the auspices of the American Anti-Slavery Society to solicit material for his proposed pamphlet. *Letters of Theodore Dwight Weld, Angelina Grimké Weld, and Sarah Grimké, 1822–1844*, Vol. II, ed. Gilbert H. Barnes and Dwight L. Dumond (New York and London: D. Appleton-Century Company, Inc., 1934), 717.

25. For example, Teresa A. Goddu, *Gothic America: Narrative, History, and Nation* (New York: Columbia University Press, 1997); Stephen Browne, "'Like Gory Spectres': Representing Evil in Theodore Weld's *American Slavery As It Is*," *Quarterly Journal of Speech 80* (1994): 277–92; and Richard O. Curry and Joanna Dunlap Cowden, eds., *Slavery in America: Theodore Weld's* American Slavery As It Is (Itasca, Illinois: F. E. Peacock Publishers, 1972). In Goddu's reading, Gothic texts in which darkness is racialized often exist in complex and contradictory relation to the antislavery effort. Referring specifically to *American Slavery As It Is*, she writes, "Nature's testimony against slavery is not the scene itself but the white viewer's response to it.... Paradoxically, the gothic effect subsumes the gothic event even as it testifies to its horrors" (135). For a differing analysis of the politics of the Gothic in antislavery discourse, see Kari J. Winter, *Subjects of Slavery, Agents of Change: Women and Power in Gothic Novels and Slave Narratives, 1790–1865* (Athens, Georgia: University of Georgia Press, 1992).

26. The classic example appears in *Uncle Tom's Cabin*, where Cassy "haunts" Simon Legree. For readings of the Gothic in *Uncle Tom's Cabin*, see Sandra M. Gilbert and Susan Gubar, *The Madwoman in the Attic: The Woman Writer and the Nineteenth-Century Literary Imagination* (New Haven: Yale University Press, 1978), and Karen Halttunen, "Gothic Imagination and Social Reform: The Haunted Houses of Lyman

Beecher, Henry Ward Beecher, and Harriet Beecher Stowe," in *New Essays on Uncle Tom's Cabin*, ed. Eric J. Sundquist (Cambridge and New York: Cambridge University Press, 1986), 107–134. In "Memories of Theodore Dwight Weld: The St. John of the Abolitionists" (unpublished manuscript, Grimké-Weld Collection, William L. Clements Library, University of Michigan), Weld's daughter Sarah Grimké Hamilton reports that Harriet Beecher Stowe "told Mrs. Weld that she kept that book [*American Slavery As It Is*] in her work-basket by day and slept with it under her pillow at night till its facts crystallized into 'Uncle Tom'" (Hamilton, 11: 289).

27. The Poe-like qualities of the story — in particular its use of the Gothic motif of burial and disinterment — are unmistakable. For an excellent contextualization of Poe's "The Black Cat" in the discourses of pro- and antislavery (including *Slavery As It Is*) and pet abuse, see Lesley Ginsberg, "Slavery and the Gothic Horror of Poe's 'The Black Cat,'" in *American Gothic: New Interventions in a National Narrative*, ed. Robert K. Martin and Eric Savoy (Iowa City: University of Iowa Press, 1998), 99–128.

28. Day, 19–23.

29. Marianne Noble, "An Ecstasy of Apprehension: The Gothic Pleasures of Sentimental Fiction," in *American Gothic: New Interventions in a National Narrative*, eds. Robert K. Martin and Eric Savoy (Iowa City: University of Iowa Press, 1998).

30. See also Cathy Davidson, *Revolution and the Word: The Rise of the Novel in America* (New York: Oxford University Press, 1986).

31. Terry Heller, *The Delights of Terror: An Aesthetics of the Tale of Terror* (Urbana and Chicago: University of Illinois Press, 1987), 2–3.

32. "Try him," writes Weld; "clank the chains and tell him they are for *him*. Give him an hour to prepare his wife and children for a life of slavery. Bid him make haste and get ready their necks for the yoke, and their wrists for the co°e chains, then look at his pale lips and trembling knees, and you have *nature's* testimony against slavery" (*TDW* 7).

33. Sarah M. Grimké to Jane Smith, 24 Jan. 1839, Grimké-Weld Collection, William L. Clements Library, University of Michigan.

34. The sentimental fantasy, therefore, can be seen as a version of what Margaret Morse terms the logic of "incorporation." "Unlike identification," writes Morse, "incorporation does not depend on likeness or similarity or mirrors in order to mistake the other as the self; in an 'oral-sadistic' or 'cannibalistic' fantasy, the introjected object ... is occluded and destroyed, only in order to be assimilated and to transform its host" (Morse 160).

35. Julie Ellison, *Cato's Tears and the Making of Anglo-American Emotion* (Chicago and London: University of Chicago Press, 1999), 48.

36. Saidiya V. Hartman, *Scenes of Subjection: Terror, Slavery, and Self-Making in Nineteenth-Century America* (New York: Oxford University Press, 1997), 19. For another reading of the problematic politics of racializing sentiment, see Laura Wexler, "Tender Violence: Literary Eavesdropping, Domestic Fiction, and Educational Reform," in *The Culture of Sentiment: Race, Gender, and Sentimentality in Nineteenth-Century America*, ed. Shirley Samuels (New York: Oxford University Press, 1992), 9–38.

37. Halttunen, "Gothic Imagination and Social Reform."

38. See Julie Ellison's discussion of the structures of liberal guilt, *Cato's Tears*, 171–194.

Works Cited

Bailyn, Bernard. *The Ideological Origins of the American Revolution.* Cambridge, Massachusetts: Harvard University Press, 1967.

Bhabha, Homi K. *The Location of Culture*. London and New York: Routledge, 1994.

Browne, Stephen. "'Like Gory Spectres': Representing Evil in Theodore Weld's *American Slavery As It Is*." *Quarterly Journal of Speech*. 80 (1994): 277–92.

Castle, Terry. *The Female Thermometer: Eighteenth-Century Culture and the Invention of the Uncanny*. New York and Oxford: Oxford University Press, 1995.

Curry, Richard O., and Joanna Dunlap Cowden, eds. *Slavery in America: Theodore Weld's* American Slavery As It Is. Itasca, Illinois: F. E. Peacock Publishers, 1972.

Davidson, Cathy. *Revolution and the Word: The Rise of the Novel in America*. New York: Oxford University Press, 1986.

Day, William Patrick. *In the Circles of Fear and Desire: A Study of Gothic Fantasy*. Chicago: University of Chicago Press, 1985.

DeLamotte, Eugenia C. *Perils of the Night: A Feminist Study of Nineteenth-Century Gothic*. New York and Oxford: Oxford University Press, 1990.

Ellison, Julie. *Cato's Tears and the Making of Anglo-American Emotion*. Chicago and London: University of Chicago Press, 1999.

Freud, Sigmund. "The 'Uncanny.'" In *The Standard Edition of the Complete Psychological Works of Sigmund Freud*. Vol. 17. Edited by James Strachey. London: Hogarth Press, 1959.

Gardner, Jared. *Master Plots: Race and the Founding of an American Literature, 1787–1845*. Baltimore: Johns Hopkins University Press, 1998.

Gilbert, Sandra M., and Susan Gubar. *The Madwoman in the Attic: The Woman Writer and the Nineteenth-Century Literary Imagination*. New Haven: Yale University Press, 1978.

Ginsberg, Lesley. "Slavery and the Gothic Horror of Poe's 'The Black Cat.'" In *American Gothic: New Interventions in a National Narrative*. Edited by Robert K. Martin and Eric Savoy. Iowa City: University of Iowa Press, 1998.

Goddu, Teresa A. *Gothic America: Narrative, History, and Nation*. New York: Columbia University Press, 1997.

Halttunen, Karen. "Gothic Imagination and Social Reform: The Haunted Houses of Lyman Beecher, Henry Ward Beecher, and Harriet Beecher Stowe." In *New Essays on Uncle Tom's Cabin*. Edited by Eric J. Sundquist. Cambridge and New York: Cambridge University Press, 1986.

Hamilton, Sarah Grimké. "Memories of Theodore Dwight Weld: The St. John of the Abolitionists." Unpublished manuscript. Grimké-Weld Collection, William L. Clements Library, University of Michigan.

Harper, Phillip Brian. *Are We Not Men? Masculine Anxiety and the Problem of African American Identity*. New York and Oxford: Oxford University Press, 1996.

Harper, William. *Memoir on Slavery, Read Before the Society for the Advancement of Learning of South Carolina at Its Annual Meeting at Columbia, 1837*. In *The Ideology of Slavery: Proslavery Thought in the Antebellum South, 1830–1860*. Edited by Drew Gilpin Faust. Baton Rouge: Louisiana State University Press, 1981.

Hartman, Saidiya V. *Scenes of Subjection: Terror, Slavery, and Self-Making in Nineteenth-Century America*. New York: Oxford University Press, 1997.

Hegel, G. W. F. *Phenomenology of Spirit*. Translated by A. V. Miller. Oxford: Oxford University Press, 1977.

Heller, Terry. *The Delights of Terror: An Aesthetics of the Tale of Terror*. Urbana and Chicago: University of Illinois Press, 1987.

Jackson, Rosemary. *Fantasy: The Literature of Subversion*. London and New York: Methuen, 1981.

Letters of Theodore Dwight Weld, Angelina Grimké Weld, and Sarah Grimké, 1822–1844, Vol. II. Edited by Gilbert H. Barnes and Dwight L. Dumond. New York and London: D. Appleton-Century Company, Inc., 1934.

Locke, John. *An Essay Concerning Human Understanding*, Vol. 1. Edited by Alexander Campbell Fraser. New York: Dover Publications, 1959.

Lott, Eric. *Love and Theft: Blackface Minstrelsy and the American Working Class.* New York: Oxford University Press, 1993.

Maier, Pauline. *American Scripture: Making the Declaration of Independence.* New York: Knopf, 1997.

Morgan, Edmund S. *American Slavery, American Freedom: The Ordeal of Colonial Virginia.* New York and London: Norton, 1975.

Morrison, Toni. *Playing in the Dark: Whiteness and the Literary Imagination.* Cambridge, Massachusetts: Harvard University Press, 1992.

Morse, Margaret. "What Do Cyborgs Eat? Oral Logic in an Information Society." In *Culture on the Brink: Ideologies of Technology.* Edited by Gretchen Bender and Timothy Druckrey. Seattle: Bay Press, 1999.

Noble, Marianne. "An Ecstasy of Apprehension: The Gothic Pleasures of Sentimental Fiction." In *American Gothic: New Interventions in a National Narrative.* Edited by Robert K. Martin and Eric Savoy. Iowa City: University of Iowa Press, 1998.

Patterson, Orlando. *Slavery and Social Death: A Comparative Study.* Cambridge, Massachusetts: Harvard University Press, 1982.

Sedgwick, Eve Kosofsky. *The Coherence of Gothic Conventions.* New York: Methuen, 1980.

Smith-Rosenberg, Carroll. "Black Gothic: The Shadowy Origins of the American Bourgeoisie." In *Possible Pasts: Becoming Colonial in Early America.* Edited by Robert Blair St. George. Ithaca and London: Cornell University Press, 2000.

Washington, George. *Writings.* Edited by John Rhodehamel. New York: Library of America, 1997.

Weld, Theodore Dwight. *American Slavery As It Is: Testimony of a Thousand Witnesses.* 1839. Salem, New Hampshire: Ayer Company, Publishers, Inc., 1991.

Wexler, Laura. "Tender Violence: Literary Eavesdropping, Domestic Fiction, and Educational Reform." In *The Culture of Sentiment: Race, Gender, and Sentimentality in Nineteenth-Century America.* Edited by Shirley Samuels. New York: Oxford University Press, 1992.

Whitman, Walter. *Franklin Evans; or, The Inebriate: A Tale of the Times.* Edited by Jean Downey. New Haven: College and University Press, 1967.

Winter, Kari J. *Subjects of Slavery, Agents of Change: Women and Power in Gothic Novels and Slave Narratives, 1790–1865.* Athens, Georgia: University of Georgia Press, 1992.

3

Cane: Jean Toomer's Gothic Black Modernism

Daphne Lamothe

Introduction

Jean Toomer, a writer of the Harlem Renaissance, recognized that in the America of the 1920s, the racial hybrid was viewed as monstrously unknowable because the mulatto was proof of the violation of social sanctions and boundaries against miscegenation. Yet Toomer also recognized that the national myth of racial and social purity co-existed with a long, complex history of racial encounters and exchange (both private and public, violently oppressive and benign). In his work, Toomer identifies the Gothic tradition as the literary form capable of capturing this paradox; in particular, he considers the transgressive figure of the mulatto as the vehicle with which to both explore America's repression of difference *and* to refuse entrenched notions of social and racial fragmentation. Toomer's interest in the mulatto as inscrutable and terrifying Other places him firmly in an American Gothic tradition that positions race at the center of its imaginative universe.

Scholars have long noted Toomer's Harlem Renaissance masterpiece, *Cane* (1923), for its sensitive and insightful portrait of the South and its Negro inhabitants. Toomer wrote this cycle of short stories, vignettes and poems after having lived for two years in Sparta, Georgia, serving as the temporary head of an industrial and agricultural school for Negroes. In a letter to *The Liberator*, he describes the experiences that inspired him:

A visit to Georgia last fall was the starting point of almost everything of worth that I have done. I heard folk-songs come from the lips of Negro peasants. I saw the rich dusk beauty that I had heard many false accents about, and of which till then, I was somewhat skeptical. And a deep part of my nature, a part that I had repressed, sprang suddenly to life and responded to them. Now, I cannot conceive of myself as aloof and separated. My point of view has not changed; it has deepened, it has widened.[1]

Toomer describes being moved by the beauty of Southern black culture, and he tells of that culture speaking to a long buried part of himself, inspiring him to find his voice as a writer. In stating that his point of view had not changed but had "deepened" and "widened," he suggests that his time in the South tapped an artistic vein within that had previously been unacknowledged, presumably because he had not recognized or fully accepted, up to the point of his travels to the South, his connection to Southern black history and culture.[2]

Toomer's multi-racial heritage[3] has been the source of considerable attention, primarily as a means of comprehending the author's reasons for and process of writing the text and explaining the narrator's point of view, which alternates between detached observation and engaged participation in the community he describes.[4] Often these discussions revolve, often implicitly, around questions of racial authenticity and passing. This inclination in the criticism is fueled by Toomer's declaration, prior even to the publication of *Cane*, that he was not black but a member of a new American race, which commingled all of its racial and ethnic elements.[5] In a letter to *The Liberator* dated August 19, 1922, Toomer declares:

From my point of view I am naturally and inevitably an American. I have striven for a spiritual fusion analogous to the fact of racial intermingling. Without denying a single element in me, with no desire to subdue, one to the other. I have sought to let them function as complements. I have tried to let them live in harmony [Rusch 15–16].

Charles R. Larson argues that, "by saying that he was a member of a new race, the American race, he was also stating that he was not a Negro and that he wanted nothing to do with negritude, although he probably could not admit this to himself at the time."[6] Darwin Turner offers a professional, rather than personal, motivation for Toomer's rejection of his blackness: it may have been the fear "that the racial identification caused publishers to reject as un–Negro the literature he wanted to create" (xxiii). The larger social implications of Toomer's insistence on recognizing his racial hybridity, which he explores in *Cane* primarily through his use of Gothic imagery, prove more illuminating, however, than his personal or professional investment in claiming or denying his blackness.

While it is certainly legitimate to read Toomer's travels to Georgia as a symbolic homecoming, it is also clear that his interests were more than regional and in fact centered on the intersections of Northern and Southern, Black and White American experiences. Toomer divided *Cane* into three parts, with the first part set in the South, the second in the North, and the third returning to the South. The first section consists of a series of poems and prose vignettes about individuals, primarily women, living in a small community in Georgia. The Northern section consists largely of stories about urban men and women whose profound alienation and disconnectedness is figured through their failed romantic relationships. It also includes some poems that extend the theme of alienation, while celebrating the vibrancy of urban life. The final section is a dramatic piece that attempts to resolve the conflicts set up in the first two sections. It revolves around a Northerner, Kabnis, who grapples to find his place in the South and to accept the relevance of its history to his personal experience. Toomer's modernist experimentation with the genre fits neatly within Teresa Goddu's understanding of the Gothic as a mutable and unstable genre. She writes, "cobbled together of many different forms and obsessed with transgressing boundaries, it [the Gothic] represents itself not as stable but as generically impure."[7] Toomer's interest in generic *and* genetic impurity (for example, the U.S. history of miscegenation) places him firmly within the territory of the Gothic, as does his exploration of the history and meaning of slavery and the modern insistence on uniformity and conformity that he associates with industrialization. Rather than detracting from his focus on the function of the mulatto, Toomer's interest in history and modernity illuminates this topic, the former because of slavery's institutionalization in both civic and legal terms of absolute racial difference and the latter because it reveals the continuation of an ideology of enforced fragmentation and difference.

Nonetheless, this Gothic contextualization of Toomer's text is not without its problems because *Cane* is so far removed in time, space and culture from a literary tradition that originates in the late eighteenth-century period of English Romanticism.[8] *Cane* has more commonly been read in terms of its narration of the Great Migration from rural South to urban North,[9] of its figuring of the beauty of the South through complex portraits of its women,[10] or as being the first expression of Toomer's spiritual quest for wholeness, which comes to its fullest expression in his post–*Cane* career when he becomes a follower of spiritualist Gurdjieff.[11] This last critical approach comes under scrutiny in the sole book-length study of *Cane* that recognizes Toomer's use of the Gothic, Charles Scruggs and Lee Vandemarr's *Jean Toomer and the Terrors of American History*. Scruggs and

Vandemarr dismiss those critics who focus on Toomer's quest for "whole-ness," arguing that the "'spiritual' always appears in *Cane* within a polit-ical context..." (4). While it may be an overstatement to call Toomer's emerging spiritual interests "irrelevant to *Cane*'s meaning," Scruggs and Vandemarr astutely and convincingly argue for the necessity of reinsert-ing the social and political contexts that inform the text.[12] They view Toomer's venture into the popular genres of Gothic horror and detective fiction as evidence of the author's primary concern with the social and his-torical, arguing that these forms share a "concern with the past" (135). This reading takes on enhanced meaning within the context of Goddu's argument for the association between the Gothic and history: "through the African American version, the gothic's relationship to history is fully revealed" (12). In other words, in Goddu's formulation the history of slav-ery haunts America, disrupting its national myths of innocence and demo-cratic egalitarianism.

Certainly Scruggs and van de Marr are correct in arguing that Toomer's concern with race and American identity, and, in particular, the history of miscegenation, lead him to experiment with the Gothic, a lit-erary form that emphasizes secrets and their excavation. But Toomer's Gothicism requires additional explanation because the genre was not an obvious influence within the American literary traditions embraced by Toomer. Allan Lloyd-Smith points to some of the material artifacts tradi-tionally found in Gothic fiction and notes their absence in the United States: "without a feudal past and those relics so convenient for the Euro-pean Gothicist, castles and monasteries and legends, the American land-scape seemed an unlikely place for such fictions."[13] Indeed, Toomer's turn to Gothic tropes in *Cane* underscores the fact that as late as the 1920s, there was no vocabulary native to this country with which to refer to the horrors of slavery, race and racism.[14]

Nonetheless, an American variant of the Gothic does exist, with race proving to be an organizing concept central to its development. Smith identifies race as one of four elements "indigenous" to America that has proven decisive in "producing a powerful and long-lasting American vari-ant of the Gothic..." (109).[15] In a similar vein, Toni Morrison has argued in *Playing in the Dark: Whiteness and the Literary Imagination* that the "Africanist" presence, found often but not exclusively in the American Gothic Romance (for example, Poe and Hawthorne), makes possible:

> an exploration of anxiety imported from the shadows of European culture
> ... Americans' fear of being outcast, of failing, of powerlessness; their fear
> of boundarylessness, of Nature unbridled and crouched for attack; their
> fear of the absence of so-called civilization; their fear of loneliness, of

aggression both external and internal. In short, the terror of human freedom — the thing they coveted most of all.[16]

Where Smith argues that uneasiness with contradictions between demo-
cratic ideals and racial subjugation gives rise to the literary emergence of
the racialized subject as the Gothic Other, Morrison argues that a much
wider array of anxieties have been projected in canonical literature onto
"conveniently bound and violently silenced black bodies" (38).

If, as Morrison elucidates, Euro-Americans employed the Gothic
Other as a racialized figure for a myriad of social and metaphysical anxieties ("the terror of human freedom"), we find that African American writers typically make use of the Gothic to convey the terrors of American
social history. African American Gothicisms evoke experiences of absence,
fragmentation and loss, characteristic of "the black experience." In Harriet Jacobs's slave narrative, *Incidents in the Life of a Slave Girl*, for example, Jacobs repeatedly describes slaveowners and the institution of slavery
as demonic and characterizes her period in hiding as a live burial. Goddu
has identified the Gothic as a typical feature of the American slave narrative: "With descriptions of slavery as a feudal institution, horrifying scenes
of torture and entrapment, lascivious masters and innocent slave girls,
and curses on many generations, the slave narrative reads like a gothic
romance with a single, crucial difference: the scenery is not staged but
real" (137). Another example of Gothicism in African American literature
is Richard Wright's *Native Son* in which he inverts the "American Africanism" that Morrison describes by depicting whites and whiteness as signifiers
of death and dread.

Toomer's concern with issues of race, then, combine with his investment in the emerging "New Negro" philosophy, enabling him to create a
particular brand of Gothic black modernism, a modernism with Gothic
evocations. The New Negroes' espousal of the twentieth century as the
dawn of an era in which African Americans would free themselves from
past assumptions of racial inferiority and subordination echoes the tenets
of the Enlightenment era.[17] Alain Locke asserts in his 1925 manifesto, "the
mind of the Negro seems suddenly to have slipped from under the tyranny
of social intimidation and to be shaking off the psychology of imitation
and implied inferiority. By shedding the old chrysalis of the Negro problem we are achieving something like a spiritual emancipation."[18] This statement and Locke's distinction between "old" and "new" Negroes echo the
notions of eighteenth-century writers who "liked to refer to their present
as 'modern' and thus distinct from both a classical antiquity appreciated
in its historical continuity and a feudal past regarded as a barbaric and

primitive stage, the dominance of which had been discontinued."[19] Black modernists like Toomer were eager to leave behind and rise above a recent past of racial oppression to which they attributed many of the same characteristics associated by Enlightenment philosophers with the medieval Goths (barbarism, lack of reason) and to articulate a continuity with an African past that constituted their particular "classical antiquity." In *Cane* then, Toomer seizes hold of certain Gothic motifs in order to explore the relationship between past and present, to express the horror of acts of racial violence such as slavery and lynching, and to meditate on the terror brought about by the recognition of racial hybridity.[20]

One source of the uneasy subversiveness that typifies the Gothic is the Gothic tendency to transgress boundaries and categories. Within American culture and the new American Gothic, which draws upon the social reality of racial categories, the most unsettling example of racial transgression proves to be the mulatto, whose existence acts as proof of miscegenation, the emblem of subversion of racial categories. Toomer draws upon the figure of the mulatto/a as Gothic Other, the figure that transgresses comforting racial categories. In *Cane,* the impossibility of establishing certain boundaries, of creating racial purity (both socially and individually), is evidenced by the racial and social intermixture. Toomer acknowledges that American culture figures the mulatto as transgressive and horrific, but ultimately he rejects this paradigm, refuses the horror of the hybrid Other and, instead, embraces the figure of the mulatto as capable of harmonizing differences and pointing to a new America of racial synthesis.

American Identities and the Specter of Race

The mulatto is, in *Cane,* the object of furtive secrecy, demonization and horrified speculation when he or she is exposed. Toomer proves miscegenation to be what Freud has called the *unheimlich,* or unhomely, "everything that ought to have remained ... secret and hidden but has come to light."[21] Scruggs and Vandemarr identify miscegenation, which Toomer examines through the Gothic, as that element which American society seeks to repress; they provide a detailed survey of the historical and social contexts which made that phenomenon the thing that is "not named but always there" (139). I extend their analysis by arguing that Toomer's concern with social and psychic confrontations with the repressed Other within bodies extends not only to the collective, but occurs in individuals as well. To focus on the personal or psychical is not, as Scruggs and

Vandemarr suggest, to exclude or diminish the public arena, for personal and communal and private and public are shown in *Cane* to be intimately connected. Indeed, Homi Bhabha identifies the "unhomely" moment in literature as the vehicle by which private and public, past and present, are bridged in that it "relates the traumatic ambivalences of a personal, psychic history to the wider disjunctions of political existence."[22] The unhomely moment erupts in those passages in *Cane* that are most inspired by Gothic tradition, resulting in the disruption of perceived order and stability and, most importantly, forcing a confrontation with the repressed Other within individual and collective bodies. The mulatto's mixed racial heritage proves to be the secret whose revelation would transgress and destabilize social norms. Characters continually hide the signs of racial miscegenation from others, and practice various forms of self-denial, only to have the evidence of racial "impurity" laid bare before the terrified, outraged gazes of their communities.

Toomer explores the terrain of the uncanny and unhomely in the first vignette in the collection, "Karintha," offering a portrait of fading Southern glory that can only hint at a parallel Southern experience of racial miscegenation and the brutal erasure of its effects. Karintha, who carries "beauty, perfect as dusk when the sun goes down," embodies all that is beautiful and tragic not only about the South but also about the nation.[23] Karintha's physical beauty is celebrated by Toomer's narrator, who associates her with the Southern landscape. Yet her splendor is marred by the overattentive, sexually charged actions of the men who "counted the time to pass before she would be old enough to mate with them" (1). Karintha, who "ripened too soon" (2) grows into a woman who eventually gives birth to a child: "A child fell out of her womb onto a bed of pine-needles in the forest. Pine-needles are smooth and sweet. They are elastic to the feet of rabbits…. A sawmill was nearby" (2). Toomer's elusive prose forces the reader to draw connections between Karintha's seemingly easy and "natural" childbearing, the ominous image of the sawmill smoldering for a year as its sawdust pile burns and Karintha's return home weeks later, apparently alone (the child is never mentioned in the vignette's remaining lines). Scruggs and Vandemarr argue persuasively that miscegenation, "is the unspoken thing, the missing fact, that is crucial to the story's 'mystery.' Who gave Karintha that child?" (140). The Gothic effect is enhanced in the reader's recognition that the sawdust pile is the child's funeral pyre, compounded by the fact that the "horror of the child's death goes unrecognized" (141). Yet Toomer renders this gruesome example of the societal pressure to repress, or more accurately in this case, to efface the Gothic Other, in the form of the unknown and unknowable mullato child, in imagistic prose that suggest the baby's birth and death are unrepresentable.

The historical and cultural blindness to America's synthesized multicultural heritage, the refusal to accept the fusion of many races, proves to be the background against which we can read and understand Karintha's horrific narrative. Karintha's story veers into the Gothic because her experience is repressed and denied. Barbara Christian argues that the nation, "in denying its own self-composition, ... also evades a true definition of self."[24] Toomer repeatedly emphasizes that this process occurs on the individual as well as the national levels in his depiction of individual characters; the reader is thus compelled to make the connection between private lives and public/communal conditions. The most striking articulation of Toomer's belief in the necessity of reckoning with personal and national history, in denying Gothic repression of the past, can be found in "Kabnis," the most autobiographical piece in *Cane*. "Kabnis" is a dramatic piece about a Northerner in Sempter, Georgia (a fictional Sparta), who works first at an industrial and agricultural school for Negroes, and then as an assistant in Fred Halsey's workshop. He is forced to live in and become a part of a community that confuses, terrifies and repulses him because it reminds him of a Negro heritage that he attempts to forget or diminish, forcing him to see himself, in other words, as the racial Other so demonized by society.

Kabnis's "thin" hair and "lemon face" signify his racial hybridity (and his inhuman otherness); his elitist remarks signal his inclination, if not to pass as white, then to distance himself from the black proletariat (81). He languishes in the town, indulging in drink and sex, but never finding intellectual or spiritual fulfillment. Kabnis's emptiness stems in large part from his inability to find personal meaning in a Southern history that he considers irreversibly marred by the legacy of slavery. Yet he cannot remain detached from his surroundings because he is literally haunted by the legacy that he attempts to deny and by his belief that blackness can only signify abjection. Kabnis is literally haunted by the repressed past; in one scene, we find him, "plastered with red Georgia mud," trying desperately to escape the ghosts that he believes hold lynching ropes. He runs into his cabin, exclaiming:

> God Almighty, they're here. After me. On me. All along the road I saw their eyes flaring from the cane. Hounds. Shouts ... I stumbled on a rope. O God, a rope. Their clammy hands were like the love of death playing up and down my spine. My spine.... My legs .... Why in hell didn't they catch me? [91].

"They" are not only the white lynchers of his imagination but also the African American ancestors he refuses to acknowledge, even as he is coated with the red earth that Toomer identifies with Southern blacks. Kabnis becomes the Gothic Other in this hallucinatory scene, wailing his unwilling acceptance of the dominant culture's message of Negro monstrosity and the need to repress it; he is at once haunted by ghosts and a ghost himself.

The apparent submission to racist ideology is temporary, however. Kabnis ultimately reasserts his hatred of the Southern cultural heritage. He appropriates for himself the role of the centered subject and vehemently rejects a blind old man, whom Lewis, Kabnis's doppelganger, recognizes to be "symbol, flesh, and spirit of the past." The elder, the epitome of the inscrutable Other as he remains silent until his final sphinx-like declaration at the very end of the text, represents a community of people descended from slaves, yet nonetheless full of the capacity to endure and transcend their own subjugation (107). Lewis calls on Kabnis to recognize in this ghostly figure of the past, the "dead blind father of a muted folk who feel their way upward to a life that crushes or absorbs them" (105). But where Lewis sees a prophetic "Father John," Kabnis sees only a "father of Hell," portent of a feudal past (105), from which he wants to distance himself.

Kabnis imagines that the only way to escape from slavery's horrific reach is to disavow his kinship with its victims; thus, he insists that his "ancestors were Southern blue-bloods." He responds to Lewis's prompting that they were also black, by stating, "Aint much difference between blue and black." Lewis's reply returns us to Toomer's central theme, the struggle to reconcile a history and identity characterized by heterogeneity and hybridity:

> Enough to draw a denial from you. Cant hold them, can you? Master; slave. Soil; and the overarching heavens. Dusk; dawn. They fight and bastardize you. The sun tint of your cheeks, flame of the great season's multicolored leaves, tarnished, burned. Split, shredded; easily burned. No use ... [107].

Kabnis's fear lies in his inability to recognize anything other than bastardization and subordination in the mixed legacy of American history, so he attempts to "whiten" his background by rejecting the blackness within. Yet Lewis's challenge suggests the possibility of turning "the horror of [one's] own history into the source of [one's] power" (Goddu 143). Lewis suggests that Kabnis find liberation and redemption through the acceptance of his heritage in all of its complexities and contradictions, through the embrace of his blackness as well as his acceptance of his whiteness. Lewis proposes that this personal acceptance would lead to his community's confrontation and reclamation of their blended and conjoined pasts. Thus, through his use of the Gothic, a genre that insists on a reckoning with history, Toomer offers a narrative of a multicultural nation that locates the "useful" in an honest assessment of the ways that cross-racial and cultural encounters tarnish, burn, split and shred, and yet fundamentally form its citizens.

The Mulatto as Social Ideal

Toomer offers multiple examples of the cultural tendency to take on Gothic forms and to demonize the racial Other, in particular the mulatto who carries that otherness within. It is important to note that this form of exclusion is practiced by both black and white communities depicted in the book, although only whites have the institutional power to enforce this ideology through juridical and large scale means (anti-miscegenation laws, lynching). Toomer's deployment of the trope in his representation of Paul in "Bona and Paul," a story appearing in the second section of *Cane*, allows him to interrogate the psychology of racialization by exploring the inner world of an individual who passes as white and the processes by which society polices the racial borders. The result is a story rife with hauntings by the racial Other of Paul and his community by his secret blackness.

Paul's possible/probable (yet never openly acknowledged) blackness haunts all his exchanges in an exclusively white, Northern environment. The Gothic trope of darkness signifies here the Negro heritage that shadows and presumably denigrates Paul. His roommate, Art, thinks, for example, "Christ, but he's getting moony. Its his blood. Dark blood: moony" (72). Even when Bona—who flouts her inherited Southern conventions by flirting with Paul—associates Paul's darkness with erotically thrilling transgression, the result is psychically damaging; Paul is forced to confront rigid expectations about appropriate racial behavior. For example, when he does not return Bona's "love" with enough fire, she thinks to herself, "Colored; cold. Wrong somewhere" (74). The heat that Toomer associates elsewhere in the collection with Southern-bred earthiness is here turned against Paul in a demand for him to fit Bona's stereotypical assumption of "typical" Negro behavior. While the rejection of Paul based on his "mooniness," "coldness" and "wrongness" is relatively benign, it forms a link between this story that takes place in the Northern section of the book and others in the first, Southern section in which characters ensure the separation of the races through brutally violent means.

In fact, the description of Paul's "red-brown" face as a inhuman, otherworldly "harvest moon" draws the reader's attention back to the last vignette in Part One, "Blood-Burning Moon." In that Southern story, a relationship between a black woman (Louisa) and a white man (Bob) results in Bob's murder by a jealous rival named Tom and Tom's lynching at the hands of a white mob. In that story, the crossing of racial strictures operates on multiple levels, from the interracial relationship to Tom's refusal to maintain a position of subservience and weakness in the face of a white man. Both transgressions are met with a violence that is meant to enforce racial distinctions and divisions. To Toomer, this aspect of Southern history *is* Gothic; thus, his depiction of the violence is realistic, lyrical, although devoid of the supernatural elements that one might expect in a Gothic tale. In fact the description of the lynchers' onslaught begins by drawing on natural imagery, but moves quickly to a description of machine-like efficiency that Toomer associates with the Gothic insistence on convention and conformity:

> White men like ants upon a forage rushed about. Except for the taut hum of their moving, all was silent. Shotguns, revolvers, lights. They came together. The taut hum rose to a low roar. Then nothing could be heard but the flop of their feet in the thick dust of the road. The moving body of their silence preceded them over the crest of the hill into factory town. It flattened the Negroes beneath it [34].

The mechanistic and violent restitution of large scale racial hierarchy is precipitated by a single act of violence. This economy of scale anticipates Toomer's depiction of an industrial, urbanized modern existence for black migrants to the North who lose all sense of connection to the spirituality of the South. In "Box Seat," the houses in Washington, D.C. symbolize social and institutional structures that are authoritarian and repressive. Toomer's imagery calls up the figure of the cold, mechanized factory, refusing difference in the goods it produces. In this case, the product is the transplanted Southerners like Dan, who displays blunted individuality and materialistic aspirations: "Dan's eyes sting. Sinking into a soft couch, about him. It is a sharp-edged, massed, metallic house. Bolted" (57). The Southern obsession with racial purity is, in this story, replaced with a Northern preoccupation with enforcing social and class conformity. The dominant culture of the North, like that of the South, views difference as a social threat that merits repression and suppression.

Where "Box Seat" concerns itself with socioeconomic conformity, "Bona and Paul" interrogates the racial fragmentation that links North to South. Even though the kind of ferocious rejection and subjugation of the racial Other found in "Blood Burning Moon" is absent in "Bona and Paul," clearly the characters are still ruled by the same racial ideologies as their Southern antecedents. Close scrutiny of the white characters' thoughts reveals that the true terror lies in the condition of not knowing with any degree of certainty the racial identity of their peers and, implicitly, of themselves. The scene revolving around the Crimson Gardens nightclub, for example, centers as much on Art's bewilderment and frustration over Paul's racial indeterminacy as it does on the protagonist's self-consciousness about his difference. Art thinks, "Hell of a thing, that Paul's dark: youve [sic] got to always be answering questions" (72). Toomer renders Paul as a ghost whose unspoken and unspeakable racial hybridity literally haunts the proceedings: "His dark face is a floating shade in evening's shadow" (73).

Yet Toomer combines the anxiety aroused by the Gothic Other with a nascent understanding of the ability of the Other to "haunt back," to reappropriate subjectivity. Toomer's characters haunt back, or hold out the possibility of doing so, not through the public act of writing but through private acts of self-recognition.[25] For example, the spectators' intrusive looks eventually allow Paul to experience an internal transformation that is potentially liberating. Toomer writes:

> A strange thing happened to Paul. Suddenly he knew that people saw, not attractiveness in his dark skin, but difference. Their stares, giving him to himself, filled something long empty within him, and were like green blades sprouting in his consciousness. There was fullness, and strength and peace about it all [75].

Paul's darkness, the thing that is the cause and sign of his difference, frees him from the obligation to conform to social mores. After spending so much time trying to pass as white, Paul comes to understand that fulfillment comes not from denying his African American heritage but from accepting it as a part of himself. The enforcement of racial and social divisions, symbolized by the stares of others, turns Paul's vision inward and impels the recognition and appreciation of internal difference. In the beginning of the story, Paul suffers from the Du Boisian notion of double consciousness, "this sense of looking at one's self through the eyes of others, of measuring one's soul by the tape of a world that looks on in amused contempt and pity."[26] In this, he has internalized the message of his culture, that he is an objectified Other to be observed with contempt and pity. But whereas Du Bois describes this condition as one of "no true self-consciousness," resulting in confusion and fragmentation, Toomer posits that this awareness might lead to a kind of wholeness and a release from social tyranny; Paul finally accepts the aspect of his identity, his mixed racial heritage, that society has conditioned him to deny and repress.

Byrd views this as a moment of empowerment for Paul because he finally accepts that he is black: "Bona discovers that she cannot shake off the well-defined, controlling code of her southern upbringing. Conversely, Paul discovers a new pride in his blackness, a new faith in himself and in life's possibilities" (22). However, although Paul discovers a pride in his blackness, the passage remains intentionally vague as to whether he identifies exclusively as black. At the conclusion of the story, Paul states enigmatically, "I came back to tell you, brother, that white faces are petals of roses. That dark faces are petals of dusk. That I am going out and gather petals. That I am going out and know her whom I brought here with me to these Gardens which are purple like a bed of roses would be at dusk" (78). Larson reads this passage differently, arguing that

> in her frustration with Paul, who cannot accept his blackness, Bona runs out of the nightclub, with Paul at her heels. At the moment, the doorman realizes that Paul is passing and smiles at him, a knowing sign of recognition, but Paul says he's wrong. In his denial, Paul not only loses his heritage but Bona also [32].

Despite the different interpretations, both Byrd and Larson focus on Paul's racial identification, looking for clarity that Toomer's narrative refuses. In fact, Paul expresses appreciation for all "roses," regardless of hue, and suggests that when regarded from a certain perspective, differences of color (and race) are erased. Thus, the text remains ambiguous; the reader cannot definitely determine whether this is a moment of disavowal or moment of assertion of Negro pride.

While Paul's acceptance and celebration of his racial hybridity is personally redemptive, the transformative possibilities of this moment remain unrealized because it occurs solely on a psychological and individual level. Bona's rejection (running out of the nightclub) and the ambiguous handshake shared by Paul and the doorman, leave us with the perception of a protagonist who remains isolated. Similarly, Toomer continually ran into resistance to his vision of a racial heterogeneity, which he considered an ideal embodied by the mulatto. Toomer indicates on some level the tenuousness of his theory of complementary races, living in a multi-racial nation, especially when the racial ideology of this country is so firmly rooted in notions of racial purity. He acknowledges the difficulty of society accepting his ideas, stating in a 1935 piece, "Not Typically American":

> Though in ideal one country, united and indivisible, though our biological actuality approaches this ideal (we are undoubtedly forming an American race) we are, sociologically, a replica of Europe's mutually repellent nationalisms.... Our social psychology lags far behind our spiritual ideals on the one hand and our physical realities on the other [Rusch 96–97].

Real and utopian are paradoxically united in this essay; Toomer equates the "biological actuality" of miscegenation with American ideals of democratic pluralism. For Toomer, the mulatto symbolizes the potential for social harmony because that synthetic figure manages to contain differences within one body. Yet the transformative possibilities that he envisions, in confronting the nation's history of racial amalgamation, is only possible when society confronts and reckons with the effects of its ideology of racial separation.

Toomer imagines such a moment in "Becky," a story about a white woman with two Negro sons. The narrator describes Becky's presence as a haunting reminder to the town of its history of miscegenation. Becky is punished for her transgression by being cast out to a cabin on the outskirts of town. Eventually abandoned by her sons and shunned by her neighbors, she is never seen or heard from again; nonetheless, the townspeople watch her house from a distance and sustain her by leaving provisions at her door. Becky's association with racial "impurity" results in her being ostracized by a community that signals its ambivalence by their continued willingness to support her existence. But in a classic scene of Gothic horror, Toomer rejects the notion of the transgressive mulatto as figure to be feared, and depicts Becky, the mother, the engenderer of mulattos, as the figure besieged. Her chimney caves in inexplicably and the collapsed house permanently contains her body, the site of racial contamination. Although Becky's fate would seem to be a matter of divine retribution for committing the "sin" of miscegenation, Gothic convention offers an alternative reading of this scene. Indeed, in this ending Toomer draws on two prevalent Gothic tropes: the destruction of the house and the entrapped woman.[27] In reconstructing Becky as the imprisoned Gothic heroine, Toomer frames her as the good subject rather than the bad object. Indeed, the destruction of the house forces the community to see the very thing it attempts to push aside, the devastating and dehumanizing effects of the denial of the reality of racial amalgamation.

The narrator describes witnessing the catastrophe, emphasizing his implication in the conventionally Gothic horror unfolding in Becky's house and on her person. Toomer suggests that he and the community he represents cannot separate themselves from this private horror and must confront the fact of the Gothic Other whom they wish to deny:

> It was Sunday. Our congregation had been visiting at Pulverton, and were coming home. There was no wind.... We were just about to pass.... Pines shout to Jesus...! The ground trembled as a ghost train rumbled by. The chimney fell into the cabin.... Barlo and I were pulled out of our seats. Dragged to the door that had swung open.... The last thing that I remem-

ber was whipping old Dan like fury; I remember nothing after that — that
is, until I reached town folks crowded round to get the true word of it
[6–7].

The narrator describes himself not as a voyeur, drawn by prurient curiosity to gaze on the wreckage, but as a witness led to the tragedy by the
weight of its gravity. Just as he acts out of compulsion when he looks at
the ruins of Becky's house, so does he respond to the community's needs
when he tells the story to its members. The narrator's acts of observation
and narration are here presented as externally driven and communally ori-
ented, forcing the group to confront the very history it has sought to keep
hidden.[28] His witnessing of and testifying to the horrific obliteration of
Becky undercuts the social inclination towards racial othering and offers
proof of Toomer's resistance to the Gothic convention of demonizing the
racial Other. Toomer's use of the Gothic allows him to elucidate history's
influential reach into the present, on the relations between Southern and
Northern, urban and rural, black and white cultures. Yet ultimately, his
belief that the mulatto represents a social ideal moves him to revise Gothic
convention — and to seize upon the Gothic tendency to resist boundaries
and categories. Toomer insists that his readers grapple with the complicated, amalgamated histories of all Americans.

Notes

1. Frederick L. Rusch, ed., *A Jean Toomer Reader: Selected Unpublished Writings*
(New York: Oxford University Press, 1993),16.
2. Toomer's mixed racial heritage and his complicated reactions to it led him to con-
coct a personal history that was based partly on fact and partly on speculation. He
identified at times with his grandfather, P.B.S. Pinchback, who was the only African
American to have served as acting governor of Louisiana, and was an advocate of Negro
civil rights during the Reconstruction era. Yet because he did not know his father, he
fashioned a personal history of being the son of a wealthy Georgia landowner that suggests a youthful idealization of and identification with white Southern gentility.
3. Toomer described his background as such: "It is possible that there are Negro
and Indian bloods in my descent along with English, Spanish, Welsh, Scotch, French,
Dutch, and German. This is common in America; and it is from all these strains that
the American race is being born" (Rusch, 105).
4. Darwin Turner writes, for example, in his introduction to the 1975 edition of
Cane that in 1920, returning to Washington D.C. after trying his hand at a number of
schools and universities, "…Toomer engrossed himself with racial matters…. In order
to deepen his understanding, he read books on race and race problems" (Darwin
Turner, Introduction to "*Cane*" by *Jean Toomer* [New York: Boni and Liveright, 1975],
xv). Turner also argues that Toomer's belief that his father may have been the son of
a wealthy, Georgia plantation owner may have contributed to his narrator's detached
and objective point of view. He writes, "If Toomer identified emotionally with the

plantation-owner class, perhaps he subconsciously established distance between himself and the Black peasants" (xi). Scruggs and Vandemarr expand this observation by arguing that the narrator shifts from the perspective of spectator to that of witness, in other words, from distanced to engaged and invested in the community that he describes (for example, Charles Scruggs and Lee Vandemarr, *Jean Toomer and the Terrors of American History* [Philadelphia: University of Pennsylvania Press, 1998], 145).

5. It is important to note that Toomer's publishers pressured him to publicly identify as black because they believed it would ensure *Cane's* positive reception by an audience that was displaying a growing a taste for "race" literature. In a letter dated September 5, 1923, Toomer wrote to Horace Liveright, "My racial composition and my position in the world are realities which I alone may determine.... As a B[oni] and L[iveright] author, I make the distinction between my fundamental position and the position which your publicity department may wish to establish for me in order that *Cane* reach as large a public as possible.... Feature Negro if you wish, but do not expect me to feature it in advertisements for you. For myself, I have sufficiently featured Negro in *Cane*" (Rusch 94). Toomer's reputation as a black writer was therefore set, because he left his racial designation up to his publisher's publicist.

6. Charles Larson, *Invisible Darkness: Jean Toomer and Nella Larsen* (Iowa City: University of Iowa Press, 1993), 13.

7. Teresa Goddu, *Gothic America* (New York: Columbia University Press, 1997), 5.

8. Michelle Massé remarks on how Gothic criticism has been transformed to accommodate the dynamism of this tradition: "There is a similar transition in criticism from the early focus upon the Gothic novel, a genre with certain distinctive features that was prominent between 1764 (Horace Walpole's *The Castle of Otranto*) and 1820 (Maturin's *Melmoth*). In the second stage, however, 'Gothic' increasingly becomes an adjective as well as a noun, a literary mode as well as a genre. Texts written in different periods and cultures (particularly the United States) are regularly discussed as 'Gothic,' albeit far removed from the historical events that helped to spawn the first generation" ("Psychoanalysis and the Gothic," in *A Companion to the Gothic*, ed. David Punter [London: Blackwell Publishers, 2000], 235).

9. Farah Jasmine Griffin, *Who Set You Flowin': The African American Migration Narrative* (New York: Oxford University Press, 1995).

10. Barbara Christian, *Black Women Novelists* (Westport, CT: Greenwood Press, 1980), and Alice Walker, *In Search of Our Mothers' Gardens: Womanist Prose* (New York: Harcourt Brace, 1984).

11. Rudolph P. Byrd, *Jean Toomer's Years with Gurdjieff: Portrait of an Artist 1923–1936* (Athens: University of Georgia Press, 1990).

12. Examples of the contexts that Scruggs and Vandemarr seek to excavate include the influence of Waldo Frank on Toomer's development as a writer, his earliest published writing and the national and regional histories that are alluded to in the book.

13. Allan Lloyd-Smith, "Nineteenth-Century American Gothic," in *A Companion to the Gothic*, 109.

14. I am grateful to Cheryl A. Wall for this insight. In addition, Goddu states that "the gothic's typical association with the 'unreal' and the sensational ... has created a resistance to examining African American narratives in relation to the gothic" (139).

15. According to Smith, the frontier, the Puritan legacy and political utopianism are the three other features prominent in the American Gothic.

16. Toni Morrison, "Romancing the Shadow," in *Playing in the Dark: Whiteness and the Literary Imagination* (New York: Vintage, 1993), 36–37.

17. A time that, Terry Castle notes, curiously gave rise to the irrational Gothic, *The*

Female Thermometer: Eighteenth Century Culture and the Invention of the Uncanny (New York: Oxford University Press, 1995).

18. Alain Locke, "The New Negro," in *The New Negro* (New York: Simon & Schuster, 1997), 4.

19. Fred Botting, "In Gothic Darkly: Heterotopia, History, Culture," in *A Companion to the Gothic*, 3.

20. Here I distinguish between Gothic horror as an external, often supernatural, phenomenon and terror as an internalized fear or anxiety projected outward onto another figure (often young and female in traditional Gothic literature). One could argue, for example, that the hauntingly passive and silent women that populate the first stories in *Cane* carry the burden of death and stasis that haunts the mostly male figures associated with the modern city. In all sections of the book, however, anxiety is projected onto the mulatto, whose racial indeterminancy reflects back to society its own repressed hybridity.

21. Sigmund Freud "The 'Uncanny'" (1919), in *Standard Edition of the Complete Psychological Works*, ed. J. Strachey et al. 24 vols (London: Hogarth Press/Institute of Psycho-Analysis) Vol. XVII, 217–56.

22. Homi K. Bhabha, *The Location of Culture* (New York: Oxford University Press, 1994), 9–11.

23. Jean Toomer, *Cane* (New York: Boni and Liveright, 1923), 1.

24. Barbara Christian, *Black Women Novelists* (Westport, CT: Greenwood Press, 1980), 55.

25. Goddu locates this possibility in the slave narrator's appropriation of the Gothic narrative in order to represent and thereby free herself from the unspeakable horrors of slavery (131–152).

26. W.E.B. Du Bois, *The Souls of Black Folk* (New York: Literary Classics of the United States, 1986), 364.

27. He also pointedly evokes a version of this theme developed by Poe — the entombment of the body in the destroyed property as, for example, in "The Fall of the House of Usher." [Ed. Note]

28. Barbara Christian has observed that "the soil of Georgia is an intense mingling of black and white culture, its cane a manifestation of the horror and beauty that is America. Miscegenation, the illicit union of black and white, is a dominant motif in the book and in many ways acts as a prism through which the observer might perceive the truth of the land" (55).

Works Cited

Bhabha, Homi K. *The Location of Culture*. New York: Oxford University Press, 1994.

Botting, Fred. "In Gothic Darkly: Heterotopia, History, Culture." In *A Companion to the Gothic*. Edited by David Punter. London: Blackwell Publishers, 2000.

Byrd, Rudolph P. *Jean Toomer's Years with Gurdjieff: Portrait of an Artist 1923–1936*. Athens: University of Georgia Press, 1990.

Castle, Terry. *The Female Thermometer: Eighteenth Century Culture and the Invention of the Uncanny*. New York: Oxford University Press, 1995.

Christian, Barbara. *Black Women Novelists*. Westport, CT: Greenwood Press, 1980.

Du Bois, W.E.B. *The Souls of Black Folk*. 1903. New York: Literary Classics of the United States, 1986.

Freud, Sigmund. "The 'Uncanny.'" 1919. In *Standard Edition of the Complete Psycho-*

logical Works. Edited by J. Strachey et al. 24 vols. London: Hogarth Press/Institute of Psycho-Analysis. Vol. XVII, 1953–74.

Goddu, Teresa. *Gothic America.* New York: Columbia University Press, 1997.

Griffin, Farah Jasmine. *Who Set You Flowin': The African American Migration Narrative.* New York: Oxford University Press, 1995.

Larson, Charles. *Invisible Darkness: Jean Toomer and Nella Larsen.* Iowa City: University of Iowa Press, 1993.

Lloyd-Smith, Allan. "Nineteenth-Century American Gothic." In *A Companion to the Gothic.* Edited by David Punter. London: Blackwell Publishers, 2000.

Locke, Alain. "The New Negro." In *The New Negro.* New York: Simon & Shuster, 1997.

Massé, Michelle. "Psychoanalysis and the Gothic." In *A Companion to the Gothic.* Edited by David Punter. London: Blackwell Publishers, 2000.

Morrison, Toni. "Romancing the Shadow." In *Playing in the Dark: Whiteness and the Literary Imagination.* New York: Vintage, 1993.

Rusch, Frederick L., ed. *A Jean Toomer Reader: Selected Unpublished Writings.* New York: Oxford University Press, 1993.

Scruggs, Charles, and Lee Vandemarr. *Jean Toomer and the Terrors of American History.* Philadelphia: University of Pennsylvania Press, 1998.

Toomer, Jean. *Cane.* New York: Boni and Liveright, 1923.

Turner, Darwin Introduction to *Cane* by Jean Toomer. New York: Liveright, 1975.

Walker, Alice. *In Search of Our Mothers' Gardens: Womanist Prose.* New York: Harcourt Brace, 1984.

4

Mixed Blood Couples: Monsters and Miscegenation in U.S. Horror Cinema

STEVEN JAY SCHNEIDER

Introduction

Forbidden love, illicit sex, the mysterious seductiveness and appeal of the villain — a family of familiar, practically ubiquitous themes in Gothic fiction past and present. The Byronic anti-hero, besides being moody, reflective, and tortured by inner demons, was undeniably superior in passion and power to the common man, reminiscent of Milton's Satan, he who "above the rest / In shape and gesture proudly eminent / Stood like a tower. His form had yet not lost / All her original brightness, nor appeared / Less than archangel ruined, and th' excess / Of glory obscured ... Cruel his eye, but cast / Signs of remorse and passion...."[1] In "The Vampyre," John Polidori's 1819 short story, the protagonist Lord Ruthven merely takes the sexual potency of his predecessors to another, more monstrous level. As Gothic scholar David Punter argues, Ruthven "transgresses the social norms, but he does so with the collaboration of his victims; he merely acts as a catalyst for repressed tendencies to emerge into the light of day."[2] In other words, what nowadays would surely be considered a very un-politically correct line of thought, the objects of Ruthven's malefaction effectively "ask for it."

Fast forward almost 175 years to Bernard Rose's 1992 feature film

Candyman, based on a story ("The Forbidden") by contemporary horror-meister Clive Barker. Here, the monster — a strapping, 6'5" African American male (Tony Todd) with Barry White bass in his voice and a phallicized hook for a hand — generates ample disgust in both victims and viewers, but he only comes to visit if you look into a mirror and call his name five times. It is all too easy to locate in this film confirmation of certain racist assumptions, as Judith Halberstam does when she concludes that "ultimately the horror stabilizes in the ghastly body of the black man whose monstrosity turns upon his desire for the white woman."[3] But neither does it require a reading against the grain to see that, in this well-received film and its subsequent sequels (two of them to date), the Candyman's predominantly white, predominantly female prey must want a date with this sweet-sounding devil pretty badly to invite him into their boudoirs so purposively: "Candyman. Candyman. Candyman. Candyman. Candyman!" Clearly, more than just black male desire for white women is at stake here; the inverse also seems to be in place. Which leads one to wonder whether there aren't other *horrors* being evoked in this film as well, or perhaps other affects altogether.

Not least because of its elastic conventions and the room it provides for exploring (or else exploiting) the darker sides of human nature, the Gothic mode is alive and well, even flourishing, in a variety of narrative and visual forms ranging from architecture and art to comic books and daytime television.[4] Especially in the horror film, Gothic themes have found a happy home, and the theme of the sexually appealing villain — now in the guise of monster — has remained a virtual constant throughout the genre's history. Whether the monster in question is figured as suave seducer (Dracula; Hannibal Lecter; the Dust Devil[5]), animal magnet (Jack Nicholson's middle-aged carnivore in *Wolf*; the Brando-esque Henry in *Henry: Portrait of a Serial Killer*; Jeff Goldblum's "Brundlefly" in the 1986 David Cronenberg vehicle, at least before pieces of his face start falling off), or literally fatal femme (*Cat People*'s Irena Dubrova; *Fatal Attraction*'s Alex Forrest; Hammer Films' eponymous "Twins of Evil"), what does not change is the culturally, often biologically transgressive nature of the romantic and sexual possibilities opened up. This in addition to the victim's decision, or compulsion, to "go for it" against his or her better (that is, rational, socially sanctioned) judgment, and the viewer's own investment in that decision, or compulsive act.

Robin Wood, in a seminal essay on the American horror film, places unfettered sexual energy on the top of his list of that which our society must repress — never wholly successfully — in order to maintain the interests of alienated labor and patriarchy: "in a society built on monogamy and family there will be an enormous surplus of sexual energy that will have to be repressed; and ... what is repressed must always strive to return,"[6] typically in the form of the monster. Although Wood holds that "the release of sexuality in the horror film is always presented as perverse, monstrous, and excessive" (189), he goes on to argue that his theory of surplus repression affords a means of categorizing individual horror films along political lines as either progressive or reactionary. Relevant characteristics for making such a determination include the following: the extent to which the film's monster is designated as *simply* evil; the capacity of the monster to arouse sympathy in the film's human characters (and in the audience); and "the confusion (in terms of what the film wishes to regard as 'monstrous') of *repressed* sexuality with sexuality itself" (193). While admitting that this last distinction is by no means always clear cut, Wood's aim here is to provide a way of identifying those reactionary horror films in which the fear and shock effects are premised on and motivated by a disgust with sexuality *per se*.

This essay will take focus on the Gothic theme of "seductive villainy" as it has manifested itself in a particular transhistorical (and broadly construed) subgenre of American horror cinema: the "race horror" film.[7] Specifically, I will be looking at the complex dynamics of interracial coupling in a number of race horror films across three decades: the 1970s, 80s, and 90s. Usually, though not always, such coupling occurs between a "monster" explicitly marked as either African or African American, and a more or less willing white "victim." I have placed the terms "monster" and "victim" in quotation marks precisely in order to anticipate my argument that, in the horror films in question (more than is typical for the genre as a whole), these terms are ambiguous, shifting in meaning, and open to multiple, even contradictory, interpretations. *Contra* the view of such film scholars and cultural critics as Halberstam and, to a lesser extent, Harry M. Benshoff and Isabel Cristina Pinedo, in the context of twentieth-century Gothic fiction, race does *not* become "a master signifier of monstrosity," one that, when invoked, "blocks out all other possibilities of monstrous identity" (Halberstam 5).[8] As I have argued elsewhere, in a discussion of the early 1970s cycle of blaxploitation horror films, "If we want to discover anything of interest about [this] subgenre *per se* as opposed to the rest of 1970s horror cinema, the way to do this is not (at least not primarily) through an analysis of blaxploitation horror *monsters*, who form far too heterogeneous and racially ambiguous a lot to justify any general claims concerning their allegorical import."[9] The same can be said of earlier and later race horror films as well.

Whether or not one buys into the entire psychoanalytic apparatus underlying Wood's "return of the repressed" thesis, the *prima facie* utility of his explanatory scheme can hardly be denied. By focusing not just on the ontological properties of particular African and African American monsters, but on their capacity to elicit sympathy from viewers by virtue of the sexual and romantic relationships they enter into with white men and women, we shall discover a whole host of politically and ideologically loaded motifs. These include (but are not limited to) the following: an exaggerated treatment of familiar and entrenched social anxieties surrounding miscegenation; an interrogation of, and response to, white male fears of black male virility; and a variant of the rape-revenge theme seen in a number of feminist horror films of the 1970s and 80s. The following discussion bears important parallels to Gina Marchetti's argument concerning American silent cinema's depiction of Asia and Asians, the false/romantic memory of which — replete as it is with "diabolical villains and yielding, exotic beauties"— serves to "obscure the far more complex fantasy world Hollywood actually offered viewers at that time."[10] As Marchetti reveals in her close reading of Sidney A. Franklin's *The Forbidden City* (1918), "silent films often simultaneously warn against miscegenation while celebrating romantic love, [and] cry for the separation of the races while condemning racial intolerance..." (257). A survey of race horror films across the decades shows them to be similarly complex, as they frequently depict Gothicized seductive villains whose powers of horror stem as much from their capacity to fulfill the not-so-repressed fantasies of typically white "victims" as from their own unnatural (and in that sense, monstrous) desires.

Race Horror Predecessors

Recently, Elizabeth Young has argued that in James Whale's 1935 horror classic *Bride of Frankenstein*, "the monster appears as a marker of racial difference, and his sexualized advances to the film's women encode racist American discourse of the 1930s on masculinity, femininity, rape, and lynching."[11] Young defends this claim as follows:

> If the monster's behavior implicitly links criminality with contemporary images of black violence, so too does his physical appearance gather force from racist stereotypes. His large, black-clad, awkward form embodies the racist association of blackness with subhumanity, as does his facial appearance [323].

Similar readings, even more intuitively plausible than Young's, have been made concerning King Kong, that "epitome of the white man's daydream of the brute black, the heartless, mindless foreigner, feasting on violence and rapine."[12] According to Harvey Roy Greenberg, "we discern in [Kong's] persona the raw sexuality which the ingenuous, racist bumpkin Driscoll has repressed, and which Ann has aroused" (344). And Fatimah Tobing Rony asserts that "the filming, capture, exhibition, photographing, and finally murder of Kong takes its cue from the historic exploitation of native peoples as freakish 'ethnographic' specimens by science, cinema, and popular culture.... [T]he monster Kong's attraction to Ann is transgressive: Kong, a hybrid figure, a manlike beast, threatens the taboo on interracial sex."[13]

There can be little doubt that the ostensible monsters in *Bride of Frankenstein*, *King Kong* (1933), *Island of Lost Souls* (1933), and other U.S. horror films of the early sound era are indeed coded along the lines suggested by Young, Greenberg, and Rony, primarily because of their savage (murderous, animalistic, lustful) and transgressive (specifically, cross-species) sexual desires. And to the extent that such coding embodies racist stereotypes of the black male as sexual monster (the "brutal Black buck," in Donald Bogle's terms[14]), these monsters provide support for Halberstam's claims concerning the irredeemably conservative/reactionary nature of Gothicized race horror. It is worth pointing out, however, that in the case of both Kong and the Frankenstein monster, their "embodiment" and "epitomizing" of racist stereotypes is mitigated, at the very least problematized, by the nature of their allegorically interracial relationships with Ann Darrow (Fay Wray) and the Bride (Elsa Lanchester), respectively.

Thus, although Greenberg describes Ann's first encounter with Kong as "redolent with rape imagery" (344), he goes on to acknowledge the "curious, tender transformation" undergone by the beast while in beauty's company: "Kong dwindles away into a clumsy knight errant, more interested in battle to protect his lady fair than making love to her" (346). Similarly, Rony points to the "noble side" of Kong: "as in ethnographic exposition, the boundaries between viewer and viewed were at times broken through, allowing the viewer of *King Kong* to see the world from Kong's eyes" (180). Recently, Thomas Wartenberg has presented the most coherent and extended argument to date in support of this reading: "*King Kong* initially presents its monstrous ape in terms that fit the racist stereotype dominant in Hollywood representations of Black males. Then, rather than maintain this view of Kong, the film employs a romantic narrative in which Kong figures as a tragic hero.... Through its identification of Kong with the stereotypical view of Black male sexuality, the film is able to criticize the racism of this stereotype."[15]

With respect to *Bride of Frankenstein*, Young claims of the Bride's famous shrieks that they "metaphorically encode a rejection by the white woman of the black man's sexual advances" (326). But what makes these shrieks so memorable, I would argue, is their very excessiveness — the monster just is not *that* threatening and repulsive. In their brief face-to-face meeting near the end of the film, the monster walks slowly towards the Bride, smiling and muttering "Friend... Friend...." He touches her softly on the arm and she reacts with a scream, running straight into the arms of her white male creator-protector, Dr. Frankenstein (Colin Clive). A few moments later, the monster again approaches the Bride as she sits on a bench in the laboratory. He sits down next to her and — like the perfect gentleman caller — pets her gently on the hand. Encouraged by her lack of resistance, the monster makes a slight move to kiss her. But she screams again, and it is at this point that her would-be mate declares, "She hate me."

Simply stated, the Bride protests too much. Thus, we would do well to consider the following alternative interpretations of the scene in question. If her manifest disgust in the face of the monster's symbolically interracial desire is read (or rather, heard) as unambiguous, then *contra* Young, it can be understood as encoding less "a rejection by the white woman of the black male's sexual advances" than a fulfillment of the white man's wish to bear *witness* to such a rejection, performed for him in hyperbolic terms. This makes narrative sense when one considers that, like the monster himself, the Bride has been animated by white male fantasy/energy all along. It also makes historical sense: as Kathy Russell explains, although sexual relations between white male slave-owners and black female slaves was tolerated in colonial America, "concern was greatest when ... the interracial relationship involved a White woman and a Black man." This was largely due to the fact that "there were far too few White females in the colonies for White authorities to tolerate their being sexually active with Black men, and lawmakers meted out stern punishments for such transgressions."[16] Of course, these punishments were much more stern for the black men found guilty of miscegenation than for their white female lovers.

Alternatively, is it not possible that what we have been calling disgust on the part of the Bride serves to lump together a whole complex of affective and cognitive responses, including astonishment, excitement, even a degree of awe in the face of an artificially endowed creature whose potency and appetites are truly prodigious? This latter interpretation is the one successfully picked up and run with by Mel Brooks and Gene Wilder in their 1974 parody *Young Frankenstein*, where the familiar stereotype of black male virility and hypersexuality is played for laughs in the rape-turned-seduction of Madelaine Kahn's randy Bride by Peter Boyle's concupiscent monster. Here, the Bride's initial screams of terror seamlessly and comically bridge into an operatic song of ecstasy, thereby casting doubt on the sincerity of her initial, supposedly "instinctive" negative reaction. One might compare this scene with the mesmerizing effect black prison escapee Charles Murray (Marlo Monte) has on the white wives of his racist enemies in *Welcome Home, Brother Charles* (1975). In this blaxploitation-era retelling of the Frankenstein tale, the stereotype in question is explicitly thematized via the restriction of scientific experimentation to Murray's genitalia — experimentation which results in monstrous growth and unnatural (one might even say Gothicized) powers of seduction.

As was the case with American cinema generally, lead roles for black men and women in the horror genre prior to the 1970s — as monsters, much less as humans (as victims, much less as heroes) — were few and far between. Until that decade, almost all of the horror films with a discernible racial component kept the black presence contained within narratives featuring exotic island locales, white interlopers, and uninhibited natives ("savages") practicing voodoo and experiencing zombification. Instead of keeping black people confined to urban settings "so that they don't trouble us with their 'otherness'" (Wood 170), horror films such as *White Zombie* (1932), *Ouanga* (1936, remade three years later as *The Devil's Daughter*, this time with an all-black cast), *I Walked with a Zombie* (1943), *Voodoo Devil Drums* (1944), *Voodoo Island* (1957), and *Voodoo Blood Bath* (a.k.a. *I Eat Your Skin*, 1964) simply substituted the jungle for the ghetto.[17] As a result, the prospects for interracial coupling in these films were extremely limited, and visible hints of its occurrence practically non-existent.

One interesting if trashy exception is the AIP drive-in feature *Voodoo Woman* (1957). Here, an obsessive mad scientist sets up a lab deep in the jungle, smack in the middle of a native village. Exploiting the local witch doctor, Dr. Roland Gerard (played by Val Lewton regular Tom Conway) uses voodoo spells and modern science to create an indestructible being whom he can control with his very thoughts. Owing more to Whale's *Bride of Frankenstein* than Mary Shelley's original Gothic novel, director Edward L. Cahn has the mad doctor use a woman from the tribe as his guinea pig. Once transformed into monster mode — a huge beast with a shock of silver hair and thick hide — she effectively (if ambivalently) satisfies traditional white male fantasies of possessing and controlling "other"/black women. As opposed to Dr. Gerard's unruly white wife, who must be kept imprisoned to prevent her from running away — back to "civilization," no doubt — the Voodoo Woman exists (in theory, if not in practice) for the sole purpose of obeying his every command she is the perfect female slave;

all he needs to do is *think* about what he wants and she will make it a reality. In a pregnant line that hints at multiple levels of miscegenation, not to mention incest and polygamy, Gerard responds to a question regarding what he plans on doing with his creation by declaring, "She may mother a whole race of new beings!" Although he does not state who the father of this new race of beings would be, the narrative offers no reason for supposing that Gerard has in mind anyone but himself.

Blaxploitation Horror

Briefly, and by way of introduction to a cycle of films whose ideological commitments, generic boundaries, and mixed-bag legacy remain controversial topics to this day: blaxploitation pictures were low- to mid-budget commercial productions released in the United States between the years 1969 and 1976 (approximately), that possessed some degree of African American creative input (via actors, directors, crewmen, or more rarely, producers); that specifically targeted African American audiences (through ad campaigns, distribution strategies, and the celebration of various aspects of 70s black culture, including Afrocentricism, jazz music, Black Nationalism, and ghetto style); and that typically presented stronger, more successful, more militant images of black men and women triumphing over white, frequently racist, adversaries (thus making genre films the favored format).[18] By around 1975, the blaxploitation craze was essentially over, having burned itself out on formulaic sequels that saw the cycle's once-proud black action heroes and heroines deteriorate into comic book caricatures of their former selves.

The first and by far the most popular blaxploitation horror film was (and still is) William Crain's *Blacula*, released in 1972 and followed by a sequel of sorts, *Scream, Blacula, Scream!*, a year later. The central romantic relationship in the original picture is that between Prince Mamuwalde (William Marshall)—transformed into a vampire and renamed "Blacula" by the racist Count Dracula (Charles McCauley) in 1780—and Tina (Vonetta McGee), modern-day reincarnation of Mamuwalde's African wife Luva, now living in urban Los Angeles. Although miscegenation is not one of the film's central themes, the possibility/threat of interracial coupling does arise early on (in the opening scene, in fact), and bears crucially on *Blacula*'s not unambiguous ideological project as a whole.

This scene serves as a historical preface to what will follow, and takes place in Dracula's Transylvanian castle in the late eighteenth century. Mamuwalde and Luva have made the trip from Africa to discuss with the supposedly progressive Count the prospect of obtaining his support in the effort to abolish the slave trade. Though Luva calls her husband "the crystallization of our people's pride," it is *she* who is fully decked out in traditional African garb and jewelry while Mamuwalde wears a tuxedo, looking and sounding every bit the European gentleman.[19] In racist (and sexist) recognition of Luva's exotic appeal, Dracula remarks, "I would willingly pay for so beautiful an addition to my household as your delicious wife." Observing Mamuwalde's shocked and appalled reaction to this admission, he continues: "it is a compliment for a man of my stature to look with desire on one of your color." With that, a lengthy fight ensues, whereupon Dracula reveals his vampire status. Biting his enemy on the neck — an erotic and interracial act of same-sex penetration — Dracula thereby transmits his affliction to Mamuwalde ("I curse you with my name; you shall be ... Blacula!"). Interestingly, for all of his conventional Gothic charm, sophistication, and professed heterosexual desire, the white Count Dracula ultimately proves doubly impotent: Luva never expresses even a hint of reciprocal sexual interest, and, rather than force the issue, he chooses instead to lock her away with her now-undead husband's coffin. Not only does *Blacula* mark blaxploitation cinema's successful co-optation of a traditional horror film subgenre; Blacula himself succeeds in co-opting for the black male monster his white predecessor's role as seductive Gothic anti-hero.[20]

A number of scholars have commented on the symbolic resonance of having an aristocratic European vampire capture, infect, and finally rename a once-proud African ruler. Benshoff, for example, argues that "[*Blacula's*] central figure must mediate his African heritage with his Westernized vampirism.... This situation parallels the historical deculturization process of the slave industry, which denied African prisoners their families, religions, and even names" (39). Leerom Medovoi concurs: "The legacy of the slave trade is figured not only by the vampire's victims, of course, but also by the vampire himself, in the transition from Mamuwalde, a wise, noble and humane African leader, to Blacula, a creature cursed with a violent desire for human blood."[21] Such a reading is undeniable because it is so manifest. However, Medovoi wants to take this even further, arguing of Crain's film that it depicts the internalization of oppression in the psyche of twentieth-century African American males: "...the humiliation inflicted by the slave trade, as figured in Dracula's humiliation of Mamuwalde before his wife, has led to a loss of black men's authority — embodied in homosexuality, miscegenation and black women's insubordination — that in turn leads them to a violent, sadistic rage against that humiliation, one that may be tragically misdirected" (8).

Leaving aside the question whether Mamuwalde is really "humili-ated" by Dracula before his wife — insulted and angered would seem more precise descriptions of his reaction — Medovoi supports the above claim with reference to *Blacula*'s subsequent scene in the historical present cen-tering on Bobby (Ted Harris) and Billy (Rick Metzler), "a mixed race gay couple whom the film depicts as degenerate and ridiculous.... Bobby, the black queen, and the first contemporary black man to appear in the film, comes to embody the loss of African pride and a degeneration into mod-ern sexual decadence" (7). However, Medovoi's symptomatic reading of *Blacula* is weakened by at least the following two considerations. First, Billy — the *white* queen — is only slightly less "ridiculous" than Bobby, so there is no good reason to attribute the latter's effeminate manner to slav-ery's negative impact on black male authority as opposed simply to con-temporary gay stereotypes prominent in mass cultural forms. And second, the black male (heterosexual) protagonist of the film, Dr. Gordon Thomas (Thalmus Rasulala), is proud, intelligent, authoritative, and apparently uninterested in interracial coupling.

Aware that the positive representation of Dr. Thomas poses a prob-lem for his overall interpretation of the film, Medovoi retreats to the realm of unmoored speculation. Citing Eve Sedgwick's theorization of the Gothic as a site of homosexual panic, he asserts that "the sexual humiliation that Blacula himself experienced at the hands of the seemingly noble Count Dracula threatens to repeat itself for Thomas if he cannot kill the mon-ster.... The vampire's conflation of antiquity, blackness and charisma therefore works to constitute an anxiety about contemporary black emas-culation through a homosocial current of racial desire for an originary black masculinity" (13). I have already suggested two reasons why sexual humiliation is not an accurate characterization of Mamuwalde's experi-ence with Dracula early in the film: Dracula proves all talk and no action when it comes to Luva (who is in no sense seduced by him); and, in any case, Mamuwalde displays shock and outrage rather than shame or dis-grace when confronted with Dracula's true views on race and slavery. Medovoi's argument here is even less compelling due to the fact that, although Thomas and Blacula are fighting over the same black woman (Tina/Luva), they are not in competition for her sexually, since Thomas is actually dating Tina's sister. In short: Medovoi's attempt to locate the historical meaning of miscegenation as just one more psychological result of humiliations inflicted on black males during the slave era fails due to a far-fetched and overly politicized reading of *Blacula*.

Turning quickly to other blaxploitation fare, in the Kafkaesque race-transformation film *Watermelon Man* (1970), directed by Melvin Van Peebles, and in each of the following blaxploitation horror movies—*Abby* (a.k.a. *Possess My Soul,* 1974); *Sugar Hill* (a.k.a. *Voodoo Girl,* 1974); *The House on Skull Mountain* (1974); *The Omega Man* (1971); and *Welcome Home, Brother Charles* (a.k.a. *Soul Vengeance,* 1975)—the prospect of interracial coupling is explicitly raised and addressed. In not *one* of them is the sexual union between black character and white character (whether actual or merely potential) represented in unproblematic terms. Considering the decade, this is none too surprising: studies indicate that, between the years 1970 and 1980, black-white marriages in the United States increased by roughly 125%, from a mere 65,000 couples to more than 165,000.[22] The anxiety experienced in both population groups as a result of this dramatic increase in size and visibility was reflected in the blaxploitation horror subgenre in a number of different ways.

In both the *Exorcist* rip-off *Abby* and the zombie/gangster hybrid *Sugar Hill,* potent black women invert the Gothic gender code, using their charms—sexual as well as supernatural—to seduce white men, albeit for instrumental rather than romantic purposes. Abby Williams (Carol Speed), possessed by the African demon Eschu, cruises a white guy at an otherwise all-black bar while on the lookout for possible victims. Although Abby-as-Eschu seems totally unconcerned with the race of her male victims—in the previous scene, she has sex with a black undertaker before killing him—Abby-as-black-woman evinces the expected (for a blaxploitation film) consciousness about her prospective partner's color. Flirting with the white guy at the bar, she remarks that "you would just be out of sight if you had a couple more inches," ostensibly referring to his height but also comparing him unfavorably to black men through her allusion to another racial stereotype. Meanwhile, voodoo-practicing Diana "Sugar" Hill (Marki Bey) woos the white gangsters responsible for her boyfriend's death as a means of facilitating her revenge. As Sugar exits a pub with one of the gangsters in tow, the camera temporarily leaves the couple to zoom in on the Haitian demigod with whom she has joined forces; his grinning face makes it obvious (as if we did not already know) that what may look like an interracial couple is really just pretend—that there will be no consummation of this relationship.

The genders are reversed, but not the pragmatic (as opposed to romantic) motivation, in *Welcome Home, Brother Charles.* In this super low-budget production, Marlo Monte stars as Charles Murray, a reticent black man who is nearly castrated by a racist cop, then sent to prison for a crime he did not commit. While there, he is subjected to a series of bizarre medical experiments which greatly increase the size and facility of his genitalia. In the film's signature scene, Charles sneaks into the home of his antagonist's partner, quickly seduces the man's wife, and strangles him with a super-elongated, python-like penis. Despite its obvious exploitation of racial stereotypes and its numerous aesthetic and technical shortcomings, this is a complex, ambitious, and inspired film with subversive potential, insofar as it transforms a myth of black male freakishness into a fantasy of black male revenge. For among Charles's phallic powers is the Dracula-like ability to hypnotize white suburban housewives and turn them into his sexual slaves. Complicating matters further is the fact that his creators are all white men, suggesting a perverse pleasure on their part in facilitating miscegenation. Or maybe not so perverse, as the feelings of impotence and rage experienced by insecure white males is perhaps mitigated by the (illusory) sense of control over interracial couplings.

Although the possibility of an equal, loving interracial relationship at least gets considered in 1971's *The Omega Man*— starring Charlton Heston as a white man almost all alone in a world of racially ambiguous vampire-zombies— the film operates so as to undercut this possibility through bad jokes ("If I was the only boy in the world, and you were the only girl.... Well, I'm the only boy!") and convenient turns in the narrative (the first kiss between Dr. Neville [Heston] and Lisa [Rosalind Cash] gets interrupted by a surprise zombie attack; Neville dies before the couple get a chance to consummate their relationship).[23] Similarly, in Ron Honthaner's *The House on Skull Mountain*— one of the earliest "voodoo in America" race horror films (later entries include *The Possession of Joel Delaney* [1972], *The Believers* [1987], and *Headhunter* [1990])— the budding romance between white anthropologist Andrew Cunningham (Victor French) and black heiress Lorena Christophe (Janee Michelle) is spoiled by the strange-but-true fact that the two are actually cousins. This narrative rationale — or is it merely an excuse?—for eschewing interracial coupling hearkens back to Oscar Micheaux's 1920 classic *Within Our Gates*, in which a white businessman about to rape a young black woman stops when he recognizes (via a telltale scar) that his would-be victim is actually his own illegitimately-conceived daughter.

One also finds in *The House on Skull Mountain* a twist on Micheaux's controversial melodramas, in which unacceptable interracial romances were frequently "saved" with the shocking discovery that the white partner has an iota of black ancestry. By way of contrast, in Honthaner's film, Victor learns that he is actually a black man by virtue of the one-drop rule, but this fact effectively serves to rule out Lorena as a mate. Miscegenation may be a tough topic to depict in American cinema, but incest has always been the greater taboo. At least *Watermelon Man* affords an interracial couple the opportunity to have sex, but significantly the white woman Jeff

Gerber (Godfrey Cambridge) sleeps with is European, not American. Once it becomes clear that she desires him only because he is black — she has heard the stories concerning the sexual prowess of black men — and not because of any interest in him as a fellow human being, Gerber rejects her, only to have the woman reveal her true (racist) colors by accusing him of rape.

Contemporary Race Horror

It was not until the release of Wes Craven's *The Serpent and the Rainbow* in 1988 that a race horror film managed to depict a black-white relationship in romantic, mutually satisfying terms. However, despite the consummated love affair between white anthropologist Dennis Alan (Bill Pullman) and Haitian-born psychiatrist (with a minor in voodoo) Marielle Duchamp (Cathy Tyson) — as well as the liberal sensibilities evident in a number of Craven's previous works (1977's *The Hills Have Eyes* ends with the surviving members of two diametrically-opposed families forming a new, class-blind couple[24]) — *The Serpent and the Rainbow* is a film of mixed ideological messages to be sure. Shot on location in Haiti and in the Dominican Republic, Craven's film takes great pains to integrate the supernatural narrative of magic and zombification with the real-life fall from power of Haitian dictator Jean-Claude "Baby Doc" Duvalier. He even goes so far as to give the evil voodoo priest Peytraud (Zakes Mokae) a day job as leader of the Tontons Macoutes, the notorious Haitian secret police. But as Pinedo points out, even while associating "the political tyranny of the Duvalier regime with voodoo, identified as a religion that can turn dissidents into zombies and use them to terrorize others" (114), Craven's focalization of events through the eyes of a white male protagonist functions to racialize the monstrous in the form of a "primitive" and superstitious black people.

Craven offers a far less ambivalent reversal of race horror stereotypes in the unjustly neglected *The People Under the Stairs* (1992). Here, a thirteen-year-old African American boy nicknamed "Fool" (Brandon Adams) overcomes the low expectations of his family to play the part of Prince Charming to a young white "princess" trapped in the lair of a two-headed monster — really a brother-sister pair of sadistic, greedy, incestuous racists. Not unlike Dr. Gerard of *Voodoo Woman*, willing to go to any lengths to create the perfect (perfectly subjugated) bride, the murderous inbred siblings of *The People Under the Stairs* seek the perfect child to live up to their motto, "See no evil, hear no evil, speak no evil." Every time one of the couple's young kidnap victims disappoints, their new "Daddy" simply cuts out the bad parts, be it eye, ear, or tongue. Worried that her newest "little angel" has been seduced by a "filthy, ... awful" black boy who has somehow managed to sneak his way into the walls of her not-so-happy home, the nameless white woman (Wendy Robie) orders her brother (Everett McGill) to "do him like the others." In a disturbing echo of Southern white lynch mentality, the man vows castration for a (non-)crime that was never committed in the first place: "it won't be his ear I cut off!" By attributing white anxiety and disgust at the prospect of miscegenation to a wholly unsympathetic and manifestly racist couple who are themselves both the products and perpetuators of incest — a far more "serious" biological-cultural transgression which seems to have rendered them perverted as well as insane[25] — Craven is able to endow the budding (though importantly not yet sexual) interracial romance between Alice and Fool with an air of normalcy, naturalness, and healthiness.

By way of conclusion, let us return once more to the world of Candyman. Despite obvious drop-offs in direction, acting, and script quality from the original to the sequels, looked at in unison the three *Candyman* films (1992, 1995, and 1999) present by far the most complex and extended treatment of the Gothic "seductive villain" theme in race horror cinema. As explained in the first entry in the series, and then again (with slight variations) in each of the latter, the eponymous monster is a late-nineteenth century African American portrait artist — significantly, not a slave — who was tortured and killed by a racist mob for impregnating the daughter of a white landowner. A century later, Candyman returns for the body and soul of his reincarnated lover. Concerning the relationship between Candyman and Helen Lyle (Virginia Madsen), Pinedo asserts that "as the interracial romance of the past once conjured up disgust and loathing in the white mob, so the suggestion of intimate contact with Candyman conjures up body horror in the audience" (129). Pinedo is here recapitulating the work of Halberstam, quoted near the beginning of this essay. Claims such as these are supported by the fact that, upon kissing Helen for the first time, Candyman's mouth and coat open to reveal (to Helen as well as the audience) a multitude of swarming bees.

As is so often the case with race horror films from all periods, however, an alternative, even contradictory interpretation to what is perhaps the most obvious one may reasonably be proffered. Considering how much Candyman suffered as a result of sleeping with a white woman in the first place, it comes as something of a surprise to discover that — like Imhotep (the original Mummy) and Blacula/Mamuwalde before him — Candyman hunts his prey *not* out of hatred or revenge, but out of a desire to (re-)unite.

In order to lure Helen to his fortress-tenement, he kidnaps a black infant, thereby providing the final member of an (admittedly dysfunctional) inter-racial family, and sending a message — to viewers, as well as to those within the diegesis— that *nothing*, not even the most horrible acts of racial violence, will prevent such families from coming into being. As with *Welcome Home, Brother Charles* and *Sugar Hill* (at the conclusion of which a bride-seeking Haitian demigod carries off the scantily-clad white girlfriend of Sugar's main antagonist), white male fears of a black man-beast come to take their women right out from under them are exposed and critiqued in *Candyman*, precisely *because* of the way these fears are hyperbolically, even monstrously, concretized. What we have here is an African American-initiated "return of the repressed" with a vengeance, and it must be noted that, at least according to Freud, such returns inevitably bring with them concomitant releases of anxiety.

Notes

1. John Milton, *Paradise Lost* (New York: Macmillan, 1993), ll. 589–608.
2. David Punter, *The Literature of Terror: A History of Gothic Fictions from 1765 to the Present Day. Volume 1: The Gothic Tradition* (London and New York: Longman, 1996), 103–104.
3. Judith Halberstam, *Skin Shows: Gothic Horror and the Technology of Monsters* (Durham: Duke University Press, 1995), 4.
4. See, for example, Mark Edmundson, *Nightmare on Main Street: Angels, Sado-masochism, and the Culture of the Gothic* (Cambridge, MA: Harvard University Press, 1997); Christoph Grunenberg, ed., *Gothic: Transmutations of Horror in Late Twentieth Century Art* (Boston: The Institute of Contemporary Art, 1997); and Brigid Cherry, "Dark Wonders and the Gothic Sensibility," in *Kinoeye: A Fortnightly Journal of Film in the New Europe* 2.1 (7 January 2002): <http://www.kinoeye.org/02/01/cherry01.html>.
5. In Richard Stanley's 1992 film of the same name.
6. Robin Wood, "An Introduction to the American Horror Film," in *Planks of Reason: Essays on the Horror Film*, ed. Barry Keith Grant (Metuchen, NJ: Scarecrow Press, 1984), 171.
7. Isabel Cristina Pinedo, in *Recreational Terror: Women and the Pleasures of Horror Film Viewing* (Albany: State University of New York Press, 1997), restricts her use of the term "race horror" to cover just those American horror films which (1) "explicitly code the monster as a racial Other," and (2) are set "in the city rather than the suburban or rural retreat favored by contemporary horror films" (112). My own use of this term is broader than Pinedo's insofar as I am interested in those films which make racial difference the primary or underlying source of horror, regardless of whether the monster is coded as black or white or whether the locale is the inner city or suburbia.
8. See also Harry M. Benshoff, "Blaxploitation Horror Films: Generic Reappropriation or Reinscription?" *Cinema Journal* 39.2 (2000): 31–50; and Pinedo, *Recreational Terror*, 111–31.
9. Steven Jay Schneider, "Possessed by Soul: Generic (Dis-)Continuity in the Blax-

ploitation Horror Film," in *Shocking Cinema of the Seventies*, ed. Xavier Mendik (Hereford: Noir Publishing), 2002.

10. Gina Marchetti, "Tragic and Transcendent Love in *The Forbidden City*," in *The Birth of Whiteness: Race and the Emergence of U.S. Cinema*, ed. Daniel Bernardi (New Brunswick: Rutgers University Press, 1996), 257–70.

11. Elizabeth Young, "Here Comes the Bride: Wedding, Gender and Race in *Bride of Frankenstein*," in *The Dread of Difference: Gender and the Horror Film*, ed. Barry Keith Grant (Austin: University of Texas Press, 1996), 310.

12. Harvey Roy Greenberg, "*King Kong*: The Beast in the Boudoir — or, 'You Can't Marry That Girl, You're a Gorilla!'" in *The Dread of Difference: Gender and the Horror Film*, ed. Barry Keith Grant (Austin: University of Texas Press, 1996), 338.

13. Fatimah Tobing Rony, *The Third Eye: Race, Cinema, and Ethnographic Spectacle* (Durham, NC: Duke University Press, 1996), 159, 165. See also James Snead, "Spectatorship and Capture in *King Kong*: The Guilty Look," *Critical Quarterly* 33.1 (1991): 53–69.

14. Donald Bogle, *Toms, Coons, Mulattoes, Mammies, and Bucks: An Interpretive History of Blacks in American Films* (New York: Viking, 1973).

15. Thomas E. Wartenberg, "Humanizing the Beast: *King Kong* and the Representation of Black Male Sexuality," in *Classic Hollywood, Classic Whiteness*, ed. Daniel Bernardi (Minneapolis: University of Minnesota Press, 2001), 158. Crucially, however, Wartenberg notes the film's lingering racist undertones: "Even as it strives to criticize the stereotype of Black men's monstrous sexuality, *King Kong* endorses a racist and Eurocentric system of aesthetic valuation, one that specifically denigrates Black women" (175).

16. Kathy Russell, *The Color Complex: The Politics of Skin Color Among African Americans* (New York: Harcourt Brace Jovanovich, 1992), 13.

17. See Ken Gelder, "Postcolonial Voodoo," *Postcolonial Studies* 3.1 (April 2000): 89–98.

18. See Harry M. Benshoff, "Blaxploitation Horror Films," in *Framing Blackness: The African American Image in Film*, ed. Ed Guerrero (Philadelphia: Temple University Press, 1993), 69–112.

19. William Marshall was a trained Shakespearean stage actor before moving into film.

20. As Chris Norton explains, "The term co-optation signifies a strategy of appropriation that operates beyond a simple borrowing of tropes or homage. It incorporates a level of critique and response to the very things it cites." See Norton, "*Cleopatra Jones: 007*: Blaxploitation, James Bond, and Reciprocal Co-Optation," *Images: A Journal of Film and Popular Culture* 4 (July 1997): <*http://www.imagesjournal.com/issue04/features/blaxploitation.htm*>.

21. Leerom Medovoi, "Theorizing Historicity, or the Many Meanings of *Blacula*," *Screen* 39.1 (Spring 1998): 8.

22. Robert McNamara, Maria Tempenis, and Beth Walton, *Crossing the Line: Interracial Couples in the South* (Westport, CT: Greenwood Press, 1999), 5.

23. Another "last person(s) on earth" film which makes a point of thematizing interracial union is Geoff Murphy's sci-fi drama, *The Quiet Earth* (New Zealand, 1985).

24. For discussion of this film, see Steven Jay Schneider, "*The Hills Have Eyes*," CTEQ Annotation on Film, in *Senses of Cinema* 19 (March–April 2002): <*http://www.sensesofcinema.com/contents/01/19/cteq/hills.html*>.

25. See the above discussion of *The House on Skull Mountain*.

88   Part I: Demonizing the Racial Other, Humanizing the Self

Works Cited

Benshoff, Harry M. "Blaxploitation Horror Films: Generic Reappropriation or Rein-scription?" *Cinema Journal* 39.2 (2000): 31–50.
"Blaxploitation Horror Films." In *Framing Blackness: The African American Image in Film.* Edited by Ed Guerrero. Philadelphia: Temple University Press, 1993.
Bogle, Donald. *Toms, Coons, Mulattoes, Mammies, and Bucks: An Interpretive History of Blacks in American Films.* New York: Viking, 1973.
Cherry, Brigid. "Dark wonders and the Gothic sensibility." *Kinoeye: A Fortnightly Journal of Film in the New Europe* 2.1 (7 January 2002). <*http://www.kinoeye.org/02/01/cherry01.html*>.
Edmundson, Mark. *Nightmare on Main Street: Angels, Sadomasochism, and the Culture of the Gothic.* Cambridge, MA: Harvard University Press, 1997.
Gelder, Ken. "Postcolonial Voodoo." *Postcolonial Studies* 3.1 (April 2000): 89–98.
Greenberg, Harvey Roy. "*King Kong*: The Beast in the Boudoir — or, 'You Can't Marry That Girl, You're a Gorilla!'" In *The Dread of Difference: Gender and the Horror Film.* Edited by Barry Keith Grant. Austin: University of Texas Press, 1996.
Grunenberg, Christoph, ed. *Gothic: Transmutations of Horror in Late Twentieth Century Art.* Boston: The Institute of Contemporary Art, 1997.
Halberstam, Judith. *Skin Shows: Gothic Horror and the Technology of Monsters.* Durham: Duke University Press, 1995.
Marchetti, Gina. "Tragic and Transcendent Love in *The Forbidden City.*" In *The Birth of Whiteness: Race and the Emergence of U.S. Cinema.* Edited by Daniel Bernardi. New Brunswick: Rutgers University Press, 1996.
McNamara, Robert, Maria Tempenis, and Beth Walton. *Crossing the Line: Interracial Couples in the South.* Westport, CT: Greenwood Press, 1999.
Medovoi, Leerom. "Theorizing Historicity, or the Many Meanings of *Blacula.*" *Screen* 39.1 (Spring 1998): 1–21.
Milton, John. *Paradise Lost.* New York: Macmillan, 1993.
Norton, Chris. "*Cleopatra Jones: 007*: Blaxploitation, James Bond, and Reciprocal Co-Optation." *Images: A Journal of Film and Popular Culture* 4 (July 1997). <*http://www.imagesjournal.com/issue04/features/blaxploitation.htm*>.
Pinedo, Isabel Cristina. *Recreational Terror: Women and the Pleasures of Horror Film Viewing.* Albany: State University of New York Press, 1997.
Punter, David. *The Literature of Terror: A History of Gothic Fictions from 1765 to the Present Day. Volume 1: The Gothic Tradition.* London and New York: Longman, 1996.
Rony, Fatimah Tobing. *The Third Eye: Race, Cinema, and Ethnographic Spectacle.* Durham, NC: Duke University Press, 1996.
Russell, Kathy. *The Color Complex: The Politics of Skin Color Among African Americans.* New York: Harcourt Brace Jovanovich, 1992.
Schneider, Steven Jay. "*The Hills Have Eyes.*" CTEQ Annotation on Film. *Senses of Cinema* 19 (March–April 2002). <*http://www.sensesofcinema.com/contents/01/19/cteq/hills.html*>.
____. "Possessed By Soul: Generic (Dis-)Continuity in the Blaxploitation Horror Film." In *Shocking Cinema of the Seventies.* Edited by Xavier Mendik. Hereford: Noir Publishing, 2002.
Snead, James. "Spectatorship and Capture in *King Kong*: The Guilty Look." *Critical Quarterly* 33.1 (1991): 53–69.
Wartenberg, Thomas E. "Humanizing the Beast: *King Kong* and the Representation of Black Male Sexuality." In *Classic Hollywood, Classic Whiteness.* Edited by Daniel Bernardi. Minneapolis: University of Minnesota Press, 2001.

Wood, Robin. "An Introduction to the American Horror Film." In *Planks of Reason: Essays on the Horror Film*. Edited by Barry Keith Grant. Metuchen, NJ: Scarecrow Press, 1984.

Young, Elizabeth. "Here Comes the Bride: Wedding, Gender and Race in *Bride of Frankenstein*." In *The Dread of Difference: Gender and the Horror Film*. Edited by Barry Keith Grant. Austin: University of Texas Press, 1996.

5

Diseased States, Public Minds: Native American Ghosts in Early National Literature

Renée L. Bergland

Washington Irving did not write much about Native Americans. For the most part, his American romances are haunted by glassy-eyed Dutchmen and knock-kneed schoolmasters rather than by Indians. But Irving's few evocations of Indians have special significance to Native American literary history, in part because his essay "Traits of Indian Character," published in 1811 in the *Analectic Magazine*, was an important source for the Pequot writer William Apess. Apess seized on the sweet and wispy shadows of Indian ghosts that Irving had conjured forth, and turned them to his own radical purposes, as I have discussed elsewhere. When Apess tried to remake Irving's Indian ghosts as political agents, he was, in effect, trying to undo Irving. For Irving had constructed his gentle romantic phantoms out of the terrifying, bloody and violent Indian figures that haunted the American polity described by Charles Brockden Brown.

In this essay, I examine the repressions and displacements of early nineteenth-century American literature — the period when Indian Removal becomes American Romance. The removals that I discuss occur on many levels; I focus here on textual displacements, as the bloody savages of *Edgar Huntly* become the romantic, neo-classical shades of Irving's *Sketchbook*, and then, remarkably, these Indian ghosts become the fathers of the new nation. Voila! According to Samuel Woodworth's 1818 novel,

Champions of Freedom, the eponymous Indian Ghost is actually a figure for the "Father of our Country," George Washington himself. When Woodworth transforms a dead Indian into a dead President, he offers us a startlingly clear example of the logic of Indian spectralization. Indian ghosts (removed, repressed, half-remembered dead Indians) father the American nation.

Although Charles Brockden Brown wrote and published *Edgar Huntly* in 1799, he set the novel in 1787, the year the U.S. Constitution and Philip Freneau's "Indian Burying Ground" were written and published. Throughout the novel, Brown continuously confounds the national constitution, the human constitution and his narrator's private constitution, as he plays on the contemporary notion that white American men embody their nation and simultaneously are possessed by it.

In the first pages of the novel, the narrator exclaims, "What light has burst upon my ignorance of myself and of mankind!"[1] It is notable that Huntly speaks of his illuminated ignorance rather than any newfound self-knowledge or understanding. It is also important that Huntly acknowledges both particular and universal ignorances; he is equally in the dark about self and mankind. The novel that follows narrates a journey into the "modern darkness" that haunts the rationalist conception of mind, both privately and publicly. Brown announced in his preface that his purpose was "to exhibit a series of adventures growing out of the condition of our country" (3). The country's condition reflects its constitution.

As Norman Grabo puts it, the novel characterizes 1787 as a "somnambulistic year."[2] Further, it can be said to characterize the American constitution itself as somnambulistic. "No one knows what powers are latent in his constitution" (159), Huntly exclaims as he recalls the mad fury that drives him to kill a panther and devour it uncooked in a dark cave. Later, when he falls into a dead faint that averts his reunion with his friends, he declares, "Such is the capricious constitution of the human mind!" (188). The political significance of describing constitutions as mysterious, even capricious entities full of unknown latent powers, cannot be ignored. Neither can the private meanings. Here, as throughout the novel, private subject and national subject are, as Carroll Smith-Rosenberg might say, fused and confused.[3]

In order to depict the somnambulistic, mysteriously constituted American condition, Brown explained in his preface that he would replace the "puerile superstition and exploded manners; Gothic castles and chimeras" common to European novels with "the incidents of Indian hostility, and the perils of the western wilderness" (3). The novel's Americanness depends upon Indian wars and a perilous frontier. In this respect, the novel accurately reflects the nation. Although the "tawny and terrific" savages of *Edgar Huntly* represent internal mental and cultural constructs, they also represent historical figures, real Native American people who were engaged in violent conflict with the United States (183).

The age of Indian Removal is often demarcated as the period between 1820 and 1850. However, the United States was actively engaged in Indian removal and Indian war almost continuously from its inception. The Pequot War in 1637 set a pattern of genocidal violence from which the United States never deviated. During George Washington's presidency, war with western Native Americans was pursued relentlessly. According to Bill Christopherson, Indian wars and treaties "accounted for five-sixths of all Federal expenses between the years 1790 and 1796."[4] By this economic measure, the main purpose of the federal government in these years was to define the relationship of the United States to Native Americans. Citizens of the republic laid claim to their citizenship by joining in the public financing of, or active military duty in, an almost ceaseless war against the Indians.

The wars were bloody and real; people died and homes burned. But they were fought (as most wars are) for the sake of abstractions. Like the earlier wars between the Puritans and the Indians, the war that the United States waged against Native Americans often conflated reality and abstraction. The goal, both physical and metaphysical, was to secure America's borders, to define the national territory and hence the nation. United States citizens struck out into the unknown western wilderness, hoping to map it, document it, write titles for it and grant themselves possession of it. It was a violently physical war. Citizen-soldiers laid their own bodies on the line, and they grew intimately familiar with the corpses of conquered Native Americans. But it was also metaphysical. In the European-American mind, as in *Edgar Huntly*, only Indian corpses had concrete reality. Before they were dead, Native Americans were representatives of the great unknown.

Ghosts haunt the frontiers between the visible and the invisible worlds, partaking of both, belonging to neither. In some sense then, ghosts can be understood as frontier-beings. Taking issue with Frederick Jackson Turner, who thought of a frontier as a "clearly discernible line between 'us' and 'them,'" Arnold Krupat defines frontier as a "shifting space in which two *cultures* encounter one another." Krupat's definition is based on James Clifton's formulation that "a frontier is a social setting," not fixed or mappable, but, rather, "a culturally defined place where peoples with different culturally expressed identities meet and deal with each other."[5]

The lore and language of ghostliness are particularly appropriate for describing the encounters that take place within the mysteriously shifting grounds of American cultural frontiers.

The dominant discourses of American nationalism at the close of the eighteenth century presumed that Indian removal was inevitable and completely effective, and that the borders around the United States were impenetrable barriers that would eventually exclude all people of darkness. Analogously, merchants, farmers and lawyers assumed that novels and poems could be effectively banished from the national discourse of laws, political tracts and constitutions, and that impenetrable borders could be erected around the realm of reason. These are the assumptions of willful blindness, repression, intentional amnesia and sleepwalking. Brown challenged this repressive nationalist rationalism by writing a novel peopled with somnambulists and spectral Indians who prove harder and harder to distinguish from each other, in a region that proves harder and harder to define.

The plots and characters in *Edgar Huntly* mirror and double each other again and again, each storyline and character offering ever more distorted reflections of its others. At the least, the novel is a house of mirrors. Since the novel projects fearsome and ghostly images before its audience, it may even be described as a phantasmagoria. *Edgar Huntly* presents a somnambulistic writer who describes an errand into a hallucinatory wilderness peopled by shadowy Indian warriors who are both the writer's enemies and his doubles, and from whom his friends and family cannot distinguish him. When he uses spectral Indians to attack rationalist, republican Americanism, Brown questions the supremacy of reason. When he uses an epistolary novel and an unreliable narrator to tell his story, he also questions the use of the written word as a vehicle for rationalist authority. Like the apparitional images of a phantasmagoria, the novel's specters work to interrogate rationalist subjectivity. Finally, *Edgar Huntly* forces the reader to question the sanity and presumed reasonableness of the narrator, the novel and the American nation itself.

Insanity and nationhood are perennial themes in Brown. None of his novels enters as deeply into the realm of mental illness— public, private, and projected onto the landscape — as *Edgar Huntly*. As the novel progresses, the very act of writing is implicated in the insanity that it documents. The subtitle of *Edgar Huntly, or, Memoirs of a Sleepwalker* gives the reader the first clue that the novel will be narrated by an unreliable (or even mentally ill) figure. Huntly begins the book by expressing agonizing doubts over his own sanity. "Am I sure that even now my perturbations are sufficiently stilled for an employment like this...? That emotions will not be re-awakened by my narrative, incompatible with order and coherence?" (5). But Huntly is a child of the Enlightenment, and he believes, as romantics and rationalists also believe, that one must be a little bit insane to write. "In proportion as I gain power over words," he explains, "shall I lose dominion over sentiments; in proportion as my tale is deliberate and slow, the incidents and motives which it is designed to exhibit will be imperfectly revived and obscurely portrayed" (5–6).

This internal dialogue dramatizes the author's preoccupation with the impossibility of being an imaginative writer in republican America. In the course of the story, the protagonist, Edgar Huntly, the Indian-fighter who is also the writer of the long letter that constitutes the manuscript, finds himself increasingly identified with the phantom-like Indians who threaten his own well-ordered community. Edgar is implicated in and suspected of every act of violence that takes place, and his written words are subject to so many changes, concealments, misinterpretations and unintended exposures that they are finally equally implicated and even more suspect. His attack on the Indians turns to an attack on himself. As the madness escalates, the entire narrative begins to call itself into question. Readers are left wondering whether the novel's villains — a host of nameless Indians and a demented Irishman — exist outside of Huntly's manuscript, or whether Huntly is the sole author of every phantomlike being that he describes.

His friends and neighbors mistake him for a corpse, an Indian, and finally, a ghost. First, Clithero recoils from him "as from a spectre" (31). Next, a good woman gazes at him "as if a spectre had started into view" (196). As he nears home, he describes himself as an "apparition" about to "present itself" before his family (227). His mentor, Sarsefeld, shrinks from him, he writes, "as if I were an apparition or an impostor" (232). Huntly is haunted to be sure, but he also haunts his fellows.

In *Love and Death in the American Novel*, Leslie Fiedler applies the terms of Freudian psychoanalysis to *Edgar Huntly*, compares Brown's American Gothic to the European version, and argues that the transposition deeply changes the genre. Fiedler writes that "the European Gothic identified blackness with the superego and was therefore revolutionary in its implications; the American Gothic (at least as it followed the example of Brown) identified evil with the id and was therefore conservative at its deepest level of implication."[6] When cliffs are substituted for castle towers, and caves for dungeons, the threats and dangers of the natural world replace the threats and dangers of ancient aristocratic power structures. When Indians and panthers take the place of villainous Italian nobles and Catholic priests, the predatory hierarchies of the Old World are replaced by the natural and wild predators of the New. In Europe, Gothic novels were fundamentally radical stories about modern people fighting ancient regimes. As Fiedler would have it, the great departure of Brown's American Gothic from the European is that while European Gothic novels worked to show the destruction of traditional power structures, the American version works to show the formation of new power structures in the wilderness. In America, Fiedler argues, Brown reimagines the Gothic protagonist as one who struggles to establish order in the chaotic and savage world of his own soul.

Fiedler's introduction of psychoanalytic criticism is appropriate for a novel whose central concern is haunted subjectivity. Smith-Rosenberg also takes a psychoanalytic or at least psychohistorical approach to *Edgar Huntly* in "Subject Female," arguing that "quite self-consciously," *Edgar Huntly* explores "a novel late eighteenth-century construction — the American subject." But Smith-Rosenberg rejects Fiedler's premise that *Edgar Huntly* is a proponent of Enlightenment rationalism and the new American order. To the contrary, she argues that "*Edgar Huntly*'s refusal of rational and cohesive subjectivity suggests that the European-American is always a divided self" (Smith-Rosenberg 481, 495). I would go further; the novel suggests that the European-American subject is founded on its own haunted ambivalence.

But Jared Gardner objects to psychoanalytic readings of *Edgar Huntly*, in which "the landscape is internal, the shadows and doubles are projections of the divided self of the narrator, and the Indians are figures for the 'dark' (uncivilized, savage) nature with which Edgar must do violent battle to claim his civilized self." Instead, Gardner argues that "the question of identity in *Edgar Huntly* is importantly national rather than (generally) human or (particularly) individual."[7] Although Gardner is right to emphasize the importance of national politics to the plot of *Edgar Huntly*, it is equally important to realize that the novel collapses the national and the personal, and that its central theme is the collapse of both. To some extent, this reflects the spirit of the times. In 1786, Benjamin Rush asserted that every young man must "be taught that he does not belong to himself, but that he is public property." His life "belong[s] to his country." Similarly, John Adams declared that the Republic required "a positive Passion for the public good, the public interest.... Superior to all private Passions."[8] Brown examines the consequences of fostering such public passions in a nation whose foundational ethos eschews passion for reason.

In *Edgar Huntly*, Native Americans are ghostly figures of the irrational. Christopherson points out that they are "phantoms of the mind first; phantoms of the culture second; and only third, Leni Lenapes living in late-eighteenth-century Pennsylvania" (Christopherson 156). Queen Mab, the leader of Edgar's Indian enemies, is presented in all three guises. She is meant to be a real Indian: Edgar Huntly describes her as a woman who "originally belonged to the tribe of Delawares or Lennilennapee" (197). She is also, indisputably, a cultural phantom; Huntly whimsically names her "Queen Mab" in order to liken her to the "fairies' midwife," queen of dreams and nightmares, who is described in *Romeo and Juliet*.[9] The implication is that her measure of her own significance and political rights is delusional, but also that she is somehow correct about her importance — at least in the realm of delusions.

In the hallucinatory world of *Edgar Huntly*, dreams and nightmares are far more constant than reason. Huntly's own constitution, which he believes to be rational and enlightened, is actually capricious and haunted by irrationality. Queen Mab's constitution, on the other hand, is solid and unchanging, "a constitution that seemed to defy the ravages of time and the influence of the elements" (200). She is inhuman, linked with fairies on the one hand, and on the other, with the rocky cliffs and vastnesses of the land itself. Like the land, she defies the elements.

With the almost inevitable logic of a bad dream, Huntly explains that the phantom queen, leader of his enemies, is "wonderfully prepossessed" in his favor, because he is the only white resident of Norwalk who has taken the pains to learn her native language, and to "discourse with her on the few ideas which she possessed" (200). Notably, the discussion of her emotions and her thoughts is framed in terms of "possession." Since Huntly figures her as the queen of dreams, and since he is a sleepwalker, the language of possession grows multivalent. When he takes up tomahawk and fusil, Huntly can be said to be possessed by Queen Mab, or at least by some Indian spirit. At the same time, the root of the conflict is contested possession of the land itself. Insofar as Queen Mab represents the land, she is Huntly's mother, and that which he longs to possess. As she represents her tribe, she is his enemy, and a threat to his title to the land. The iconography of the period often depicted America as a fecund and mysterious Indian woman, who beckoned and threatened white settlers. Queen Mab is like this icon. But she is also the queen of dreams. In this respect, she is the one who possesses Huntly, the supremely rational, enlightened and educated young man whose faulty reason and untrustworthy (somnambulistic) constitution leads him into an orgy of killing which he cannot end even when he is "satiated and gorged with slaughter" (190).

Queen Mab is invisible throughout the text. Nonetheless she is credited with directing the attacks of the "terrific" Indians who do appear. She may also direct the sleepwalker Huntly. Much of the violence takes place in her cottage, and on her land. Huntly and the girl whom he has rescued take refuge there. Then the Indians approach, and overcome by the "desperate impulse of passion," Huntly hides himself in Queen Mab's oven. He contemplates "the consequence of shrouding myself in this cavity," reflecting, "How strange is the destiny that governs mankind!" (181). The oven is womb and grave at the same time. When he emerges from the oven, he has taken on the guileful strategies of an Indian warrior. A bullet grazes his cheek, blood dyes his face red, and Huntly is impossible to distinguish from his Indian enemies. Like a revolutionary soldier or an Indian warrior, he feints, rolls and slides across the land, and defeats his enemies by trickery.

After the showdown at Mab's hut, Huntly's friends mistake him for dead, and leave him pillowed upon "the breast of him whom I had shot in this part of the body" (189). Coated in blood, Huntly rises, and goes for water. At the spring, he glimpses a movement that he instantly identifies as an Indian: "my startled fancy figured to itself nothing but a human adversary," he explains (191). The native adversary is a figure of his fancy, as much imagined as real. As the man comes closer, his form and movements mark him as bestial and savage. "He moved on all fours.... His disfigured limbs, pendants from his ears and nose, and his shorn locks, were indubitable indications of a savage" (191).

The encounter exposes the fallacies at the heart of the nightmare logic of conquest. Huntly begins by proclaiming his own innocence and his peaceful nature. "My abhorrence of bloodshed was not abated," he says, "but I had not foreseen this occurrence.... The mark was near, nothing obstructed or delayed; I incurred no danger and the event was certain." An Indian presents himself as a "mark" or a target. There is no danger to Huntly, and he will surely be able to kill his victim. Presented with this opportunity, Edgar asks, "Why should he be suffered to live...? Fate has reserved for him a bloody and violent death. For how long a time soever it may be deferred, it is thus that his career will inevitably terminate." The man's death, after all, is inevitable. Once Huntly has reminded himself of this, he cocks his gun, and the Indian catches sight of him. At this juncture, Edgar writes, "I saw that forbearance was no longer in my power; but my heart sunk while I complied with what may surely be termed an indispensable necessity" (191–2). In the space of a moment, the Native American man has been transformed from a figure of fancy to a bestial savage, then a target, then a being fated for a bloody death, and finally someone whose murder "may surely be termed an indispensable necessity."

But Edgar is a reluctant murderer. After his first shot, he writes, "Horror, and compassion, and remorse were mingled into one sentiment and took possession of my heart" (192). Possessed by strange, regretful passion, he shoots again, and finishes the job with his bayonet. Then he comments, "The task of cruel lenity was at length finished. I dropped the weapon and threw myself on the ground; overpowered by the horrors of the scene. Such are the deeds which perverse nature compels thousands of rational beings to perform and to witness!" (193). Edgar is not unique. Since nature itself is perverse, "thousands of rational beings" find themselves compelled by "cruel lenity" to perform and to witness acts of horrifying brutality. These are the perils of the western wilderness, writ small. Rational and brutal, cruel and kind, perverse and natural, savage and civilized, red and white — *Edgar Huntly* encompasses the dire ambivalence of the American constitution.

As he began his career, Washington Irving struggled against the hallucinatory artistic vision of Charles Brockden Brown. Brown's haunted landscapes and his inchoate narratives painted a gloomy picture of an American subject that was dangerously close to madness. Irving hoped to contain the madness, to unify the American subject, and to construct a national literature. "In the early chronicles of these dark and melancholy times," Irving wrote, "we meet with many indications of the diseased state of the public mind."[10] He refers to the long, Rowlandsonian tradition of ambivalent jeremiads, but he seems also to be writing about more recent compositions such as *Edgar Huntly*. The diseased and unsettled state of the public mind, is after all, Brown's central theme. In order to cure the American disease, Irving was compelled to return to the ghostly figure of the Native American. His essay "Philip of Pokanoket," published in the *Analectic Magazine* in 1813, focuses specifically on the Wampanoag leader King Philip (or Metacom) and more generally on the role of Native Americans in American literature. But Irving's comments can be applied directly to *Edgar Huntly*. His words about King Philip's War also describe Queen Mab's War. In fact, Irving seems to invoke Brown's vision explicitly. Like Brown's, his Indians are figures that "stalk, like gigantic shadows in the dim twilight of tradition" (Irving, "Philip of Pokanoket" 1014), while his description of Philip seems lifted from the pages of Brown's novel:

> Philip became a theme of universal apprehension. The mystery in which he was enveloped exaggerated his real terrors. He was an evil that walked in darkness; whose coming none could foresee, and against which none knew when to be on the alert. The whole country abounded with rumours and alarms. Philip seemed almost possessed of ubiquity, for, in whatever part of the widely extended frontier an irruption from the forest took place,

Philip was said to be its leader. Many superstitions were circulated concerning him. He was said to deal in necromancy and to be attended by an old Indian witch or prophetess, whom he consulted and who assisted him with her charms and incantations [Irving "Philip of Pokanoket" 1021–2].

Irving's sketch on Philip is usually paired with his "Traits of Indian Character," which was also published first in the *Analectic Magazine*. The second essay, as I have discussed elsewhere, conjured forth its own Indian ghost, in the shape of the Sachem of Passonagessit's mother. The two sketches, both of which depicted spectral Indians who were justifiably angry but nonetheless threatening, were later published side-by-side in *The Sketchbook of Sir Geoffrey Crayon*. Like many contemporary essays and speeches, the sketches call for Americans to take advantage of Native American sources and themes to differentiate Anglo-American writing from English.

Curiously, however, Irving ignored his own advice. Beyond these two, both of which call on American writers to write about Indians, there are no other Native American sketches or tales in *The Sketchbook*. In fact, Irving would not treat Native American themes again until he published *A Tour on the Prairie* in 1835. In light of these omissions, it seems that when Irving writes of ghostly or demonic Indians in *The Sketchbook*, his purpose is more to lay their ghosts to rest than to invoke them himself.

Although Irving hopes to quiet the horrors of Brown's American Gothic, the new American Romanticism that he proposes also relies on presenting Native Americans as ghosts, and it also assumes the inevitability of Indian disappearance.

They will vanish like a vapour from the face of the earth; their very history will be lost in forgetfulness; and "the places that now know them will know them no more forever." Or if, perchance, some dubious memorial of them should survive, it may be in the romantic dreams of the poet, to people in imagination his glades and groves, like the fauns and satyrs and sylvan deities of antiquity.[11]

The real Indians are forgotten; the tawny and terrific phantoms of *Edgar Huntly* may give way to the classically inflected romantic dreams of Irving's "Traits of Indian Character," but either way, the Native Americans disappear into the minds of white American men.

In the *Sketchbook* itself, Irving's technique is one of displacement. When Rip Van Winkle ventures into the wilderness, for example, he seems to expect that he will encounter an Indian, or perhaps an Indian ghost. Instead, Rip finds the bumptious spectres of Hudson and his crew, who have taken the place of the Indian spirits the reader has been led to expect. Later, when Rip returns after his long and dreamless sleep, he finds that

President George has replaced King George on the tavern sign, though their faces remain eerily the same. The displacement of Native Americans with early settlers in Irving's work is parallel to the replacement of Hanover by Washington. It is central to the drama, and, at the same time, it is silently passed over. This is how repression works. Native Americans are not forgotten in Irving's texts, but they are civilized and controlled, clothed in the odd garments of Dutchmen, and made into tame and unfrightening figures.

In the writings that follow *The Sketchbook*, Native American phantoms continue to appear and reappear, while each apparition reinforces the notion that Indians must inevitably vanish. Sometimes the spectral Indians reveal the horrors of American nationalism as they do in *Edgar Huntly*. Sometimes they reveal the unique aesthetic possibilities of America, as they do in Irving's *Sketchbook*. Often, ghostly Indians are simultaneously horrific and aestheticized.

Of all the Indian ghosts I have come across, I am fondest of the Mysterious Chief who haunts Samuel Woodworth's 1818 novel, *The Champions of Freedom, or, The Mysterious Chief*. This Native American ghost functions directly as the mouthpiece of American nationalism, and simultaneously as a young man's conscience. Although he seems to be a Miami warrior, at the climax of the story Woodworth enacts a displacement that was surely inspired by Irving and reveals, startlingly, that the chief is actually George Washington himself, appearing as a spectral Indian.

The mysterious chief appears at every dramatic turn of the story to advise his young protégé, George Washington Willoughby, an army captain fighting on the Canadian border in the War of 1812 . The chief advocates the moral duties of patriotism, and prophesies that if Willoughby follows his advice, he will defeat a host of enemies single-handedly. But since the novel is based on a factual history of the Canadian front, there are few opportunities for glory. As the war closes, Willoughby asks his ghostly mentor about the unfulfilled prophecy. The chief explains that although his military record is only average, the promise has been fulfilled: "You have at length become all I can wish — you have adhered to my precepts and defeated a host of internal foes that were more dangerous to your peace than the British were to your country."[12]

This interchange points to many of the most important aspects of Indian spectralization. First, Indian ghosts show that the most important American battlefields are within the heads of white American men, while the most dangerous enemies are "internal foes." Next, the Indian ghost acts as a revisionist historian, turning America's historical indignities into spiritual or mental glories. Finally, it will turn out that the Indian ghost is none other than the father of his country. The Mysterious Chief's explanation of Willoughby's unnoticed triumph over evil is not the novel's climax. The last scene is written as a script:

> George. What then am I to think of you?
> M.C.Think of me as an ALLEGORY — and let it be recorded in your journal, that it is the duty of every parent to believe that his children are *specially* destined by Heaven for a life of *peculiar usefulness* — in order that he may be thereby induced to prepare them for such a life. I repeat — that, as the instrument of heaven I achieved every victory which graces your Journal; because (let it be recorded) whenever Americans would succeed, either in peace or in war, their counsels must be actuated and their heroes inspired by the *Spirit of Washington* [Woodworth 2:336].

The Indian ghost turns out to be George Washington, the father of his country. His last words reflect on his role as spiritual father of every American, and counsel every father to prepare every child for a life of *"peculiar usefulness,"* as he has prepared George Washington Willoughby. The transformation of the Indian ghost into the spirit of the first president works to remove Indians completely from the text — they were never really there at all. But also, more importantly, it establishes Indian ghosts as fathers of their country, thereby constituting young Americans as the children and spiritual heirs of the Native Americans. The slippage between the Indian Chief and the Great White Father makes young George Washington Willoughby into the legitimate heir of Indian lands, and revises history in order to remove the stains of injustice from the American legacy.

Edgar Huntly, *The Sketchbook*, and *The Mysterious Chief* employ Native phantoms for vastly different ends. In Brown's work, the specters undermine the American Constitution and question national sanity. In Irving's writing, similar specters cast a classic glow over the American landscape, and establish the gentle pleasures of American Romanticism. For Woodworth, the supernatural capacities of the Mysterious Chief enable George Washington to act as father to a new generation of American boys. But no matter how they use the figure, all three writers seem to find Native American phantoms an inevitable corollary to American nationalism.

Brown, Irving, Woodworth, and their peers based their constructions of Indian ghosts on the poetry of Philip Freneau and Sarah Wentworth Morton, on the silences of the Constitution and on the bloody and almost unceasing Indian wars of the period. In different ways, these writers were attempting to write nationalist fiction and to draw on American history and nationhood in their work. Their Indian ghosts were certainly shaped by the recent historical past; by the Revolution, the Constitution, and the

Indian wars and treaties of the late eighteenth century. Just as importantly, their Indian ghosts shaped the nation and the national literature, constructing America as a haunted community rather than a simple imagined one.

Notes

1. Charles Brockden Brown, *Edgar Huntly, or, Memoirs of a Sleep-Walker* (1799: New York: Penguin Books, 1988), 6. Subsequent citations will be included parenthetically in the text.

2. Norman Grabo, introduction to *Edgar Huntly, or, Memoirs of a Sleep-Walker* by Charles Brockden Brown (1799: New York: Penguin Books, 1988), xxi.

3. Carroll Smith-Rosenberg, "Subject Female: Authorizing American Identity," *American Literary History* 5, no. 3 (Fall 1993): 491. Her exact words are, "Fusion is confusion."

4. Bill Christopherson, The Apparition in the Glass: Charles Brockden Brown's American Gothic (Athens: The University of Georgia Press, 1993), 11, 12.

5. Arnold Krupat, *Ethnocriticism: Ethnography, History, Literature* (Berkeley: University of California Press, 1992), 5.

6. Leslie Fiedler, *Love and Death in the American Novel* (New York: Anchor Books, 1992), 160–1.

7. Jared Gardner, "Alien Nation: Edgar Huntly's Savage Awakening," *American Literature* 66 (1994): 429.

8. Isaac Kramnick, "The 'Great National Discussion': The Discourse of Politics in 1787," *The William and Mary Quarterly* 45 (January 1988): 15–16.

9. *Romeo and Juliet*, 1.4.50–114.

10. Washington Irving, "Philip of Pokanoket," in History, Tales, and Sketches (New York: Library of America, 1983), 1018.

11. Washington Irving, "Traits of Indian Character," in *History, Tales, and Sketches* (New York: Library of America, 1983), 1011–12.

12. Samuel Woodworth, *The Champions of Freedom, or The Mysterious Chief, A Romance of the Nineteenth Century*, 2 vols. (New York: Charles M. Baldwin, 1818), 2:336.

Works Cited

Brown, Charles Brockden. *Edgar Huntly, or, Memoirs of a Sleep-Walker*. 1799. New York: Penguin Books, 1988.

Christopherson, Bill. *The Apparition in the Glass: Charles Brockden Brown's American Gothic*. Athens: The University of Georgia Press, 1993.

Fiedler, Leslie. *Love and Death in the American Novel*. New York: Anchor Books, 1992.

Gardner, Jared. "Alien Nation: Edgar Huntly's Savage Awakening." *American Literature*. 66 (1994): 429.

Grabo, Norman. Introduction to *Edgar Huntly, or, Memoirs of a Sleep-Walker* by Charles Brockden Brown. New York: Penguin Books, 1988.

Irving, Washington. "Philip of Pokanoket." In *History, Tales, and Sketches*. New York: Library of America, 1983.

____. "Traits of Indian Character." In *History, Tales and Sketches.* New York: Library of America, 1983.

Kramnick, Isaac. "The 'Great National Discussion': The Discourse of Politics in 1787." *The William and Mary Quarterly* 45 (January 1988): 15–16.

Krupat, Arnold. *Ethnocriticism: Ethnography, History, Literature.* Berkeley: University of California Press, 1992.

Smith-Rosenberg, Carroll. "Subject Female: Authorizing American Identity." *American Literary History* 5.3 (Fall 1993): 491.

Woodworth, Samuel. *The Champions of Freedom, or The Mysterious Chief, A Romance of the Nineteenth Century.* 2 vols. New York: Charles M. Baldwin, 1818.

6

Yellow Peril, Dark Hero: Fu Manchu and the "Gothic Bedevilment" of Racist Intent

Karen Kingsbury

Midway through *The Insidious Dr. Fu-Manchu* (1913), the narrator, Dr. Petrie, describes a confrontation between Fu, "the head of the great Yellow Movement," and Nayland Smith, "the man who fought on behalf of the entire white race":

> At last they were face to face — the head of the great Yellow Movement, and the man who fought on behalf of the entire white race. How can I paint the individual who now stood before us— perhaps the greatest genius of modern times?
>
> Of him it had been fitly said that he had a brow like Shakespeare and a face like Satan. Something serpentine, hypnotic, was in his very presence.... Together, chained to the wall, two mediaeval captives ... we crouched before Dr. Fu-Manchu.[1]

Is this racist nonsense, pure and simple, and does the series's appeal depend on nothing more than this? But what then of the Poe-like exaggerations, the Walpole-like setting — Fu as "the greatest genius" of the era, with his Shakespearian cranium and Satanic mien, filling the "mediaeval" torture chamber with his "serpentine, hypnotic" presence? How might these strains of Gothic fantasy have shaped and sustained the Fu Manchu myth?[2]

It is clear that some force of great power has sustained Fu. In 1912, the British writer Arthur Sarsfield Ward (1883–1959), under the pen name Sax Rohmer, published the first Fu story in a London magazine; by the following year, the story had grown to a book-length adventure tale published in both New York and London. The series kept growing throughout Ward's lifetime and beyond, and was even more popular in the U.S. than in Great Britain. At the height of his fame in the 1920s and 30s, Fu Manchu was a household name in English-speaking homes around the globe, including Calvin Coolidge's White House.[3] By the early 1980s, the Fu corpus included thirteen print volumes in numerous editions, at least five radio-play serials, a TV series, and dozens of films.[4] In the last few decades, as sensitivity to racism in literary and media representations has increased, Fu has been relegated to the cult-figure margins, where he circulates actively in new print editions, in digital-download format, on video, and even in heavy-metal music — but also, as Asian American observers have noted, as a figure who still haunts the political imagination of white America.[5]

From the very outset, critics of the Fu Manchu series objected to its negative stereotypes, and it was not long before more benign Chinese figures (Charlie Chan, for example) were created to counter the negative impression produced by Fu. Ward himself, at least as portrayed in the 1972 biography written by his wife and a close family friend (*Master of Villainy: A Biography of Sax Rohmer*), generally maintained a half-bemused stance toward the character who financed his often-lavish lifestyle. On occasion, however, he did rise to the defense of the Fu series. The portrayal of a strong Chinese leader as a criminal mastermind was fundamentally truthful, he said, because criminality was in fact rampant among the Chinese — especially in Limehouse, London's Chinatown district at the turn of the twentieth century.[6]

The trend among Fu's recent admirers (most notably, Douglas G. Greene, author of the introduction to the Dover edition, but also a large number of commentators on various websites) is to shy away from Ward's unabashed China-bashing and argue instead that Fu should not be seen as a representation of the Chinese or anyone else; instead, he is fantastic, with no particular real-world referents at all. Though this latter line of argument can be even more insulting than the first, it nonetheless helps us delve deeper into the sources of Fu's continuing appeal.

A critical look at the historical and cultural conditions in which Fu was produced, and at certain key features of *The Insidious Dr. Fu-Manchu*, shows us that the Fu Manchu myth was indeed built on an all-too-familiar framework of racist, imperialist assumptions regarding Asians. But Ward drew also on his long-standing interests in hermeticism and Orientalism, both strongly flavored with Gothic fantasy. As a result, his Fu became far more than a soulless stereotype: the Gothic dimensions altered and elaborated the Devil Doctor's basic form, till a white-identified reader might well find in Fu not only the demonized features of the conventional dark Gothic Other, but also the exhilarating presence of a dark Hero-Self. The multiple, contradictory identifications implicit in this half-conscious fantasy, as the reader's decoding of the Fu figure shuttles rapidly between Other and Self, animate what would otherwise be a flat, dull character, and breathe life into an otherwise predictable, conventional narrative.

Thus, as this essay proposes to show, in a typical Fu story, Gothic fantasy magnifies, undermines, sweetens, and destabilizes racist content, till the whole narrative fairly writhes with unresolved tension. We may fairly say that Gothic fantasy "bedevils" racist content in the Fu figure. A focus on this "Gothic bedevilment" leads us, moreover, to a fuller understanding of Fu's vitality than can be found by attributing his success to racism or escapism alone.

The Boxers, the Illuminati, and Fu as "Master of the Show"

Ward may have defended his characterization of a Chinese leader as a criminal mastermind as an exaggerated but fundamentally truthful idea, but what really interested him was the commercial potential of the idea. "Conditions for launching a Chinese villain on the market were ideal.... The Boxer Rebellion had started off rumors of a Yellow Peril which had not yet died down. Recent events in Limehouse had again drawn public attention eastwards" (Van Ash and Rohmer 75). Working from these two basic elements, a foreign uprising against Western influence and a local immigrant community viewed with increasing suspicion by white Londoners, Ward played on his white readers' most self-serving fears regarding the Chinese. But perhaps because he himself could not take these fears with perfect seriousness, Ward transformed London's Limehouse into a scenic, if seedy, backdrop (as the next section of this essay will show in greater detail), while using the Boxer scare to conjure, as in a lantern-show, a figure as menacing as he was shadowy and (apparently) foreign, thus infusing real political anxieties with fantastic Gothic motifs.

The Boxer Rebellion (1899–1900) was a largely spontaneous series of attacks on Christians in China (both native and foreign), carried out by a rough assortment of poor peasants who prepared themselves for battle by means of shamanistic ritual (including the martial-arts exercises for which they were named). As Joseph W. Esherick notes in *The Origins of the Boxer Uprising*, the Boxers offered "a dramatic example of ordinary

Chinese peasants rising up to rid China of the hated foreign presence. As such, they were an important episode in the emergence of mass nationalism in China."[7]

In the West, as Esherick also notes, the Boxers provided "ample copy," both for the sensationalist press of the time, and for Hollywood script-writers half a century later (xiii). One of the films he had in mind, no doubt, is the 1963 blockbuster, *55 Days at Peking*, in which Charlton Heston leads a hardy band of beleaguered whites as they fend off hordes of dark-skinned natives. These cinematic images, like many other aspects of Yellow Peril mythology, American-style, seem to have been directly inspired by the frontier myth of peaceable settlers suddenly attacked by unruly Indians, that is, a direct confrontation between two races, with political maneuvering a distinctly background phenomenon. But for Ward there were distinctly European, more subtly political ways of imagining the Yellow Peril threat, informed in great part by his experience with hermeticism and secret societies.

According to his biographers, Ward was a member of the Hermetic Order of the Golden Dawn, and quite possibly a member of the Rosicrucian society also. As they note, "here, obviously, is the source from which he obtained the idea of a secret brotherhood holding arcane knowledge" (Van Ash and Rohmer 30). But while the occult always fascinated Ward, in the end he tended to prefer some form of rationality. Both strands of this interest run through the Fu Manchu series, as the Devil Doctor displays various strange powers whose mechanisms, while often exotic, are later given full explanation. (For instance, the deadly "Zayat Kiss" that dispatches various targets of Fu's ire turns out to be the work of a hitherto-unknown, highly poisonous insect.)

An even deeper influence, however, can probably be found in the legends of the Illuminati, the 18th-century secret society that was viewed by conspiracy theorists as the motivating force behind many crucial political events, from palace coups to the French Revolution,[8] and that inspired Romantic writers as well. "The Gothic imagination," according to Pascal Nicklas (citing Shelley's *St Irvyne, or, The Rosicrucian* as a case in point), "is stimulated less by the reforming intentions of the Illuminati and other secret societies than by their subversive and mysterious character.... Gothic treatment [of these societies] tends to emphasize eerie paraphernalia, political subversion, and repression."[9]

All of these Gothic elements may be found in the Fu tales, and together they deepened the sense of fantastic things afoot in the politically mysterious Orient. This sense of vast foreboding was a significant part of the series's appeal, a fact which the movie-makers were quick to exploit. When

Metro Goldwyn-Meyer made *The Mask of Fu Manchu* (1932) the first Fu adventure to be given full-fledged cinematic treatment, the choice no doubt was influenced by the sheer magnitude of Fu's ambitions, as well as the secrecy with which they were cloaked, ambitions that certainly had contemporary resonance for its audience. Smith and his companions have to hunt long and hard to find Fu's hidden headquarters in China, but when they do, they find that he has assembled an army of slave-soldiers and, following in the footsteps of his putative ancestor, Genghis Khan, is preparing for world conquest.

In *The Insidious Dr. Fu-Manchu*, Fu's immediate domain is much smaller, consisting mostly of secret hide-outs dotted through the English landscape. But the claim to a much greater domain, and even to a commanding position in world affairs, is perfectly clear in scenes like the mid-story encounter in which Fu stands triumphant over his "mediaeval captives," Smith and Petrie, chained to a cellar wall and awaiting imminent death. "You have presumed," he sneers, "...to meddle with a world-change! Poor spiders—caught in the wheels of the inevitable!" (84). Then he scoffs at the notion that he is working on behalf of so limited a project as the Young China Movement (a reference to the Chinese Nationalist Party, which overthrew the Manchu dynasty in 1911). Instead, as we learn later, Fu is the leader of a mysterious "Third Party," neither Manchu nor Republican (and entirely an invention of Ward's). In later installments this "Third Party" evolves into the even more ominous Si-Fan, a secret international committee that, as in *The Mask of Fu Manchu*, amasses both slave armies and occult devices until foiled, as usual, by Smith and Co.

Thus, in both its nascent and its fully formed phases, Fu's secret organization is indebted to the Gothic conceit of dark powers functioning behind the screen of daily events. By fusing contemporary fears of a Boxer-inspired Yellow Peril with the old, European secret-society traditions, Ward created a powerfully nuanced, highly ominous worldview that both frightened and titillated his readers.

From a post-colonial perspective, however, the most striking thing about this view is its complete inversion of the actual power relations between East Asia and the West, as in this passage from *The Insidious Fu-Manchu*:

> To Smith and me, who knew something of the secret influences at work to overthrow the Indian Empire, to place, it might be, the whole of Europe and America beneath an Eastern rule, it seemed that a great yellow hand was stretched out over London [122–3].

This reversal of historical relations constitutes the fundamental underpinning of the whole narrative, and provides the justification for incessant vilification of the Chinese.

But a reversal of this sort is far from stable; it requires constant reitera-
tion and magnification, hence the evocation of the conventionally repetitive
and excessive Gothic apparatus. Indeed, the attendant exaggerations sometimes grow so wild that they threaten to tip over the story's basic premises. A
basic problem in story-logic is revealed, for instance, in the conception of Fu
as "the Master of the Show," a notion that Petrie borrows from *The Rubaiyat
of Omar Khayyam*, as an explanation for Fu's power to shape not only world
events, but the whole organization of the tale that Petrie is telling. "[I]ts scheme
is none of mine," he exclaims, for it is Fu who directed every move:

> Often enough, in those days, I found a fitness in the lines of Omar:
>
> > We are no other than a moving show
> > Of Magic Shadow-shapes that come and go
> > Round with the Sun-illumined Lantern held
> > In Midnight by the Master of the Show.
>
> But the "Master of the Show," in this case, was Dr. Fu-Manchu! [155].

The problem, of course, is that omnipotence of this magnitude makes the
heroes the puppets of their foe, with no scope for autonomous thought or
perception, let alone independent action. In order to avoid the consequences
of such a hyper-inflation of Fu's powers, he has to be contained somewhat,
and so, whatever his claims in moments of triumph (or the narrator's claims
in moments of intense melodrama), he is usually a "would-be Master of the
Show." This turns out to be a comfortable enough solution, Fu thus assuming his rightful place in the long line of distinctly Miltonic Gothic Satan-
heroes, enormously powerful in the mundane scheme, but foiled in the end
by Christian, Anglo-Saxon decency (and, in this case, a traitor in the ranks).

But trouble comes again, this time at a subtler level, because this fundamental reliance on Western mythology leads to phrases like Petrie's key
description of Fu as having "a brow like Shakespeare and a face like Satan."
While certainly a resonant description, the phrase must give pause to all
but the most hurried readers: can the head of the Yellow Peril have the brow
of the Bard? At moments like this, as he reaches for the peaks of suspense,
Ward's Gothic exaggerations undermine his own racist anomosity, till he
has to prove all over again that the Devil Doctor really is a foreigner, really
is a yellow-skinned Chinese.

Limehouse, Orientalist Fantasy, and the Ever-Elusive Karamanèh

Turning back to the "recent events in Limehouse," we can see that
Rohmer meant this as an allusion to criminal activity and police response

in London's Chinese immigrant community. By 1911, according to Chinese diaspora historian Lynn Pan, some 1,319 Chinese had left their homes in the Canton area and settled in British ports, including London's Lime-house district, where they ran small service businesses like laundries, shops, and restaurants.[10] For most Chinese migrants, the journey abroad was provoked by duress, for the Chinese economy and political system were in great turmoil (the Boxer indemnities being a major contributing factor). The pressure of white prejudice was felt all the more directly in cities like London, where immigrant Chinese communities were subjected to raids, prosecutions, and investigations. According to Pan, there were three main factors leading to resentment of the Chinese in British ports: fear of sexual liaisons between Chinese men and white women (the ratio of Chinese men to Chinese women being approximately 8:1); fear of cheap labor (no doubt the critical motive here), and fear of the opium habit and associated drug trade (85–93).[11]

Taken one by one, these fears highlight several notable features of the Fu character, at least in his first appearances. First, he is made to seem rather cold and asexual (no doubt to make the series suitable for general audiences, though nowadays it is hard to ignore the hints of homoeroti-cism in his encounters with the white heroes). Secondly, both Smith and Petrie are gentlemen-professionals, so the potentially explosive labor issues are thoroughly sidelined. With these two issues heavily blanketed, the full force of apprehension is channeled into the opium-phobia. Thus, as we might have guessed, Fu himself is an addict, so that the aura of drug-induced dementia makes his already Gothicized character even darker and more ominous (without ever interfering with his powers of cold intellect).

More broadly significant, however, is the opium-den setting that the drug immediately connotes. Indeed, the first direct encounter with Fu occurs only after the heroes have successfully negotiated a secret opium den.[12] They must bluster their way through the filthy barbershop that fronts for the den, then blend into the scene by pretending to smoke. They must also avoid detection by the hunchbacked usher who, after pulling back the heroes' eyelids to make sure they are asleep, escorts Fu's other servants out of the den and into an even more secret room — the master's headquar-ters. When Smith and Petrie make a mad dash into the inner sanctum and are treated to their first full glimpse of Fu Manchu's baleful mien, the opium den, itself a scene of intense iniquity, turns out to be the gateway to even greater horrors. They plummet to certain death — if not by water, then by fire — falling through a trapdoor and into a water-filled pit just as the building above bursts into flames.

How do they escape? Well, fortunately Fu Manchu has a Near Eastern slave-girl, Karamanèh, who has somehow grown fond of Petrie, and unbeknownst to her master, she finds ways to aid the heroes, on this and on many other occasions. In this initial escapade, it turns out that the hunchbacked usher in the opium den is none other than Karamanèh in disguise. After the heroes have fallen into the pit, she scrambles down a ladder, guides them past a knife-edged beam designed to sever their fingers, then gives Smith her pigtail-wig to serve as a rope whereby Petrie can be hauled to safety. To Petrie, at least, her motives are as clear as they are unexpected:

> I think it was my wonder at knowing her for the girl whom [I had encountered once before] which saved my life.
> For I not only kept afloat, but kept my gaze upturned to that beautiful, flushed face, and my eyes fixed upon hers—which were wild with fear ... for me! [39].

When Petrie finally swoons, Karamanèh disappears; he later learns that Smith, grateful for her help, has connived at her escape.

Though Smith half-blames himself for letting Karamanèh go, the heroes are clearly much better off with her working for Fu, but on their side. Karamanèh works for Fu under duress (he has taken her beloved brother hostage), but she has "formed a sudden predilection, characteristically Oriental, for [Petrie]" (11). Thus, in moments of crisis, she repeatedly aids and rescues both the narrator and the action-hero. Then, in a flash, she vanishes. Smith and Petrie often sigh over her mysterious ineluctability: she is never attainable, never knowable, and always desirable.[13] In a cast of characters that ostensibly falls into three categories: the heroes (Smith and Petrie); the villains (Fu and his minions); and the victims (careless eccentrics, valuable specialists, and sometimes their beautiful daughters as well), Karamanèh could be seen as the only liminal figure, for she operates in all three of these categories. And yet, for all this functional complexity, she undergoes no real development, no real change in status or outlook. Instead, she remains a distant, mysterious figure who, by and large, is just an animated part of the stage-apparatus, a personification of the Oriental décor, the female personification of the Oriental Other.

Karamanèh clearly grows out of Ward's long-standing interests in the customs and lore of the Levant, especially Egypt. Though he eventually made two extended trips to the region, his views never developed much past an eye for the exotic, a taste for adventure, and a ready grasp of the comfortable cliché. When it came to the rapid reproduction of stereotyped imagery, he clearly had a gift of sorts, for his Oriental Gothic settings are sketched with tight economy, effortlessly evoking the shadowy depravity and gold-lamé luxury of the Oriental despot. Thus we have the filthy, decrepit opium-smokers' den; the camouflaged cabaret with its divans, draperies, and exotic dancers; and the sumptuous residence protected by a labyrinthine entrance. Sometimes the characters find inner rooms (and traps) within these settings, and in every case there is a truly motley assortment of artifacts and persons. In the cabaret, for example, one can find Turks, Egyptians, Greeks, Chinese, and a "negress"—not to mention the two heroes, both in disguise.

Though this surface complexity can be quite dazzling, the basic intent, as several decades of anti–Orientalist critique have shown, is reductive and inimical. Generally speaking, characterizations like these serve to minimize, flatten, and condescend to Asian cultures. In the Fu tales, these Orientalist details add color and variety, but their underlying purpose is to "prove" that Fu Manchu is indeed culturally and racially Other, that he belongs to some significantly foreign category of being, toward which the reader need feel little or no responsibility. Since, as we have seen, quite a few bits of highly familiar Western mythology are attached to Fu, such reminders of foreignness are often needed.

Freedom from responsibility toward others is a key result also of the Orientalist treatment accorded to the Karamanèh character. In *The Insidious Dr. Fu-Manchu*, the following dynamic can be discerned: first, when pursuing Fu and his beautiful slave, the heroes are transported to another realm; then, when things get too hot in that faraway spot, the girl comes to the rescue. While perhaps not quite in keeping with the chivalric tradition, this dynamic helps explain why Karamanèh is so alluring and so elusive. As a signifier for romantic, Oriental Otherness, she has to remain out of reach; then, as a savior who guides the heroes home, she has to disappear the moment that danger is past, so that both of these ego-satisfying experiences—exotic allure and homeward return—can come blessedly free of commitment on Petrie's part.

Fu and the "Armchair Adventurer"

To Ward, the Boxer Uprising and the raids in Limehouse signaled a climate ripe for the rise of a villainous Chinese figure; to us, they are more likely to seem signs of an imperialist discourse, and Fu Manchu to be a manifestation of racial animosity deepened (but also undermined) by Illuminati undertones, and sweetened (but also strengthened) with Orientalist fantasies. It is therefore not surprising that, in an era marked by the ascendancy of post-colonial critiques, Fu Manchu's defenders have found it difficult to justify his existence as a representational figure. They have turned instead to a different argument: real-world reference is irrelevant, because what the series inspires is enjoyment of "pure fantasy." This approach can be seen most clearly in Douglas G. Greene's introduction to the Dover reissue of *The Insidious Dr. Fu-Manchu*:

> Rohmer's novels remain popular not because they say anything about what was going on in the world in his time or in ours, but because they are almost pure fantasy, appealing to the armchair adventurer, the ones for whom Rohmer's Asians are as imaginary as J.R.R. Tolkein's Orcs, Frank Baum's wicked witches, or the various inhabitants of Edgar Rice Burrough's Barsoom.[14]

The claim that Ward's "Asians" have no greater claim to real-world referents than do imaginary creatures like Orcs and witches is specious, of course. It is, moreover, even more insulting than Ward's assertion that the inhabitants of Limehouse were basically criminals—for while Ward states a position that can be rebutted, Greene tries to vaporize the whole history of modern race relations, refusing to see any connection between Fu and "what was going on in the world in his time or in ours."

And yet, without dismissing history as thoroughly as Greene has, it is worth trying to define the "pure fantasy" that the Fu tales offer the "armchair adventurer," especially since these fantasies are, as we have seen, predicated on and complicated by several slippery strains of Gothicism.

Greene himself does not say exactly what sort of fantasies he thinks the Fu tales embody. Instead, he emphasizes surface technique, arguing that Ward was "above all a splendid storyteller" (vii). Ward clearly did have a strong grasp of all the usual techniques for producing suspense: cliffhanger chapter endings, terse dialogue, sudden disappearances, mysterious messages and so on. The most pervasive device, however, is a tone of relentless Gothic excess, the constantly quivering tension of melodrama. Opened nearly at random, the text presents us with a barrage of exclamations: "Good heavens!" I cried, "what's that...?" "Miss Edmonds went into violent hysterics...!" "My God! Yes. Go on" (66–7). Alternating with these exclamations are longer, more ominous musings on the nature of the enemy and the enterprise: "I may have mentioned the fact before, but on this occasion it became so peculiarly evident to me that I am constrained to record it here — I refer to the sense of impending danger which invariably preceded a visit from Fu-Manchu" (97–8).

Thus, throughout the story, the level of tension is kept as high as possible, with only the briefest of reprieves when a victim dies or the narrator goes home to re-work his notes. The strain is both warping and liberating, in that any attempt by the reader to locate authenticity amid these entertaining-yet-exhausting exaggerations is most probably abandoned: in typical Gothic form, the text relieves the reader of responsibility for applying any ordinary sense of scale and perspective. This is not to say that a reader need be taken in by these shenanigans; a good deal of the enjoyment comes from the awareness that one is being bombarded with and to excess. Still, in fairness to the series, we have to admit that its appeal is rooted in something deeper than melodramatic tone and the consequent opportunities for humor. To discover why Ward's work has attained such fame, we must find the source of the "bedevilment" that so animates and enlivens the text.

Oriental Other, Dark-Hero Self

Paralleling Karamanèh's infatuation with Petrie, but in a more covert, internalized manner, is Fu Manchu's own interest in the doctor. Indeed, if there is any thematic line of development running through *The Insidious Dr. Fu-Manchu*, it is the struggle by the good guys not merely to foil the Devil Doctor, but to gain his esteem. In their first face-to-face encounter, Fu's expression reveals "pitying contempt" for Smith and Petrie (37). Halfway through the book, Smith, always the leader in their efforts to thwart Fu Manchu, comes close to admitting defeat: "His contempt is justified. I am a child striving to cope with a mental giant" (97). But in the end, Petrie surpasses his mentor — another satisfying thought, is it not? — and his reward is to have won from their opponent "some kind of admiration or respect" (191). Even the soft, amorous glances of the gorgeous Karamanèh seem less flattering than this. Thus, underlying the text is a seduction narrative in which the subject-center narrator — and, presumably, the reader as well — is the focus of thrilling and flattering multiple lines of desire.

But at this point we must again wonder how entirely Fu is Other, for are there not many indications that he is also some glorified version of Self? The swirling mix of racist animosity, melodramatic suspense, and authentic as well as feigned dread is lit also with longing, with suppressed, narcissistic desire for a figure of great power and cunning; it cannot be too surprising to find that Ward invested Fu with many of his own characteristics, both real and imagined. Apparently Ward was quite famous for the intensity of his eyes, by some accounts "the eyes of a murderer," and Fu's most notable feature is, of course, his long, narrow, green eyes. When it came to mental equipment, Fu is always portrayed as a superhuman genius, and Ward apparently enjoyed fostering the impression that he too had "the trained mind of a master criminal." Even in the arena of action there are moments of marked consonance. Drug-dealing is Fu's stock in trade; Ward, besides selling several novelistic treatments of the drug trade, once tried to market a brand of perfume called "Honan," in the belief that this Chinese province was "notorious for the cultivation of the opium poppy." Or again, Ward's wife is said to have goaded him into writing by deliberately provoking him until "he finally reached the stage of readiness to wring her neck, [whereupon] he would go and work it off in a Fu Manchu scheme to wring the neck of a Prime Minister" (Van Ash and Rohmer 42, 86, 112, 104).

In using himself as a model for Fu Manchu, Ward may have simply succumbed to the narcissistic urge that has shaped many a protagonist of detective/suspense fiction. According to Shuchin Lin, in her dissertation work[15] on hard-boiled detective fiction, a remarkable number of detective-heroes — Dashiell Hammett's Sam Spade and Continental Op, Raymond Chandler's Philip Marlowe, and Ross Macdonald's Lew Archer — bear a striking physical and/or intellectual resemblance to their creators, with Macdonald even going so far as to pose as Archer for the book-jacket illustrations. But in the more sophisticated tales, Lin argues, the relationship between character and author extended far beyond surface playfulness. Macdonald in particular uses his look-alike creation as a "psychoanalytic instrument that enables the author to face and revisit his traumatic experiences," a therapeutic turn that Macdonald himself recognized and acknowledged in his autobiographical writings. Ward, in contrast, seems to have tried quite hard never to take Fu altogether seriously, much less as a "psychoanalytic instrument." But in this he did not fully succeed.

The notion that the Fu-Smith dyad could be seen as a complementary pair of self-portrayals, a set of matching masks that could be worn by the writer — or by the reader — must have hovered at the edges of many minds long before Peter Sellers made the game explicit in *The Fiendish Plot of Fu Manchu* (1980). In this black comedy, Sellers plays both Smith and Fu, both of whom, now aged and declining, recognize each other as alter egos. In Sellers's interpretation, a decrepit Fu and an equally decrepit Smith play Self and Other back and forth, over and over again. In the end, Fu even offers Smith a comradely draught of the life-restoring elixir that will, in the last scene, restore his youth and transform him into a Elvis-style rock star. (Smith, however, shakes his head sadly and prepares for death). Throughout this last big sequel to Ward's series, Fu is at least as much a hero as Smith. In retrospect, Sellers has made clear that even in Ward's telling, Fu was always a "hero-villain."

The hero-villain, or dark hero, is a basic conceit of Gothic literature, and a figure who usually elicits as much sympathy as fear or revulsion on the part of the reader. Ward's Fu differs, however, from such representative hero-villains as Vathek,[16] Melmoth, and Heathcliff, by eliciting not sympathy but envy or admiration — at least for those readers willing to admit, at some level or another, an attraction to the notion of occult powers and worldwide domination. This pull of admiration is kept in careful tension with the distancing effects of the Devil Doctor's immunity from suffering which — far more than his rather-garbled ethnicity — keeps him at a distance, and accentuates his Otherness. As Helen Stoddart has pointed out, the swing between attraction and replusion is a general feature of this type of character: "...though the hero-villain may temporarily function as a vehicle for fantasies of unregulated desire and ambition ... the undeniable nature of his 'otherness' ... always ultimately provides a means of distancing and disavowing his actions as unfeasible or illegitimate."[17] Any stable, sympathetic identification with Ward's Fu Manchu is thus averted just when the figure has grown most compelling. Instead, the reader of a Fu Manchu tale is offered, simultaneously, the pleasing power of disavowal (of a demonized Oriental Other) and the thrill of covert identification (with a darkly heroic image of Self). Hence, for many readers, the Fu Manchu tales offer a fantastically motile locus of identification, a shu°ing play of attraction and repulsion that disrupts the borders between Other and Self.

Conclusion

Fu Manchu, as we have seen, rose to fame on the tides of Yellow Peril fear and hatred, but that fame was maintained by more than a mere fanning of racist animosity. Similarly, though surface melodrama and constant plot suspense keep the stories moving, the action that keeps the reader involved operates at a much deeper level. By drawing on Gothicized versions of the Illuminati, the mysterious Oriental girl, and the hero-villain, Fu's creator magnified, undermined, sweetened, and destabilized his own basically racist intent. These Gothic strains do not transcend the story's basic racism, much less transform it, but by offering multiple, irrepressible reminders that the Other may not really be Other, but only another side of Self, they turn the urge to vilify back upon itself, and create a fundamentally dynamic story-basis. From this "Gothic bedevilment," Fu gained a vitality and staying power that a simpler villain could not have attained.[18]

Notes

1. Sax Rohmer [Arthur Sarsfield Ward], *The Insidious Dr. Fu-Manchu: Being a Somewhat Detailed Account of the Amazing Adventures of Nayland Smith in His Trailing of the Sinister Chinaman* (New York: P.F. Collier, 1913. Dover Mystery Classics. New York: Dover, 1997), 84.

2. In the first three volumes of the series, the title-character's two-part name is hyphenated; it usually is not hyphenated in general discussion. ("Fu" is a plausible surname in Chinese, but "Manchu" was probably chosen for the rhyme, and for the English-language reference to China's last imperial dynasty). As a form of resistance to the author's personal myth-making, this essay breaks with usual practice by using his legal name, Arthur Sarsfield Ward, rather than his pen name, Sax Rohmer.

3. Frank Luther Mott, *A History of American Magazines, 1885–1905* (Cambridge: Harvard University Press, 1957), 4:471. Quoted by Knapp, Lawrence. The Page of Fu Manchu: The Sax Rohmer Research Web Site (15 June 2001 <http://www.njin.net/~knapp/FuManchu.html>).

4. Knapp's well-documented website lists four U.S. radio serials; the biography by Van Ash and Rohmer mentions one additional radio series, and also notes that the BBC shied away from the material (240, 241, 273). There are three film serials (usually running to 15 episodes each) and 14 feature-length films in English, plus another half-dozen in other languages. According to Knapp's website, Fu Manchu tales have been published in 29 different countries. It is worth noting that none of these editions is in Chinese; Singapore is the only country listed that has a significant Chinese population, and the Fu Manchu stories published there are written in Malay.

5. Eric Liu, *The Accidental Asian: Notes of a Native Speaker* (New York: Vintage, 1998), 133–135.

6. Cay Van Ash and Elizabeth Sax Rohmer, *Master of Villainy: A Biography of Sax Rohmer*, ed. Robert E. Briney (Bowling Green: Bowling Green University Popular Press, 1972), 73.

7. Joseph W. Esherick, *The Origins of the Boxer Uprising* (Berkeley: University of California Press, 1987), xiii.

8. Robert A. Gilbert, "'Two Circles to Gain and Two Squares to Lose': The Golden Dawn in Popular Fiction," in *Secret Texts: The Literature of Secret Societies*, eds. Marie Mulvey-Roberts and Hugh Ormsati-Lennon (New York: AMS Press, 1995), 320.

9. Pascal Nicklas, "Illuminati Novels," in *The Handbook to Gothic Literature*, ed. Marie Mulvey-Roberts (New York: New York University Press, 1998), 275.

10. Lynn Pan, *Sons of the Yellow Emperor: A History of the Chinese Diaspora* (New York: Kodansha, 1994), 85.

11. With regard to this last factor, we can hardly forget that, half a century earlier, the British had resorted to war to protect exactly that trade and the profits it brought them — but of course, that was in China.

12. For a detailed study of the Orientalist apparatus crammed into the barbershop and opium den, see Ng.

13. Apparently the mysterious Oriental girl was a figure of personal significance for Ward. Ten years prior to the launching of Fu Manchu, flush with his first success as a commercial fiction-writer, he tried to write a novel about Egypt. The novel was never completed, but while searching for the details needed to complete his portrait of an Egyptian-princess-turned-banquet-dancer, he had a vivid dream that supplied the missing material: the make-up, the nail color, the gauzy dress, the floral girdle. The already long tradition of such representations notwithstanding, Ward took this image

as a clairvoyant revelation, and apparently believed that he had prognosticated Egyptology's later findings (Van Ash and Rohmer 29).

14. Douglas G. Greene, "Sax Rohmer and the Devil Doctor," introduction to *The Insidious Dr. Fu-Manchu: Being a Somewhat Detailed Account of the Amazing Adventures of Nayland Smith in His Trailing of the Sinister Chinaman* by Sax Rohmer [Arthur Sarsfield Ward] (New York: P.F. Collier, 1913. Dover Mystery Classics. New York: Dover, 1997), vii.

15. Lin, Shuchin, "Ross Macdonald's Innovations in the Hard-Boiled Tradition of Dashiell Hammett and Raymond Chandler." Dissertation in progress. University of Newcastle.

16. An earlier Oriental figure.

17. Helen Stoddart, "Hero-Villain," in *The Handbook to Gothic Literature*, ed. Marie Mulvey-Roberts (New York: New York University Press, 1998), 114.

18. I am indebted to Marcus Bingenheimer for careful reading and helpful comments during the drafting of this essay.

Works Cited

Esherick, Joseph W. *The Origins of the Boxer Uprising.* Berkeley: University of California Press, 1987.

The Fiendish Plot of Dr. Fu Manchu. Dir. Peter Sellers and Richard Quine. Perf. Peter Sellers and Helen Mirren. 1980. Videocassette. Warner Home Video, 1996.

55 Days at Peking. Dir. Andrew Martin and Guy Green. Perf. Charlton Heston and Ava Gardner. 1963. Videocassette. Best Film and Video 2, 1998.

Gilbert, Robert A. "'Two Circles to Gain and Two Squares to Lose': The Golden Dawn in Popular Fiction." In *Secret Texts: The Literature of Secret Societies.* Edited by Marie Mulvey-Roberts and Hugh Ormsby-Lennon. New York: AMS Press, 1995.

Greene, Douglas G. "Sax Rohmer and the Devil Doctor." Introduction to *The Insidious Dr. Fu-Manchu: Being a Somewhat Detailed Account of the Amazing Adventures of Nayland Smith in His Trailing of the Sinister Chinaman* by Sax Rohmer [Arthur Sarsfield Ward]. New York: P.F. Collier, 1913. Dover Mystery Classics. New York: Dover, 1997.

Knapp, Lawrence. *The Page of Fu Manchu: The Sax Rohmer Research Web Site.* 15 June 2001. <*http://www.njin.net/~knapp/FuManchu.html*>.

Lin, Shuchin. "Ross Macdonald's Innovations in the Hard-Boiled Tradition of Dashiell Hammett and Raymond Chandler." Dissertation in progress. University of Newcastle.

Liu, Eric. *The Accidental Asian: Notes of a Native Speaker.* New York: Vintage, 1998.

The Mask of Fu Manchu. Dir. Charles Brabin. Perf. Boris Karloff and Myrna Loy. 1932. Videocassette. Warner Home Video, 1992.

Mott, Frank Luther. *A History of American Magazines*, 1885–1905. Cambridge: Harvard University Press, 1957.

Ng, Maria Noelle. "Representing Chinatown: Dr. Fu-Manchu at the Disappearing Moon Café." *Canadian Literature* 163 (1999 Winter): 157–75.

Nicklas, Pascal. "Illuminati Novels." In *The Handbook to Gothic Literature.* Edited by Marie Mulvey-Roberts. New York: New York University Press, 1998.

Pan, Lynn. *Sons of the Yellow Emperor: A History of the Chinese Diaspora.* New York: Kodansha, 1994.

Rohmer, Sax [Arthur Sarsfield Ward]. *The Insidious Dr. Fu-Manchu: Being a Somewhat*

Detailed Account of the Amazing Adventures of Nayland Smith in His Trailing of the Sinister Chinaman. New York: P.F. Collier, 1913. Dover Mystery Classics. New York: Dover, 1997.

Stoddart, Helen. "Hero-Villain." In *The Handbook to Gothic Literature*. Edited by Marie Mulvey-Roberts. New York: New York University Press, 1998.

Van Ash, Cay and Elizabeth Sax Rohmer. *Master of Villainy: A Biography of Sax Rohmer.* Edited by Robert E. Briney. Bowling Green: Bowling Green University Popular Press, 1972.

7

A Return to the Caves: E.M. Forster's Gothic Passage

Douglas L. Howard

To the extent that the Gothic typically involves, "a kind of despair about any direct use of the language,"[1] as Eve Kosofsky Sedgwick points out in her seminal study, *The Coherence of Gothic Conventions*, the Gothic is a genre that implicitly relies upon context to deliver "the horror, the horror." Within the framework of the "unspeakable," the reader is left to project the horrifying products of his or her own imagination into the gaps caused by such moments of linguistic ambiguity and to illuminate textual darkness with those biases or those timely cultural associations that terrify him or her the most.[2] What becomes most frightening in the Gothic is created through the fears of the interpreter, but those fears need context to give them substance.

Political, social, and historical context was certainly key to the initial reception of E.M. Forster's *A Passage to India* (1924), a novel, at once both modern and Gothic, constructed around a textual omission demanding interpretation. When Forster began work on the project in 1913, he had only a vague notion of how this break would figure into the text as a whole. As he later admitted in an interview, all he "knew was that something important happened in the [Marabar] Caves, and that it would have a central place [...]—but [he] didn't know what it would be."[3] In fact, he was evidently troubled by this "central something" because, as Nicola Beauman points out, "of [the] one hundred rejected but preserved sheets of [the] manuscript, fifty-five [were] drafts of the caves episode."[4] From his

120

first visit to India between 1912 and 1913, he clearly wanted to speak out against the prejudice that he witnessed firsthand and to use the incident in the caves to make this statement, but the changing state of Anglo-Indian relations sharply contrasted with the novel's development. Upon returning to India in 1921, he found that "the gap between India remembered and India experienced was too wide"[5] and that his earlier work "seemed to wilt and go dead" (Forster *Devi* 238). By ignoring, denying, and displacing the disparity between memory and experience, he finished the book, but the attack upon Adela Quested in the caves and the resulting gap in the text, in and of themselves creations of implied Indian Gothic, never inspired the horror that they could and should have because they never reached their ideal readership, the pre-war English readers who had been bred to believe in the nature of Indian evil and who would, in context, have seen Indian villainy within the blankness of Forster's missing "central something."

There was already an extensive history of Anglo-Indian tension prior to 1924, a history dating back, at the very least, to the beginning of England's colonization of the country. At the end of the eighteenth century, Lord Cornwallis, the British Governor-General of India through the East India Company, deliberately excluded natives from positions of power within the government following England's occupation, a move that socially as well as economically separated the Indian from other British subjects. Their presence, he maintained, could undermine "moral integrity as the basis of good government"[6] since extended contact with the Indian, in any form, could only lead to corruption. Although Cornwallis's successors in the nineteenth century worked vigorously to expand the development of the country, the Indian people, impoverished and crowded into slums, rarely benefited from this progress and English leaders continued to ignore the value of Indian culture.[7] By the mid–1800s, this insensitivity led to violence. Outraged by a rumor that British soldiers were using "the fat of cows (sacred to Hindus) or pigs (sacred to Muslims)"[8] to grease their guns, Indian factions began killing Europeans in 1857 until they were physically suppressed. The British essayist Thomas De Quincey described the horrors that took place in Gothic terms as "things not utterable in human language or to human ears— things ineffable — things to be whispered — things to dream of, not to tell."[9] This "Indian Mutiny" or "Sepoy Rebellion"[10] sparked further mistrust in the English, who became even more inclined to dismiss Indian behavior as foreign and inexplicable. The English press largely blamed the incident on the Indian natives, who "were ignorant and credulous, like savages or children."[11] The races themselves were more conspicuously separated as new towns and suburbs, with wide roads to accommodate British soldiers in the event of trouble, "were [specifically] built for British officials and their wives."[12] In addition, though it essentially governed India through the East India Company's administration, the Crown officially stepped in and took control of matters in 1858, proclaiming Lord Charles Canning England's first Viceroy of India.

For all of the structural improvements that were made in the country thereafter by men like Lord Curzon (British Viceroy of India 1899–1905), who provided famine relief to afflicted Indian territories, investigated land and agricultural issues, increased public works programs and modernized the transportation system by building more railways,[13] the English, generally speaking, still maintained a belief in their social and cultural superiority through the Edwardian era, both at home and abroad. This belief, according to K.M. Panikkar, was largely the reason why "they remained strangers in the country" (119) until the end of British rule. Lord Kitchener, commander-in-chief of the Indian Army, proudly suggested that no military rank could make the Indian native "the equal of the British officer" (116). Moreover, when Indian radicals began to protest for *swaraj*, or "self-rule," prior to World War I, English officials dismissed their cries because Indian terrorism reaffirmed more derogatory perceptions. In 1909, "Sir Curzon Wyllie, an India Office official, was gunned down"[14] in London by an Indian assassin, and in 1913 the British Viceroy Lord Hardinge was severely injured by an Indian bomb attack. While many Indian natives believed that they could enjoy a relationship with their colonizers that was based upon mutual respect and equality, the British attitude at this time continued to be characterized by suspicion, mistrust and contempt.

By the time that *A Passage to India* was published in 1924, the dynamic between the Indians and the English had changed dramatically. After more than a century of British control (and British racism and discrimination) in one form or another, India, no longer the complacent colonial satellite of a larger empire, now bitterly demanded the right for self-rule. Not only had the Indian people enthusiastically supported the English campaign against the Central Powers in World War I, but "over two million Indian combatants and support staff" (Keay 470) went off to Egypt, France, and Iraq to aid the Allied effort. After the war, Edwin Montagu, the Secretary of State of India, and Lord Chelmsford, the British Viceroy, drafted a number of reforms which officially recognized "self-government as the goal of British policy in India,"[15] and which, among other significant measures, devolved political authority from the central government to the provinces. While "these provisions," as historian John Keay points out, "would have caused a sensation [before the war], by 1921 [the year that they were inaugurated] they were barely acceptable" (480).

However, Indian loyalty during the war merited a greater reward than the insulting, mistrustful Rowlatt, or "Black Acts," which were passed in March 1919 "over the universal opposition of elected Indian [Legislative Council] members" (Wolpert 298). The Acts attempted to maintain wartime curfews and to allow officials to dispense with jury trials in order to suppress sedition. And the Indian people still mourned for their dead at Amritsar, where British soldiers opened fire on a group of unarmed protesters campaigning against the Rowlatt measures and killed hundreds. For Gandhi, who had emerged as a spiritual and political leader in this time, and for members of the Indian National Congress, which had transformed itself from a modest political and social organization to the nation's pre-eminent governing body, the constitutional changes that these Montagu-Chelmsford Reforms offered, coming on the heels of such a tragedy, were simply feeble attempts to delay an independence that was long overdue and to appease a people who had become disenchanted with the mystique of English rule. As Forster himself described the new state of their relationship, English "manners" in India "improved wonderfully," but now the Indians did not want "social interaction with [them] any longer" (Forster *Devi* 237).

Rather than reflecting this conciliatory attitude, many of Forster's English characters in *A Passage to India* are readily inclined to believe the worst of their Indian counterparts—Mrs. Callendar coldly conceives that "the kindest thing one can do to a native is to let him die,"[16] and, following the attack in the caves, Mr. McBryde, the District Superintendent of Police, affirms that "all unfortunate natives are criminals at heart, for the simple reason that they live south of latitude 30" (184)—and their opinions are more consistent with pre-war attitudes, when Indian prejudice, miscegenative fears, and more negative historical examples continued to encourage such harsher voices. The English literary representations of the Indian prior to World War I, moreover, inspired, and were reciprocally inspired by, this discourse. As he more and more became the owner of the worst vices that the Victorian and Edwardian mind could conceive –cruelty, treachery, barbarity and debauchery—the Indian's otherness became an accepted convention within the fiction of the times, a fiction that, as Edward Said notes, was specifically designed "to keep the empire more or less in place" (74) and that provided moral/political support for the reality of occupation. In his 1838, novel *The Tremendous Adventures of Major Gahagan*, Thackeray, for example, describes the half-caste wife of his Colonel Jowler as "a hideous, bloated, yellow creature, with a beard, black teeth, and red eyes; she was fat, lying, and stingy—she hated and was hated by all the world."[17] Even more fearsome and inhuman is the mad Indian fakir that Bithia Croker's heroine, the fair Juliet Carwithen, stumbles upon in the 1894 novel *A Family Likeness: A Sketch in the Himalayas*:

> His hair, plastered with dirt, stood stiffly erect, like horns; his face and chest were daubed with wood ashes and of a bluish-white color. From his unearthly white face gleamed a pair of devilish eyes that glowed like carbuncles. He was partly clothed in panther's skin. In one hand he held the dripping carcase of a headless kid, and in the other the enormous sacrifical knife. [...] He looked insane. [...] At first sight [...], he burst into a low peal of demoniacal laughter.[18]

Although Shere Ali, the Indian protagonist of A.E.W. Mason's 1907 *The Broken Road*, receives a respectable education at the best schools in England, he orchestrates a vicious revolt against English forces in India after he returns home and accepts his place among a people for whom "treachery was a point of honour ... and cold-blooded cruelty a habit."[19] In his 1907 historical novel, *The Red Year*, Louis Tracy specifically reminds Edwardian readers of the horrors of 1857 and describes, in detail, "the most unheard-of atrocities"[20] that were perpetrated by "ghoulish" Indian mutineers. The phantasmagoric productions of the prolific I.A.R. Wylie, who based her Indian novels "entirely from second-hand sources and her [own] lurid imaginings"[21] also did little to change such negative perceptions of the Indian. The Hindus in her 1912 novel *The Daughter of Brahma* are idolatrous fiends, "evil-faced, with wild disheveled hair and torn filthy garments,"[22] and they conduct orgiastic rituals for the pleasure of the evil god Siva. And in Margaret Peterson's 1913 *The Lure of the Little Drum*, the villainous Indian Prince Ishat Khan, fueled by his childhood hatred of the English, viciously seduces and ruins the wife of a British noble as "a way of hurting the pride of the English [... and] insulting his enemies."[23]

Even Rudyard Kipling's portrayal of the Indian, which often suggested a nobility that previous authors had ignored, was tainted by a bias that was perhaps even more damaging than the horrifying caricatures that came before or after him. Natwar-Singh maintains that all of Kipling's talk about "the white man's burden and the stiff upper lip [and his blindness to imperialist economics] only widened the gulf between India and Britain,"[24] and Said agrees that Kipling implicitly, hierarchically contrasts "white Christian Europe" with "lesser, inferior, dependent, subject [races]" (134). Gunga Din may be "a better man than" the British soldier who recites the poem, but even in the afterlife, his socioeconomic inferiority is still acknowledged. His servitude will continue, as he gives "drink to poor damned souls" and to the speaker who has admittedly "belted and flayed" him.[25] Kipling's masterwork, *Kim*, also offers readers a decidedly skewed version of history that perpetuates the portrayal of the Indian as brutish and savage. Recounting his experiences during the 1857 Indian Mutiny, an old Indian soldier whom Kim and the Tibetan lama meet on the road remembers that "a madness ate into all the Army, and they turned against their officers"[26] and killed their wives and children. When British reinforcements finally arrived, the Indian rebels were, in the soldier's words, called into "most strict account" (52), a version of events that, as Said explains, makes the Indians appear "naturally [...] delinquent [and] the white man a stern but moral parent and judge" (148).[27] From this point of view, the Indians should, like the old soldier, appreciate the British occupation of their country because they clearly cannot be left to their own devices. They desperately require the supervision of a more noble, sophisticated authority. Moreover, as Thackeray and Wylie and these other authors imply through their horrific depictions of Indian vice and villainy, English readers should, in turn, "take up the white man's burden" and endorse Indian colonization because it is both a moral and political imperative; inasmuch as they are "half devil and half child,"[28] the Indian people need to be saved from themselves and their own destructive instincts.

For Forster, however, these exaggerated portrayals were inconsistent with his early experiences with India and its people. In 1906, several years before his first visit to the country, he began tutoring and fell in love with Syed Ross Masood, the son of the Indian reformer Sir Syed Ahmed Khan. Even though these feelings were not returned, their friendship, a friendship that Forster honored in the dedication to *A Passage to India* and that formed the basis for the relationship between Aziz and Fielding, continued until Masood's death in 1937.[29] From his first visit to India in the fall of 1912, in fact, he "viewed the British presence in India with intense distaste."[30] While the Islington commission, formed under Lord Hardinage in 1912 to consider the possibility of admitting Indians into the higher ranks of civil service and defuse growing Anglo-Indian tensions, was still deliberating, Forster was consistently reminded "that the educated 'native' didn't count; he was only a drop in the ocean."[31] After a bombing incident in Delhi, he learned that "several Englishman — officials of high position, too — were anxious for the [British soldiers] to be turned to fire at the crowd, and seemed really sorry that the Viceroy [Lord Hardinage] had not been killed because then there would have been a better excuse for doing such a thing" (Forster *Devi* 27–28). This violent vision anticipated the grim realities at Amritsar; news of that tragedy contributed to Forster's "growing sense of indignation against his country" (Furbank II: 59). Stung by his experiences with British imperialism, he informed his countrymen, in a painfully honest assessment of "the English character" in 1920, that they were all members of "perfide Albion, the island of hypocrites, the people who have built up an Empire with a Bible in one hand, a pistol in the other, and financial concessions in both pockets."[32]

By 1921, Forster believed that the English were getting better and that their "manners" had "improved wonderfully," but that now the Indians did not want "social interaction with [them] any longer" (Forster *Devi* 237). Critics initially attacked *A Passage to India* because they believed that Forster failed to represent this change in his novel,[33] but as Forster himself admitted and as his friend Rose Macaulay points out, the book "deals with the India of one period, is written largely from material collected and from a point of view derived from that period and was published twelve years later, when Indians and English had got into quite another stage."[34] In spite of the social changes that had occurred, then, the novel and its characters should not be read so much as a commentary upon the state of Anglo-Indian affairs in post-war India, but, primarily, as a delayed response to the horrors of pre-war India, when the English prejudice toward the Indian that had reached its height appeared justified.[35]

To this end, Forster turns to the Gothic. Although critics sparingly associate him with the tradition,[36] he consistently juxtaposes his novelistic realism with Gothic elements—malevolent foreigners, manipulative ghosts, and mysterious forces—that often defy specific linguistic descriptions, playing "the seen" off of "the unseen," and he is clearly intrigued by the conflict and the contrast that is created when his practical Edwardian protagonists are confronted with the unexplainable and forced to deal with the paranormal. He finds a variety of spirits and haunted mansions out on the English countryside. In *The Longest Journey* (1907), Mrs. Failing goes so far as to warn her nephew Rickie that the fields of Wiltshire — the very heart, we are told, of England — are littered with the remains of dead soldiers and "full of ghosties"[37] who worship the devil. His aunt's house, moreover, inspires Rickie with "the most awful feeling of insecurity" (109) because it is the focal point for so many family scandals, just as it also bears witness to the revelation of Rickie's coarse half-brother, Stephen. After Rickie is killed by a passing train at the end of the novel and becomes, in effect, yet another ghost of the landscape, Stephen, "the future of our race" (310), can only contemplate and question that ambiguous spiritual world around him, "the dead who had evoked him, the unborn whom he would evoke" (310). The eponymous Howards End likewise is a living "spirit"[38] and a place for spirits. Throughout Forster's 1910 novel, Margaret feels Ruth Wilcox, "ever a welcome ghost" (166),[39] guiding her toward her destiny as the heir to Howards End. And when the eccentric charwoman Miss Avery, a woman whom Dolly compares to "a spook" (202), conceives that Margaret, as "Mrs. Wilcox," has come to claim ownership of the empty house, she is noticeably shaken by the realization of the maid's prophecy, an effect that illustrates, according to John Colmer, Forster's manipulation of the Gothic "to produce supernatural vision through physical shock."[40] At the end of the novel, she does unite the Schlegels and the Wilcoxes at Howards End, just as she inherits the house as per Ruth Wilcox's original request, but even Margaret must admit that "things that [she] can't phrase have helped [her]" (339) and she literally shivers when she sees herself as the object of such metaphysical forces at work.

If England is haunted by its own history, however, Forster finds (in true English Gothic tradition) equal if not greater Gothic terrors awaiting the Englishman abroad. The foreign and the exotic are also the unknown and, for all of the cultural richness that the characters in his Italian novels and short stories would experience in their travels, he additionally exposes them to a host of horrors born from their own stereotypes, misconceptions, and outright ignorance. The Italian town of Monteriano, in *Where Angels Fear to Tread* (1905), for example, is alternately described as "a magic city of vice"[41] and a place of "solid enchantment" (96). Though the impetuous Lilia Herriton takes pleasure in escaping to it and in rebelling against her family by marrying the vulgar Gino Carella, she is soon horrified to discover that her husband has "plenty of brutality deep down in him" (58)—he later tortures Philip Herriton by twisting his broken arm — and that he would, in accordance with Italian custom, keep her from walking out alone, just as he would assert his manhood by being unfaithful. Essentially imprisoned like so many Gothic heroines,[42] she learns, only too late, that Gino, whom Caroline Abbott refers to as "thoroughly wicked"(89),[43] "cruel," and "vicious" (136), married her for her money and she dies fulfilling his final wish, giving birth to Gino's son. Italy's otherness is also reaffirmed in *A Room with a View* (1908), as the inexperienced Lucy Honeychurch struggles to make sense of its mysteries without the able guidance of her Baedeker and has difficulty distinguishing the saints from a statue of Machiavelli. Rejecting the advice of her chaperones, who like Gino would discourage her from seeing the country alone, especially in the evening, she wanders out into the Piazza Signoria and witnesses a violent murder near the Loggia, an edifice that is compared to "the triple entrance of a *cave* [...] wherein dwelt many a deity, shadowy, but immortal."[44] From this traumatic incident, she momentarily comes to an understanding of "the nature of ghosts" (46). And in the same way that Adela Quested is transformed by her experience in a cave, she develops a greater understanding of herself and is perhaps brought more fully into a world of pain and love, but even the love that she gets from the roguish George Emerson, and that they finally celebrate in their

Italian pensione at the end of the novel, is tempered by a vague awareness of forces beyond their control and "a love more mysterious than this" (204).[45] Moreover, as "The Story of a Panic" (1904) and "The Story of the Siren" (1920) remind us, Italy is a place where mythological legends live to terrorize the unsuspecting, where the god Pan horrifies a group of English tourists—the narrator confesses that he is unable "to describe [the encounter] coherently"[46]—and makes the quiet adolescent Eustace abandon his countrymen in favor of his baser, animal instincts and where Guiseppe's glimpse of the Siren — a glimpse that neither Guiseppe nor the narrator can adequately put into words— leads to his own ruin and throws a local village into chaos.

Although part of the British Empire and caught under "the net Great Britain [has] thrown over [it]" (*Passage* 13), the India of Forster's *Passage* is still a wild, untamed country, a land of magic and wonder to the open-minded and a land of physical dangers and spiritual peril to the uninformed or the uninitiated. While it does not boast haunted houses or secluded castles, at least in the traditional sense, it is indeed a Gothic place. As in Italy, English travelers are discouraged from walking out alone at night because of the awful fates that could befall them. Aziz warns Mrs. Moore that "there are bad characters about and leopards [and ...] snakes" (19). Crocodiles eat the dead bodies that float down the Ganges. And ghosts inhabit the landscape. Sitting in a mosque, the sober Aziz concedes that a "belief in ghosts ran in his blood" (17). When Ronny Heaslop and Adela Quested have a car accident that they believe was caused by a hyena, Mrs. Moore is quick to attribute it to "a ghost!" (104), and their car's owner, Nawab Bahadur, fears that it is the spirit of a drunken man that he ran over nine years earlier "who had been waiting for him ever since" (106). The dead live. After her visit to the caves, Mrs. Moore thinks that she rides in a train full of corpses. During the Gokul Ashtami that marks the birth (or rebirth) of God, Aziz contemplates the legend of the Mohammedan saint who carried out his mother's wishes even though his head had been cut off, and Ralph Moore is convinced that he sees the Rajah out on the lake, though, as Aziz notes, the Rajah had just died. Even Mrs. Moore, who dies onboard a steamer and is buried at sea, appears to live on. "A ghost," we are told, "follow[s her] ship up the Red Sea" (285); tombs are reportedly built containing her remains; and the Indians develop a cult dedicated to worshipping the ongoing influence of "Esmiss Esmoor."

Forster most dramatically invokes the Gothic genre when he leads Adela Quested and his readers into the Marabar caves, those legendary landmarks that conceal forbidden experience and become the novel's most pronounced physical as well as verbal source of horror. In a tone that suggests admiration as much as apprehension, the narrator conceives that the caves "are older than all spirit.... [T]he shrines are unfrequented, as if pilgrims, who generally seek the extraordinary, had here found too much of it.... Nothing, nothing attaches to them and their reputation — for they have one — does not depend upon human speech" (136–7). Even sound cannot escape them, as their "terrifying echo," another conventional element of the Gothic,[47] reduces all spoken language to a monotonous, monosyllabic "boum" and robs "infinity and eternity of their vastness" (165). The caves thus contain some sort of primordial power that actively annihilates language. They, like the tourists' meeting with Pan or Guiseppe's vision of the Siren, not only defy the visitor's ability to describe them in words, inside as well as outside the caves, but they also defy the narrator's ability to explain them to the reader adequately. They have a reputation, but the narrator never tells us what it is, just that it exists, and this indefinable aspect is what keeps the narrator, the characters, and even the reader literally and figuratively fumbling in the dark because they do not have the comfort of language to show them the way.[48] Are visitors confronted by their own demons in the caves or demons that are manifested externally through some supernatural force? Or are the dangers within the caves simply the product of talented tour guides and immoral assailants? In true Gothic fashion, the caves conspire against a definite answer.

This linguistic breakdown apparently extends to the author as well and is largely responsible for the controversy surrounding Adela Quested's experience in the caves, an experience that Forster deliberately "muddles"[49] (his word). In the manuscript version of the novel, Adela enters a cave after her conversation with Aziz and suddenly finds herself fighting off an assailant whom she does not see, but whom she believes is the Indian doctor:

> At first, she thought that <she was being robbed,> he was <holding> [...] her hand [...] to help her <out>, then she realized and she shrieked at the top of her voice [...]. She struck out and he got hold of her other hand and forced her against the wall, he got both her hands in one of his and then felt at her [...] \breasts/. "Mrs. Moore" she yelled. "Ronny — don't let him, save me." The strap of her Field Glasses, tugged suddenly, was drawn across her throat. She understood — it was to be passed once round her neck, [...] she was to be throttled as far as necessary [...]. Silent, though the echo still raged up and down, she waited and when the breath was on her wrenched a hand free, got hold of the glasses and pushed them [...] \into/ her assailant's mouth [...].He let go and then with both hands \on her weapon/ she smashed [...] \at him again/ [...].She gained the entrance ... of the tunnel.[50]

Given the narrator's earlier references to the caves' historical/mythical significance and the extent of Adela's peril, the scene certainly qualifies as that masochistic vision of being raped by a stranger that is consistent with conventional Gothic.[51] Although the reader does not know the identity of her attacker, the presence of language here eliminates a number of other possibilities and allows the reader to make a few definite statements about Adela's experience. There is little doubt that she is assaulted in this version, that her assailant is male (based upon the pronouns used to describe him) and that, from his attempt to push her against the cave wall and grab at her breasts, he obviously does have violent sexual intentions. The narrative, in fact, specifies the extent to which her attacker will go, even choking her with the strap to her Field Glasses to assure that she will keep quiet during the ordeal. Knowing this, the reader is more inclined to feel sympathy for Adela and her story and perhaps even forgive her if her assumption, that her attacker is Aziz, proves to be incorrect. Since the reader knows that a crime has been committed, readerly attentions now focus more on the "who" as opposed to the "what."

In the wake of Joyce's *Ulysses*, Eliot's *The Waste Land*, and Woolf's *Jacob's Room* as well as his own previous fictional use of Gothic conventions, however, Forster conducts his own linguistic experimentation and paradoxically voices his own "despair about the direct use of the language,"[52] a despair that clearly is both modern and Gothic, by removing the rape scene from the novel proper. He forces the reader to engage the text on a more active level by collaborating with the author and replacing this crucial gap.[53] Following her conversation with Dr. Aziz at the end of Chapter 15, Adela goes into "a cave, thinking with half her mind 'sightseeing bores me,' and wondering with the other half about marriage" (169). Her experience in the caves takes place outside the text, between Chapters 15 and 16.[54] When Chapter 16 begins, the narrative refocuses on Aziz, who fears that Adela has gotten lost in one of the caves, and the next glimpse that we get of her is not through her own interior narrative that marked the conclusion to the previous chapter, but rather through Aziz's eyes: "Miss Quested wasn't lost. She had joined the people in the car — [...] there she was quite plain, framed between rocks, and speaking to another lady" (171).

Not only must the reader in this version now speculate as to the character and intentions of the assailant, but they must also recreate the details of the attack and weigh the credibility of Adela's story afterwards. Did Adela indeed hallucinate? Was she, like Nawab Bahadur, terrorized by a ghost, an idea that she also entertains and that seems plausible given the presence of ghosts in the novel? Was she physically attacked by Aziz or, as

Fielding later suggests, was she accosted by some other Indian guide? What, moreover, did her attacker, assuming that she was attacked, do to her?[55] In any case, her experience as well as her recollection of that experience become more than simply the sum of her fears and perceptions; they become the product of the reader's psychology, fears and perceptions, since the reader has no verbal cues to direct judgment. Any explanation becomes valid and the appeal of one explanation over another becomes a matter of individual discretion. In trying to illuminate the dark walls of Marabar, then, the readers ultimately reveals more about themselves and, even if only for a moment, frames the fearful symmetry of Adela's attacker from the dark side of their own imagination, conjuring up that image that disturbs them the most.[56]

More than likely, Aziz is not Adela's attacker, if, in fact, she is attacked. Such a reading would run contrary to Forster's dedication to Masood and seem absurd given his connection to the Indian people. Aziz's behavior after the incident also does not coincide with this explanation. He fears that Adela is lost in the caves and that losing his guest will be "the end of [his] career" (171), concerns that would make little sense if he had just tried to rape her. He even strikes their guide for failing to keep track of her. More than likely, the incident is the result of some kind of hallucination based upon what Frederick Crews calls "her unvoiced desire for physical love"[57] or what Freud more technically defines in his essay on "The Uncanny" as an "emotional affect [that] is transformed by repression into morbid anxiety."[58] Her story functions, as Jenny Sharpe explains, within the tradition of the "dark rapist" colonial narrative that "is commonly explained as the projection of white fantasies onto a racial Other" (Sharpe 3).[59] Prior to her entrance into the caves, Adela, who is engaged to a man that she is admittedly not attracted to and does not love, notes that Aziz is "a handsome little Oriental" with "beauty, thick hair, [and] a fine skin" (169). And though she maintains that she has no "personal warmth" for Aziz because "there was nothing of the vagrant in her blood" (169), she cannot help contemplating his appeal to "women of his own race" and wondering if Aziz has more than one wife. In the same way that Adela feels that she must marry Ronny Heaslop for propriety's sake, she consciously denies her sexual attraction to the exotic Indian because it is socially as well as politically unacceptable. Yet, clearly, on some level, she views him as a potent sexual figure.[60] Within the darkness of the caves these desires that are a part of the subtext of their conversation surface. If the incident is a fabrication, Adela's desire, which results in the rape vision, enables her to experience the sexual contact she so desperately craves by channeling it through an acceptable outlet. If she is forced by Aziz, the handsome, foreign, unknown and therefore dangerous man that she wants but should not have, then she, as a victim and a "respectable English lady," is freed from responsibility for the encounter, a masochistic attitude that is an inherent part of the Gothic and "the end result of a long and varyingly successful cultural training" (Massé 3).

In spite of such rational explanations and in spite of what probably happened in the caves, however, Forster deliberately leaves the question unanswered. He could have openly exonerated Aziz and the Indian people and eliminated or, in Fielding's words, "resisted the supernatural" explanation, but that alternative probably would not have addressed the racial and cultural issues behind the novel at their source — in the minds of his readers. Prejudice cannot be changed by rhetoric alone; acceptance requires awareness and belief and, in order to force his readers to confront the character of their biases, Forster deliberately constructs his novel around a linguistic gap that demands an active participation on their part. The question is never resolved and the reader is left unsatisfied because this dissatisfaction inevitably and inexhaustibly stimulates further debate, one of the by-products of effective fiction.

And while contemporary readers certainly must evaluate their judgment of "what happened in the caves" in terms of their own personal beliefs and prejudices, the question would have been particularly relevant to prewar readers because they would have had to consider their reading of this textual silence in light of the long and seemingly justified history of English prejudice and the more popular, derogatory representations of the Indian in the literature of the times.[61] As he initially envisioned and developed the novel, before "the gap between India remembered and India experienced" grew "too wide," Forster was almost certainly daring his Edwardian readers — without the lessons of World War I and Rowlatt and Amritsar and Gandhi that are conspicuously absent from the novel — to bring their skewed perceptions of the Indian as sinful and lascivious to the caves and to conjure up figures like Croker's menacing fakir, Wylie's idolaters, and Peterson's vengeful prince. He was daring them to contemplate the possibilities, to assume that Aziz, for all of his civility toward Adela and his other English guests, was vicious enough to attack her inside of the caves and then cold enough to maintain his innocence afterwards, or to believe that some other Indian, who was just as cold and vicious, was capable of this horrific crime. Rather than perpetuating the mutually exclusive narratives of fear that Aziz condemns at the end,[62] Forster wanted these readers to wrestle with his "subversively" unresolved question so that they, too, might see themselves on those cave walls and come out ready for that debate that could lead to tolerance and that was perhaps more pressing than the complicated questions of independence and empire that kept men like Fielding and Aziz from being friends. Unfortunately, his audience could never reap the benefits of Forster's experiment because they came to the novel under different circumstances—after the misunderstandings, mismanagement, violence, and bloodshed that characterized postwar Anglo-Indian relations and that anticipated Indian independence two decades later—and, therefore, would be inclined to different interpretations. Since the Indians and the English had moved "into quite another stage" and the context for their relationship had changed, they would not and could not receive his message in quite the same way. To this extent then, *A Passage to India* is a Gothically modern text that bears the burden of what Perry Meisel has called "the paradox of belatedness that is its precondition"[63] inasmuch as it nostalgically considers a world that no longer exists, yet speaks to one that does.

Notes

1. Eve Kosofsky Sedgwick, *The Coherence of Gothic Conventions* (New York: Metheun, 1986), 14.

2. Norman N. Holland essentially makes this point in his essay "Unity Identity Text Self" when he states that readers generally "will find in the literary work the kind of thing [they] characteristically wish or fear the most." Norman N. Holland, "Unity Identity Text Self," in *Reader-Response Criticism*, ed. Jane P. Tompkins (Baltimore: Johns Hopkins University Press, 1980), 124.

3. E.M. Forster, "E.M. Forster," in *Writers at Work: The Paris Review Interviews*, ed. Malcolm Cowley (New York: Viking, 1958), 27.

4. Nicola Beauman, *E.M. Forster: A Biography* (New York: Knopf, 1994), 276.

5. E.M. Forster, *The Hill of Devi* (New York: Harcourt, 1953), 238.

6. C.A. Bayly, *Indian Society and the Making of the British Empire*, part I, vol. II of *The New Cambridge History of India*, gen. ed. Gordon Johnson (New York: Cambridge University Press, 1988), 78.

7. H.L. Malchow points out that this fear of Indian corruption extended, in the 1800s, to Eurasians, who, from the perspective of "the white establishment," epitomized the dangers of miscegenation by horrifically combining "the vices of the 'native' ... with those of the particularly debased 'European 'stock' ... 'the worst of both races'" (H.L. Malchow, *Gothic Images of Race in Nineteenth Century Britain* [Stanford: Stanford University Press, 1996], 201).

8. Francis Watson, *A Concise History of India* (New York: Charles Scribners' Sons, 1975), 110.

9. Thomas de Quincey, "Hurried Notices of Indian Affairs," in *The Uncollected Writings of Thomas de Quincey*, Vol. 1, ed. James Hogg (Plainview Books for Libraries, 1972), 303.

10. As Edward Said explains in *Culture and Imperialism*, the uprising was described in different terms by both sides, a fact that clearly reflected the differing political attitudes toward the English occupation. While British authors and historians discussed "the Indian Mutiny of 1857," Indian writers were more inclined to refer "to [it]

as a 'Rebellion.'" Edward Said, *Culture and Imperialism* (New York: Vintage, 1994), 146.

11. Thomas R. Metcalf, *The Aftermath of Revolt: India 1857–1870* (Princeton: Princeton University Press, 1964), 75.

12. Stanley Wolpert, *A New History of India*, 5th ed. (New York: Oxford University Press, 1997), 245.

13. It should be noted that Curzon was, as K.M. Panikkar notes, "the apostle of imperialism," and these reforms were not implemented with the idea of liberating India or making it self-sufficient. Rather, Curzon's intent was to increase English control and suppress anti-imperialist Indian sentiments (K.M. Panikkar, *Asia and Western Dominance: A Survey of the Vasco da Gama Epoch of Asian History* [New York: Collier, 1969], 117).

14. John Keay, *India: A History* (New York: Atlantic Monthly, 2000), 468.

15. Percival Spear, *A History of India* (Baltimore: Penguin, 1965), II: 340.

16. E.M. Forster, *A Passage to India* (New York: Harcourt, 1924), 25.

17. William Makepeace Thackeray, *The Tremendous Adventures of Major Gahagan* (London: Smith, Elder & Co., 1887), 13. I am indebted to Malchow's *Gothic Images of Race in Nineteenth Century Britain* for bringing this reference to my attention.

18. Bithia Croker, *A Family Likeness: A Sketch in the Himalayas* (London: Chatto & Windus, 1894), 205. By demonizing the Indian Other in this way, Croker is perhaps expressing an ongoing English concern toward what Lizabeth Paravisini-Gerbert refers to as "the nation's exposure to colonial societies, nonwhite races, non–Christian belief systems, and [even] the attendant horror of interracial sexuality" (Lizabeth Paravisini-Gerbert, "Colonialism and Postcolonial Gothic: The Caribbean," in *The Cambridge Companion to Gothic Fiction*, ed. Jerrold E. Hoyle [Cambridge: Cambridge University Press, 2002], 230). Described in such graphic physical terms, the fakir is thus not only a "devil" for religious reasons, but also because of the dangerous forbidden sexual experience that he represents. Jenny Sharpe, moreover, believes that this kind of narrative, which pits an English white woman against a threatening native, also deliberately recalls the 1857 Mutiny because, for the British, "the Mutiny was remembered as a barbaric attack on innocent white women" (Jenny Sharpe, *Allegories of Empire: The Figure of the Woman in the Colonial Text* [Minneapolis: Minnesota University Press, 1993] 2.)

19. A.E.W. Mason, *The Broken Road* (New York: Scribner's, 1907), 3.

20. Louis Tracy, *The Red Year: A Story of the Indian Mutiny* (New York: Grosset and Dunlop, 1907), 22.

21. Benita Parry, *Delusions and Discoveries* (Berkeley: California University Press, 1972), 82. I am indebted to Parry for bringing both Croker and Wylie's novels to my attention.

22. I.A.R. Wylie, *The Daughter of Brahma* (Indianapolis: Bobbs-Merrill, 1913), 55.

23. Margaret Peterson, *The Lure of the Little Drum* (New York: G.P. Putnam's Sons, 1913), 98–99.

24. K. Natwar-Singh, "Only Connect....: Forster and India," in *Aspects of E.M. Forster*, ed. Oliver Stallybrass (New York: Harcourt, 1969), 39.

25. Rudyard Kipling, "Gunga Din," in *The Portable Kipling*, ed. Irving Howe (New York: Penguin, 1982), 618.

26. Rudyard Kipling, *Kim* (Oxford, Oxford University Press, 1987), 52. I am indebted to Said's *Culture and Imperialism* here for bringing this reference to my attention.

27. Said also points out that, although many Indians viewed the Rebellion as a nationalist response to oppressive British rule — Panikkar, in fact, describes it as India's

"last effort on a national scale to recover [its] freedom" (111) — Kipling puts this sympathetically British version of the uprising "in the mouth of an Indian" (148), which adds to its credibility and implies a more harmonious relationship between the two countries since that time than was clearly the case.

28. Kipling, "The White Man's Burden," in *The Portable Kipling*, 602. For all of his noble intentions, Kipling, like Croker, demonizes the Indians and other "silent, sullen people" like them and, in the process, reaffirms the explicit social and cultural differences between the "devilish" natives and their "humane" white "saviors." And to the extent that miscegenative fears fueled English contempt toward the Indian and that miscegenation was, according to Malchow, "seen as evidence of moral weakness on the part of the white, Christian male," Kipling's description here suggests that the Indian and other colonized races like them, as combinations of both viciousness and innocence, of both devil and child, were already moral half-breeds of sorts and thus inferior to those who would bring them "toward the light" (Malchow, 202).

29. Forster even contributed an elegy to Masood's memorial, in which he alluded to their "affection," but could not speak of it because it was "not the time or the place." E.M. Forster, "Syed Ross Masood," in *Two Cheers for Democracy* (New York: Harcourt, 1979), 292.

30. According to William Walsh, Forster's "analysis of the mentality of the officials sent there showed them to be under such internal and external strain that they were liable in a crisis to break out into a brutish, stampeding hysteria." William Walsh, *Indian Literature in English* (London: Longman, 1990), 171.

31. P.N. Furbank, *E.M. Forster: A Life* (New York: Harcourt, 1978), I: 230.

32. E.M. Forster, "Notes on the English Character," in *Abinger Harvest* (New York: Harcourt, 1964), 11.

33. For example, in his 1924 review, H.W. Massingham, commenting on the outdated nature of Forster's portrayal of India, considered it to be "the image of a phantasm, almost a joke of the Time-spirit. If India is governed from the bridge-tables and tennis-courts of Chandrapore — well, the day is coming when she will be so no longer." H.W. Massingham, "The Price of India's Friendship," in *A Routledge Literary Sourcebook on E.M. Forster's A Passage to India*, ed. Peter Childs (New York: Routledge, 2002), 55.

34. Rose Macauley, *The Writings of E.M. Forster* (London: Hogarth, 1938), 188.

35. Dating the action and the attitude of the novel continues to be an issue for critics. Although he believes that *A Passage to India* incorporates Forster's experiences from both his pre-and post-war visits to the country, David Medalie agrees that "the final version, far from simply replacing a 1914 perspective with that of 1922, retains many of the preoccupations of the earlier period and charts their fate" (David Medalie, *E.M. Forster's Modernism* [New York: Palgrave, 2002], 159).

36. While a few critics like John Colmer, whom I mention here, briefly refer to Forster and the Gothic, his use of the genre is largely ignored. Even Denis Godfrey's book *E.M. Forster's Other Kingdom*, which specifically considers "Forster's mysticism and ... the relationship of [the supernatural] world to this one," disregards the extent to which his work is informed by the literary Gothic (Denis Godfrey, *E.M. Forster's Other Kingdom* [London: Oliver and Boyd, 1968], 4).

37. E.M. Forster, *The Longest Journey* (New York: Vintage, 1962), 140.

38. E.M. Forster, *Howards End* (New York: Vintage, 1921), 98.

39. Ruth Wilcox is the predecessor of the ghostly Mrs. Moore in *A Passage to India*.

40. John Colmer, *E.M. Forster: The Personal Voice* (London: Routledge, 1975), 107.

41. E.M. Forster, *Where Angels Fear to Tread* (New York: Vintage, 1920), 87–88.

42. As Sandra M. Gilbert and Susan Gubar explain in *The Madwoman in the Attic*,

female Gothic heroines "characteristically inhabit mysteriously intricate or uncomfortably stifling houses [and] are often seen as captured, fettered, trapped, even buried
alive" (Sandra M. Gilbert and Susan Gubar, *The Madwoman in the Attic: The Woman
Writer and the Nineteenth Century Literary Imagination* [New Haven: Yale University
Press, 1979], 83). The dominating, tyrannical male figure is also consistent with the genre.

43. In this context, in fact, she compares Gino to the corrupt Rodrigo Borgia, also
known as Pope Alexander VI and head of the vicious Borgia family, in order to illustrate that "thoroughly wicked men have loved their children."

44. E.M. Forster, *A Room with a View* (New York: Bantam, 1988), my italics, 39–40.

45. Though Forster never specifically explains exactly what this "love" is or why it
is so "mysterious," Claude Summers believes that it refers to the "fated pairing of arche-
types […] that may yield a new society rising phoenixlike from the ashes of a dying
one," a suggestion that essentially makes the characters, as in *The Longest Journey* and
Howards End, subject to the deliberate, yet largely unknowable, machinations of a universal order. (Claude Summers, *E.M. Forster* [New York: Frederick Ungar, 1983], 100).

46. E.M. Forster, "The Story of a Panic," in *The Collected Tales of E.M. Forster* (New
York: Knopf, 1966), 11.

47. In listing the elements of conventional Gothic, Eve Kosofsky Sedgwick refers to
the presence of "unnatural echoes or silences" (Sedgwick, *Gothic Conventions*, 9).

48. A number of works in the Gothic canon rely upon linguistic ambiguity to
describe some building, edifice, or pivotal scene of horror. As Isabella wanders through
the subterranean catacombs of *The Castle of Otranto*, the narrator explains that "words
cannot paint the horror of [her] situation" (Horace Walpole, *The Castle of Otranto*
[New York: Macmillan, 1963], 37). When Raymond in *The Monk* encounters the Bleeding Nun, he gazes "upon the spectre with horror too great to be described" and his
"blood [freezes] in [his] veins" (Matthew Lewis, *The Monk* [New York: Modern Library,
2002], 126). Victor Frankenstein cannot "describe [his] emotions [after creating the
monster nor] delineate the wretch whom with such infinite care and pains [he] had
endeavoured to form" (Mary Shelley, *Frankenstein* [New York: New American Library,
1983], 56). And upon first seeing Roderick's home, the narrator in "The Fall of the
House of Usher" is likewise struck by "a sense of insufferable gloom" that he cannot
explain and must accept as "a mystery all insoluble" (Edgar Allan Poe, "The Fall of the
House of Usher," in *Selected Writings of Edgar Allan Poe*, ed. Edward H. Davidson
[Boston: Houghton Miꟷin, 1956], 95). Since language is the means through which the
reader first comes to the text, the author's admission that language cannot adequately
compensate for the experience at hand or describe the incident in question forces the
reader to replace the gaps imaginatively and to reconstruct the ambiguity with his or
her own personal definition of horror.

49. In 1934, Forster told novelist William Plomer that Adela's experience in the
caves was "an unexplained muddle." In an earlier 1924 letter to his friend Goldswor-
thy Lowes Dickinson, he more candidly admitted, "In the caves it is either a man, or
the supernatural, or an illusion. And even if I know!" (Furbank, *Life* II: 125).

50. E. M. Forster, *The Manuscripts of A Passage to India*, vol. 6a of *The Abinger Edition of E.M. Forster*, ed. Oliver Stallybrass (London: Edward Arnold, 1978), 243. Words
within slashes are Forster's insertions; those within angle brackets are his deletions.

51. In her analysis of the genre, Michelle Massé believes that this kind of secretly
desired violence toward women is "at the center of the Gothic" (Michelle Massé, *In
the Name of Love* [Ithaca: Cornell University Press, 1992], 2).

52. This despair, in fact, is one of the central themes in the novel. Mrs. Moore bitterly refuses to describe the echo in the caves, "[a]s if anything can be said" (222).

53. According to Wolfgang Iser, all texts contain "inevitable omissions" that demand

the reader's input in order to replace them. In this case, though, replacing the gap is not only part of the reader's response, but it is part of the narrative imperative, inasmuch as the gap is the focal point of the novel. (Wolfgang Iser, "The Reading Process," in *Reader-Response Criticism*, 55).

54. Again this narrative gap is consistent with the genre. As Sedgwick points out, "a fully legible or an uninterrupted narrative is rare" (14).

55. Both Medalie and Jenny Sharpe discuss the case of Miss F. Marcella Sherwood in connection to the attack upon Adela in the caves, but, as Medalie reminds us, it is "not referred to directly" in the novel and contributes more to the backdrop "of colonial anxiety itself" (162). In response to the massacre at Amritsar, the Indian people rioted and, according to Sharpe, a missionary, "was dragged off her bicycle[, ...] beaten with sticks[, ... and] left for dead" (114). While the missionary incident does indeed add to the context of *A Passage to India*, Forster is probably not thinking of her specifically, inasmuch as the circumstances here and the character of Adela herself are different. Whereas the attack upon the missionary is a matter of historical record and not in doubt, Adela's story and the broken narrative are open to question.

56. This kind of effect, still typical of the Gothic, was used masterfully in the 1999 independent blockbuster *The Blair Witch Project*. Although the filmmakers, Daniel Myrick and Eduardo Sánchez, did not dazzle audiences with a creature based upon elaborate special effects and although audiences never actually saw the witch, the film's intensity revolved around the reactions of the characters and this visual absence of menace, forcing the viewers to imagine the nature of the threat and, in effect, scare themselves.

57. Frederick Crews, *E.M. Forster and the Perils of Humanism* (Princeton: Princeton University Press, 1962), 159.

58. Sigmund Freud, "The Uncanny," in *Gothic Horror*, ed. Clive Bloom (New York: St. Martin's, 1998), 50.

59. Sharpe, however, finds this type of reading problematic because of "the historical erasure it performs." In her chapter on the novel, she considers *A Passage to India* in light of the 1857 Mutiny and sees the racial and gender politics of the incident in light of "a colonial discourse of power" (Sharpe 125).

60. David Lean clearly reads the novel this way, based upon his interpretation of events in the film version of *A Passage to India*. Although Lean, like Forster, never shows the audience Adela's entire experience in the cave, Judy Davis's Adela Quested, sweaty and weary from their climb up the mountain, looks longingly at Victor Banerjee's Aziz before she enters the cave. And Lean, as Jenny Sharpe points out, adds a scene prior to Adela's visit to the caves involving sexual temple carvings and wild monkeys that symbolizes her sexual arousal and overtly suggests that she has "suffered a bout of sexual hysteria" (119).

61. In his recent analysis of the manuscripts, David Medalie similarly sees the "the indeterminacy of the final account [... as] an effective way of commenting upon Anglo-Indian paranoia" (176).

62. Aziz sarcastically tells Fielding that he foresees the same "old story of 'We will rob every man and rape every woman from Peshawar to Calcutta,' [...] which you will get some nobody to repeat and then quote every week in the *Pioneer* in order to frighten us into retaining you!" (Forster 361). He refers to the kind of fictions and imperialist narratives that Forster is debunking through the novel.

63. Perry Meisel, *The Myth of the Modern: A Study in British Literature and Criticism After 1850* (New Haven: Yale University Press, 1987), 5.

Works Cited

Bayly, C.A. *Indian Society and the Making of the British Empire. Part I, vol. II* of *The New Cambridge History of India*. Gen. ed. Gordon Johnson. New York: Cambridge University Press, 1988.

Beauman, Nicola. *E.M. Forster: A Biography*. New York: Knopf, 1994.

Colmer, John. *E.M. Forster: The Personal Voice*. London: Routledge, 1975.

Crews, Frederick. *E.M. Forster and the Perils of Humanism*. Princeton: Princeton University Press, 1962.

Croker, Bithia. *A Family Likeness: A Sketch in the Himalayas*. London: Chatto & Windus, 1894.

De Quincy, Thomas. "Hurried Notices of Indian Affairs." In *The Uncollected Writings of Thomas De Quincy*. Vol. 1. Edited by James Hogg. Plainview: Books for Libraries, 1972.

Forster, E.M. "E.M. Forster." In *Writers at Work: The Paris Review Interviews*. Edited by Malcolm Cowley. New York: Viking, 1958.

____. *Howards End*. New York: Vintage, 1921.

____. *The Hill of Devi*. New York: Harcourt, 1953.

____. *The Longest Journey*. New York: Vintage, 1962.

____. *The Manuscripts of A Passage to India*. Vol. 6a of *The Abinger Edition of E.M. Forster*. Edited by Oliver Stallybrass. London: Edward Arnold, 1978.

____. "Notes on the English Character." In *Abinger Harvest*. New York: Harcourt, 1964.

____. *A Passage to India*. New York: Harcourt, 1924.

____. *A Room with a View*. New York: Bantam, 1988.

____. "The Story of a Panic." In *The Collected Tales of E.M. Forster*. New York: Knopf, 1966.

____. "The Story of the Siren." In *Collected Tales*.

____. "Syed Ross Masood." In *Two Cheers for Democracy*. New York: Harcourt, 1979.

____. *Where Angels Fear to Tread*. New York: Vintage, 1920.

Freud, Sigmund. "The Uncanny." In *Gothic Horror*. Edited by Clive Bloom. New York: St. Martin's, 1998.

Furbank, P.N. *E.M. Forster: A Life*. 2 vols. New York: Harcourt, 1978.

Gilbert, Sandra M., and Susan Gubar. *The Madwoman in the Attic: The Woman Writer and the Nineteenth Century Literary Imagination*. New Haven: Yale University Press, 1979.

Godfrey, Denis. *E.M. Forster's Other Kingdom*. London: Oliver and Boyd, 1968.

Holland, Norman N. "Unity Identity Text Self." In *Reader-Response Criticism*. Edited by Jane P. Tompkins. Baltimore: Johns Hopkins University Press, 1980.

Iser, Wolfgang. "The Reading Process." In Tompkins.

Keay, John. *India: A History*. New York: Atlantic Monthly, 2000.

Kipling, Rudyard. "Gunga Din." In *The Portable Kipling*. Edited by Irving Howe. New York: Penguin, 1982.

____. *Kim*. Oxford: Oxford University Press, 1987.

____. "The White Man's Burden." In Howe.

Lean, David, dir. *A Passage to India*. Perf. Peggy Ashcroft, Judy Davis, James Fox, Victor Banerjee, and Alec Guinness. Columbia Pictures, 1984.

Lewis, Matthew. *The Monk*. New York: Modern Library, 2002.

Macauley, Rose. *The Writings of E.M. Forster*. London: Hogarth, 1938.

Malchow, H.L. *Gothic Images of Race in Nineteenth Century Britain*. Stanford: Stanford University Press, 1996.

Massingham, H.W. "The Price of India's Friendship." In *A Routledge Literary Source-book on E.M. Forster's A Passage to India.* Edited by Peter Childs. New York: Routledge, 2002.

Massé, Michelle. *In the Name of Love.* Ithaca: Cornell University Press, 1992.

Mason, A.E.W. *The Broken Road.* New York: Scribner's, 1907.

Medalie, David. *E.M. Forster's Modernism.* New York: Palgrave, 2002.

Meisel, Perry. *The Myth of the Modern: A Study in British Literature and Criticism After 1850.* New Haven: Yale University Press, 1987.

Metcalf, Thomas R. *The Aftermath of Revolt: India 1857–1870.* Princeton: Princeton University Press, 1964.

Myrick, Daniel, and Eduardo Sánchez, dirs. *The Blair Witch Project.* Perf. Heather Donahue, Joshua Leonard, Michael Williams. Artisan Entertainment, 1999.

Natwar-Singh, K. "Only Connect....: Forster and India." In *Aspects of E.M. Forster.* Edited by Oliver Stallybrass. New York: Harcourt, 1969.

Panikkar, K.M. *Asia and Western Dominance: A Survey of the Vasco da Gama Epoch of Asian History.* New York: Collier, 1969.

Paravisini-Gerbert, Lizabeth. "Colonialism and Postcolonial Gothic: The Caribbean." In *The Cambridge Companion to Gothic Fiction.* Edited by Jerrold E. Hoyle. Cambridge: Cambridge University Press, 2002.

Parry, Benita. *Delusions and Discoveries.* Berkeley: California University Press, 1972.

Peterson, Margaret. *The Lure of the Little Drum.* New York: G.P. Putnam's Sons, 1913.

Poe, Edgar Allan. "The Fall of the House of Usher." In *Selected Writings of Edgar Allan Poe.* Edited by Edward H. Davidson. Boston: Houghton Miᶜin, 1956.

Read, Anthony, and David Fisher. *The Proudest Day: India's Long Road to Independence.* New York: Norton, 1998.

Said, Edward. *Culture and Imperialism.* New York: Vintage, 1994.

Schmitt, Cannon. *Alien Nation: Nineteenth-Century Gothic Fiction and English Nationality.* Philadelpha: University of Pennsylvania Press, 1997.

Sedgwick, Eve Kosofsky. *The Coherence of Gothic Conventions.* New York: Methuen, 1986.

Sharpe, Jenny. *Allegories of Empire: The Figure of the Woman in the Colonial Text.* Minneapolis: Minnesota University Press, 1993.

Shelley, Mary. *Frankenstein.* New York: New American Library, 1983.

Spear, Percival. *A History of India.* Baltimore: Penguin, 1965.

Summers, Claude. *E.M. Forster.* New York: Frederick Ungar, 1983.

Thackeray, William Makepeace. *The Tremendous Adventures of Major Gahagan.* London: Smith, Elder & Co., 1887.

Tracy, Louis. *The Red Year: A Story of the Indian Mutiny.* New York: Grosset and Dunlop, 1907.

Walpole, Horace. *The Castle of Otranto.* New York: Macmillan, 1963.

Walsh, William. *Indian Literature in English.* London: Longman, 1990.

Watson, Francis. *A Concise History of India.* New York: Charles Scribners' Sons, 1975.

Wolpert, Stanley. *A New History of India.* 5th ed. New York: Oxford University Press, 1997.

Wylie, I.A.R. *The Daughter of Brahma.* Indianapolis: Bobbs-Merrill, 1913.

PART II

Demonizing the Religious Other, Humanizing the Self

8

Gothic Routes, or the Thrills of Ethnography: Frances Calderon de la Barca's *Life in Mexico*

SOLEDAD CABALLERO

In 1838 Angel Calderon de la Barca traveled to Mexico as its first Spanish ambassador and with his visit officially recognized Mexico, formerly the colony of New Spain, as an independent nation. His Scottish wife, Frances Erskine Inglis, traveled with him and lived in the country for two years exploring and investigating its culture and people. During her residence, Frances Calderon de la Barca produced a huge correspondence that she gathered at the end of her travels and, using these letters and her private journals as a foundation, she edited, rearranged, and published them as a travel narrative entitled *Life in Mexico, During a Residence of Two Years in That Country* (1843).

By the mid-nineteenth century, the number of British women traveling to and writing about imperial and economically significant locations was on the rise.[1] Although domestic ideology aimed to separate women from political activity, their travel writings tended to examine the domestic cultures of foreign places, often supporting British imperial and political interests abroad, and were instrumental in creating and disseminating information about foreign locations to the English reading public.[2] This was particularly true of women who traveled to what was again called the "New World," or the Americas, in the early-to-mid-nineteenth century.

Alexander von Humboldt's thirty-two volume "natural science" investigations of the Americas, entitled *Personal Narrative of Travels to the Equinoctial Regions of the New Continent* and published throughout the 1810s and 1820s, sparked European entrepreneurial interest in the Americas. This and other travel narratives provided public and readily available information to the many merchants, investors, adventurers, naval officers, sailors, and governmental officials interested in the New Continent.[3] The women who traveled with these governmental and economic emissaries wrote narratives about these locations; their narratives must be examined not only within the context of the domestic sphere and women's writing but also within the larger political, economic context of English/American relations during the early part of the nineteenth century.[4] It is this framework that suggests the significance of Frances Calderon de la Barca's 1843 travel narrative and her representations of Mexican social, cultural, and political life.[5] De la Barca's narrative is exhaustive in its focus, commenting in detail about Mexican political, social, and domestic life. While her narrative spans vastly different topics, large portions of it focus upon the varied and various Catholic ceremonies and rituals of the country, especially initiations of novice nuns and penance rituals.

Significantly, while de la Barca attempts to follow in Humboldt's path and produce a narrative about Mexico that engages with emerging scientific discourses, particularly ethnography and anthropology, she also unexpectedly follows in the footsteps of Gothic writers of a generation before her, particularly Ann Radcliffe and Matthew Lewis, producing a proto-ethnography of Mexico through a Gothic lens. Not surprisingly, de la Barca's Gothicism manifests itself in a specific version of the Gothic that posits the Catholic as Other and at the same time, "spectacular." Thus, in a narrative that positions itself to be a truthful, accurate account of Mexican culture and the writer's experiences in it, we find a literary diagnosis that systematically differentiates between the civilized Protestant observer and the superstitious, underdeveloped Catholic. The Catholic and that which is associated with Catholicism function as figures for what is Other and othered in her narrative. This othering process suggests that, rather than illustrate the divide between anthropological and literary writing, de la Barca's text demonstrates how specifically Gothic resonances not only complicate scientific attempts at objectivity but also how these literary echoes, as she uses them, actually form the basis of the emerging scientific discourses of the nineteenth century. Though she attempts to authorize her narrative via scientific discourses, de la Barca deploys Gothic tropes such as the young female victim and the mysteries and horrors of the Catholic Church; these tropes are used in the service of differentiating a civilized self in relation to an unknown, Catholic Other. Ultimately, de la Barca's text unveils the literary thrills at the heart of ethnographic discourses.

Ian Duncan notes and explains the tendency to represent the political Other in the Gothic, suggesting that the political debate around the Gothic in the late eighteenth century centers around "the myth of national secular experience" in England.[6] In Duncan's view, while certain "proto-nationalist" sectors considered England's true, Gothic past to have been "usurped by the Norman Conquest and subsequent aristocratic rule," (read Catholic invaders) those in power "held that the 1689 Constitution marked the final defeat of Gothic Barbarism [which stood for] the *alien* forces of oppression, those of Pope and Pretender."[7] Historically, it appears that the valence of the term Gothic suggests both the Gothic purity of English culture before "foreign" Catholic influence and, paradoxically, the infestation of that culture by Gothic, meaning Catholic sources. This political debate highlights the fact that whether the term Gothic is used to describe indigenous English or foreign institutions, that which is foreign and other within this paradigm is always that which is Catholic.

Significantly, both Lewis and Radcliffe, representing both the male and female poles of the Gothic, structure their narratives around this resistance to the foreign (Catholic). Whether it is expressed through Ambrosio's hypocritical piety in Matthew Lewis's *The Monk* or the nefarious collusion between the Marchesa and the Abbess in Ann Radcliffe's *The Italian*, there is an inherent oppositional relationship between the presumed English, Protestant reading subject and the Catholic Other of the text. For this reason, in the work of both authors, protagonists like Emily, Ellena, Lorenzo, and Vivaldi maintain a critical distance from their own Catholic environment and beliefs. In *The Italian*, for example, Ellena Rosalba eschews the confines of the veil despite the powerful means that have trapped her within the convent walls. When shown what the Abbess calls the "generosity" of the Marchesa and "indulged" with a choice of taking the veil or marrying a partner selected by the Marchesa, Ellena rejects both choices and rejects the Abbess who here functions as an emissary of Catholic authority. Instead Ellena argues that she will not "condemn [her]self to the cloister" and that her "voice never shall sanction the evils" she has been subjected to by its power.[8] Ellena rejects the power of the Abbess and the Church and exclaims that she has the right to "condemn" and speak up against the injustices inflicted upon her precisely because the Abbess has corrupted whatever was holy about her religion. In fact, Ellena suggests that she is, as a religious subject, able to interpret the commands of the Church herself and more significantly, that she is able to determine how to perform her faith as an individual thinking subject outside the strictures of Church dogma; in other words, she embodies what in English culture would be deemed the antidote to the Catholic hierarchy, an individual relationship to faith. When Ellena exclaims that the "sanctuary" of the Church has "become a prison" and that when commanded by the Abbess to "revere" her religion by obeying the Abbess's will, Ellena instead passionately claims that the Abbess's conduct "urges" Ellena to "condemn" the Abbess. As such, Ellena rejects precisely what the Abbess, the emblem of the Church, argues is the unquestionable power of Catholicism; she is instead arguing for her own individualized relationship with church and God, what we can think of as an oppositional coded "Protestant" response to the "Catholic" irrational, power hungry Abbess. Along the same schema, in *Udolpho*, when Emily St. Aubert finds comfort in a convent, it is precisely because the Abbess who oversees this convent, unlike the Abbess in *The Italian*, does not follow the strict scriptures of Catholicism, again exhibiting what has been recognized within the text as particularly un–Catholic behavior. What we see, then, is that the central characters in these texts, although identified as Catholic, tend to be veiled representations of the rational, modern, and gendered subjects who confront a residual, ancient Gothic past and discard it in favor of an individualist, modern, Protestant ethic.

However, if the Catholic is necessarily Other within Gothic literature, this process of othering takes different forms in the female Gothic of Radcliffe and the male Gothic of Lewis. As Maggie Kilgour suggests, "in the female version of development, the female individual is usually brought safely into a social order which is reaffirmed at the end."[9] In Radcliffe, the power and strangeness of the Catholic church in all its manifestations, though tangible and threatening, are, by the end of the narratives, usually diffused and revealed to be benign, as in Vivaldi's experience with an unexpectedly just Inquisition or with Ellena's eventual return with Vivaldi to her mythic and mythologized childhood home. And Schedoni's terrifying power, the masculine and Catholic horror that he engenders, is, even in its most potent moments, subject to being subdued; it is Ellena's passive beauty as she sleeps that inspires him to observe the locket on her neck and in turn, discover, or rather mis-recognize her as his daughter, thus stopping him from killing her.

Furthermore, while heroines in Radcliffe's texts are continuously bombarded with evil prognostications and continual attempts upon their chastity and honor, they are able to remain untouched, either by virtue of the strength of their capacities or due to the inept strategies of those around them. This does not suggest that there is no danger in the lives of the female protagonists in Radcliffe's novels. This danger, however, as feminist critics like Diana Hoeveler and Michelle Massé have argued, is not a danger of what is unknown or ghostly, or even finally Catholic. It is, rather, the danger of quotidian female life: the social and political power that men have over the bodies of the women they rule and govern. Indeed, as Massé has effectively suggested of Gothic plots and heroines, "the Gothic plot is ... not an 'escape' from the real world ... both the nightmare stasis of the protagonists and the all-enveloping power of the antagonists are extensions of social ideology and real-world experience."[10] Ellena and Emily, Radcliffe's heroines, are then traumatized by their experiences, but what is particularly Catholic about these experiences does not kill the heroines. By the end of the text, the specifically Catholic power is relegated to the realm of the bizarre but finally contained curiosity. Their unpleasant experiences have served to prepare Ellena and Emily for the life of the subjugated but functioning adult woman within the patriarchy.

Radcliffe's "explained supernatural," most famously in *The Mysteries of Udolpho*, works to deflate or naturalize the actual threat to the female protagonist, including the danger of Catholic authority. Terry Castle argues that the ghostliness or the supernatural elements of Radcliffe's *The Mysteries of Udolpho* emerge and emanate not from what is ghostly and unknown, and for our purposes from that which is Catholic, but rather from what she calls "the supernaturalization of everyday life."[11] By the end of *Udolpho*, "old-fashioned ghosts, it is true, have disappeared ... but a new kind of apparition takes their place" (123). And for Castle this new ghostliness means that "to be a Radcliffean hero or heroine" is to find oneself "obsessed by spectral images of those one loves" and "to be haunted, according to the novel's romantic myth, is to display one's powers of sympathetic imagination; the cruel and the dull have no such hallucinations" (123). Thus, within Radcliffe's mythic world of the strange, that which is Catholic and outside of oneself is strange. Yet the protagonist's virtuous strength, and her ability to recognize that the "real" ghosts in her life as the beloved dead who are still present in her life, allows her to subdue the threat of the Catholic Church. The Church is rendered harmless, representing more the figurehead of power rather than power itself; this power is instead transferred to the happily rational heterosexual couple, surrounded by the benign ghosts of their dead.

And though Castle has argued that the supernatural in Radcliffe is not explained but rather "displaced" or "diverted — rerouted, so to speak, into the realm of the every day," this nonetheless indicates that in Radcliffe's narratives, danger and in particular, Catholic danger and terror, are diffused and do not permanently disrupt the heroine's future bliss and tranquility (124). Though Ellena is imprisoned by the Abbess, and by extension, the power of the Church, she is not a sacrifice to its authority, and, in the end, she marries and return to her childhood home. And though Emily is frightened senseless by the effigy of a dead corpse, a literal materialization of Catholic practice, our "Protestant" heroine endures by practicing her individual reading and writing of poetry and contemplating sublime, natural vistas. Indeed, this Radcliffean formulation of Catholic otherness suggests that once the Catholic elements in Ellena's and Emily's lives are classified as alien, Other, they lose their threat.

Nevertheless, for Radcliffe, Catholicism (although relegated to the margins of the text) is not ultimately demystified or normalized. The wax figure Emily finds, although explained as artificial, is nonetheless strange and finally inexplicable to the Protestant mind as an actual practice of the Catholic devotion; this relic ultimately signifies "that fierce severity, which monkish superstition has sometimes inflicted on mankind" (662). Similarly, the Abbess who imprisons Ellena is, although benign, a figure of religious aberrance; we know, through Ellena's condemnation of her, that the Abbess has corrupted true faith by her strict adherence to Catholic hierarchy.

Like de la Barca who follows her, Radcliffe's rational explanation of Catholic horror functions akin to ethnographic explanations, serving to rationally categorize, classify and therefore limit the power of the Catholic Other. Thus in *The Mysteries of Udolpho*, Emily is rendered senseless by the dead figure that she thinks she sees underneath the veil in the first third of the novel: "after the first glance, [Emily] let the veil drop, and her terror prevented her from ever a renewal of such suffering, as she had then experienced" (664). Yet by the novel's closure, Emily, and the reader, have discovered the rational, ethnographic explanation for this still-strange phenomenon — through understanding, the fearful power of the alien culture is dissipated. However, despite the sense of deflation that this ending consciously offers, the explanation does not erase or clarify what is finally understood to be the materially *other* aspects of that which is Catholic. Indeed, the effigy, when revealed to be nothing more than a wax body, is nonetheless strangely discordant to the Protestant, non–Catholic, sensibility. Although disempowered by the closure of the novel, the Catholic is still strange, still Other.

In Lewis's *The Monk*, the exemplar of the horrifying male Gothic, the violently threatening supernatural reality of Catholicism is not contained. The Catholic Other in Lewis brings to the surface that which is repressed in Radcliffe's novels. The suspense generated by Lewis's novel foreshadows the materialization, in the end, of a horrible reality that has been anticipated from the beginning. Unlike Radcliffe, who attempts to close the gap between the imagined and the possible with regard to the dangers of Catholicism by positing a rational, Protestant ending, Lewis "rationally" allows for the supernatural and inexplicable to be part of the vision presented in his text. Indeed for Lewis, the power, horror, and violence is manifest in the quotidian elements of the lives that he traces and finally destroys. Happy endings are tempered by deaths, and not simply natural deaths, but death by Catholic imprisonments and at the hands of the Church's instruments. In Lewis's novel, unlike Radcliffe's texts, the horror infliction by the demonized Catholic Church is real and enduring.

For Lewis, then, that which is Catholic intrudes upon the realities of the characters and not just on their imaginings, intervening in their lives in tangible, corrupt ways. These disruptions and interventions are not separate from the daily lives of the characters, but rather ground the very realities that they must contend with and suffer through. Agnes's irreverent drawing of the Bleeding Nun comes back to haunt Raymond in the form of the actual Bleeding Nun, thwarting his marriage to Agnes.

Unlike Radcliffe's Ellena, who is fully released from the confines of the Church, Agnes never fully escapes; her imprisonment marks her future because her baby dies in the dungeons of the Church. Unlike Radcliffe's Montoni and Schedoni, who are defeated at the end of their narratives, Lewis's Catholic villains exude an uncontainable power. While they have performed vile acts in the past, they do not gather to themselves the power to rule over and win against the virtue and justice expected and anticipated in Radcliffe's texts. Lewis's Ambrosio, however, is ultimately defeated. It is the Church's schooling that leads Ambrosio to a path of prideful piety. While Montoni arranges for Emily's seduction and Schedoni attempts to kill Ellena, Ambroiso consummates his plan — to rape and kill his victim — because the Devil does actually exist in bodily form as his tempter.

The representation of the Church in the novels of Radcliffe and Lewis confirm Anne Williams's suggestion, "whereas the female tradition of Gothic explains the ghosts, the male formula simply posits the supernatural as a 'reality,' a premise of this fictional world."[12] To use the paradigm established by Radcliffe: her female Gothic delights in the "terror" that ultimately leads her characters from suspense to the world of bliss; Lewis, however, capitalizes on the tendency of the male Gothic toward actual consummated "horror." What Radcliffe and Lewis have in common is that in both "formulas," Catholicism represents the source of terror and horror. And more significantly, it represents an otherness that is either foreign or strange, even when ethnographically contained and understood.

Gothic Relations: Enjoying the Show

In de la Barca's travel narrative, the two seemingly distinct traditions of male and female Gothic are fused together and work in concert to present the "real truth" of Catholicism as it functions in her understanding of Mexican religious practices. For de la Barca, what initially appears to be the Radcliffean Catholic terror, safely unconsummated, presenting the possibility of classification and containment, ultimately materializes as actual horror and violence. In fact, de la Barca deploys both strains of Gothic to convey her meaning. Radcliffe's narrative model allows her to call attention to what she considers to be the spectacle, strangeness, and beauty of the religious events she witnesses, while Lewis's narrative trajectory allows her to highlight what she considers to be the actual primitivism, horror, and violence that seem inherent in Catholic rituals of worship.

Thus, de la Barca has two seemingly oppositional responses to Catholic religious displays. She produces descriptions through what seems to be the distanced, objective stance of the Radcliffean ethnographer at the same time that she focuses upon the Lewisian titillating sensationalism of the foreign Others. De la Barca's narrative oscillates, then, between the Radcliffean allusion to violence and the Lewisian actualization of that violence. In each mode of representation, de la Barca sustains the mysterious and what she views as the inherently Gothic elements of their quotidian Catholic lives; the Radcliffean structure allows her to enjoy the spectacle and feel titillated by it though she is not in any "real" danger, while the Lewisian model highlights the potential horror, in de la Barca's case, the pain of watching that which, if spectacular, is also horrifying.

One of de la Barca's first encounters with Mexican religious traditions, described in *Life in Mexico*, exemplifies and influences later representation of these encounters in her novel. During a visit to a wealthy Mexican lady, she begins to describe cultural practices in Mexico:

> I paid a visit the other day, which merits to be recorded. It was to the rich Señora de Aguero, whose first visit I had not yet returned. She was at home, and I was shown into a very large drawing room, where to my surprise I found the lamps, mirrors, &c. covered with black crepe, as in cases of mourning here. I concluded that some one of the family was dead, and that I had made a very ill-timed first visit. However, I sat down, when my eyes were instantly attracted by *something awful* placed directly in front of the sofa where I sat. There were six chairs ranged together, and on these lay stretched out a figure, apparently a dead body, about six feet long, enveloped in black cloth. Oh, horror! Here I sat, my eyes fixed upon this mysterious apparition, and lost in conjecture as to whose body it might

be. The master of the house? He was very tall, and being in bad health might have died suddenly. My being received argued nothing against this, since the first nine days after a death the house is invariably crowded with friends and acquaintances, and the widow or orphan or childless mother must receive the condolences of all and sundry in the midst of her first bitter sorrow. There seems to be no idea of grief wishing for solitude.[13]

De la Barca is so overtaken by and involved with the "mysterious apparition" that when Señora de Aguero enters the room she involuntarily "starts up." She is further unhinged when the lady of the house receives her in blue muslin, which, as de la Barca recognizes, shows "no signs of mourning" (*Life* 178). It is only after a very uncomfortable and anxious visit that de la Barca discovers that the figure in the corner is a San Cristo effigy for the chapel and as the señora explains, "for which reason this room is, as you see, hung with black" (*Life* 179).With the revelation that the figure in the corner is an effigy of Christ that accounts for the room's decorations, de la Barca ends the description and declares happily, "I never felt so relieved in my life, and thought of the *Mysteries of Udolpho*" (*Life* 179), evoking, of course, Emily's misunderstanding with the black veil.

Thus, amidst this proto-ethnographic analysis, de la Barca constructs her experience in the drawing room as if she were a heroine in a Gothic novel encountering a horrible unknown. David Punter points out that "above all, the gothic has to do with terror" and there appears to be plenty of that for de la Barca in the drawing room.[14] Like Emily St. Aubert who believes that she has seen a dead body hidden behind a veil, de la Barca suggests that there is something ominous in the drawing room under the black veil. An inexplicable excess, what Cannon Schmitt calls a "generalized paranoia," is embedded and lingers within the materiality of mourning even before de la Barca is aware of the effigy.[15] Although de la Barca is relieved to discover that the figure in the corner is not a dead body, the effigy nonetheless represents a practice that reveals, even when explained, the foreign, other reality of Mexican Catholicism. Thus, like Radcliffe, de la Barca diminishes the power of the cultural Other without diminishing its strangeness. The señora's explanation of the apparition offers de la Barca a marker by which to recognize the foreignness of the scene and to figure Catholicism as Other. In aligning herself with Emily St. Aubert, de la Barca recognizes that she, too, will return to the stasis of safety by the end. The strange figure of Mexican Catholicism is labeled and categorized as interesting but not actually threatening.

As in Radcliffe's *The Mysteries of Udolpho*, then, what is behind the veil in de la Barca's narrative is not nearly as central to the description as the heightened anxiety and suspense, followed by relief, that it generates.

As Maggie Kilgour suggests, in Radcliffe's novels "the gap between the drawn-out suspense and the perfunctory revelation itself reveals that the author's real interest is not in revelation but in suspense" (130). Significantly, Eve Sedgwick argues that the valence of the veil in Gothic novels is as much about the veil itself as what it covers up or conceals: "The characters in gothic novels fall in love as much with women's veils as with the women" (143). De la Barca's investment in the veil, then, in the "black cloth," and the evocative possibility that a dead body *could* be underneath it, argues for the fact that she locates titillation in the veil itself and in the suspense before the revelation that it provokes; the veil, emblemizing suspense, is, thus, of more interest than the actualization of the cause of suspense. In other words, for de la Barca, like Radcliffe, the suspense before the revelation functions as the central component of the Gothic experience. By simultaneously foregrounding the connection between the terror and pleasure of the veil (the dramatic "Oh, horror" that it elicits), and the "rational explanation" of what the veil covers, de la Barca employs the "revelatory sciences," the developing human social sciences like ethnography and anthropology. These sciences are constituted by a "truth revealing intention" that is, in actuality, grounded in a Gothic literary tradition based upon the attenuation of that truth. De la Barca, though mesmerized by the body under the veil, and structuring her analysis around the mysterious apparition, nonetheless proceeds to explain Mexican visiting-mourning customs, describing for her audience the social interactions and expectations between grievers and guests. The description of this visit interweaves what I call proto-ethnographic descriptions of Mexican social rituals with the Gothic sensationalism that appears to inform the structures of the customs de la Barca describes. And for de la Barca, even as she scientifically describes the "mourning customs," she uses the Radcliffean Gothic trope of the attenuation of "the truth" to extend the pleasure of not knowing what is underneath the veil. However, if de la Barca finds "relief" in the final scientific explanation,[16] a narrative overflow persists beyond the final rational revelation. The residue that Ian Duncan identifies as "a spiritual orientalism in the British Protestant imagination" (24) lingers on. In essence, although all is explained, the otherness of Mexican Catholicism remains the central component of this visitation scene, even as the potential terror of a dead body in the corner is diffused. The consequences of this narrative ghostliness, this residual lingering otherness, are multifold.

One consequence of this narrative ghostliness is that de la Barca clearly indicates that her initial encounter with and understanding of Catholicism is already determined by and structured within a Gothic novelistic rubric. The apparition may not be a dead body, but it is, literally, a figurative embodiment of the strangely Gothic way that Mexicans perform their religious devotions. Indeed, rather than explain away, through science, the titillating terror that de la Barca "imagined," the explanation at the end of this visit actually reinscribes Radcliffean Gothic formulations that structure Catholicism with inherently exotic, although safe, otherness. The proto-ethnographic analyses that she attempts to use owe their rhetorical formulations not to disinterested, objective observations that argue for conclusions based upon rational explanations, but instead have as a basis of their rhetorical structures a subjective Gothic tradition that heightens, suspends, and denies access to the truth by focusing upon the pleasure and titillation produced precisely because the "truth" is suspended. And we see this in de la Barca's descriptions which, as they strive to tell her readers about the room and her observations about religious practices, are organized around the apparition in the room and her subjective response.

The tradition of ethnography and anthropology — initially articulated by scientists and travelers like Carl Linneaus, Alexander von Humboldt, Erasmus Darwin, and James Prichard in the eighteenth and nineteenth centuries and developed in the twentieth century by anthropologists and ethnographers like Franz Boaz, Claude Levi-Strauss, James Clifford and feminist anthropologists like Micaela di Leonard and Margery Wolf — has in large part been based upon the revelation of similarities and relationships between human societies. Paradoxically, this tradition has been structured around the idea of classifying and explaining in some kind of quantifiable terms the foreignness and strangeness of others within a framework of the ethnographer's making, that is to say, based upon the value systems of the recorder. Thus, while it may seem that the tenets of these revelatory sciences disclose and present in explicit terms the "truths of a culture," or how they relate to our culture and "our" understanding of social and cultural systems (as de la Barca deploys them), they actually rely upon and are narratively driven by maintaining and sustaining what is unknowable or impenetrable, indeed different and Other, about that culture. Anthropologists, then, deal in the shock moment of contact, the moment of encounter with the strange or bizarre about a culture as defined by the ideological understanding of the ethnographer. It is precisely this central shock moment that connects anthropological discourses to Gothic discourses that suspend the "shock" in favor of the thrills of what is unrevealable.

In de la Barca's narrative, we see how the seeds of this tradition begin with an attempt to defamiliarize social rituals like those of mourning and prayer by invoking their Gothic strangeness and unknowability even in the face of a proto-ethnographic explanation. In this example, de la Barca focuses upon the mystery at the center of a cross-cultural encounter and the pleasure and titillation it provokes even as the circumstances are finally "explained." And though de la Barca "explains" Mexican mourning and praying practices, she organizes them within specifically Gothic terms, or the still unknowable aspects of these rituals in Mexico. In light of this strategy of representation, one can see that de la Barca's other descriptions of Catholic rituals contain this Gothic approach in less self-consciously recognized ways; her descriptions of novice ceremonies offer such an example.

Just Visiting: Convents, or Houses of Fun

De la Barca observes three different novice inaugurations and visits at least two convents. In her description of these visits, she demonstrates that the basis of her understanding of Catholicism evolves out of the literary conventions of the Gothic that mystifies and produces a religious, socially inferior "Other." In these visits, de la Barca aspires to produce accurate representations of Mexican Catholicism; however, in light of her literary influences, de la Barca also participates in the delights of suspending the "truths" of Catholicism in favor of attenuating these pleasures. Finally, de la Barca records the transformation of the Radcliffean pleasure of watching the terrifying spectacle of Catholic rituals into the Lewisian reality of horrifying violence that is no longer titillating and pleasing but is rather bloody and intensely real.

The Radcliffean pleasure that de la Barca takes in observing and attending inaugurations and visiting convents is evident in her narrative.[17] As de la Barca herself acknowledges to her reader, "You will think I pass my time in convents, but I find no other places half so interesting and you know I always had a fancy that way" (*Life* [1931] 273). When she describes the inaugurations, de La Barca sets herself up as an objective, outside observer. All is spectacle; each "scene" is "striking," and has a mixture of Gothic tropes and proto-ethnographic analysis. There are "nuns, all ranged around and carrying lighted tapers in their hands" and "churchmen near the illuminated and magnificently-decked altar [that] formed, as usual, a brilliant background to the picture" of the ceremony. And most importantly, there is "the girl, kneeling in front, and also bearing a heavy lighted taper, [who] looked beautiful with her dark hair and rich dress, and the long black lashes resting on her glowing face" (*Life* [1931] 266).

By stabilizing her subject position in relation to the scene before her, and by presenting the otherness of the figures on stage, de la Barca attempts to make authoritative claims about her distance from the victimhood of the novice. This ceremony, is "next to death ... the saddest event that can occur in this nether sphere" (*Life* [1931] 258), a scene of sacrifice that she "dislike[s] more and more upon trial" (*Life* [1931] 263), but it does not directly impact upon her; to de la Barca, the scene bears the pleasures of narrative. Significantly, the "back story" of one novice reads very much like the stories of Ellena and Agnes. She, too, is being forced into convent life: "The whole affair ... was entirely against the mother's consent, though that of the father had been obtained" (*Life* [1931] 197). De la Barca even sees "the confessor whose influence had brought it about" (*Life* [1931] 197). De la Barca finds pleasure in watching because, as in Radcliffe's novels, that which is Catholic is Other and strange; even after explanations, it is the non-threatening delight of watching that organizes her inauguration extravaganza.

And yet, de la Barca, like Lewis's characters, finds herself being implicated in the spectacle that she witnesses. The very pleasure and discomfort that she takes in her observations comes to implicate her within her own Gothic narrative; she cannot sustain her status as untouched observer. Like the young novice, de la Barca takes center stage in her narrative, glowing in her "victimization" as the unwilling Protestant observer forced to watch "the sacrifice." Though she has declared after her first two novice ceremony experiences that she "had almost made up [her] mind to see no more such scenes," de la Barca needs little convincing to attend the next one *(Life* [1931] 195); her feigned resistance inscribes de la Barca as an "unwilling" participant in the scene she describes. Like so many young girls in Mexico whom de la Barca claims are "more ... smitten by the ceremony than anything else," de la Barca is herself unknowingly "smitten" by the pleasures of the scene despite her objections to it *(Life* [1931] 190).

And this pleasant fascination endures despite, or because of, the discomfort evoked by these scenes. The novice's victimhood, her status as "human sacrifice" and her separation from daily cultural life, reflect de la Barca's own sense of displacement and alienation in a culture she does not completely comprehend. And yet, as cultural spectacle, the novice, "the cynosure of all approving eyes," solidifies de la Barca's separation from the nun, her own sense of empowerment as the ambassador's wife and as a European woman in a land of inferior beings (*Life* [1931] 190). Thus, when de la Barca observes and describes convent life and novice ceremonies, her responses oscillate between horror and revulsion and pleasure and "fancy." Although in her narrative, de la Barca attempts to relate the realities of these religious rites "as they really are," her desire is directed towards participating in and being seduced by the very sacrifice and spectacle that she claims to detest. As such, de la Barca becomes an unwilling participant in the Gothic story that she is writing, following the Lewisian pattern.

Though she attempts to stabilize her authority via social scientific discourse and distance, the Gothic at the center of these discourses produces de la Barca as the heroine of her own Gothic romance, playing the part of the adorned and adored victim. Rather than being the distant, Radcliffean, objective "I/eye" watching the Catholic Other from afar and unequivocally castigating convent practices in Mexico, de la Barca appears to immerse herself in the beauty of the spectacle and the sensations it elicits. She unconsciously positions herself as an active participant in the scene of sacrifice she claims to deplore. And we see that embedded within her attempts to employ the emerging rhetoric of revelatory sciences, to "explain" the Catholic Other, is the narrative pleasure derived from withholding the constitutive truth-telling components of these discourses. For de la Barca, this suggests that, though she attempts to reveal the strangeness of Catholicism and classify its central components, ultimately she uses tropes that suspend the revelation in favor of the thrill of not knowing but imagining the horrific possibilities and inscribing herself as a victim of these possibilities.

In the following instance, we see an example of the process whereby de la Barca becomes implicated by her own narrative strategies:

> But the other night I was present at a much stranger scene, at the discipline performed by the men—admission having been procured for us by certain means, *private but powerful*. Accordingly, when it was dark, enveloped from head to foot in large cloaks—and without the slightest idea of what it was—we went on foot through the streets to the church of San Agustin. When we arrived a small side door apparently opened of itself, and we entered—passing through long vaulted passages and up steep winding stairs, till we found ourselves in a small railed gallery looking down directly upon the church [*Life* (1963) 336].

De la Barca presents herself as a passive Gothic heroine. Though her presence at the men's "discipline" has been "procured" by "private but powerful" means, which suggest her own powerful status in Mexico as someone capable of observing usually secretive events, de la Barca attempts to construct for herself a passive unknowingness that is the essence of the conventional Gothic heroine. She suggests that what is unusual and Gothic about her situation originates from outside herself and that she is not actually a part of it. Thus, as she attempts to present herself as the distanced observer of the events as they transpire before her, de la Barca simultaneously becomes a Gothic heroine. Through her uses of Gothic devices to present the situation, de la Barca merges the personae of the Gothic heroine and the objective, passive, distant observer.

De la Barca is clearly part of the event as it transpires before us; it is she who is hooded and dressed in large cloaks; passively led through the streets, she is nonetheless a willing participant in light of her desire to see and witness the discipline ritual. In this way, though what she is being led to is supposedly what is strange about Mexican Catholicism, the scene elucidates the ways in which de la Barca's own presence, her desire to see, to witness, and to record Mexican society are also in and of themselves strange, are in fact part of the strangeness of the scene itself.

What is finally most compelling about this scene is that in observing the men's discipline, de la Barca finds herself moving from the female Gothic of the nun's rituals to the male Gothic of the monks. Having entered into San Agustin, de la Barca proceeds to describe the penance ritual before her:

> The scene was curious. Above one hundred and fifty men, enveloped in cloaks and sarapes, their faces entirely concealed, were assembled in the body of the church. A monk had just mounted the pulpit, and the church was dimly lighted....
>
> His discourse was a rude but very forcible and eloquent description of the torments prepared in hell for impertinent sinners. The effect of the whole was very solemn. It appeared like a preparation for the execution of a multitude of condemned criminals. When the discourse was finished they all joined in prayer with much fervor and enthusiasm, beating their breasts and falling upon their faces. Then the monk stood up, and in a very distinct voice read several passages of scripture descriptive of the sufferings of Christ. The organ then struck up the *Miserere*, and all of a sudden the church was plunged into profound darkness— all but the sculptured representation of the Crucifixion, which seemed to hang in the air illuminated. I felt rather frightened, and would have been very glad to leave the church, but it would have been impossible in the darkness.
>
> Suddenly a terrible voice in the dark cried, "My brothers! When Christ was fastened to the pillar by the Jews, he was *scourged!*" At these words, the bright figure disappeared, and the darkness became total. Suddenly, we heard the sound of hundreds of scourges descending upon bare flesh. I cannot conceive of anything more horrible. Before ten minutes had passed, the sound became *splashing*, from the blood that was flowing.
>
> We could not leave the church, but it was perfectly sickening; and had I not been able to take hold of the Senora de Adalid's hand, and feel something human beside me, I could have fancied myself transported into a congregation of evil spirits [*Life* (1963) 336–7].

Again de la Barca attempts proto-ethnographic descriptions but she is quickly confined by her own narrative, trapped in the church like Lewis's

Agnes and subject to the physical sensations of actual horror. The actuality of this scene allows us to realize that, although de la Barca herself does not endure the fate of the novices, their fate is, nevertheless, actual and consummated and, thus, more Lewisian than Radcliffean. According to her, there is an alarming "frequency of these human sacrifices," the initiation of a young girl to church life, when she "knows nothing of the world [and] from childhood is under the dominion of her confessor" (*Life* [1963] 258). For de la Barca, then, the danger suggested by Radcliffe's novels plays itself out in the Lewisian "nether sphere" of Mexico. In de la Barca's representation, then, the figure of the novice, like those of the scourged monks, embodies the real violence and oppression of Catholicism; implicit in her presentation is de la Barca's suggestion that, like Agnes in her living tomb, young girls perish in the bowels of Mexican Catholic convents. Thus within the scene of female Gothic terror, de la Barca locates actual male horror.

We see, then, that de la Barca's Gothicism combines the styles of Radcliffe's female Gothic and Lewis's male Gothic. The ambiance of the scene heightens the suspense *à la* Radcliffe, while the final revelation details the horrible truth *à la* Lewis. What appears to be the most barbaric, Gothic, and yet very real aspect of the penance performance is the revelation of what is actually done to the flesh during penance. Less explicit, but equally real, is the fate of the nun after her induction. De la Barca's Lewisian shift, then, is one of emphasis; what is pleasurable, the sense of excited suspense, is not as central as that which is painful. Through the tautology of de la Barca's Gothic literary proto-ethnography, the "truth" of scourging (and to a lesser degree, the truth of the nun's experience) is "revealed" to be the Catholic Gothic horror that has been foretold; in fact, for de la Barca this Catholic Gothic horror and the otherness of these religious practices are precisely the reality of Mexican culture "as it really is," and it is here that she uses a Lewisian model to highlight that which is Catholic horror.

Thus de la Barca's use of the Gothic in her attempts to present the reality of Mexican culture functions in two related ways: The embedded Gothicism of the "revelatory sciences" suspends the revelation of the truth rather than discloses it; when a truth is "disclosed," the embedded Gothicism of the "revelatory sciences" reconstitutes the foreignness of the Catholic Other at the moment when "the truth" is supposedly "revealed." We see that the revelatory sciences, as expressed by de la Barca, are based upon Gothic literary traditions that represent the Catholic as categorically Other; in de la Barca's narrative this takes either of two forms, the Radcliffean or the Lewisian. Catholicism is presented as a beautiful, impenetrable and delightful spectacle that alludes to but does not actualize its violent possibilities, or as a primitive, consummated, violent reality that presents the truth of Mexican moral deprivation and barbarism. In each case, the Catholic is the irreducible Other. De la Barca's use of the Gothic in writing ethnography reveals that the objective, dispassionate, disinterested, civilized, and in her case, Protestant observer is always an implicated and subjective participant.

Notes

1. For more on gender and travel including continental travel and the Grand Tour, see James Buzard, *The Beaten Track: European Tourism, Literature, and the Ways to Culture, 1800–1918* (Oxford: Clarendon Press, 1993), and Chloe Chard, *Pleasure and Guilt on the Grand Tour: Travel Writing and Imaginative Geography 1600–1830* (New York: St. Martin's Press, 1999).

2. Much has been written about women and empire. For more see Vron Ware, *Beyond the Pale: White Women, Racism, and History* (New York: Verso, 1992); Clare Midgely, "Anti-Slavery and the Roots of 'Imperial Feminism.'" In *Gender and Imperialism*, ed. Clare Midgely ([New York: St. Martin's Press, 1998], 161–179); Margaret Strobel, *European Women and the Second British Empire* (Bloomington: Indiana University Press, 1991); Gayatri Chakravorty Spivak, "Three Women's Texts and a Critique of Imperialism," *Critical Inquiry* 12 (1985): 243–261; Deidre Hall, *Rule Britannia: Women, Empire, and Victorian Writing* (Ithaca: Cornell University Press, 1995); Billie Melman, *Women's Orients: English Women and the Middle East, 1718–1918* (Ann Arbor: The University of Michigan Press, 1992). For more on women travel writers and women travelers see Sara Mills, *Discourses of Difference: An Analysis of Women's Travel Writing and Colonialism* (New York: Routledge, 1991); Susan Morgan, *Place Matters: Gendered Geography in Victorian Women's Travel Books About Southeast Asia* (New Brunswick: Rutgers University Press, 1996); Mary Louise Pratt, *Imperial Eyes: Travel Writing and Transculturation* (New York: Routledge, 1992); Maria Fawley, *A Wider Range: Travel Writing by Women in Victorian England* (Rutherford: Fairleigh Dickinson Press, 1994); and Karen Lawrence, *Penelope Voyages: Women and Travel in the British Literary Tradition* (New York: Cornell University Press, 1994). This is by no means an exhaustive list.

3. Alexander von Humboldt's narratives include *Personal Narrative of Travel to the Equinoctial Regions of the New Continent* and his *Political Essay on the Kingdom of New Spain* both of which were important in reinvigorating European interest in the forming independent nations of the Americas. Travel narratives like Mark Beaufoy, whose journey to Mexico in 1825–1827 culminated in a narrative entitled *Mexican Illustrations* (1827), blamed "Humboldt for having conveyed through his popular writings on Latin America too rosy a picture of the prospects offered to enterprising Europeans" (Desmond Gregory, *Brute New World: The Rediscovery of Latin America in the Early Nineteeth Century* [New York: British Academy Press, 1992], 148).

4. In his descriptive and often pro–European analysis, Desmond Gregory (*Brute New World* discusses English/Latin American relations during the nineteenth century by using travel narratives written by British subjects traveling to Latin America. He discusses the most widely read and used narratives, most of which are written by men, but de la Barca is included in his survey. She is, in fact, one of two female travel writers he mentions.

5. For more on Latin American and English relationships in the nineteenth cen-

tury, see Alan Knight, "Britain and Latin America," in *The Oxford History of the British Empire* (Oxford: Oxford University Press, 1999), 122–145; Leslie Bethell, "Britain and Latin America in Historical Perspective," in *Britain and Latin America: A Changing Relationship*, ed. Victor Bulmer-Thomas (Cambridge: Cambridge University Press, 1989); Desmond Gregory and Andrew Graham-Yooll, *The Forgotten Colony: A History of the English Speaking Communities in Argentina* (Washington: Washington State University Press, 1999); Charles Waddell, "International Politics and Latin American Independence," in *From Independence to 1870*, vol. 3 of *The Cambridge History of Latin America*, ed. Leslie Bethell (Cambridge: Cambridge University Press, 1984), 197–228; and Rory Miller, *Britain and Latin America in the Nineteenth and Twentieth Centuries* (New York: Longman Group, 1993).

6. Ian Duncan, *Modern Romance and Tranformations of the Novel: The Gothic, Scott, Dickens* (Cambridge: Cambridge University Press, 1992), 23.

7. Duncan, 21, 23–24. Emphasis mine.

8. Ann Radcliffe, *The Mysteries of Udolpho* (New York: Oxford University Press, 1966) 84.

9. Maggie Kilgour, *The Rise of the Gothic Novel* (New York: Routledge, 1995), 37.

10. Michelle A. Massé, *In the Name of Love: Women, Masochism, and the Gothic* (Ithaca: Cornell University Press, 1992), 18.

11. Terry Castle, *The Female Thermometer: Eighteenth-Century Culture and the Invention of the Uncanny* (New York: Oxford University Press, 1995), 123.

12. Anne Williams, *Art of Darkness: A Poetics of the Gothic* (Chicago: The University of Chicago Press, 1995), 102.

13. Frances Calderon de la Barca, *Life in Mexico: The Letters of Frances Calderon de la Barca, With New Material from the Author's Private Journals*, annotated and ed. Howard T. Fisher and Marion Hall Fisher (Garden City, NY: Doubleday and Company, Inc., 1966), 178. Emphasis in the original. I have used this expanded edition unless otherwise noted. The Fishers reinserted unpublished material into the published text at their own discretion.

14. David Punter, *The Literature of Terror, the Gothic Tradition: The History of Gothic Fiction from 1765 to the Present Day* (New York: Longman Group, 1996), 13.

15. Cannon Schmitt, *Alien Nation: Nineteenth Century Gothic Fiction and English Nationality* (Philadelphia: University of Pennsylvania Press, 1997), 44.

16. Like Catherine Morland in Jane Austen's *Northanger Abbey*, she is chided for her outlandish speculations.

17. Frances Calderon de la Barca, *Life in Mexico During a Residence of Two Years in That Country* (New York: E. P. Dutton and Co., Inc., 1931), 199.

Works Cited

Austen, Jane. *Northanger Abbey*. Hertfordshire, England: Wordsworth Editions Limited, 1993.

Bethell, Leslie. "Britain and Latin America in Historical Perspective." In *Britain and Latin America: A Changing Relationship*. Edited by Victor Bulmer-Thomas. Cambridge: Cambridge University Press, 1989.

Buzard, James. *The Beaten Track: European Tourism, Literature, and the Ways to Culture, 1800–1918*. Oxford: Clarendon Press, 1993.

Calderon de la Barca, Frances. *Life in Mexico During a Residence of Two Years in That Country*. New York: E. P. Dutton and Co., Inc., 1931.

_____. *Life in Mexico: The Letters of Frances Calderon de la Barca, With New Material From the Author's Private Journals.* Annotated and edited by Howard T. Fisher and Marion Hall Fisher. Garden City, NY: Doubleday and Company, Inc., 1966.

Castle, Terry. *The Female Thermometer: Eighteenth-Century Culture and the Invention of the Uncanny.* New York: Oxford University Press, 1995.

Chard, Chloe. *Pleasure and Guilt on the Grand Tour: Travel Writing and Imaginative Geography 1600–1830.* New York: St. Martin's Press, 1999.

Clemens, Valdine. *The Return of the Repressed: Gothic Horror From The Castle of Otranto to Alien.* New York: State University of New York Press, 1999.

Duncan, Ian. *Modern Romance and Transformations of the Novel: The Gothic, Scott, Dickens.* Cambridge: Cambridge University Press, 1992.

Fawley, Maria. *A Wider Range: Travel Writing by Women in Victorian England.* Rutherford: Fairleigh Dickinson Press, 1994.

Ferris, Ina. *The Achievement of Literary Authority: Gender, History, and the Waverly Novels.* Ithaca, NY: Cornell University Press, 1991.

Gregory, Desmond. *Brute New World: The Rediscovery of Latin America in the Early Nineteenth Century.* New York: British Academy Press, 1992.

_____, and Andrew Graham-Yooll. *The Forgotten Colony: A History of the English Speaking Communities in Argentina.* Washington: Washington State University Press, 1999.

Hall, Deidre. *Rule Britannia: Women, Empire, and Victorian Writing.* Ithaca: Cornell University Press, 1995.

Hoeveler, Diane Long. *Gothic Feminism: The Professionalization of Gender from Charlotte Smith to the Brontës.* University Park: The Pennsylvania State University Press, 1998.

Kilgour, Maggie. *The Rise of the Gothic Novel.* New York: Routledge, 1995.

Knight, Alan. "Britain and Latin America." In *The Oxford History of the British Empire.* Oxford: Oxford University Press, 1999.

Lawrence, Karen. *Penelope Voyages: Women and Travel in the British Literary Tradition.* New York: Cornell University Press, 1994.

Lightman, Bernard, ed. *Victorian Science in Context.* Chicago: University of Chicago Press, 1997.

Massé, Michelle A. *In the Name of Love: Women, Masochism, and the Gothic.* Ithaca: Cornell University Press, 1992.

McLane, Maureen. *Romanticism and the Human Sciences: Poetry, Population, and the Discourse of the Species.* Cambridge: Cambridge University Press, 2000.

Melman, Billie. *Women's Orients: English Women and the Middle East, 1718–1918.* Ann Arbor: The University of Michigan Press, 1992.

Midgely, Clare. "Anti-Slavery and the Roots of 'Imperial Feminism.'" In *Gender and Imperialism.* Edited by Clare Midgely. New York: St. Martin's Press, 1998.

Miller, Rory. *Britain and Latin America in the Nineteenth and Twentieth Centuries.* New York: Longman Group, 1993.

Mills, Sara. *Discourses of Difference: An Analysis of Women's Travel Writing and Colonialism.* New York: Routledge, 1991.

Morgan, Susan. *Place Matters: Gendered Geography in Victorian Women's Travel Books About Southeast Asia.* New Brunswick: Rutgers University Press, 1996.

Pearson, Jacqueline. *Women's Reading in Britain 1750–1830.* Cambridge: Cambridge University Press, 1999.

Pratt, Mary Louise. *Imperial Eyes: Travel Writing and Transculturation.* New York: Routledge, 1992.

Punter, David. *The Literature of Terror, the Gothic Tradition: The History of Gothic Fiction from 1765 to the Present Day.* New York: Longman Group, 1996.

Radcliffe, Ann. *The Italian.* New York: Oxford University Press, 1968.

____. *The Mysteries of Udolpho.* New York: Oxford University Press, 1966.

Richter, David H. *The Progress of Romance: Literary Historiography and the Gothic Novel.* Columbus: Ohio State University Press, 1996.

Schmitt, Cannon. *Alien Nation: Nineteenth Century Gothic Fiction and English Nationality.* Philadelphia: University of Pennsylvania Press, 1997.

Sedgwick, Eve Kosofsky. *The Coherence of Gothic Convention.* New York: Metheun & Co., Ltd., 1986.

Shteir, Ann. *Cultivating Women, Cultivating Science: Flora's Daughters and Botany in England 1760–1860.* Baltimore: Johns Hopkins University Press, 1996.

Spivak, Gayatri Chakravorty. "Three Women's Texts and a Critique of Imperialism." *Critical Inquiry* 12 (1985): 243–261.

Stocking, George. *Victorian Science.* New York: Free Press, 1987.

Strobel, Margaret. *European Women and the Second British Empire.* Bloomington: Indiana University Press, 1991.

Waddell, Charles. "International Politics and Latin American Independence." In *From Independence to 1870.* Volume 3 of *The Cambridge History of Latin America.* Edited by Leslie Bethell. Cambridge: Cambridge University Press, 1984.

Ware, Vron. *Beyond the Pale: White Women, Racism, and History.* New York: Verso, 1992.

Williams, Anne. *Art of Darkness: A Poetics of the Gothic.* Chicago: The University of Chicago Press, 1995.

9

The Infamous Svengali: George Du Maurier's Satanic Jew

RUTH BIENSTOCK ANOLIK

> The wild-dove hath her nest, the fox his cave,
> Mankind their country — Israel but the grave!
> Byron, "Oh! Weep for Those"

The Diabolic Svengali in *Trilby*

Like Frankenstein's monster and like Dracula, the figure of Svengali — another darkly demonic human monster who threatens to overwhelm his hapless victim — expands his power by escaping the boundaries of the text that confines him, stalking his way into the popular imagination.[1] Indeed, Svengali, even more than his fellow monstrous creatures, is so much more famous than his text of origin, so detached from the text that engenders him, that his origin in George Du Maurier's *Trilby* (1894) is not commonly known.[2] This was not the case when Du Maurier first published his sensational novel; *Trilby* was a great success, becoming "the first modern best seller in American publishing."[3] Indeed, in a trend that prefigured the excesses of twentieth-century popular culture, "Trilby [the eponymous heroine of the novel] generated a craze — 'Trilby-mania' — that went beyond the novel itself. Socialites performed *tabeaux vivants* from the book, and sang Trilby's songs to raise money for charity; art galleries exhibited the manuscript, illustrations ... manufacturers vied to produce Trilby products from ice-cream to shoes; and a town in Florida named its streets after characters in the book" (Showalter ix–x).

163

Trilby's author, George Du Maurier, although now consigned to the ranks of former sensations, was in his time a popular novelist as well as a successful illustrator. Of French and English lineage and raised as a bilingual child in Paris and London, Du Maurier turned to writing when his eyesight weakened. Having achieved moderate success as a journalist and magazine illustrator, he wrote *Trilby* during a period in his life when eye problems kept him from his drawing. Showalter locates this biographical detail as the source of the preoccupation of Du Maurier's text with sight and seeing — both in the eyes of the artists who populate his book and in the mesmerizing and penetrating eyes of the villainous Svengali. Du Maurier's mixed genetic and linguistic lineage also finds a place in his novel, in his fixation upon the cultural and geographic rootlessness and linguistic hybridism of Svengali.[4]

Many of the essentials of Svengali's persona — his dark foreignness; his quasi-supernatural, mesmerizing powers, deployed to influence a young impressionable female performer — still append to the popular conceptions of this mysterious figure. However, one essential trait of Du Maurier's Svengali has been lost in the translation from text to mythic figure: the essence of Du Maurier's monstrous Svengali is that he is a Jew. And this fact of racial and cultural identity is an essential element of Du Maurier's Svengali, his primary identifying feature, the sole source of his malevolence. When Svengali intrudes upon the text, heretofore populated by proper British types, Du Maurier informs his reader that he is "a tall bony individual of any age between thirty and forty-five, of Jewish aspect, well-featured but sinister" (11). Nor does Du Maurier allow his reader (or the characters of the novel) to forget this essential identifying feature of his villainous "Oriental Israelite Hebrew Jew" (234) whose "real name is Adler" (165). Svengali displays the physical attributes stereotypically associated with the Jew: he is possessed of a "long shapely Hebrew nose" (230),[5] "thick, heavy, languid, lusterless black hair ... bold brilliant black eyes, with long heavy lids, a thin, sallow face, and a beard of burnt-up black, which grew almost from under his eyelids; and over it his moustache, a shade lighter, fell in two long spiral twists" (11). Additionally, "he was both tawdry and dirty in his person ... greasily, mattedly unkept..." (39). Nor does Svengali's behavior temper his offensively Jewish exterior. His manners, too, are those of the stereotypically obtrusive Jew: "He would either fawn or bully, and could be grossly impertinent. He had a kind of cynical humour, which was more offensive than amusing and always laughed at the wrong thing, at the wrong time, in the wrong place ... his egotism and conceit were not to be borne" (39).

Du Maurier is very careful to distinguish this physically and morally offensive foreigner from the Englishmen who are the heroes of his novel. Before Svengali sullies the novel with his entrance, Du Maurier works to establish in the persons of "three well-fed, well-contented Englishmen" (4), the various types of the "normal Englishman" (11) against whom Svengali is clearly opposed: Taffy, the Yorkshireman, "big ... [and] fair, with kind but choleric blue eyes, and the muscles of his brawny arm were strong as iron bands" (4); Sandy, the Scotsman, "with a face ... blithe and merry and well pleased" (6) and Little Billee, the small, delicate and sensitive artist "with large dark blue eyes, delicate, regular feathers ... he was also very graceful and well built, with very small hands and feet" (6).

And yet, in the description of Little Billee, some slippage occurs in Du Maurier's scheme, his attempt to separate and oppose the British and the foreign types; this slippage reveals the anxieties that inform the text. For Billie, the "winning and handsome" Englishman displays in his face:

> just a faint suggestion of some possible very remote Jewish ancestor — just a tinge of that strong, sturdy, irrepressible, indomitable, indelible blood which is of such priceless value in diluted homeopathic doses, like the dry white Spanish wine called montijo, which is not meant to be taken pure ... or like the famous bulldog strain, which is not beautiful in itself, and yet just for lacking a little of the same no greyhound can ever hope to be a champion. So, at least, I have been told by wine merchants and dog-fanciers.... Fortunately for the world, and especially for ourselves, most of us have in our veins at least a minim of that precious fluid, whether we know it or show it or not [6–7].

After the initial shock of reading this egregious passage, structured upon race prejudice and twisted eugenics, the modern reader may take comfort in noting the discomfort of the writer. Du Maurier, too, is shocked and troubled by the paradoxical situation that he formulates. His racist paradigm indicates a serious flaw: the vexing, the repulsive Jew is also the source of art. Indeed, it is Billee and not the other racially pure Englishmen, who succeeds in becoming a great artist just as it is Svengali, who "had been the best pianist of his time at the Conservatory in Leipsic" (39). To complete the stereotype, Du Maurier later tells us that Billee benefits in more practical ways from his healthy dose of Jewish blood; upon achieving financial success he becomes "an excellent man of business. That infinitesimal dose of the good old Oriental blood kept him straight.... He loved to make as much money as he could, that he might spend it royally in pretty gifts to his mother and sister..." (151).

We see, then, in Du Maurier's anxious description of little Billee, a demonstration of the anxieties generated by the "*peculiar nature* of the threatening otherness of the Jew.... Whereas in general the Other's most threatening aspect seems to reside in an identifiable difference, the most ominous aspect of the Jewish threat appeared as related to sameness. The Jews' adaptability seemed to efface all boundaries and to subvert the possibilities of natural confrontation. The Jew was the *inner* enemy *par excellence*."[6] This fear manifest in another fact that we learn about Billee: "Little Greek that he was, he worshipped the athlete..." (170). Since we already know that little Billee is also a little Jewish, the association in this phrase jolts us once again. For in this tiny character, Du Maurier appears to capture a synthesis between Hebrew and Hellene — the two cultures that Arnold works so hard to disentangle in his influential work *Culture and Anarchy* (1869). In his chapter on "Hebraism and Hellenism," Arnold sets up an opposition between Hebraism, associated with morality and devotion to work and mechanical accomplishment, and Hellenism, the cultivation of aesthetic and intellectual understanding of life. In confusing the two within the figure of Billee and in further confusing Arnold's distinction by associating the Hebrew with aesthetic virtuosity, the Greek with athletic prowess, Du Maurier exposes his fear of the destabilizing disruptiveness of Jewish blood — in even small doses — indicating his concern regarding Arnold's project to "absorb Hebrew culture in English culture [through a] kind of conversion."[7] Thus the assimilation that represented a positive move to the British liberal imagination — the hope expressed in the *Spectator* in 1868 (quoted by Modder): "Day by day families drop away, inter-marry, subside, often half consciously, into the mass and we see no guarantee that in a couple of centuries more if the world advances on its course, the Jews will be in any way a separate or a noticeable people, more distinct than Unitarians among ourselves"[8] — represents Du Maurier's great fear, a fear that the already elusive boundary between English Christian and Jewish Other will be effaced, as the blood of the latter infests that of the former, to a vexingly paradoxical good effect. Indeed, it is this problem that locates this late–Victorian realistic novel within the Gothic tradition, the tradition that is driven by the anxiety of separating the "normal" and socially acceptable subject from the horrifying otherness of the outside world.

In creating the inhumanly repulsive Jew, the foreigner equipped with quasi-supernatural powers, Du Maurier attempts to solve the problem of separation. Whereas Billee is a troubling figure, disrupting the distinct categories that buttress Du Maurier's theories of racial and cultural purity, Svengali is visibly and absolutely not English, in appearance or in behavior. Every time he opens his mouth to speak, he asserts his foreign and transgressive nature, mangling the English language with his "Hebrew-German accent" (88). His voice, in fact, clearly establishes that Svengali is not only non–English but non-human as well. He speaks with a "throaty rook's caw, his big yellow teeth baring themselves in a mongrel canine snarl" (88).[9]

Yet Du Maurier goes even further in establishing the otherness, the non–Englishness and non-humanness of Svengali, the Jew, working to establish securely the certainty of separate categories. Not only is Svengali the Jewish Other, Svengali is also established in the novel as the Satanic Other. Like Satan, Svengali is a fallen angel, glorious in heaven, a source of evil upon falling from heaven: "Svengali playing Chopin on the pianoforte ... was as one of the heavenly host.... Svengali walking up and down the earth seeking whom he might cheat, betray, exploit, borrow money from, make brutal fun of, bully if he dared, cringe to if he must — man, woman, child, or dog — was about as bad as they make 'em" (40). Du Maurier deploys his talent as a graphic artist to reinforce this theme. In the illustrations that accompany the text, Svengali is figured as the icono-graphic devil with a dark and pointed beard (17, 43) and pointed (Pan-like) ears (249) wielding his tool of power, the baton (202). The long hair "so offensive to the normal Englishman" (11), which associates him with the image of the disreputable artist–Jew, also refers to devil iconography; his "beard of burnt-up black" (11) announces that he hails from realms of fire. Wistrich's description of the iconography of the Devil in Christian art certainly resonates with the figure of Svengali: the Devil is "an unde-niable repulsive figure with an oversized head, bulging eyes, horns, a tail, and long, flamelike hair."[10]

Wistrich adds an additional fact of demonic iconography long used to link the Devil and the Jew that is most relevant to *Trilby*: "Moreover Jews, like the Devil, were also identified with the sin of unbridled lech-ery" (4). For it is Svengali's physical and spiritual possession of the beau-tiful and innocent Trilby that links him most explicitly to the figure of Satan. From the first, their interchanges are tainted by a troubling sexual subtext. In his light moments with Trilby, Svengali's "playfulness [is] like that of a cat with a mouse — a weird ungainly cat, and most unclean; a sticky, haunting, long, lean, uncanny, black spider-cat, if there is such an animal outside a bad dream" (70). In this description Du Maurier moves from describing Svengli as merely animalistically lecherous toward align-ing Svengali with the sexual potency of the dark supernatural, with the stuff of bad dreams. From Trilby's perspective, "he seemed to her a dread pow-erful demon, who ... oppressed and weighed on her like an incubus" (88). In evoking the image of the incubus, the demon who sexually possesses the sleeping woman, then, Du Maurier taps into two related tropes of anti–Semitism: Jew as demon; Jew as lecher.

Svengali is established as the lecherous Jew, unnaturally focused upon Trilby's body in a number of interchanges with her. His examination of Trilby's singing apparatus is conducted in language that at once decomposes and fetishes Trilby's body (a tendency Svengali shares with all the men who idolize Trilby in the novel) and sexualizes her singing organs:

> The roof of your mouth is like the dome of the Panthéon; there is room in it for "toutes les gloires de la France...." The entrance to your throat is like the middle porch of St. Sulpice when the doors are open for the faithful ... and not one tooth is missing — thirty-two British teeth as white as milk and as big as knuckle bones: and your little tongue is scooped out like the leaf of a pink peony, and the bridge of your nose is like the belly of a Stradivarius ... and inside your beautiful big chest the lungs are made of leather...! And you have a quick, soft, susceptible heart ... [48].

When Svengali is angered by Trilby's rejection of his attentions, he also fetishes and sexualizes her body, although in a more openly hostile way. He warns her that she will end up in the city morgue where "the cold water shall trickle, trickle, trickle all the way down your beautiful white body to your beautiful white feet until they turn green.... And people of all sorts, strangers, will stare at you through the big plate-glass window" including himself (72). Once Svengali takes charge of Trilby, abandoned as she is by her English champions, he takes full possession of her body. Svengali's eventual appropriation of Tribly is, in addition to the more explicit demonic possession that dominates the narrative, certainly sexual — she becomes his mistress although he refuses to marry her.

Du Maurier also clearly establishes Svengali as the demonic Jew in his relationship to Trilby. Svengali enacts Satanic possession of Trilby though his powers of "mesmerism" (50). When Trilby is overcome with "neuralgia in her eyes" (46),[11] Svengali cures her with his powers, demonstrating the control over her that those powers bring him: "Trilby was spellbound, and could not move," until "'I will now set her free,' said Svengali" (47). He reminds her of the continuing presence of his power, encouraging her to return to him for future cures, telling her, "'...*you shall see nothing, hear nothing, think of nothing but Svengali, Svengali, Svengali!*'" (50). Once Trilby becomes "La Svengali," the intermittent demonic possession becomes constant; she completely loses possession of herself to Svengali. After she leaves Billee and his friends because Billee's family deems her an unsuitable match (thereby consolidating her representation of the symbol of goodness and innocence), Trilby, friendless and poor, is taken under Svengali's wing. Although when we first hear Trilby sing, her performance is "grotesque" and "funny," "it was as though she could never once have deviated into tune, never once have hit upon a true note" (18);

upon becoming Svengali's disciple, Trilby is transformed into "La Svengali," whose singing is the toast of Europe. That this transformation is the result of demonic power rather than effective voice tutoring is made eminently clear. As Gecko, Svengali's closest comrade, reveals in responding to Taffy's comment that Tribly was an artist, "'Yes! But all that was Svengali, you know. Svengali was the greatest artist I ever met! Monsieur, Svengali was a demon, a magician!'" (284). Thus, the nature of Svengali's possession of Trilby locates him as the Devil; as he sings through her, she becomes the conventional possessed soul, speaking (singing) with the voice of the Devil. Possessed, Trilby is reduced to being a singing-machine — an instrument upon which Svengali plays, "the unconscious voice that Svengali sang with" (288).

Du Maurier further develops the Satanic trope in Svengali's possession of Trilby by gesturing to a number of Devil narratives. Svengali is Satan tempting Eve in Paradise: "One jarring figure in her little fool's paradise, a baleful and most ominous figure that constantly crossed her path, and came between her and the sun, and threw its shadow over her, and that was Svengali" (70). Svengali is also the Devil seducing Trilby with a Faustian bargain: her body and soul in exchange for her musical success. In hearing Trilby sing as "La Svengali" the narrator recounts, "It was Faust! It was the most terrible and pathetic of all possible human tragedies..." (205).[12]

Significantly, the set of related anti–Semitic tropes— Jew as lecher; Jew as demon — that Du Maurier draws upon for his representation of Svengali is also later tapped and conflated in "Hitler's chilling fantasy about the devilish Jew seeking to bastardize the white Germanic race and poison its blood through sexual intercourse" (Wistrich 7). The continuing power of these related twin tropes serves to identify a specific anxiety generated by the repulsive and yet compelling Svengali: the threat of miscegenation, referred to in the description of Billee. As Rosenberg argues, "the crime at the heart of the novel is not really one of occult sorcery but the specifically 'Jewish' crime to which the Germans have since given the name *Rassenschande*, the ... mating of the inferior racial type with the higher" (7).[13]

The Diabolic Jew in History

As Hitler's twentieth-century reinvention of the trope of the lecherous and demonic Jew indicates, there is much in this representation of the Jew that anchors it to the real and actual world of history; the trope thus seems to be very much at home in the realistic novel, as it was at home in the actual world of history and culture in late-nineteenth-century Europe.

By the mid-nineteenth century, Jews in Western Europe had achieved emancipation, that is "removal of civil disabilities."[14] Modder elaborates: "Eventually, late in the nineteenth century, through the influence of the liberal and more tolerant elements among both Jews and gentiles, the English Jews emerged into political emancipation and social acceptance" (Modder 347). As a result, the population of Jews in England expanded: in 1800, there were eight thousand Jews in London; by 1900 the Jewish population of London was 160,000 (348). Modder goes on to quote Dean Milman's *History of the Jews* (1870): by his time "'all the higher offices of the city of London have been filled by Jews.'" France too, an important setting in *Trilby*, experienced an upsurge in the Jewish population in the nineteenth century. "Around the time of the French Revolution, there were 40,000 Jews in France; one hundred years later, there were close to 100,000. The rapid increase in number and influence of the Jewish population led to the prevalence of the anti–Semitic notion that the Jews were 'les rois de l'époque.'"[15]

This, of course, indicates the paradoxical problem of Jewish success in Europe; as Jews became more successful and more visible, they became a larger and more inviting target for anti–Semitism, evoking sentiments that have been present in Western culture since early Christian times. In fact, it was not until the emancipation and attendant success of the Jews that the concept of anti–Semitism was updated and reified. Carmichael notes that, although after the emancipation of the Jews, the "'Jewish Question' preoccupied the summits of opinion in the mid-nineteenth century, it was not until the last third that broad gauge opposition to the Jews began to be organized.... The process was signaled by the coinage of a new word, 'anti–Semitism,' in the 1870's. Before the middle of the nineteenth century the notion of 'race' had not meant much."[16] That is, Judaism, before the inauguration of "anti–Semitism," was identified correctly as a religion. Then Judeophobia began to take on racial overtones; "the word 'Semite' almost immediately came to mean nothing more than a Jew" (126). This new quasi-scientific racial definition of the Jew — "the word 'anti–Semitism' [was] polite and socially acceptable ... in harmony with the scientific temper of the age" (129) — "made the whole question of 'reforming' the Jews downright senseless: if they were condemned to pernicious inferiority by their own biology, that is, their *nature*, what could be done about it? The race view eliminated all hope" (130). Wistrich, too, notes the intransigence of the racial category[17]: "They were the counter-type, the paradigmatic 'other' race unassimilable by definition" (3). This quasi-scientific version of Judeophobia also served to naturalize a hatred that had existed in various forms throughout Western culture — giving it an acceptable form and meaning in a newly enlightened world. "When theology becomes obsolete through the cooling of faith and atheistic indifference, the Jews become *pure* Evil.... They no longer *meant* anything [theologically] ... the Jews were simply monsters and nothing else" (Carmichael 133).

The construction of the Jews as scientifically and racially defined (as opposed to theologically defined) monsters served a useful political purpose in the formation of national identity, a topic of great interest in nineteenth-century Europe. Ragussis notes that "by depicting the persecution of the Jews, including the attempt to convert them, at a critical moment in history — the founding of the English nation —*Ivanhoe* located 'the Jewish question' at the heart of English national identity" (12). Shapiro notes a similar tendency in the formation of German national identity: "For nineteenth-century Germans, so unsure of their own 'Germanness,' the Jewish Question was ultimately the German Question. It was, in effect, another way of asking 'What is German': and receiving the satisfying answer —'whatever is not Jewish.'"[18] Henri Zukier's essay "The Transformation of Hatred" also shows the uses of anti–Semitism as a means of constructing national identity.[19]

It is not, however, a mundane variety of race hatred that makes itself available to abject the Jew and thereby define national identity in nineteenth-century Europe. The version of anti–Semitism revived for nationalistic purposes is, in fact, the culmination of "a rich bimillennial tradition that went back to the Gospels and their depiction of the Jews as a pariah people, as the murderers of Christ ... in league with Satan himself" (Wistrich 3). As Wistrich suggests, abjection of the Jew through association with the Devil has a long tradition within the history of ideas and of Western culture. Indeed, the Jews have the dubious distinction of being the first group set up as the Other, and the demonic Other, in the Western tradition; the representation of the Jew as Other works, in fact, as the paradigm for representations of other abjected groups that follow.[20] Many scholars note that this pattern begins during the time of early Christianity — another moment when a group, the sect of early Christians, is seeking to define itself in opposition to the Other, the Jew. Pagels, arguing that the idea of Satan is largely Christian and that the figure of Satan takes on importance at the time of the early Christians, examines "the *social* implications of the figure of Satan: how he is invoked to express human conflict and to characterize human enemies within our own religious tradition ... Satan as a reflection of how we perceive ourselves and those we call 'others.'

Satan, has, after all made a kind of profession out of being the 'other' and so Satan defines negatively what we think of a human" (xviii). This, Pagels argues, is part of a larger pattern, the "virtually universal practice of calling one's own people human and 'dehumanizing' others" (xix).

As Pagels indicates, this *dehumanization* of the Other is often bound up with the *demonization* of the Other. And this is certainly the pattern in the case of the figure of the Jew. Since the social and cultural categories were inextricably interwined with the religious categories in the time of the early Christians, the association of the Other with Satan, the theological, supernatural Other, is a logical next step: if "we," early Christians, are on God's side, then "they," the Jews (and all enemies of Christ), must be on the side of Satan. And once set, the pattern endures: Pagel argues that "because Christians as they read the gospels have characteristically identified themselves with the disciples, for some two thousand years they have also identified their opponents, whether Jews, pagans, or heretics, with forces of evil, and so with Satan" (Pagels xxiii). Wistrich too argues for the endurance of this pattern: "In the lower depths of Western culture, in its collective subconscious, the kinship of the Jews with Satan was firmly established by the late Middle Ages" (3–4).

This theological cast, then, allows for a mystical, supernatural framing of the category of otherness. Indeed, a great many scholars notice that Judeophobia, the abjection of the Jewish Other is frequently framed as what Carmichael characterizes as "mystical anti–Semitism" (vii),[21] unique among outsider-hatred in its associations with supernatural potency, with "the world of God and the world of the Devil. Since the Jews have not accepted the Christian God, they have ipso facto been arrayed alongside the Devil in Christendom.... It is surely this concept of essential Evil, plus occult power, that distinguishes anti–Semitism from all other group hatreds" (viii–ix).[22] Wistrich's collection, *Demonizing the Other: Anti-semitism, Rascism, and Xenophobia* is a useful addition to this discussion, working to contextualize the tendency to cast the Other as demon. In his Introduction, Wistrich also distinguishes the "sacral, quasi-metaphycial quality of anti–Semitism" (2), the demonization of the Jew, the association of the Jew with the Satanic Other.

Susan Shapiro's essay, "The Uncanny Jew" works to further clarify the utility of the trope of Jew as Satanic Other in the Western tradition. Shapiro teases out the tendency in Western Christian culture to see the figure of the Jew as vexing categorical certainties of identity. Shapiro evokes the story of the Wandering Jew, that construes the Jew as a "living corpse, a dead man who has not yet died."[23] In Shapiro's formulation, then, the Jew is figured as the uncanny Other, "as occupying an indistinguishable and undecideable borderline between life and death" (64). Associating her model of the figure of the Jew with Freud's representation of the uncanny, Shapiro defines Uncanny Jews "as spectral, disembodied spirits lacking a national home and, thus, as unwelcome guests and aliens wandering into and within other peoples' homes, disrupting and haunting them, making them '*Unheimliche*'" (65).

This fear of the uncanny — that which transgresses protective categories, that which seems like but is, in fact, different — translates in political discourse into the fear of assimilation, the fear that the Jew will no longer be identifiable, transgressing the borders between Christian and Jew, a fear that we have identified in *Trilby*. Shapiro quotes Alain Finkielkraut: "The more they hid their Jewishness, the more terrifying they became to others. As Jewish appearance gave less and less hint of ethnic background, the evils charged to Jews by anti–Semitic opinion grew worse and worse.... For the myth of Jewish omnipotence to take hold, the people of Zion first had to pass unnoticed, merge with the general populace."[24]

It is then possible to see the potent appeal of the association of the Jew and Satan in the nineteenth century, when the uncanniness of the Jew, always capable of unsettling categories of life and death, of Christian and Other, becomes even more powerful through the dual processes of emancipation and assimilation. If the uncanny Jew represents the resistance of the Jew to the containment of categories, the Satanic Jew is the ideal solution to this particular Jewish Problem. Framed as Satan, the quintessential, visible Other, the Jew is less able to secretly infiltrate and disrupt categories. Thus the identification with Satan is a strategy to identify and contain the Jew. The figure of Satan endures, thus, as a way to contain that elusive Jewish Other, the people who are "*inclassable*, outside the natural hierarchy of races, beyond the human pale. Not even a race strictly speaking (since they were 'unnatural'), perverse, demonic, the intriniscially evil 'other' — in a word, the Jews [who] were the Devil incarnate in human form" (Wistrich 3).

Thus, when used for political purposes, the figure of the Jew as Satan is a practical and utilitarian solution to a political and social problem. It is this construct to which Du Maurier refers when he creates a monstrously diabolic Jew to inhabit his realistic novel. In the figure of Svengali, Du Maurier creates a seemingly realistic reflection of the political realities of his time and place. In constructing the Jew as demonic Other, Du Maurier relies less on artifice than on convention, less on creation than on mimesis.

The political efficacy and endurance of this trope, its potency in the actual world of history and politics, during Du Maurier's time, becomes visible in the Dreyfus case that emerged in the year 1894, significantly the year in which *Trilby* was published. As narrated by Carmichael, "At the end of the nineteenth century the 'Dreyfus Affair' highlighted and focused the tension surrounding the Jews.... Captain Alfred Dreyfus, son of a rich textile manufacturer, had a position in the French War Ministry; in 1894 he was charged with treason (selling military secrets to the Germans); on 22 December he was convicted and sentenced to life imprisonment on Devil's Island.... The tone of the press, however, was unusually vindictive; its theme was that Dreyfus symbolized the inherent disloyalty of French Jews to France. Anti-Semitic elements led the chorus of outrage.... This coupled with severe doubt raised by extraordinary irregularities in the trial, created a violent counter-movemement.... For twelve years all France ... was polarized.... Dreyfus's innocence [was] demonstrated a few years later..." (140–41). In the enactment of the Dreyfus Affair, it is possible to see the political use of the trope of Satanic Jew. Wistrich notes, "the myth of the all-powerful Jew ... acquired a new lease on life: so did the medieval fantasies of the Jew as Antichrist, agent of Satan and corruptor of morals. The traitor Dreyfuss [was construed] as a reincarnation of Judas" (9). The mechanics of the Dreyfus Affair demonstrate, then, the naturalization of the demonization of the Jew in nineteenth-century Europe, the translation of millennia of theological and supernatural tropology into normative political practice. It was, in part, the brave demystification of this process on the part of Dreyfus supporters (including Émile Zola) that led to the ultimate reversal of the sentence.

We can see then, that in the actual world inhabited by George Du Maurier, there was nothing at all unnatural in figuring the Jew as Satan. This trope informed political discourse and action with little resistance as it had for thousands of years. Even after the figure of Satan loses its supernatural potency in a post–Enlightenment world, long practice had worked to naturalize the trope. As Carmichael suggests, "mystical anti–Semitism, even when secularized remains anchored in the division of the universe into the the Light and the Dark" (203).

The Diabolic Jew in the Realistic Novel

Because the Devil has been demystified by the Enlightenment and because the trope of Jew as Devil had been naturalized by long use in the actual political and social world, the presence of Svengali, the Satanic Jew, does not immediately seem to vex the realism of the text that frames him; Du Maurier seems to accomplish a neat balancing act, managing to adhere to the imperatives of realism while simultaneously injecting his text with a whiff of the sensational and always entertaining "uncanny" (201—Du Maurier's word). Just as the British types or stereotypes convey a realistic portrait of expatriate artists in the Paris of la vie bohème, so does Du Maurier's portrait of Svengali draw upon the accepted tropology of the Jew, invoking the strategies of realism and the contexts of history to naturalize and encode the figure of supernatural, transcendent evil — to create a realistic representation of the Jewish Devil, the figure of the Other contained by realism, and by the realistic text.

The commitment of Du Maurier to realism, the dominant literary mode of his time, is evident. With the exception of Svengali, his characters are all realistically drawn. Du Maurier takes great care in locating his particular characters within a precise place and time. Paris and London are drawn with great visual particularity and Du Maurier, or his narrator, is quite insistent on locating the narrative in a particular time. The reader is told repeatedly that the first episodes of the book occur in "the fifties" (68, 86). At one point the narrator explicitly addresses the need of the reader to keep the chronology of the narrative in mind: "The fin de siècle reader ... must remember that it happened in the fifties" (114). As this instruction indicates, Du Maurier is also careful to locate his *reader* in time. He also takes care in indicating the time of the *writing*; describing a picture painted during the 1850s episode in Paris, the narrator writes, "Last year ... (more than thirty-six years after it was painted)..." (139). The chronology of the narrative is thus carefully framed between the late 1850s and late 1890s. And within the narrative, Du Maurier is careful to sprinkle various markers that indicate the exact placement of his narrative in historical time: his favorite "'cinq ans après,'" "in emulation of the good Dumas" (185). The sense of the great obligation Du Maurier displays to the imperatives of realism is best revealed in a statement of the narrator. Contemplating the closure of his narrative, he expresses his subordination to the demands of truth and realism, despite his own wishes: "It is a great temptation ... to enrich [the] hero beyond the dreams of avarice and provide him with a title and a castle and park...!" — by killing off the many relatives who stand between him and his fortune — in "a Shakespearean holocaust.... But truth is inexorable" (278).

Like other realist writers who dwell on the superficial appearance of things, Svengali sets his narrative among artists and concerns itself with problems of visual art. Set in the art world of Paris,[25] Trilby is suffused with images of the pictorial arts. The eponymous character is a sometime model, "she surpassed all other models … and was equally unconscious of self with her clothes on or without!" (64). Du Maurier's proper English heroes are all visual artists—and all realist artists as well. Du Maurier faithfully re-presents their art: Sandy's "lifelike Spanish toreador[s] (5), Taffy's realism's (for Taffy was a realist)" (9) and Billee's "funny little pen-and-ink sketches … so lifelike, so real, that you could almost hear the beautiful things they said" (9). Indeed, *Trilby* follows a pattern similar to that noted by Byerly who notices that in Eliot's novels "the association of individual characters with specific arts produces a moral hierarchy in which visual art is exposed as a detached and static simplification of reality, theatrical art is linked with a dangerous deception of self and others, and music alone is capable of representing truth."[26] Like Eliot,[27] Du Maurier creates a moral hierarchy of the arts, differing from Eliot, however, in his more predictable ranking of the various art forms, valorizing the visual arts, as he does, in his realistic novel. In *Trilby,* the "good" characters are associated with the visual arts. Evil and decadence typify the musical arts and their most visible practitioners in the book: Svengali and his assistant, Gecko. Byerly's reading helps to define Du Maurier's association of music with moral turpitude by noting the contemporary significance of music as posing the threat of the loss of self-possession: "The mesmeric control that Svengali has over Trilby's music in Du Maurier's novel is a late manifestation of the nineteenth-century cultural preoccupation with the idea of music as a kind of sexual hypnotism. The popular movements of mesmerism and spiritualism were both tangentially associated with music" (139).[28] Another way to account for Du Maurier's hierarchy is to contextualize it within the anti–Semitism that suffuses the novel. From the earliest times of the emancipation and assimilation of the Jews into European culture, Jewish contributions to the arts were more prominent in the musical arts. This discrepancy was likely due to the roots of Jewish culture that valorized music in liturgical forms while disparaging the visual arts as a violation of the second commandment prohibition of graven images. Du Maurier's valorization of the visual arts, the arts most distant from Jews, over the musical arts, the forms associated with the Jews,[29] and his moralization of this hierarchy is one of the strategies he deploys in discrediting his Jewish villain.

Yet despite all this evidence for the moral, artistic and economic power of visual representation through painting and drawing (a valorization of the visual that promotes the realistic project), the most powerful visual image in the novel is a photograph of Svengali, which mysteriously appears from beyond the grave. After Svengali dies, as Trilby lingers on her deathbed, depleted by the sudden withdrawal of his artistic and psychic energies, she receives a mysterious package containing "a large photograph, framed and glazed of Svengali ... looking straight out of the picture, straight at you.... His big black eyes were full of stern command" (271). The shock of the "you" is the first indication of the power of this photograph; until now, the reader has been politely addressed in the third person, as "the reader." Yet here, not only is Trilby implicated in the glance of her mentor — and of course, Svengali's power in life was located in the power of his gaze — so too, is the reader.

In the photograph, then, we see the vexing and supernatural uncanniness of Svengali as well as his power: the photograph effaces the distinction between reality and representation, working to destabilize the realism of Du Maurier's text. Indeed the photograph is ultimately not a representation of Svengali but Svengali himself. Like Svengali, the photograph is of dubious Eastern origins and has wandered though Europe before arriving at its destination. "From the postmarks on the case, [the photograph] seems to have traveled all over Europe to London, out of some remote province in eastern Russia — out of the mysterious East! The poisonous East — birthplace and home of an ill wind that blows nobody good" (271). The photograph further effaces the distinction between realistic representation and real object by enacting Svengali's power over Trilby. Trilby speaks to the photograph, responding to it as if it were addressing her. As in life, the photograph of Svengali — as seen by Trilby although not by the narrator or the reader — commands her to sing. Addressing the mute photograph, Trilby asks it, "Encore une fois?"[30] and responds, "Bon! Je veux bien! Avec la voix blanche alors...," continuing in this vein, seemingly repeating the musical instructions that Svengali in his photographic form is conveying to her through his photographed, still powerful eyes. More evidence of the power of the photographic representation of Svengali: when Trilby begins to sing, her voice has the old power given to it by Svengali in his life. "It was as if breath were unnecessary for so little voice as she was using, though there was enough of it to fill the room — to fill the house — to drown her small audience in holy, heavenly sweetness" (272). After her uncanny solo, Trilby speaks her last words before dying, again addressed to Svengali: "Et maintenant, mon ami, *je suis fatiguée — bon soir!*" and a final "'*Svengali ... Svengali ... Svengali...*'" (272), echoing, ventriloquistically, Svengali's early spell (50). In her dying repetition of the spell that Svengali uses to enact his mesmeric powers over her, Trilby dies as she has lived, the empty vessel of Svengali's ventriloquistic voice. It is Svengali's troubling power that endures, mysteriously and supernaturally located in the photograph, the image that *should* operate as the icon of realism.

Nancy Armstrong's recent study on realism — that accounts for the pervasiveness of realism, with its valorization of objective, visual representation during the late nineteenth century, as exemplified by the valorization of the visual arts in *Trilby*— also works to explain the power of Svengali's photograph. Armstrong connects the move toward literary realism with "the sudden ubiquity of photographic images in the culture at large..." (6). The rise of photography during the period of Victorian fiction, she suggests, changed the terms of meaning from the word to the image: "'the image'— or more accurately, a differential system thereof— supplanted writing as the grounding of fiction" (3). Literary realism prevailed within Armstrong's paradigm because it "referenced a world of objects that either had been or could be photographed ... [supplying readers] ... with [the] kinds of visual information" (7), for which they had developed a desire by virtue of the dominance of the visual image in popular culture. Thus the move to realism, a "fiction [that] equated seeing with knowing and made visual information the basis for the intelligibility of a verbal narrative" (7).

Thus the uncanny power of Svengali's photograph: it violates the equation of seeing with knowing that Armstrong locates in the realist tradition. Svengali's final appearance, in which he is reincarnated as a photograph, in which he exerts his now explicitly uncanny power, expresses a number of complementary anxieties, the coalescing of new fears anchored by old anxieties. We see new fears engendered by the new technologies of reproduction, the fear that these technologies may be used to replicate evil, evil that can transcend death and endure beyond death. And yet, this new set of fears is still encoded in the old way, as the fear of the Satanic Jew, the Wandering Jew, the uncanny Jew whose evil evades death. We see thus the convergence of the new and old anxieties engendered by realistic visual representation: the fear that the image is a ghost of sorts, that like more quaint ghosts, the photographs of the dead have the power to continue their haunting influence upon the living. In the image of the photograph, then, Du Maurier deploys the anxiety-provoking figure of the uncanny Jew — the figure that already vexes the problem of genre and category — to complicate the questions regarding the distinction between representation and reality that haunt the realist tradition: "how can art evoke reality?"[31] (Byerly 2). That is: how can representation capture and reenact reality without losing its privileged status as art? How can a literary mode that valorizes the actual, exist as a literary mode at all unless it creates though convention and artifice, some separation from reality?

Many critics note that the realist text is always a little unstable, a little inconsistent, struggling to maintain its own generic identity by fending

off the temptations of Romantic literature, keeping at bay the messy com-
plications of the Gothic and of revolutionary politics. There is a critical
consensus that the movement toward realism in the late nineteenth century was—as George Levine suggests in his influential critical analysis—
"a self-conscious rejection of certain conventions of literary representation
and of their implications" (5), "in pursuit of the unattainable unmediated
reality" (8). In particular, the reaction was against the subjective excesses
of the Romantic tradition, including the Gothic mode, that had typified
literature of the late eighteenth century and early nineteenth century, characterized, as Levine notes, by "excesses, both stylistic and narrative of various kinds of romantic, exotic or sensational literature" (5). As a result,
the realist writer has to work to accomplish generic containment, resulting in a focus upon boundaries—generic and otherwise—that is paradoxically opposed to the realistic project. Thus realism, although claiming
an unmediated encounter with reality, needs to embrace the boundaries
of art, turning to the limits of art like plot and closure to convey reality
that is never determined by neat plot or closure. It is this problem that
Lloyd locates as the "radical uncertainty at the heart of realism as it continually questions itself in the process of creating relative order out of a
world in social and cultural flux" (11–12). Kearns also defines the unsettling paradox at the center of the realist project: "one must guard against
reproducing exactly the effects of reality, with its welter of detail, its bewil-
dering subversions of expectation, and its capricious tendency toward a
coincidentally perfect order that would embarrass any artist worth her
salt. One the other hand, one must avoid a translation so aestheticized as
to arrest reality's disorderly conduct" (51).

   The self-imposed order of realism, then, forces the realist writer to
exclude some realities from the text, excluding from the text all transcendent and extra-natural planes, planes that are deemed "unrealistic" by
post–Enlightenment imperatives. Jenkins notes that when "the novelist
has to fall back on a negative picture of the desolation of a world without
God, it seems clear that this problem had less to do with theology than
with the technical difficulty of fitting God into the realist conventions" (6).
As we see, in *Trilby,* not only is God exiled from the realist text, the Devil
too is dispossessed from this man-made Paradise in which there is no place
for transcendent good or evil. Lloyd suggests that a self-conscious awareness of this dilemma results in a realistic tradition that is intrigued by that
which lies beyond the limits of realism, that which is Other to the realistic text (11), revealing an unwitting interest in "the monster" that in
Levine's formulation, realists fear and reject (Levine 328). Kearn suggests
that the realistic impulse to contain the transcendent, to "curb the impulse

to aggrandize such anarchic power as transcendent," results in displacement of the ineffable and unrealistic, transcendent upon the figure of the human though demonized Other, "this displacement of the enigma onto the Other" (82). This is, indeed, what Du Maurier attempts with the figure of Svengali: to introduce transcendent evil into his text in the figure of the Satanic Jew while at the same time containing this evil within the bounds of realism: the Jew, after all, is already figured as evil within political and cultural discourse. And indeed, Svengali does diminish and contain the eternal Wandering Jew; Svengali dies in a quite satisfyingly public manner, sitting in his box at the theater while Trilby performs.

It is not surprising to observe that Du Maurier's strategy of introducing and containing transcendent evil within the realistic project, resonates with Henry James's project since James was involved with the inception of the novel. In her Introduction, Showalter quotes from a conversation with James in the late 1880s, later recalled by Du Maurier, in which Du Maurier offered the plot of *Trilby* to James. "But James would not take it; he said it was too valuable a present and that I must write the story myself" (Showalter xii).[32] Rosenberg's version is, given the ventriloquistic nature of Svengali's power, even more telling. In declining Du Maurier's offer of plot, James "invited Du Maurier 'to speak for himself'" (240). The offer to James makes sense because of the Jamesian concerns expressed in *Trilby*: the problems of the expatriate exposed to the evils of the continent; the problems of personal influence and the consideration of the struggle between transcendent good and transcendent evil in the real and realistic world.[33] It is likely, however, that the James version of *Trilby* would have looked somewhat different. For while Du Maurier, looking backward to archaic forms, takes the route of locating evil within the figure of the Jew, already conveniently encoded as evil by the dominant culture, James tends to anticipate the insights of modernism — and the lessons of the twentieth century — in psychologizing and "interiorizing" evil, in suggesting that the true source of fearsome evil lies within. Thus, for example, the reader of "The Turn of the Screw" is never quite sure if the evil is located in the ghosts that the governess sees or in her psyche. So while Du Maurier contains and localizes evil (or attempts to do so) by fixing it within an easy stock figure of evil, the Satanic Jew, James complicates and problematizes the nature of evil in the modern world. In this, it is possible to see that, of the two constructions of evil, James's is, paradoxically, more real, though less superficially visual. Certainly the world, unmediated by prejudice and convention, reveals more instances of ambiguous evil, as exemplified by James's governess and her ghosts, than of absolute evil, as exemplified by Du Maurier's Svengali. Seen in this light, Svengali indeed troubles the realism of Du Maurier's text, problematizing, indeed, a realism that considers surface reality while suppressing the internal reality of human consciousness.

Turning to Dickens's Fagin (*Oliver Twist* 1837–9), it might be tempting to argue that the realist text may contain the figure of the Satanic Jew without compromising its adherence to realism. Certainly Fagin is no less Satanic than Svengali. Dickens deploys the conventional Devil iconography — red hair, fire, fork — when introducing him to the reader, as he cooks over a fire. Fagin is "a very old shrivelled Jew, whose villainous-looking and repulsive face was obscured by a quantity of matted red hair ... [with a] toasting fork in hand" (105). Many critics notice the association between Fagin and Satan. Rosenberg notes: "the epithet 'merry old gentleman,' which is repeatedly applied to Fagin, is still a well-known euphemism for the devil" (125). Many critics also draw attention to the visual nature of Dicken's description. Armstrong notes, "of all the characters in [*Oliver Twist*], only Fagin receives much in the way of pictorial elaboration" (134). "There is just enough visual detail in [the introductory] passage to call up the traditional figure of the Jew [and] relocate that figure at the infernal center of the nineteenth-century slum..." (135). Like other critics, Armstrong focuses on the visual complement of "the Cruikshank illustrations for the novel [that] operate in a supplementary relationship to Dickens's prose in lending the characters of the urban underworld the picturesque qualities that belong, at this point in cultural history, strictly to the domain of popular illustration and cartoon" (135). Kelly (117) and Rosenberg both amplify the significance of the visual representation of Fagin in drawing connections between the Cruikshank illustrations of Fagin and Du Maurier's drawings of Svengali. Rosenberg writes, "Detail for detail the two Jews run equally true to type: the same unkempt hair, the same bushy eyebrows and penetrating stare, the same protruding Hapsburg lip. The noses are beaked in the same way, not so much jutting out as resting flat against the mustaches.... The beards, too, are of identical cut, straggling Vandykes. The fingers which Fagin strikes cunningly against the side of his nose and those with which Svengali beckons toward Trilby are the same long, bony, by no means unbeautiful fingers" (234).

Yet although both Fagin and Svengali share the same visual diabolism and share the same plot functions—"Jews often act within Victorian fiction as a kind of principle of accident around which the relatively predictable unfolding of plot events is suddenly made strange and unpredictable"[34]— ultimately they are distinguished by their actions and by their contexts. For although Fagin may *look* like "a wholly sinister demon" (Rosenberg 126), he *acts* like a common criminal — admittedly a sinister, scurrilous scoundrel — but a realistically comprehensible scoundrel nonetheless. Rather than centering supernatural evil upon a single figure, as Du Maurier does, Dickens decenters evil and the supernatural. The evil Jew is matched, and even surpassed, by a number of other evil characters, including the murderous Bill Sikes. The supernaturally uncanny Jew is eclipsed by the "shade of Agnes" whose hovering spirit closes Dickens's narrative. And, on the level of plot, Fagin's evil is successfully contained by the mundane power of the state; he is imprisoned and hanged for his crimes, reduced by his punishment to a pathetic, crazed, and quite plausible, old Jewish man. And so Fagin does not trouble the realism of the text that contains him as Svengali does.

It is ultimately Du Maurier's construction of the Jew as Satan, the cynosure of supernatural evil, that taps into the inherent instability of the realist form, ultimately wrenching *Trilby* from the realm of realism and relocating it back to the world of the Gothic novel. It is Svengali's extended metaphor of Jew as Satan — the Jew who is not merely one evil character among others but the only evil and supernatural character in the text — that sets Du Maurier's Satanic Jew apart. And it is his insistent demonizing of the Jew that ultimately disables the realism of Du Maurier's text.

This is not to say that every reference to a Gothic trope results in a Gothic text. As *Oliver Twist* indicates, it is possible to populate a text with the occasional ghost and with characters who are excessively good or excessively evil — thus referencing the Gothic struggle — without losing sight of the realism of the text. In fact, Du Maurier deploys another conventional Gothic trope, the motif of the double — a trope with a long history of mediating between the fantastic and the realistic — without disabling the realism of his text. Ann Radcliffe, reputed as a mother of the Gothic tradition, often deploys the motif of the double to satisfy the competing demands of Gothic fantasy and realism, to introduce unsettling horror into the narrative in a manner that is concordant with the imperatives of realistic fiction.[35] Radcliffe uses the double to construct her famous "explained supernatural" — asserting to her reader that the uncanny hauntings of her books are explicable in a rational world governed by science and reason. Indeed, Radcliffe's deployment of the trope of the double evokes a very real and justifiable horror of her time, the fear of losing one's self (in fact, the fate suffered by Trilby). Thus, for example, in *The Mysteries of Udolpho* (1794), Radcliffe sets up the textually superfluous Blanche, living in the Chateau-le-Blanc, the bleached white counter to Radcliffe's protagonist, Emily, who has just escaped from the dark Castle Udolpho. Blanche serves no function in the plot but she does serve as the uncanny double who creates a disturbing sense of unreality and instability raising very frightening questions about individuality and identity without dislodging Radcliffe's text from the domain of realism.[36] Closer to Du Maurier's time and mode of writing, Wilkie Collins demonstrates an instance of an uncanny double who haunts a realist text without threatening its realism. In Collins's *The Woman in White* (1860), the title suggests the doubled uncanniness of the text for there are several women in white in his novel. It is the death of the one: Anne Catherick — who dies while identified as the other, Laurie Fairlie — that provides the text its moment of realist ghostliness. For when Walter, the narrator, goes to the tomb that is ostensibly Laura's, he finds Laura herself in front of him. Collins, then, uses the technique of the double to haunt his text with a rationally plausible and real ghost.

Thus Du Maurier's use of the trope of the double to insert a dose of the supernatural sanctioned by the imperatives of realism, poses no immediate threat to the realism of his text.

There are, in fact, two doubled characters in *Trilby*: Svengali and Trilby. Trilby under Svengali's control is an *other* Trilby, a (musical) instrument of Svengali who looks like Trilby but sounds like Svengali. Trilby's thoughts demonstrate this: "When I am the singer ... I am *Svengali...*" (205). It is this doubling of Trilby — the independent "real" Trilby and the Trilby under Svengali's control — that accounts for the confusion of the friends as to whether La Svengali is actually Trilby. After La Svengali, who looks like Trilby, ignores Billee, the Laird says, "It's not Tribly — I swear! She could *never have done that* — it's not *in* her! And it's another face altogether..." (225). As the friends suspect, the Trilby they see as La Svengali is not Trilby, "in fact, our Trilby was *dead*" (289). As Gecko, Svengali's assistant explains:

> *There were two Trilbys.* There was the Trilby you knew, who could not sing one single note in tune ... with a word — Svengali could turn her into the other Trilby, *his* Trilby — and make her do whatever he liked ... she suddenly became an unconscious Trilby of marble who could produce wonderful sounds ... and think his thoughts and wish his wishes ... that was the Trilby he taught how to sing.... That Trilby was just a singing-machine — an organ to play upon — an instrument of music ... a voice, and nothing more — just the unconscious voice that Svengali sang with [288].

Several critics suggest that Trilby is not the only character doubled in Du Maurier's novel. Indeed, the image of the photograph indicates the duality of his figure — real and represented. Kelly cites Edmund Wilson's essay "The Jews," in which Wilson notes that the figure of Svengali plays the "dual role of the Jew" appearing as a realistic person, a European artist, and then again "as a malignant devil, whose malignancy is hardly accounted for" (Kelly 117). Rosenberg cites Shaw who criticizes Beerbohm Tree's stage production for showing only the villainous and diabolic Svengali, ignoring "'the original Svengali, the luckless artist-cad'" (Rosenberg 248). And yet, Shaw's characterization of the original Svengali indicates the flaw in reading Svengali as a doubled figure. For although the visual figure of Svengali is doubled by the photograph, the moral figure of Svengali is not truly doubled as Shaw suggests: there is no "good" Svengali and "bad." Instead, we see shadings of the bad Svengali, a Svengali who occupies the spectrum of evil from the pole of the realistically scurrilous, in the Faginian mode, to the pole of the supernaturally evil in the Satanic mode (and it is this doubleness with which Du Maurier attempts to straddle the world of realism and the world of the Gothic). Svengali is actually centered and unified in his commitment to evil, like the Devil who is solely evil and who is in possession of all that is evil. Like Satan, Svengali represents the concentration and distillation of evil: he is not one of several evil characters; he does not reveal a benevolent side; he is the sole force of evil.

It is, then, this model of absolute evil — and the character who emblematizes it — that dislocates *Trilby* from the realist tradition and relocates it into the Gothic tradition, where the essential struggle is always between absolute goodness incarnate and absolute evil incarnate. Even more precisely, the character of Svengali relocates *Trilby* into the Gothic tradition in which absolute evil is frequently incarnated by the Devil himself. Indeed, the Devil is the central evil character in a number of influential Gothic novels including Charlotte Dacre's *Zofloya* (1806) and Matthew Lewis's *The Monk* (1796). Significantly, in both these novels, the Devil takes the form of a marginalized member of society — a black slave in *Zofloya*; a woman in *The Monk* — thus contextualizing Svengali's representation of the Devil as incarnate in the Jew.

Svengali's evocation of the figure of the Wandering Jew is another indication of his place in the Gothic tradition, in which the Wandering Jew appears as a version of the Devil, "his alliance with the superhuman powers ensured him the distinct respect which nature [and the Gothic] traditionally pays to supernature" (Rosenberg 245). The Wandering Jew, as Modder notes, "curiously persisted in English literature from an early age" (353), appearing in a number of Gothic texts including William Godwin's *St. Leon* (1779) and Lewis's *The Monk* (1795). The mid-nineteenth-century publication of the translation of Eugene Sue's *Wandering Jew* and subsequent stage adaptations revived this supernaturally immortal figure, resulting, if not culminating, in the figure of Svengali, figured by Rosenberg as "the Wandering Jew driving about London in a gilded landau, with a nice Gibson girl in tow" (235).

Another instance of a late–Victorian realist text that unleashes the Gothic in the form of Satan is Marie Corelli's *The Sorrows of Satan* (1895 — the year after the publication of *Trilby*) in which Satan is figured as the sorrowful (and thus atypically ambiguous) Prince Rimânez. Like *Trilby*, *The Sorrows of Satan* was an enormous popular success and like *Trilby*, *Sorrows* quickly vanished from the canon. Peter Keating in his Introduction to the Oxford edition of *The Sorrows of Satan* suggests that it is this very recontextualization into the Gothic tradition that accounts for the disappearance of this popular work (and hence *Trilby* as well) from the canon. "She was willing to draw on older popular traditions of sensation and horror fiction.... She was everything that the most admired [realist] late–Victorian novelists were not" (xx). Thus *Sorrows of Satan* and *Trilby* do not enter the canon because, as Jane Tompkins suggests in *Sensational Designs*,[37] texts that do not fit the dominant notions of literary form — frequently sensation texts — often are excluded from the canon.

The figure of Satan then, conveniently encoded as the Jew, destabilizes the realism of Du Maurier's text, removing it from the contexts of realism and subsequently from the literary canon. Although Du Maurier relies on history and tradition to naturalize his representation of the Satanic Jew, rendering it safely and acceptably realistic, the very process of demonization relocates his text to the realm of darkness and horror. It is the historical and cultural contexts, the preexisting naturalization of the figure of the Jew as demon — "the Jew [as] peculiarly congenial (because historically acceptable) type of supernaturalist..." (Rosenberg 251) — that allow for the realism of this depiction. And within the failure of literary realism to sustain the naturalization of this figure, arise meanings that may be applied to the strategies of culture and history.

For as the figure of the Satanic Jew tends to destabilize literature, so does it destabilize history, as does the racist figuring of all demonized Others. The dangers of the leakage of this tropology into political discourse that was, as indicated earlier, evident in the Dreyfus Affair, is recognized by both Zola and Lukacs in their writing of the Affair. Zola suggests that the Affair was certain to destabilize modern history and wrench it back to the dark past. In a letter dated 1896 (predating by two years the famous "J'accuse)," Zola evokes Gothic tropology in writing of the Affair: "It seems to me a monstrosity; by that I mean something that is altogether beyond the bounds of common sense, truth and justice, a blind and stupid thing that would drag us back centuries in time."[38] Lukacs also observes the dangerous tendency of demonizing the Other and of naturalizing this process. Writing of the Dreyfus trial, Lukacs argues that only when the tendency to naturalize demonization was resisted and reversed, was justice restored, was the course of history restabilized (at least for the moment). "When first of all an intellectual vanguard, but later followed by broad masses, no longer came to accept the fate of an individual man, the unjustly condemned Captain Dreyfus, as normal and natural, refusing to 'accustom' themselves to it, then a state crisis developed in France," leading to Dreyfus's exoneration.[39]

The danger of the unresisted Gothic, then, is that it provides a cultural frame of reference to naturalize the demonization process that buttresses racism, to encode what is unknowable, fearful and evil as the Other. "That thing which refutes all attempts at being bespoken, that thing for which the trope of visibility is always insufficient — becomes phatasmic, made of monsters, women, beasts, and Others" (Kearns 142). The counter suggested by this reading of *Trilby* is the opposing context of realism, that provides the critical distance needed to contain the Gothic impulses within art without allowing these impulses to escape into history,[40] allowing us to understand the horrifying impulse to naturalize the dehumanization of the Other and enabling us to resist this impulse in the "real" actual world. "Realism by its very nature destabilizes the convictions behind these stereotypes" and recognizes "the humanness that exceeds the sum of its parts ... the monster predicts a semantic disturbance that will work in realism to undercut rote misogyny [and racism] with uncertainty" (Kearns 93). This, as Kearns argues, is the use of realism: "realism genuinely problematizes and ultimately curbs the impulse to aggrandize such anarchic power as transcendent.... Separated from the cluttered and homely milieu of realism ... the unnameable may be ... invested in ... racist name-calling" (81). The dangers of the Gothic, as posited by Kearns is that,

> other scapegoats are postulated in an environment in which the ineffable is privileged, and they are partially disguised ... as enigmas.... This enriched, aestheticized racism is almost more egregious than its less elegant nineteenth-century counterparts, as it metaphorizes race ... as a locus for its preoccupation with the otherwise inarticulable foreignness of that unnameable energy. Realism's dubious courtesies of defensive hostility or crude caricature seem preferable because less disguised [83].

A corollary of this argument is that racism — literary and cultural — is always horrifyingly evocative of the Gothic, always relying on the trope of the dehumanized Other and always wrenching literature and history from the realm of realism's "what is" to the realm of the Gothic: "what should not be." When confined in the world of Gothic text, Gothic tropes provide the pleasures and recognitions that Burke discovers in his work on the Sublime,[41] the pleasures of pain and fear contained by art. In his novel, Du Maurier attempts to unleash the demonizing trope by locating it in a realistic text. This escape from the Gothic of the trope of demonization of the Other, effected through the naturalization of the trope, represents an early step in the relentless drift of modern history toward Gothic horror, to the Gothic nightmare of history in the twentieth century and, seemingly, in the twenty-first century as well.

Notes

1. A cursory check indicates that Svengali remains alive and well, operating as a figure of dark power in the popular imagination, although his creator's book is long forgotten. An Internet search reveals such headlines as: "Spice Svengali Celebrates Club Success" <*www.news.bbc.co.uk/hi/english/entertainment/newsid_368000/368484.stm* > (about a "former Spice Girls manager"); "Europe Ignores England's Svengali" *www.sport.news.com.au/common/story_page/0,4057,3647509%5E9755,00.html* (about a powerful European football coach); "British Svengali Behind Clash of Civilizations" <*www.larouchepub.com/other/2001/2846b_lewis_profile.html*> (about a "British intelligence senior operator"); and "Svengali of the Truth-Seeking Set" <*www.lightmind.com/thevoic/daism/sfex-02.html*> (about a charismatic cult leader). In the print media, Maureen Dowd (*New York Times* 8 May 2002, sec A, p. 31) writes of "the imperious Hollywood Svengali, Michael Ovitz." Significantly, several of these instances reveal a continued association between Svengali and the arts— the quintessential Svengali is, as is the original, a powerful figure in the field of entertainment.

2. Rosenberg also identifies this phenomenon: "Svengali has been so vastly diffused and generalized by the public media that he has passed into the popular consciousness as something of a household name, with the result that one has difficulty in remembering his exact credentials" (Edgar Rosenberg, *From Shylock to Svengali* [Stanford: Stanford University Press, 1960], 4).

3. Elaine Showalter, introduction to *Trilby* by George Du Maurier (New York: Oxford University Press, 1995), ix.

4. Kelly also suggests a connection between Du Maurier and his villain. All the talk about Jewish blood in *Trilby* and in Du Maurier's other novels indicates to Kelly that Du Maurier suspected that he might be of Jewish descent. "It may be that Du Maurier suspected that he himself had a strain of Jewish blood, for his other hero, Peter Ibbetson, has a distant Jewish ancestor..." (Richard Kelly, *George Du Maurier* [Boston: Twayne, 1983], 113). One other genealogical detail of interest is found in a discussion that locates Du Maurier within the Gothic tradition: he was the grandfather of Daphne du Maurier, the neo–Gothic writer of the mid-twentieth century. Nina Auerbach's recent study, *Daphne du Maurier: Haunted Heiress* (Philadelphia: University of Pennsylvania Press, 2000) focuses on the relationship of influence of grandfather upon granddaughter. Auerbach argues that the granddaughter's "fictional mission" is to "absorb without being obliterated by the ... history" of her predecessor (96) and locates in this struggle the "obsessively genealogical" (14) nature of Du Maurier's work. Interestingly Auerbach identifies within Daphne a tendency toward "decomposition" of women (99), a tendency that also evidences in *Trilby*.

5. Given the detail that Du Maurier draws upon anti–Semitic tropology in asso-ciating Svengali with sexual lasciviousness, it is tempting to think that the long asso-ciation of the Jew with a long "shapely" nose is a code for the phallus of the Jew (the association between nose and phallus in Sterne's *Tristram Shandy*, for example, with its attendant anxieties of loss of nose/castration — another anxiety associated with Jew-ish sexuality — is another example of this encoded metaphor).

6. Saul Friedländer, "'Europe's Inner Demons': The 'Other' as Threat in Early Twentieth-Century European Culture," in *Demonizing the Other: Antisemitism, Racism, and Xenophobia*, ed. Robert S. Wistrich (Amsterdam: Harwood, 1999), 213.

7. Michael Ragussis, *Figures of Conversion: "The Jewish Question" and English National Identity* (Durham: Duke University Press, 1995), 224.

8. Montagu Frank Modder. *The Jew in the Literature of England to the End of the 19th Century*. 1939. (Reprint, New York: Meridien, 1960), 349.

9. Rosenberg notes that in this description, Du Maurier "recovers ... the often potent medieval metaphor [of anti–Semitism], that of the dog" (256).

10. Robert S. Wistrich, "Introduction: The Devil, the Jews, and Hatred of the 'Other,'" in *Demonizing the Other: Antisemitism, Racism, and Xenophobia*, ed. Robert S. Wistrich (Amsterdam: Harwood, 1999), 4.

11. Showalter, noting the significance of eyes and sight in this novel, attributes Du Maurier's pre-occupation with his own "severe eye-problems and migraine headaches [that] kept Du Maurier from his drawing board" (xv).

12. Kelly argues for another association of Svengali with the devil. He notes that when Little Billee first hears about La Svengali from another famous singer, "her voice is described in terms of an instrument: 'Everything that Paganini could do with his violin she does with her voice — only better...' (258 — [Kelly's citation]). Legend had it that the only way Paganini could have achieved his virtuosity on the violin was by selling his soul to the devil. Du Maurier's association of Svengali with the devil is sub-tly reinforced through this allusion." Kelly also cites the conversation between Trilby and the conductor when Svengali dies. "The references to God, the devilish musicians and the Satanic music further strengthen the relationship between Svengali's demonic character and the music" (99).

13. In fact, the anxiety associated with Svengali's mesmerism is an anti–Semitic ver-sion of a more generalized Victorian anxiety. "One of the great anxieties among Vic-torian critics of hypnotism arose from a sense of the potential danger ... the implicit anxiety was a sexual one" (Kelly 91).

14. Modder 310.

15. Richard I. Cohen, "Recurrent Images in French Antisemitism in the Third Republic," in *Demonizing the Other: Antisemitism, Racism, and Xenophobia*, ed. Robert S. Wistrich (Amsterdam: Harwood, 1999), 185.

16. Joel Carmichael, *The Satanizing of the Jews: Origin and Development of Mysti-cal Anti-Semitism* (New York: Fromm, 1992), 125.

17. The quality that Wistrich argues made the Jew so vexing to Nazi ideological cat-egories.

18. Susan Shapiro, "The Uncanny Jew: A Brief History of an Image," *Judaism* 46 (1997): 65, 63–78. This observation, of course, echoes the argument that Toni Morrison makes in "Romancing the Shadow," regarding the utility of the figure of the American Other — the dark slave — in defining the white free American ("Romancing the Shadow," in *Play-ing in the Dark: Whiteness and the Literary Imagination* [New York: Vintage, 1993].)

19. Henri Zukier, "The Transformation of Hatred: Antisemitism as a Struggle for Group Identity," in *Demonizing the Other: Antisemitism, Racism, and Xenophobia*, ed. Robert S. Wistrich (Amsterdam: Harwood, 1999), 120.

20. Zukier states that "I would like to argue that the Jew in modern times has become the privileged and essential 'other' in the Western mind" (121). However, it appears that this role of the Jew, although culminating in modern times, began millennia ago.

21. A suspicion shared by Leo Pinsker in his essay, "Auto-Emancipation: An Appeal to His People by a Russian Jew": "A fear of the Jewish ghost has passed down the generations ... Judeophobia is a variety of demonopathy with the distinction that it is not peculiar to particular races but is common to the whole of mankind ... this fear of ghosts [is] the mother of Judeophobia" ("Auto-Emancipation: An Appeal to His People by a Russian Jew," in *Modern Jewish History: A Source Reader*, ed. Robert Chazan and Marc Lee Raphael [New York: Schocken Press, 1969], 163–4).

22. Of course, as this collection indicates, while the concept of associating the Other with darkly supernatural forces, might have begun with Christian constructions of the Jew, it is a tendency that finds expression all too commonly at other cultural moments.

23. It is, of course, the figure of the Wandering Jew that invites scholars to see in the figure of Dracula, with his thirst for blood and his dangerous tendency to mix blood, the encoded Jew. Shapiro, in noting that the anti–Semite perceives the Jew living "parasitically on other nations" (66), indicates another connection between the figure of the Jew and the vampire.

24. Alain Finkielkraut, *The Imaginary Jew*, trans. by David Suchoff and Kevin O'Neill (Lincoln: University of Nebraska Press, 1994), quoted by Shapiro (64–65).

25. An interesting and relevant discussion of the figure of the artist's model in nineteenth-century French literature may be found in Marie Lathers's *Bodies of Art*. Lathers considers "how the female model is narrated and read by readers and spectators" (*Bodies of Art: French Literary Realism and the Artist's Model* [Lincoln: University of Nebraska Press, 2001], 1) and the relation of the figure of the artist's model to realism. "Through the figure of the model ... realist authors were able to produce and dispute claims concerning representation, mimesis, and the real, as well as sexual and other forms of difference" (2). Lathers shows that the ethnicity of the model comes into play, tracing an evolution "in the preference for different racial and ethnic model types, from the Jewish model, most popular in the 1830s and 1840s, to the Italian immigrant model favored by painters in the 1850s, 1860s, and 1870s, to the Parisian poser ... of the1880s and 1890s" (15–16). This discussion becomes relevant when we remember that Trilby is an Anglo/Irish artist's model and that Du Maurier sets the opening scenes of his story in the 1850s. Of further interest: Lathers identifies "the novel of the artist's life as a 'popular subgenre of French literature' (4) and also identifies an English strain, exemplified by Hawthorne's *The Marble Faun* and Wilde's *The Picture of Dorian Gray*. Of great significance to the discussion of this essay is that both Hawthorne's and Wilde's texts (like Du Maurier's as we shall see) veer toward the supernatural Gothic in their stories of artist life. Reading from a different perspective, Lukacs notes that the relationship that the artist has to his model is "only a special and immediately palpable case of the changed relationship between art and life in general" and indicates that "Flaubert, Baudelaire, Ibsen and Anatole France wrote of this relationship" (George Lukács, "Tribune or Bureaucrat?" in *Essays on Realism*, ed, Rodney Livingstone, trans. David Fernbach [Cambridge, Mass.: The MIT Press, 1980], 221). Of importance to our discussion is that Trilby becomes susceptible to Svengali only after her English friends can see her only in the role of unsuitable wife. Because they cannot see their way to allowing Trilby to continue as a model, she becomes a laundress and later Svengali's protégée.

26. Alison Byerly, *Realism, Representations, and the Arts in Nineteenth-Century Literature* (Cambridge: Cambridge University Press, 1997), 10–11.

27. That Eliot associates realism with moral imperatives is evident from her essay

"Realism" in which she equates realistic writing with honest writing, providing "a faithful account of men and things" (George Eliot, "On Realism," in *Documents of Modern Literary Realism*, ed. George J. Becker [Princeton: Princeton University Press, 1963], 113), finding the truth of "the secret of deep human sympathy" (115). And, indeed, it might be possible to fault Eliot's Jewish characters as demonstrating a flaw on the same plane as Du Maurier's—in each case they inhabit inhuman extremes on the spectrum of morality: Du Maurier's Svengali being inhumanly evil, Eliot's Deronda inhumanly good ("the impeccable Jew," Rosenberg calls him [6]). The ambiguous figure of Deronda's mother, however, rescues her author from this charge.

Eliot's stance toward her Jewish characters takes on additional meaning in the context of her correspondence with Harriet Beecher Stowe, whose project in deconstructing the African slave as Other mirrors Eliot's own. "It was reading Stowe's antislavery novels that Eliot began to see the dignity of 'the fellowship of race,' at which she had sneered when responding to Disraeli's trilogy in 1848.... It is under the tutelage of Stowe ... that Eliot first comes to contemplate racial and national subjects for her own work" (Ragussis 265–6). Ragussis notes that both *Daniel Deronda* and *Uncle Tom's Cabin* end with a young man dedicating himself to the cause of his race (267).

28. Kelly adds, "for Svengali, music, like mesmerism is power and control" (98).

29. An association echoed in *Daniel Deronda*; Daniel's Jewish mother is an actress and singer.

30. Part of the strangeness of *Trilby* lies in the multilingual dialogue of the text. Long passages of French conversation and some German dialogue are presented unmediated by English translation.

31. Byerly argues that this anxiety manifests in the prominence of the arts in so many realist Victorian novels including *Trilby*.

32. Showalter adds that "indeed, James himself had written in *The Bostonians* (1886) about a beautiful young woman who is mesmerized by her charlatan spiritualist father, and becomes a famous feminist orator" (xiii). Showalter also recounts that James subsequently complimented his protégé upon the "conversational naturalness of '[his] style'" (x).

33. Brooks quite convincingly locates James within the Radcliffean tradition of the Gothic, the explained supernatural, that deploys a strategy of presenting transcendent issues—the struggle between good and evil, light and dark, the individual recognition of good and evil –within a context of seeming realism (Peter Brooks, *The Melodramatic Imagination: Balzac, Henry James, Melodrama and the Mode of Excess* [New Haven: Yale University Press, 1976]).

34. Irene Tucker, *A Probable State: The Novel, the Contract, and the Jews* (Chicago: University of Chicago Press, 2000), 31.

35. And, as Clery suggests, with the imperatives of gender: "a woman wishing to publish fiction in a supernatural vein needs to be prepared to negotiate" (E.J. Clery *The Rise of Supernatural Fiction* [Cambridge: Cambridge University Press, 1995], 106).

36. Castle draws upon Freud's essay "The Uncanny" to argue that Radcliffe's characterizations reveal that, in the age of sensibility and sentimentality, the subjectivity of the other becomes unsubstantial. The other, any other, becomes the ontological and epistemological ghost, spectralized in a way that eliminates the need for supernatural sources of horror and mystery. Radcliffe's doubles, like those of Hoffman's noted by Freud, destabilize the self in a frightening way by presenting the subject with a self that is unrecognizable; in fact, Gothic characters virtually never recognize their mirrored selves. That is, the uncanny only takes visible shape when it is set against a backdrop of realism that provides contrast. Castle masterfully builds upon Freud's argument by suggesting in the Introduction to *The Female Thermometer* that the Enlightenment

valorization of reason is a necessary precondition for the invention of the uncanny (including its appearance in the Gothic) in the eighteenth century. The uncanny takes on meaning and horror only as a contradiction of a supposedly reasonable and rational universe. Thus, Radcliffe's doubles are uncanny and particularly unsettling because they occur within a text that appears to adhere to the conventions of realism (Terry Castle, "The Spectralization of the Other in *The Mysteries of Udolpho*," in *The Female Thermometer* [New York: Oxford, 1995]). Todorov, too, in discussing what he calls "the fantastic," notes the particular power found in the space between pure realism and pure unreality (Tzvetan Todorov, *The Fantastic: A Structural Approach to a Literary Genre*, trans. by Richard Howard [Cleveland: Case Western University Press, 1973]).

37. Jane Tompkins, *Sensational Designs: The Cultural Work of American Fiction, 1790–1860.* (New York: Oxford University Press, 1986).

38. Émile Zola, *The Dreyfus Affair: "J'Accuse" and Other Writings*, ed. Alain Pagès, trans. Eleanor Levieux (New Haven: Yale University Press, 1996), 2.

39. Lukacs 213.

40. The timeliness of this struggle — that is, political struggle translated into generic struggle — is indicated in a piece in the *New York Times* 17 June 2002, headlined "For an Israeli, Flights of Fancy Are Grounded: Wide Praise for a Novelist Stirred to Social Realism by Bombings." The writer, Orly Castel-Bloom, is quoted on her move from "flights of dystopian fantasy" (sec. E, p. 1) to realism, "History became so invasive that I had to stick with reality" (sec. E p. 5).

41. Edmund Burke, *A Philosophical Enquiry into the Origin of Our Ideas of the Sublime and the Beautiful* (New York: Oxford University Press, 1990).

Works Cited

Armstrong, Nancy. *Fiction in the Age of Photography: The Legacy of British Realism.* Cambridge, Mass.: Harvard University Press, 1999.

Auerbach, Nina. *Daphne du Maurier: Haunted Heiress.* Philadelphia: University of Pennsylvania Press, 2000.

Brooks, Peter. *The Melodramatic Imagination: Balzac, Henry James, Melodrama and the Mode of Excess.* New Haven: Yale University Press, 1976.

Burke, Edmund. *A Philosophical Enquiry into the Origin of Our Ideas of the Sublime and the Beautiful.* New York: Oxford University Press, 1990.

Byerly, Alison. *Realism, Representations, and the Arts in Nineteenth-Century Literature.* Cambridge: Cambridge University Press, 1997.

Byron, George Gordon. "Oh! Weep for Those." In *The Poetical Works of Lord Byron.* London: Oxford University Press, 1966).

Carmichael, Joel. *The Satanizing of the Jews: Origin and Development of Mystical Anti-Semitism.* New York: Fromm, 1992.

Castle, Terry. "The Spectralization of the Other in *The Mysteries of Udolpho*." In *The Female Thermometer.* New York: Oxford, 1995.

Clery, E.J. *The Rise of Supernatural Fiction.* Cambridge: Cambridge University Press, 1995.

Cohen, Richard I. "Recurrent Images in French Antisemitism in the Third Republic." In *Demonizing the Other: Antisemitism, Racism, and Xenophobia.* Edited by Robert S. Wistrich. Amsterdam: Harwood, 1999.

Corelli, Marie. *The Sorrows of Satan.* New York: Oxford University Press, 1996.

Dickens, Charles. *Oliver Twist.* Illustrated by George Cruikshank. Baltimore: Penguin, 1966.

Du Maurier, George. *Trilby*. Introduced by Elaine Showalter. New York: Oxford University Press, 1995.

Eliot, George. "On Realism." In *Documents of Modern Literary Realism*. Edited by George J. Becker. Princeton: Princeton University Press, 1963.

Finkielkraut, Alain. *The Imaginary Jew*. Translated by David Suchoff and Kevin O'Neill. Lincoln: University of Nebraska Press, 1994.

Friedländer, Saul. "'Europe's Inner Demons: The 'Other' as Threat in Early Twentieth-Century European Culture." In *Demonizing the Other: Antisemitism, Racism, and Xenophobia*. Edited by Robert S. Wistrich. Amsterdam: Harwood, 1999.

Jenkins, Cecil. "Realism and the Novel Form." In *The Monster in the Mirror: Studies in Nineteenth Century Realism*. Edited by D. A. Williams. New York: Oxford University Press, 1978.

Kearns, Katherine. *Nineteenth-Century Literary Realism: Through the Looking Glass*. Cambridge: Cambridge University Press, 1996.

Kelly, Richard. *George Du Maurier*. Boston: Twayne, 1983.

Lathers, Marie. *Bodies of Art: French Literary Realism and the Artist's Model*. Lincoln: University of Nebraska Press, 2001.

Levine, George. *The Realistic Imagination: English Fiction from Frankenstein to Lady Chatterley*. Chicago: University of Chicago Press, 1981.

Lloyd, Tom. *Crises of Realism: Representing Experience in the British Novel, 1816–1910*. Lewisburg: Bucknell University Press, 1997.

Lukács, Georg. "Tribune or Bureaucrat?" In *Essays on Realism*. Edited and introduced by Rodney Livingstone. Translated by David Fernbach. Cambridge, Mass.: The MIT Press, 1980.

Modder, Montagu Frank. *The Jew in the Literature of England to the End of the 19th Century*. 1939. Reprint, New York: Meridien, 1960.

Morrison, Toni. "Romancing the Shadow." In *Playing in the Dark: Whiteness and the Literary Imagination*. New York: Vintage, 1993.

Pagels, Elaine. *The Origin of Satan*. New York: Random House, 1995.

Pinsker, Leo. "Auto-Emancipation: An Appeal to His People by a Russian Jew." In *Modern Jewish History: A Source Reader*. Edited by Robert Chazan and Marc Lee Raphael. New York: Schocken Press, 1969.

Ragussis, Michael. *Figures of Conversion: 'The Jewish Question" and English National Identity*. Durham: Duke University Press, 1995.

Rosenberg, Edgar. *From Shylock to Svengali*. Stanford: Stanford University Press, 1960.

Shapiro, Susan. "The Uncanny Jew: A Brief History of an Image." *Judaism* 46 (1997): 63–78.

Showalter, Elaine. Introduction to *Trilby* by George Du Maurier. New York: Oxford University Press, 1995.

Todorov, Tzvetan. *The Fantastic: A Structural Approach to a Literary Genre*. Translated by Richard Howard. Cleveland: Case Western University Press, 1973.

Tompkins, Jane. *Sensational Designs: The Cultural Work of American Fiction, 1790–1860*. New York: Oxford University Press, 1986.

Tucker, Irene. *A Probable State: The Novel, the Contract, and the Jews*. Chicago: University of Chicago Press, 2000.

Vernon, John. *Money and Fiction: Literary Realism in the Nineteenth and Early Twentieth Centuries*. Ithaca: Cornell University Press, 1984.

Wistrich, Robert S., ed. *Demonizing the Other: Antisemitism, Racism, and Xenophobia*. Amsterdam: Harwood, 1999.

____. "Introduction: The Devil, the Jews, and Hatred of the 'Other.'" In *Demonizing the Other: Antisemitism, Racism, and Xenophobia*. Amsterdam: Harwood, 1999.

Zola, Émile. *The Dreyfus Affair: "J'Accuse" and Other Writings.* Edited by Alain Pagès. Translated by Eleanor Levieux. New Haven: Yale University Press, 1996.
Zukier, Henri. "The Transformation of Hatred: Antisemitism as a Struggle for Group Identity." In *Demonizing the Other: Antisemitism, Racism, and Xenophobia.* Edited by Robert S. Wistrich. Amsterdam: Harwood, 1999.

PART III

Dark Master, Dark Slave:
Class Hatred and Class Fear

10

The Death of Zofloya; or, The Moor as Epistemological Limit

STEPHANIE BURLEY

Charlotte Dacre's *Zofloya; or, the Moor* caused a sensation when it was published in 1806.[1] Arousing both the interest of readers and the ire of the literary establishment, her Gothic tale of seduction set in fifteenth-century Italy added to the fame — and infamy — of Rosa Matilda, Dacre's literary persona. Like many other Gothic texts (*The Castle of Otranto, Caleb Williams,* and *Confessions of a Justified Sinner,* to name a few), *Zofloya* uses the historical novel format to explore the implications of the dissolution of patriarchal power in the wake of the French Revolution. In Dacre's novel, the aristocratic Lorendini family, the emblem of *ancien régime,* is supplanted by increasingly illegitimate family ties. The crack in the patriarchal armor is occasioned by Laurina Lorendini's adulterous affair with Ardolph. The next generation of Lorendinis, already denied access to any kind of legitimate cultural inheritance by virtue of their mother's scandal, spirals away from the seat of ancestral power, downward into increasingly demonic associations with courtesans, robbers, murderers, and eventually with the Devil himself. The few recent theoretical treatments of *Zofloya* all remark on the hyperbolically libidinal and violent scale of this descent into human depravity: James Dunn states that "the most protracted description of gore in Dacre's novels occurs in *Zofloya*"[2]; Adriana Craciun describes *Zofloya* as "the vivisection of virtue" (9); and Diane Hoeveler calls it "perhaps the most eccentric female gothic ever penned."[3] Dacre's use of sex and violence is indeed striking, especially in comparison to the works of more "tame" female Gothic authors like Charlotte Brontë.[4]

Part of *Zofloya's* particular transgressiveness derives from Dacre's use of the racialized Other as Gothic spectacle: the black male servant Zofloya in league with the sexually predatory Victoria no doubt adds to the scandalous flavor of this text. Victoria and Zofloya embody the dangerous libidinal impulses that the discourses of empire prevalent during the time of Dacre's writing seek to dominate, and therefore represent the dark desires that must be penetrated, illuminated, and regulated in the name of colonization. *Zofloya* portrays the failure of such disciplinary social forces to fully understand, and therefore control, the insurrectionary Other, who knows all too well how to use his or her subordinate status to subvert the social order. However, as this reading of the title character will show, Dacre explores the revolutionary possibilities of dangerous knowledge within clearly defined, racially specified limits. Zofloya, the exoticized Moor of the title, is actually missing in action by the time he "speaks." We hear of him halfway through the novel, and then we see him only through the imaginative perspective of Victoria, whose gaze immediately fixates on and aestheticsizes his body. We find out in the closing paragraphs that the real Zofloya has been murdered shortly after Victoria's first sighting of him, and that the empty, soulless shell of his body has been inhabited by Satan throughout the narrative. The evacuated space of Zofloya's body — and the elimination of his perspective of social domination — is at the center of the text; the epistemological standpoint that social subordination produces is the necessary pre-condition for insurrection, even as its logical embodiment, the slave Zofloya, is willfully erased from the discursive landscape. The ramifications of this erasure, especially within the project of resituating knowledge through a modern literary apparatus like the Gothic novel, are the subject of this inquiry. Paying attention to the small but important narrative detail of Zofloya's death lends insight into some of the difficult epistemological problems Dacre as Rosa Matilda faced in the literary marketplace of the early nineteenth century. The epistemological standpoint of Zofloya the Moor, as opposed to Zofloya the Devil, is in fact symptomatic of the double bind that female Gothic authors like Dacre faced: namely, how can a woman who knows so much about desire, seduction, and murder, be a trustworthy producer of cultural capital?

Before turning to the unknowable Gothic Other, Zofloya, we must first understand how the pattern of Dacre's narrative contextualizes his function as a servant. Underlying the initial domestic crisis are anxieties about certain kinds of knowledge, particularly the knowledge that social subordinates have about their positioning within the patriarchal (and capitalist) power structure. In *Zofloya*, the farther down the hierarchy a character is positioned, the more dangerous is that character's knowledge. The fact that social subordinates have the ability to seduce their benefactors through dissembling creates the power implosion that leads to the downfall of patriarchal authority.

In the very first lines of *Zofloya*, the narrator prepares the reader to understand the following events as a chain reaction of disastrous proportion. Her aim is not only to "[detail] a series of events" but also to "ascertain causes, and follow progressively their effects."[5] The narrative proper begins with a birthday celebration for the "lovely and haughty Victoria," who "smiled with unchecked vivacity" as the vain object of familial and social adoration (39). We quickly learn that both she and her brother have inherited a pathological mix of good looks and pride from their mother, whose main flaw is "too great a thirst for admiration, and confidence in herself" (39). These imperfections are distinct from the fatal flaw of the father, the Marchesse di Lorendini, whose mistake, if it can be called one, is his "unsuspicious and generous nature [which] gloried in the attractions of his wife" (40). The sin of the father is his failure to discipline the roiling desires of his subordinate family members.

The language of the text makes explicit the ideological links between knowledge, power, and sexuality. One character after another is *seduced*, and therefore overthrown, by an underling. What allows these seductions to occur is the knowledge that the subordinates possess, both of themselves and of their superiors. The compact intertwining of these three ideological concepts — knowledge, power and sexuality — is emblemized by the various domestic settings of this novel in particular, and of the Gothic genre in general. The home is the anxiety-filled space where sexual struggles attain their most fevered pitch. It is also the site of intimate knowledge, where subordinate subjects gain access to the private secrets and vulnerabilities of their protectors.

The dynamic of inversion accounts for much of the uncanny effect in the novel. According to Freud, "the uncanny is that class of frightening which leads back to what is known of old and long familiar."[6] In *Zofloya* we see this in the spectacle of a happily married wife who abandons her husband, houseguests who murder their hosts, and a daughter who sells her soul to the Devil in the guise of a servant. Subordinates, who are assumed to be totally transparent to their beneficent keepers, are actually the location of disguised and threatening knowledge; in *Zofloya*, this leads to one transgression after another as social and familiar underlings use the mask of harmless, familiar submission to disguise their insurrectionary aims.

As the analog of *ancien régime* nobility, Lorendini is the first victim dispatched by those whom he is assigned to protect. Not only is his wife unfaithful to him, but he is betrayed by Ardolph, a foreign guest who places himself at the mercy of Lorendini's hospitality.[7] Significantly, here and throughout the text, the act of seduction is described in terms of power, as a kind of inverted master/slave dialectic. Rather than attempting to master the vassal-like Laurina, Ardolph seduces his victim in becoming enslaved by her physical beauty and virtue (43). Ardolph is enraged by "the ascendancy she had gained over" his jaded heart, and "felt that over *her* he could gain no triumph" (45). When he approaches her to confess his feelings, his heretofore fetching appearance has been degraded: he is "pale, haggard, and with an expression of wretchedness on his countenance" (45). A defeated victim of the "maddening passion" she has inspired in him, he is "no longer master of his violent emotions" (45). Laurina initially revels in "her brilliant triumph of captivating such a heart as his" (46). But her period of mastery over Ardolph is brief indeed.

The dialectical machinations of seduction and the narrator's foreshadowing of the evil nature of Ardolph set the scene for an almost instantaneous reversal of power. The position of the enslaved lover is fraught with violent resentment. No sooner has Ardolph cast himself as the supplicant at his beloved's feet, than he is plotting to "degrade completely in her own eyes the miserable and deluded Laurina" (47). By the time he spirits her out of the house, Laurina has become Ardolph's love slave. This rapid series of events in which subordinates overcome their unsuspecting superiors, compacted as it is into the first three short chapters of *Zofloya*, sets the stage for subsequent power inversions and foreshadows the way that subordinate knowledge works as destabilizing power in this text.

Parallels between Laurina's daughter, Victoria, and Ardolph are established as Victoria sets her sights on the home of Berenza, where she hopes to gain asylum in the wake of her family's scandal, and where she positions herself as the same kind of domestic supplicant as Ardolph has been in the house of Lorendini. The scene where she completes her seduction of Venice's most eligible bachelor is symptomatic of the uncanny power of subordinate knowledge that haunts this text. As it opens, Victoria has been feigning melancholy, moping around Berenza's abode in the hopes of convincing him that she is lovesick. Exhausted with this performance, she retires to the salon where her unsuspecting victim finds her "sleeping." "In an instant," Victoria scripts the performance that transforms her from an "imperfect" and "curious woman" into "an innocent and lovely girl" (98, 90, 99).

The literal and symbolic positioning of the characters in this scene reflects the social relations being dramatized here. Victoria finds herself in the double bind of a desiring woman a social convention which demands that she obtain a husband, but prohibits her from actively seeking him. To further emphasize Victoria's socially disadvantaged position, we should remember that she is a runaway, and so has no choice but to angle for the most legitimizing arrangement possible. Victoria's seeming feminine passivity is signaled by her reclining position, her closed eyes (she is the object, not the subject of the gaze), and her apparent lapse into artifice-less unconsciousness. Berenza relishes the opportunity to "penetrate her thoughts" as he observes her sleeping (92). He is positioned as the active masculine agent, "surprising" Victoria, sitting over her, observing her from a privileged vantage point. He, too, is aware of masculine and feminine roles in the marriage plot. He has planned all along to avail himself of the masculine power that will give him access to the desirable Victoria without having to marry her.

What turns this power hierarchy on its head is what these characters *know* about each other. As a subordinate, Victoria understands and uses to her advantage the masculinist discourse which would objectify her as a damaged commodity on the marriage market. However, as a superior, Berenza has only superficial knowledge of her: her performance of drowsy vulnerability and seemingly unconscious (and therefore innocent) love is a familiar image, one that allows Berenza to imagine Victoria as a passive female at his mercy. Victoria's knowledge of Berenza is considerably more subtle. She knows what he desires and how "to suit [her] conduct to the fastidious delicacy of his ideas" (97). This knowledge allows her to negotiate both her desire and his expectations of female modesty by objectifying herself as his passive fantasy. Her understanding of his fantasy is so on-target that all she has to do is murmur, "Indeed — indeed, Berenza — I love *thee!*" and he is instantly seized by such "violent emotion" that he is "deprived of the power of speech" (98–99). Her knowledge, which comes from her position as a subordinate, allows her to dominate Berenza at the very instant he imagines himself the master of her heart.[8]

The narrative pattern of *Zofloya* presents one such betrayal after another, all of which are enacted by the epistemological power of the menacing subordinate-turned-master. This pattern of betrayal through seduction prepares the reader for the rather belated appearance of the novel's title character, the one who occupies the lowest position on the social ladder. Enter Zofloya, the Moor servant of Henriquez, subordinate by virtue of race as well as class. The narrative logic of the text has prepared us to understand Zofloya as yet another site of subversive-because-subordinate knowledge. On one level, the novel supports this reading: Zofloya pretends to serve everyone around him, especially Victoria, while in reality plotting the ultimate demise of each. And like Victoria, his aesthetic beauty misleads his superiors, including Victoria, creating a fascinating and disarming mask behind which his true ugliness and power lie. After these two supposedly subordinate subjects—Victoria and Zofloya—use their intimate domestic knowledge to poison both an elderly chaperone and Berenza, cause the suicide of Henriquez, and abduct the innocent Lilla, the rival in love of Victoria, Zofloya suggests that he and Victoria run off into the mountains together to escape the law. If we have not yet realized that Zofloya does not have Victoria's best interests at heart, the "servant's" suggestion to remove his "master" to an even more isolated location makes the point clear: a menacing reversal of power is at hand.

Hoeveler's[9] understanding of the image of Victoria and Zofloya's spectacularly violent and unholy alliance as "sexual nausea" is useful in its reading of Dacre's work as a reaction to the threat of dispossession. It is, however, possible to push the postcolonial reading of this text even further by focusing on the limits of insurrectionary epistemology it presents. The fact that Zofloya is not really the Moor, not really a subordinate, but in fact the devil occupying the body of the black servant, is an important detail which Hoeveler glosses over. Indeed, the subplot of the murdered slave is easy to miss, since it is elliptically summarized in just a few sentences, such as when Victoria notices in passing that "Zofloya, before his sudden disappearance, and Zofloya since his return, were widely different from each other" (153), or in the parenthetical comment the demonic Zofloya makes just before casting Victoria into the abyss: "yes, *I* it was, that under semblance of the Moorish slave *(supposed the recovered favorite of Henriquez)*—appeared to thee first in thy dreams" (254, emphasis added). Thus, there are actually two Zofloyas in the text, one demonic, and one dead.[10]

The demonic Zofloya fits into the pattern of knowledge/power described above. He is the ultimate masquerading subordinate who has supernatural access to knowledge and deadly intimate proximity to his victims. He is object-turned-subjective taken to its most vicious and seductive extreme. The dead Zofloya is much more difficult to understand. What epistemological viewpoint can he represent? Why does a text so much about the insurrectionary potential of subordinate knowledge require his death? How can we place this interesting narrative detail within the kinds of colonial machinations that Hoeveler identifies in *Zofloya*? Taking a look at the psychological work that the demonic Zofloya does for Victoria is one way to begin answering these questions.

On one level, Zofloya-as-demon signals Victoria's relationship to her particularly evil ideology of self-gratification — an ideology of aristocratic pride and libidinal excess that the novel wants to critique. Following Slavoi Zizek's post–Marxist/psychoanalytic framework, Victoria seems to be mired in a pre-cynical epistemological space where ideology can be defined as "they do not know it, but they are doing it."[11] The passionate dreams where we get our first glimpse of Zofloya highlight this relationship:[12]

> She beheld advancing a Moor, of a noble and majestic form ... his arms and legs, which were bare, were encircled with the finest oriental pearl; he wore a collar of gold round his throat.... Victoria contemplated this figure with an inexplicable awe, and, as she gazed, he bent his knee, and extended his arms towards her. While in this attitude, her mind filled with terror, she looked upon him with dread, and essaying to fly, she stumbled and awoke [145–46].

The narrative pattern of the text has prepared us to understand this foray into the subconscious of Victoria as another instance of Gothic foreshadowing. The manacles of bondage are transformed into markers of wealth in anticipation of the true nature of the demonic Zofloya's pseudo-slavery. And his kneeling at the feet of Victoria signals the beginning of the master/slave reversal that eventually leads to her demise. While there is no evidence that Victoria consciously knows what her dream might mean (on the contrary, she remains unbelievably naive about the demon Zofloya until the apocalyptic ending), her immediate horror and struggle to wake up and run away at this point signals that her subconscious, at least, has registered the dangerous pattern of uncanny power transformations she has witnessed and accomplished for herself. As readers, we understand what Victoria does not: that her ideology of self-gratification as an ideological self-construct (and as something morally corrupt) has blinded her both to the horror of her own actions and to her imminent danger. Her failure to recognize the evil within, even as it is mirrored in her fantasy of Zofloya, is the Lacanian "kernel," or subconscious truth, that eludes Victoria as she wakes from her dream.[13]

In the second dream, where Victoria imagines with vicious jealousy the marriage of Henriquez, the object of her desire, to the virginal Lilla, the Moor is even more demonic, and as such, even more "symptomatic" of Victoria's ideological imprisonment. Here, he offers to break up the wedding if Victoria will become his. She readily agrees, and a condensed version of the rest of the novel plays out in her dream: Lilla is forced out of the picture, Berenza is murdered, and Victoria is briefly united with Henriquez before he turns into a skeleton. In this dream, Zofloya becomes the fetish of Victoria's ideology of self-gratification: the body of the Moor, the dreamed presence of which she explains as "merely in consequence of her beholding him daily, sometimes attending behind the chair of his master at meal times, and on other occasions," is invested with supernatural value as a demonic *deus ex machina* (147). Readers understand how Victoria's misrecognition of her image of Zofloya exemplifies her investment in her ideology. We know that she is making a pact with the Devil, but she cannot see it as such, focused as she is on her wish-fulfillment. Not surprisingly, the next day she cannot keep her eyes off the heretofore un(consciously)-noticed Moor, whom she now invests with the conspiratorial fantasy that the Devil, or the devil-within (to follow Hoeveler's reading), has brought to the surface. The fetishized image of Victoria's dreams is the "hysterical symptom" of the reality to which Victoria is blind.

In Zizek's terms, this image is the symptom that "disguises" social relations of domination and servitude by displacing them onto fetishized things (27). According to him, the symptom is most readily apparent in the "passage from feudalism to capitalism," a historical moment in which:

> the relations between domination and servitude are *repressed*: formally, we are apparently concerned with free subjects whose interpersonal relations are discharged of all fetishism; the repressed truth — that of the persistence of domination and servitude — emerges in a symptom which subverts the ideological appearance of equality, freedom, and so on. This symptom, the point of emergence of the truth about social relations, is precisely the "social relations between things" — in contrast to feudal society, where ["relations between men," not "relations between things" signified the process of social domination] [27].

Zizek's terminology is especially suggestive in the case of *Zofloya*, a work that deals with early-nineteenth-century anxieties about the insurrectionary possibilities of subjugated populations by casting the revolution back onto the rapidly decaying feudal landscape. In fact, Zizek's (and Marx's) moment of transformation — in which relations of fetishized commodities of exchange disguise social domination of "men" — is another way to describe the colonial project of slavery that underwrites this text: slavery requires the transformation of men and women into fetishized commodities of exchange; the subjugated black bodies are both the counterexample against which white entrepreneurial freedom recognizes itself and the symptomatic disjuncture that reveals the ideological construct of colonial domination. The death of Zofloya is an example of such a moment of pre-capitalist transformation. His body must be emptied out, transformed from a *man* into a fascinating *thing* so that Satan can use it as a disguise to entrap Victoria.

Certain details about the "real" Zofloya, conveyed posthumously as a kind of eulogy, highlight this moment of transformation from man to thing, from subject to Gothic Other. Zofloya is "of noble birth," and fell into the "misfortune" of slavery by "the chance of war" (150). His first master, a Spanish nobleman and friend of Henriquez, "considered him rather as a friend than an inferior, and bestowed high polish upon the education he had received" (150). Henriquez, too, recognizes "his intrinsic worth" (150). *This* Zofloya would perhaps better fit the narrative logic of the text. As a person who is temporarily reduced to the position of servitude, he would be another ideal site of rebellious knowledge. He could harbor secret resentments against his patrons and lead yet another domestic insurrection. But the text is not willing to consider this possibility, perhaps because, in light of recent bloody slave revolts in Jamaica, Haiti, and other European colonies, such a possibility was too frightening for a British audience to contemplate. Or perhaps Dacre was unwilling to make a "real" black man the ultimate villain of her novel. Instead of being the perpetrator of evil, the dead Zofloya is, like Lilla, a perfectly innocent victim. Is Dacre's often-noticed decision to name her novel after him an indication that the Moor is the ultimate demonic threat, or a symbolic encomium meant to highlight the difference between Zofloya (as Satan) and Zofloya (the Moor)?[14] In any event, the final limit placed on the insurrectionary possibilities of subjugated knowledge is the body of Zofloya, the utterly unknowable Gothic Other.

As a corporeal entity, Zofloya's black body signifies colonial anxieties about subjugated populations. By fixing identity in the body, as racial ideology does through its taxonomies of skin color, colonialism measures its moral, economic, and cultural superiority against the sign of dark otherness. The eulogized Zofloya challenges this representational schema because he is the one figure in the text who embodies the perspective of the colonized Other. A fully subjective portrayal of his psychological interiority and epistemological standpoint threatens to disrupt the black/evil metonymy by evoking the possibility of dissent or resistance to slavery. Therefore, if Dacre is to use his black body as a trope — or cultural shorthand for the frightening possibility of rebellion — she must somehow erase the knowledge, subjectivity, and humanity of his perspective and replace it with a less threatening (because less real) signifier — like the Devil — which confirms stereotypes of racial Otherness and permits no critique of slavery. Thus, the colonial Other is transformed into the supernatural Gothic Other in order for Zofloya's corpse to stand as a racially specific embodiment of evil that does not threaten to undermine colonial agendas, because unlike the other subjects, slaves, and underlings in this novel, his knowledge is thoroughly suppressed. The spiral downward along the social hierarchy that begins with the seduction of the unsuspecting great white father (or his wife, as proxy), and that passes through several levels of economic servitude and erotic enslavement, ends with Zofloya's death. If demonic Zofloya is the symptom of Victoria's ideological fixation, then dead Zofloya is the symptom of this text's ideological investment in the capitalist/colonialist project of slavery.

The troubling dead end in the epistemological trajectory of *Zofloya* fits the pattern of colonialist discourse that Gayatri Spivak identifies in other Gothic novels: the ideological construct of the subaltern Other consolidates and particularizes European subjectivity and simultaneously silences the colonized voice. As she states:

> When we come to the ... question of the consciousness of the subaltern, the notion of what the work *cannot* say becomes important. In the semiotic of the social text, elaborations of insurgency stand in the place of "the utterance." The sender — "the peasant" — is marked only as a pointer to an irretrievable consciousness.[15]

Like Bertha Mason in *Jane Eyre*, the dead Zofloya is just such an "irretrievable consciousness," and his epistemological standpoint — what he knows about slavery, seduction, power, and the capitalist transformation of black people into fetishized things — is what this work *cannot* articulate, to itself or to its audience.

Dacre uses spectacular images of seduction, torture, and murder to rewrite revolutionary violence against the patriarchy from a domestic perspective, bringing the threats of revolution into the private sphere in order to dramatize the metonomies of family and state corruption. These actions seem to fulfill the Burkean prophecy that once the illusion of traditional power is subverted by violence, there will be no controlling moral principle to keep the social fabric from disintegrating altogether.[16] Thus, we have the ending landscape of *Zofloya*, a scene devoid of fathers and husbands, where no authority exists to hold evil in check and where the corrupt aristocratic social order is cast into the eternal abyss. And yet, the conclusions *Zofloya* seems to draw about post-revolutionary society are neither as reactionary as Burke's, nor as hopeless as the apocalyptic ending suggests, for in it, we can also see the construction of an emerging disciplinary force that supplants the attenuated patriarchy as moral force; popular literature, especially the Gothic genre written and consumed in large part by women, replaces the law of the father for a class of female readers who have increasing access to literacy as the nineteenth century progresses.

In making sense of this text, it is important to account not just for the unknowable epistemological limit of the dead Zofloya, but also for the presence of the omniscient narrator, the capitalist-as-author and female educator who knows (she tells us again and again) what Victoria does not. In didactic fashion, the narrator participates in the discourse of "the conduct manual," a double-binding educational practice designed to exert capitalist discipline upon the nineteenth-century bourgeois woman. As Alan Richardson notes, the domestic ideology of the conduct manual and the domestic novel as a sub-set of this genre, "simultaneously gave women a more credible public voice and excluded them from active participation in the public sphere, valorized women as guardians of education and devalued their bodies and desires as potentially dangerous strongholds of the irrational."[17] *Zofloya's* narrator walks this fine line, interceding at regular intervals to remind readers of the immorality of the characters she presents: "Tremble, unfortunate and guilty mother, for longer and more gloomy becomes the register of thy crimes!" (136), and "Should not this lesson, then, be conveyed to the mind — that the propensity of our natures to evil should be vigilantly checked, and that the guard which should be constantly kept over the wanderings of the heart, should never be suffered to slumber on its post?" (57), are typical of her bold admonitions. She presents herself as the moral authority of the text, the disciplinary force that takes the place of the dispatched patriarchal father.

Yet, her capitalist project as a female author is vulnerable to the masculinist demonization of the literary marketplace, and requires her to negotiate a kind of double consciousness: she tells a graphic tale of immorality, and thus risks being read as a victim of the same ideology of self-gratification which clouds her heroine's moral judgement. Contemporary reception of the novel suggests that the narrator, and, by extension, the author, were not quite able to convince some critics that "Rosa Matilda" was a good woman with a bad story to tell: "Indeed, we may safely affirm, that there has seldom appeared a romance so void of merit, so destitute of delicacy, displaying such disgusting depravity of morals, as the present," opines one reviewer,[18] while another goes on to make even more explicit links between the scandalous text and its immoral author: "there is a voluptuousness of language and allusion, pervading these volumes, which we should have hoped, that the delicacy of the female pen would have refused to trace; and there is an exhibition of wantonness of harlotry, which we should have hoped, that the delicacy of a female mind, would have been shocked to imagine."[19] The narrator, who perhaps protests her morality too much and risks undermining her authority by becoming a parody of herself, falls prey to the kind of "ideological fantasy" (to use Zizek's term) that Victoria is too un-self-conscious to attain. She is obviously aware that the violent sexual spectacle she narrates threatens to expose her own libidinal desires (as the reviewers were quick to observe), and thus must reiterate (perhaps hysterically) a fantasy of her own uprightness in an attempt to structure the reality in which she is not the site of sexual knowingness, but rather the moral gatekeeper. Thus, the constant didactic interruptions are symptoms of her struggle to situate herself within the capitalist project of female education through popular literature.

The same capitalist pressures which require the death of Zofloya (to effectively demonize Victoria's investment in the ideology of self-gratification) and the narrator's pose of innocence (to support the fantasy of herself as a moral producer of white bourgeois culture) circulate around the epistemological space of the unknowable dead Zofloya. His death and subsequent inhabitation by the supernatural Devil ease the audience's anxieties about what the real Zofloya knows by placing this knowledge outside of the text and simultaneously offer the demonic Zofloya as an alternative to the spectacle of Victoria's desire for a real black man. The narrator's semblance of feminine modesty assuages a related set of fears about contaminating knowledge. Both of these tactics (the death of Zofloya and the moral fortitude of the narrator) are designed to carve out a space in the literary marketplace for white women as Gothic writers. But this dual strategy has a disturbing element. Zofloya's body, and, as Spivak argues in "Three Women's Texts and a Critique of Imperialism," the bodies of other silenced subaltern subjects like Bertha Mason are the constituent indeterminacies against which Eurocentric "feminist individualism in the age of imperialism" creates itself as its own kind of ideological fantasy,[20] the "Cult of True Womanhood" that requires both the objectification of black bodies and the reification of white, bourgeois, female innocence.[21] The narrator of *Zofloya* longs for the epistemological space of the Moor, the only character in the novel who is both knowing and innocent. The fact that the creation of the epistemological space that white womanhood longs to occupy requires the death of the black servant is as troubling as it is symptomatic of nineteenth-century codes of race and gender. This hollowed-out black space as the epistemological limit of insurrectionary knowledge is the contradiction that the Gothic genre, as proto-feminist endeavor and capitalist object of exchange, seeks to repress in figures like the murdered, mute Zofloya.

Notes

1. As Adriana Craciun notes, *Zofloya* sold 754 of 1,000 printed copies in its first six months of publication. See Craciun's "Charlotte Dacre and the 'Vivisection of Virtue.'" Introduction to *Zofloya* by Charlotte Dacre (Orchard Park, NY: Broadview, 1997), 9–31.

2. James Dunn, "Charlotte Dacre and the Feminization of Violence," *Nineteenth Century Literature* 53.3 (December 1998): 313.

3. Diane Long Hoeveler, "Charlotte Dacre's *Zofloya*: A Case Study in Miscegenation as Sexual and Racial Nausea," *European Romantic Review*, 8.2 (Spring 1997): 188.

4. In "Charlotte Dacre and the Feminization of Violence," Dunn notes that "the violence of female sexual desire [dramatized in vivid detail in Dacre's works] conforms neither to the usual masculine Romantic images of women (as evanescent temptresses or omnipresent mothers) nor to what Anne K. Mellor describes as the prevailing counter-ideology of feminine Romanticism (emphasizing the rationality of women and the values of domesticity and common sense)" (397).

5. Charlotte Dacre, *Zofloya; or, The Moor: A Romance of the Fifteenth Century*, 1806, ed. by Adriana Craciun (Orchard Park, NY: Broadview, 1997), 39. Determining the gender of the narrator is tricky. On one hand, it makes sense to read it as feminine, using Dacre's well-known pen name, "Rosa Matilda," as the basis of the narrator's identity. Yet, in the opening passage, the narrator appeals to the universally male "historian who would wish his lessons to sink deep into the heart," indicating that the following narrative sees itself as something more universal than "the discourse of ladies" (Dacre 39). One possibility to consider is that Dacre is drawing a distinction between the male preserve of historical reporting and a more feminized discourse of the novel. In any event, she certainly evokes a theoretical male audience of concerned historians who are trying to decipher the human heart. When we consider that novel readers at the beginning of the nineteenth century were already being characterized as frivolous females, it seems that here Dacre is sharing a joke between her female narrator and her readers by positioning a group of rational male historians as marginal over-hearers of their feminine discourse.

6. See Sigmund Freud's "The 'Uncanny'" in *The Standard Edition of the Complete Psychological Works of Sigmund Freud*, translated by James Strachey, 17:218–52. 22 vols. (London: Hogarth Press, 1959), 220.

7. In her particularly emphatic style, the narrator underlines the fact that the patriarchal head of the household is Ardolph's real target: his "evil eye" fixates "on the wife of his hospitable unsuspecting host!— of the man who daily and hourly showered down civilities and attention on him. It was *his* honour and *his* happiness that he sought to blight— it was *his* offspring whom he sought to destroy and to disgrace— it was *his* Wife whom he sought to seduce!" (Dacre 44).

8. While the parlor scene is where Victoria gains the heart of Berenza, the bedroom scene, where Berenza is attacked by an unknown assailant who turns out to be none other than Victoria's brother, is the scene where she fools him into finally making her his legal wife. She unwittingly sustains a minor injury during the attack and Berenza awakens just in time to surmise that Victoria has intentionally put herself in harm's way to save his life. Of course, the subtle Victoria knows this to be false, but she once again hides this knowledge behind Berenza's assumptions of her utter devotion. By the time she has recovered from the scratch, she is engaged.

9. Hoeveler's postcolonial reading of *Zofloya* describes the fraught relationship between Zofloya and Victoria as "sexual and racial nausea," and asserts that the "confluence here of the sexually predatory woman and the black male servant" enacts both gender and racial anxieties heightened at the beginning of the nineteenth century (189). (Noting that the discourses of women's rights and the anti-slavery movement were already beginning to borrow from each other's rhetoric, she sees Dacre's work as reactionary in the way it represents the menace of the "social and economic alliance of dispossessed subject populations working together, recognizing their mutual

alienation and objectification and banding as one in a maniacal and deadly pursuit of the great white father and his property" (190).

10. Hoeveler, in contrast, suggests that, on a psychological level, there may be less than one Zofloya. According to her, "Victoria's dreams, [where we first encounter the image of Zofloya] present us with the possibility that the character we recognize as "Zofloya" is actually less a real personage than the dark and demonic forces within Victoria's own psyche" (189). She sees Zofloya as a dramatic projection of Victoria's "alter-ego" (189).

11. Marx, quoted in Slavoi Zizek's *Sublime Object of Ideology* (New York: Verso, 1989), 28. Victoria's relationship to ideology never becomes the kind of "ideological fantasy" proposed by Zizek; such a relationship would require more self-consciousness than Victoria is accorded in this text. Rather than overlooking the fact that she is evil, so as to structure her everyday reality as one in which she is virtuous, it seems that Victoria is never aware (until it is too late, of course) that she has literally gone to the Devil. The narrator and the reader, however, stand on a different epistemological ground, and thus have a more "cynical" relationship to the ideological constructs of *Zofloya*.

12. Near the end of the novel our suspicions that this Zofloya is actually the Devil himself haunting Victoria's dreams are confirmed when he announces that "yes, *I* it was, that under semblance of the Moorish slave (supposedly the recovered favorite of Henriquez) appeared to thee first in thy dreams, luring thee to attempt the completion of thy wildest wishes!" (Dacre 254).

13. Here I refer to Zizek's analogy between political ideology and the psychological processes of dreaming. As he says, the Lacanian "kernel," which is the subconscious truth of our desire that is only present in the dream state, slips away as one wakes into consciousness, so that the "Real of our desire which announces itself in this dream" cannot surface (Zizek 48). In the case of Victoria, the reality of her moral depravity escapes her as she awakens from her dream of Zofloya, thus allowing her to use the waking memory of her dream to serve her deluded fantasies of conquest.

14. The sketchy biographical details known about Dacre's life do not allow us to solve the question of her sympathy, or lack thereof, with the anti-slavery cause. For an overview of the rather contradictory portrait we currently have of Dacre's political affiliations, see Craciun's introduction to the Broadview edition of *Zofloya*.

15. See Gayatri Spivak's "Can the Subaltern Speak?" excerpted in *The Post-Colonial Studies Reader*, ed. Bill Ashcroft, Gareth Griffiths, and Helen Tiffin (New York: Routledge, 1995), 28.

16. See Edmund Burke's *Reflections on the Revolution in France* (1790), ed. J. G. A. Pocock (Indianapolis: Hackett Publishing, 1987).

17. Alan Richardson, *Literature, Education, and Romanticism* (New York: Cambridge University Press, 1994), 169.

18. See *Monthly Literary Recreations* 1 (July 1806): 80, excerpted in "Appendix B" of the 1997 Broadview edition of *Zofloya*, 261.

19. Excerpted from *The Annual Review* 5 (1806): 542, in "Appendix B" of the 1997 Broadview edition of *Zofloya*, 262.

20. Gayatri Spivak, "Three Women's Texts and a Critique of Imperialism," *Critical Inquiry* (Autumn 1985): 244.

21. For a discussion of the importance of whiteness, in particular, to the emerging nineteenth-century "Cult of True Womanhood," see Hazel Carby's *Reconstructing Womanhood: The Emergence of the Afro-American Woman Novelist* (New York: Oxford University Press, 1987).

Works Cited

Burke, Edmund. *Reflections on the Revolution in France.* 1790. Edited by J. G. A. Pocock. Indianapolis: Hackett Publishing, 1987.

Carby, Hazel. *Reconstructing Womanhood: The Emergence of the Afro-American Woman Novelist.* New York: Oxford University Press, 1987.

Craciun, Adriana. "Charlotte Dacre and the 'Vivisection of Virtue.'" Introduction to *Zofloya* by Charlotte Dacre. Orchard Park, NY: Broadview, 1997.

Dacre, Charlotte. *Zofloya; or, The Moor: A Romance of the Fifteenth Century.* 1806. Edited by Adriana Craciun. Orchard Park, NY: Broadview, 1997.

Dunn, James. "Charlotte Dacre and the Feminization of Violence." *Nineteenth Century Literature.* 53.3 (December 1998): 307–327.

Freud, Sigmund. "The 'Uncanny.'" In *The Standard Edition of the Complete Psychological Works of Sigmund Freud.* Translated by James Strachey. 17: 218–52. 22 vols. London: Hogarth Press, 1959.

Hoeveler, Diane Long. "Charlotte Dacre's *Zofloya*: A Case Study in Miscegenation as Sexual and Racial Nausea." *European Romantic Review* 8.2 (Spring 1997): 185–199.

Richardson, Alan. *Literature, Education, and Romanticism.* New York: Cambridge University Press, 1994.

Spivak, Gayatri. "Can the Subaltern Speak?" Excerpted in *The Post-Colonial Studies Reader.* Edited by Bill Ashcroft, Gareth Griffiths, and Helen Tiffin. New York: Routledge, 1995.

____. "Three Women's Texts and a Critique of Imperialism." *Critical Inquiry* (Autumn 1985): 243–261.

Zizek, Slavoi. *Sublime Object of Ideology.* New York: Verso, 1989.

11

"The Vampyre": Romantic Metaphysics and the Aristocratic Other

Gavin Budge

John Polidori's short story "The Vampyre" was published anonymously in 1819. For some time afterwards, despite denials, it was believed to be the work of Lord Byron, whose traveling companion Polidori had been regularly involved in translations of his works. Byron had, in fact, written a fragment of a vampire story, a product of the same storytelling session in Geneva that famously formed the seed of Mary Shelley's *Frankenstein*; it was this story that Polidori was regarded as having plagiarized. Recent critics, however, have emphasized Polidori's own original contribution to the story, regarding it as in creative dialogue with Byronic sources, rather than a straightforward borrowing of them.[1]

The Byronic background to the story is significant, since what Polidori contributes to literary vampirism is a series of topoi which emphasize the aristocratic nature of the vampire. Polidori's vampire is called Lord Ruthven, a name borrowed from the Byron figure of Caroline Lamb's *roman-à-clef Glenarvon*, and which is in turn borrowed by Charles Nodier for his sequel *Lord Ruthven ou les vampires,* published in 1820, in which the vampire's status as an English "milord" is very much stressed. A key characteristic of Polidori's vampire is the inscrutable reserve he displays in the midst of fashionable aristocratic dissipations; his incomprehensibility fascinates the story's young hero, Aubrey. Nodier similarly draws attention to his vampire's aristocratic manners, though these are characterized in a more conventional way.[2]

Before Polidori, vampires appeared in folk tales and were almost always described as peasants; since Polidori, they have retained at least an aristocratic flavor until the present day (one could cite Anne Rice's vampire Lestat, or the upper-class English vampire Spike in *Buffy, the Vampire Slayer*). The issue this paper explores is why Polidori's association between the vampire and the aristocrat has proved so long lasting. Vampirism since Polidori, it seems, has consistently functioned in Western culture as a metaphor for the class Other; my aim is to provide some account of the late-eighteenth- and early-nineteenth-century cultural and intellectual tendencies which have made Polidori's aristocratic characterization of the vampire so powerful.[3]

As the mistaken attribution by contemporaries suggests, Lord Byron is the story's aristocratic Other, an interpretation which biographical information about the fraught personal relationship between Polidori and Byron on their tour together, which is parallelled by the tour taken by Aubrey and Lord Ruthven in the narrative, can only strengthen. The story thus exhibits, at both an intertextual and an intratextual level, the kind of paranoid structure that Eve Kosofsky Sedgwick, in *The Coherence of Gothic Conventions*, has found indicative of "homosocial panic." Aubrey's beloved Greek peasant girl, Ianthe, falls victim to the vampire, and the culminating horror of the story comes on Aubrey's return to London, when he finds Lord Ruthven, whom he has seen dead and buried, engaged to his sister. Aubrey, however, is restrained by the supernatural power of an oath from revealing Ruthven's secret. The women of the story function merely as a bond between the two men, in the way that Sedgwick describes, and the instability of the men's homosocial relationship is reflected in the way that one is constantly supplanting the other.[4]

While not denying the applicability of Sedgwick's "homosocial" reading to Polidori's narrative, I would like to explore a slightly different aspect of the text's "paranoid structure." As William Hughes has suggested, in a criticism that could be applied even to so sophisticated a critic as Sedgwick, the twentieth-century tendency to interpret the vampire in terms of the discourse of sexuality tends to obscure the extent to which the effect of Gothic "horror" is produced by a specifically textual kind of breakdown or failure:

> Something, it appears, always escapes categorization or observation: the Other is dangerous because its boundaries map over those of the perceiving culture, making it *both* an "enemy within" and an externalized (or externalizable) fear.[5]

The failure of discourse that Polidori's narrative dramatizes as "horror," then, is not so much a breakdown of the homo/hetero distinction as an indication of fiction's inability to police the distinction between the aristocratic values of Lord Ruthven and the emergent middle-class values of Aubrey and Polidori's reading audience. The figure of Polidori's vampire projects the aristocrat as an externalized threat, but the very attractiveness of the vampire hints at its status as an "enemy within," in that the reader's interest in Lord Ruthven is doubled within the text as the vampiric fascination to which Aubrey succumbs. Aubrey's enforced silence, on which the horror of the story's *dénouement* depends, in this way figures the reader's own complicity with Ruthven's vampirism, the "open secret" at which the text constantly hints.[6]

I will take as my starting point the use made of "The Vampyre" by a contemporary reviewer as a metaphor for the corrupting influence of Byron's poetry; this gesture, as we shall see, is profoundly revealing about the nature of the social anxieties about writing which are at work in Polidori's narrative. The reviewer warns against "the dangers of a thirst for poetic fame and intellectual dominion." If a writer such as Byron, who is "a man of depraved feelings," makes his aim simply "the consciousness of exciting vivid sensations in others," then "the fable of the Vampyre" will be fulfilled, in that the writer will be "renewing the life of his pleasures from the heart's blood of the principles of his victims."[7] For the reviewer, Byron's poetry is a vampiric text, in that it drains the reader of his vital "principles." The reviewer's anxiety about a kind of writing that aims merely at exciting "sensation" anticipates later nineteenth-century reviewing of "sensation fiction," and also the criticism that was directed against "penny dreadfuls": literary sensationalism is regarded as a contributing cause to mental instability, in that its encouragement of an immediate responsiveness in the reader is at the expense of the capacity for long-term rational consistency. Polidori's narrative itself figures the unhealthiness of sensational fiction in the mental collapse of Aubrey as a result of his obsession with the vampire, a collapse that reflects the mentally precarious situation that contemporary commentators would have found characteristic of the horrified reader. As we shall see, a medical model underlies these anxieties, in which the activities of writing and reading are figured as fundamentally vampiric in nature, at once weakening the mind by rendering it incapable of response to a normal stimulus and producing a craving for more of the same kind of stimulation.[8]

For the moment, however, I will confine my attention to the reviewer's assumption that writing such as Byron's, possessing "the irresistible fascination exerted by a mind of such transcendent faculties," poses the danger that it might weaken the reader's moral "principles." This argument comes easily to the reviewer because it echoes a warning about the dangers of the imagination which had been repeatedly made by members of the Scottish Common Sense school of philosophy over the previous forty years. Although not much read today, Common Sense philosophy was a dominant intellectual tendency in early-nineteenth-century Britain, so much so that Coleridge could casually refer to its most prominent popularizer as "the amiable Beattie" in his *Biographia Literaria*. Polidori's Edinburgh medical training would have made him thoroughly familiar with Common Sense philosophy, particularly since at the time it was influencing studies of the physiology of the brain. Polidori's knowledge of this intellectual tradition is established by explicit references in unpublished writings subsequent to "The Vampyre."[9]

The Common Sense school, particularly in its early phases, did not so much advance a philosophy as criticize the associationist account of the mind proposed by David Hume. It was characterized by a rejection of Hume's systematic mode of philosophizing, which it claimed contradicted "the principles of common sense," from frequent appeal to which the Common Sense school derived its name. Common Sense philosophers regarded these "principles of common sense" as an indefinite number of essentially unanalyzable intuitions on which all thought was necessarily based: one such intuition was that a real world existed outside our perceptions, a principle which Dr. Johnson illustrated, in Boswell's famous anecdote, by kicking a stone to demonstrate his agreement with the Common Sense school, and disagreement with Berkleyan idealism.[10]

The claim that Hume's philosophy is simply absurd and ridiculous presents the Common Sense school with something of a problem. How is the fact of Hume's philosophical persuasiveness, his demonstrated ability to convince readers of the truth of his philosophy, to be accounted for, given his contradiction of principles, which must be, by definition, self-evident to every individual? The Common Sense school surmounts this difficulty by pointing to the way in which Hume's writing appeals to the imagination: Hume's philosophizing, they argue, invokes a number of material metaphors for the mind, such as that of "impression," which are then illegitimately extended so as to imply that all mental operations can be explained in material terms. Thomas Reid, the founder of the Common Sense school, suggested that Hume's real talent as a writer was for poetry, where the imagination can be allowed free play, rather than for philosophy, where it must be kept on a tight rein.[11]

The Common Sense school's defense of the essential immateriality of the mind, then, involves a certain distrust of the imagination. The imaginative writing of Hume, by accustoming the mind to a purely material mode of explanation, can obscure the mind's awareness of its intuitive and immaterial "principles," an argument that is echoed by the reviewer's remark about the influence of Byron's poetry. James Beattie, whose *An Essay on the Nature and Immutability of Truth* popularized the Common Sense philosophical position, puts this argument in strong terms that antic- ipate the reviewer's use of Polidori's *The Vampyre* as a metaphor for Byron's relationship with his readers. Beattie claims that Hume's philosophy actively corrupts the minds of his readers. It is specifically Hume's detailed writing style which Beattie blames for this, since "the very act of studying discomposes our minds a little, and prevents that free play of faculties from which alone we can judge with accuracy," leading us "to mistake ver- bal analogies for real ones, and to apply the laws of matter to the opera- tions of mind." Systematic philosophical writing of the kind in which Hume engages, by the way it leads us to "fix the attention on minute and trifling objects" and so "cramp the imagination," has an inherent tendency to make us regard the mind in material terms, since it exaggerates the importance attached to material metaphors. But once the reader has been led by Hume's language inadvertently to adopt materialist forms of expla- nation, his intuitive mental principles have been fatally compromised, so that he has nothing left to oppose Hume's full-blown philosophical mate- rialism: turns of phrase that were initially accepted by the reader as mere metaphors insensibly come to be regarded as literal descriptions of the reality of mental functioning. At the end of the *Essay*, Beattie makes it clear that he regards Hume's philosophical seduction of his readers with the utmost seriousness, concluding with a ringing denunciation in which he argues that the "detestable" nature of Hume's writings is "of that pecu- liar sort" which requires exposure "in their proper colours" of Hume's "abilities and moral character," disregarding any considerations of polite- ness "which, if we are what we pretend to be, would be hypocritical at best, as well as mockery of the public, and treachery to our course."[12]

For Beattie, Hume's philosophical writing saps the mind's sources of strength (its "principles," or intuitions) and so represents a vampiric form of textuality of the kind which the reviewer finds exemplified in Byron's writing: in both cases, what is at stake is the mental health of the reader, that "free play of faculties" that is impaired by excessive stimulation of the imagination. Polidori, I will argue, describes Aubrey's mental collapse in "The Vampyre" as brought about by exactly this kind of excessive imagi- native stimulation, in terms that make Aubrey's relationship to Lord Ruthven parallel the reader's relationship to Polidori's fantastic narrative. Before making this case, however, for "The Vampyre" as a self-reflexive text that dramatizes its reader's relationship to a Romantic imagination embodied by the text itself, I am going to examine some of the thematic details in the story that suggest the relevance of the Common Sense school's account of the pernicious influence of Humean philosophy as a context for the narrative of Aubrey's fascination with, and undoing by, Lord Ruthven.

The issue of social class that is present in Aubrey's relationship with Lord Ruthven, as in Polidori's real life relationship with Byron, has an analog in the philosophical context I have been describing. One of Hume's major complaints about Beattie's *ad hominem* attack in the *Essay on the Nature and Immutability of Truth* was that Beattie had not treated him "like a gentleman," and this question of gentlemanly status is one of the major issues in the passage, included at the end of later editions of the *Essay,* which I have just summarized. Beattie there argues that Hume, whose work is, in his view, "subversive of virtue," does not deserve to be addressed with respect, and in private correspondence he complained that other members of the Common Sense school had treated Hume too much with kid gloves. It was just this kind of social deference, in Beattie's view, that had allowed Hume to continue to corrupt others through his writings.[13] Beattie does not scruple to portray Hume, in terms that are heavily indebted to Henry Mackenzie's sentimental class rhetoric, as one of the "enemies of religion" who are aristocratic debauchers of oppressed innocence:

> Caressed by those who call themselves the great, ingrossed by the formalities and fopperies of life, intoxicated with vanity, pampered with adulation, dissipated in the tumult of business, or amidst the vicissitudes of folly, they perhaps have little need, and little relish, for the consolations of religion. But let them know, that, in the solitary scenes of life, there is many an honest and tender heart pining with incurable anguish, pierced with the sharpest sting of disappointment, bereft of friends, chilled with poverty, racked with disease, scourged by the oppressor; whom nothing but trust in Providence, and the hope of a future retribution, could preserve from the agonies of despair. And do they, with sacrilegious hands, attempt to violate this last refuge of the miserable, and to rob them of the only comfort that had survived the ravages of misfortune, malice, and tyranny! [Beattie 443].

Beattie's example shows that the Common Sense school's critique of Humean philosophy possesses class overtones that parallel those in Polidori's narrative. Ruthven's status as a lord enables him to spread his vampiric corruption through society in just the same way as Beattie argues that his critics' mistaken treatment of Hume as a "gentleman" allows his writings to continue circulating their evil influence. Ken Gelder, in his 1994

Reading the Vampire, draws attention to the way in which Ruthven is immediately recognized as a vampire by the Greek peasants, but is able to pass unrecognized in polite society, commenting that "Polidori's story seems to suggest that 'society' is vampirish; its aristocratic representatives prey upon 'the people' wherever they go" (34).

If one looks at the respective social positions of Hume and the Common Sense philosophers Beattie and Thomas Reid, it becomes clear why Common Sense philosophy represented an articulation of a newly emergent middle-class outlook. Hume was financially independent, and his writings (particularly the *Treatise of Human Nature*) target a readership of "gentlemen," an orientation also reflected in the posts he occupied as a high-ranking official, which were entirely dependent on aristocratic patronage. Beattie and Reid, on the other hand, were employed as professors in Scottish universities; the students to which their writings were addressed were mostly, like Polidori himself, seeking to establish careers for themselves in the professional fields of law and medicine. The social tensions within the middle class reflected by the Common Sense philosophers' critique of Hume are also exemplified by Polidori's position at the time he wrote "The Vampyre": Polidori's acceptance of the post of Lord Byron's personal physician constituted a resort to aristocratic patronage, after his failure to establish himself professionally. In view of Polidori's personal circumstances, it is unsurprising that "The Vampyre" is characterized by a deep ambivalence about aristocratic power.[14]

The contrast between the "gentlemanly" terms in which Hume expected philosophical debate to be conducted and the Common Sense assertion of independence from "those who call themselves the great" is not just a matter of tone, but extends to substantive philosophical issues, particularly in the field of ethics. Polidori's description of the vampiric corruption spread by Lord Ruthven can be understood in these terms, as a criticism of the aristocratic ethic of "benevolence" from the middle-class standpoint articulated by Common Sense philosophy. Lord Ruthven is shown as exercising a traditional mode of aristocratic charity, of a sort that Byron himself practiced:

> His companion was profuse in his liberality; the idle, the vagabond, and the beggar, received from his hand more than enough to relieve their immediate wants. But Aubrey could not avoid remarking, that it was not upon the virtuous, reduced to indigence by the misfortunes attendant even upon virtue, that he bestowed his alms; these were sent from the door with hardly suppressed sneers; but when the profligate came to ask something, not to relieve his wants, but to allow him to wallow in his lust, or to sink him still deeper in his iniquity, he was sent away with rich charity. This

was, however, attributed by him to the greater importunity of the vicious, which generally prevails over the retiring bashfulness of the virtuous indigent. There was one circumstance about the charity of his Lordship, which was still more impressed upon his mind: all those upon whom it was bestowed, inevitably found there was a curse upon it, for they were all either led to the scaffold, or sunk to the lowest and the most abject misery [Polidori 110–111].

Ruthven's charity is shown to be superficial: by rewarding importunity rather than virtue, it simply furthers the moral corruption of the poor. Polidori's characterization of an aristocratic charity guided not by "principle" but merely by passive response to external stimulus, echoes early-nineteenth-century debates about poor relief; arguments against "indoor relief" making very similar claims about charity's moral corruption of the poor can be found in the 1834 Poor Law Report.[15]

Ruthven's apparently benevolent behavior turns out to be vampiric corruption in disguise. This, I would argue, reflects a disagreement between Hume and the Common Sense school over the nature of virtue itself. Hume had claimed that all virtuous behaviour had its origin in "benevolence." Since this is a disinterested feeling, Hume argued, it is the only emotion that can be consistently awakened by events, and so must come to predominate in our responses even though, in itself, it is a comparatively weak emotion.[16]

As Thomas Reid points out, the derivation of virtue from benevolence implies that it is the aristocrat, or gentleman of leisure, who embodies virtue. Hume's argument implicitly appeals to an aristocratic breadth of experience: the greater the range of situations to which the mind has been exposed, the more the emotion of benevolence will predominate within it. Furthermore, Hume's argument assumes that a detachment from active commitments is necessary to the practice of virtue, since a personal involvement in any particular situation will necessarily tend to excite more self-interested emotions, and this kind of detachment is available only to the aristocrat. A more mundane argument, which Reid does not employ but which is implied in Polidori's narrative, is that "benevolence," in the discourse of Sensibility within which Hume situates his ethics, is really a code word for giving money, an activity in which the aristocrat has an obvious advantage.[17]

Polidori's characterization of Ruthven's charity and its effects illustrates the way in which his narrative generally figures the aristocratic Other in terms of vampirism. Ruthven's very superficiality, his purely materialistic approach to giving, is shown simultaneously as a fascinating source of power, and as a source of moral corruption. A similar point can be made about a prominent feature of Polidori's description of Lord Ruthven, the emphasis at the beginning of the story on Lord Ruthven's fascinating gaze:

> Those who felt this sensation of awe, could not explain whence it arose: some attributed it to the dead grey eye, which, fixing upon the object's face, did not seem to penetrate, and at one glance to pierce through to the inward workings of the heart; but fell upon the cheek with a leaden ray that weighed upon the skin it could not pass ... the deadly hue of his face ... never gained a warmer tint, either from the blush of modesty, or from the strong emotion of passion [Polidori 108].

Lord Ruthven's face is completely unexpressive, in a way that links Polidori's description with late-eighteenth-century bourgeois criticisms of the insincerity of aristocratic manners. The contemporary reader might well have recalled Chesterfield's famous advice, in his *Letters to his Son*, never to betray any spontaneous emotion, a kind of behavior which eighteenth-century reviewers characterized as positively inhuman.[18]

Polidori gives his description of Lord Ruthven a more metaphysical dimension when he characterizes him as "a man entirely absorbed in himself, who gave few other signs of his observation of external objects, than the tacit assent to their existence, implied by the avoidance of their contact." Polidori echoes here one of the chief arguments of the Common Sense school for the absurdity of Hume's skeptical philosophy. Hume had argued that it was impossible to give a rational demonstration of the existence of an external world. The Common Sense school denied Hume's assumption that such extreme skepticism was inherent in philosophical rationality, using as one of their chief points the *ad hominem* argument that Hume's own behavior showed that he was in fact convinced of the external world's existence (as indeed, in their view, only a madman could fail to be) (Reid 102). Hume, in the view of the Common Sense school, tacitly assented to the existence of "external objects" in exactly the same way as Lord Ruthven is described as doing. Polidori's reference to this philosophical debate thus associates the aristocratic inscrutability that had been criticized in Lord Chesterfield with the skeptical materialism of Humean philosophy and with the unknowable mysteriousness of the Gothic Other. The uncanniness of Ruthven's gaze consists in its pure materiality, the quasi-physical way in which it "weighs upon the skin," a trope which figures the aristocratic Other as a nightmarish animated corpse.

Ken Gelder notes that the way Polidori describes Ianthe, the Greek peasant girl with whom Aubrey falls in love, is a deliberate revision of one of his Byronic sources. This gesture too can be linked to the Common Sense philosophical context that I am suggesting shapes Polidori's treatment of the aristocratic Other in "The Vampyre," as can the role assigned to women generally within the narrative. In Byron's "The Giaour," in which the belief in vampires is incidentally recounted, the heroine Leila's eyes are described:

> Her eye's dark charm 'twere vain to tell
> But gaze on that of the Gazelle
> It will assist thy fancy well;
> As large, as languishingly dark.[19]

Gelder highlights Polidori's rewriting of the comparison to a gazelle in his description of Ianthe, in a way which apparently critiques Byron:

> As she danced upon the plain, or tripped along the mountain's side, one would have thought the gazelle a poor type of her beauties; for who would have exchanged her eye, apparently the type of animated nature, for that sleepy luxurious look of the animal suited but to the taste of an epicure.[20]

Gelder uses this example to argue that "The Vampyre" is a consciously revisionist text, rather than a mere cento of Byronic motifs, but he fails to note that Polidori's reworking of Byron's simile is linked both to contemporary critical responses to Byron's poetry, and to a whole thematics of the eye within the story itself. The descriptions of women in Byron's oriental tales were frequently criticized in contemporary reviews for their concentration on external, physically feminine attributes, with reviewers commenting that Byron subscribed, poetically at least, to the Mahometan view that women had no souls. Polidori's ostentatious rejection of the gazelle comparison echoes this characterization of Byron, implicitly identifying him with the luxurious aristocratic epicure, and pointedly associates the materialism of which Byron had been accused by critics with the aristocratic *hauteur* of his vampire — and the uncanny superficiality of his gaze — whose reception in London society closely parallels that of Byron himself.[21]

This passage, however, is only one of a number of places in "The Vampyre" in which descriptions of eyes play a prominent role. Aubrey's sister, for example, is also characterized through the Romantic inwardness of her eyes:

> Her blue eye was never lit up by the levity of the mind beneath. There was melancholy charm about it which did not seem to arise from misfortune, but from some feeling within, that appeared to indicate a soul conscious of a higher realm [Polidori 120].

Aubrey's sister's eye, like that of Ianthe, is described in terms of a contrast between the superficiality of the merely material, and the "depth" that indicates consciousness of a spiritual realm. Both of these descriptions contrast markedly with the "dead grey eye" of Lord Ruthven himself, and correspond to the Common Sense school's claims for the essential immateriality of the human mind, for which they adduced the spontaneous physical expression of the human body as evidence (Reid 458).

In terms of the parallel I have been suggesting between Lord Ruthven's vampirism and the corrupting influence that the Common Sense school attributed to Humean philosophy, it is significant that expressive gazes are consistently associated with the women in Polidori's narrative. Within the context of Common Sense philosophy, the expressiveness of Ianthe and of Aubrey's sister testifies to their moral claims on the world of men, which the vampiric Lord Ruthven brutally disregards. Such disregard for women's rights is identified by Thomas Reid as a consequence of Humean philosophy: Hume's Hobbesian argument that rights are an effect of power implies that women, as the physically weaker sex, "owe the share they have in the rights of society, to the power which their address and their charms give them" rather than to any intrinsic moral claim on men, a view which Reid rejects as self-evidently immoral (660). This Humean view of relationships between the sexes as a power struggle in which there no such thing as mutuality is encapsulated in Lord Ruthven's parting words to Aubrey at the end of "The Vampyre," "Women are frail!" (125), hinting that Aubrey is powerless to prevent Ruthven's marriage to his sister because she has already been debauched.

So far, I have been suggesting that the association of vampirism with aristocracy that is fundamental to Polidori's narrative reflects the critique of aristocratic values embodied in late-eighteenth-century Common Sense philosophy, and, more generally, in the sentimental discourse of authors such as Henry Mackenzie; James Beattie, poet of Sensibility as well as Common Sense philosopher, illustrates the continuity between these two traditions. But much of the horror of "The Vampyre" comes from the way its ending stages a breakdown of the middle-class values that the reader is led to expect the narrative will embody, a breakdown that mirrors the breakdown of the middle-class narrative of professional success in Polidori's own life at the time he wrote the story. Aubrey's relationship to Lord Ruthven is a strangely ambiguous one of attraction and repulsion, and I would like to argue that this corresponds to a more general Romantic ambivalence about the social consequences of the imagination itself, a theme with which Aubrey is very strongly identified within the story.

The ambivalence of Aubrey's relation to Lord Ruthven finds a parallel in the Common Sense school's reaction to Hume, in which the category of the imagination also plays an important role. As I have already noted, members of the Common Sense school repeatedly suggest that the main fault of Hume as a philosophical writer was that he had allowed his imagination to run away with him. They link this criticism with Hume's materialistic epistemology. Hume's imagination, they argue, was so struck with material metaphors for the mind, such as that of "impression," that his conception of the mind became completely dominated by such metaphors and hence materialistic, ignoring evidence as to the non-material nature of mind.[22] However, the problem with this criticism of Hume, as the Common Sense school certainly knows, is that it is impossible to write about the mind without employing material metaphors, which are embedded in the very language we must use to describe the mind. To write about the mind at all is to risk falling into Humean materialism. It is in this context, I would suggest, that the full ambiguity in "The Vampyre," both of the imagination and of Polidori's position as an author, becomes apparent (Stewart 179–182, 447).

The moral ambiguity of Aubrey within Polidori's narrative can be identified with the ambiguity of the imagination within Common Sense philosophy. For the Common Sense school, the imagination confirms and embodies our original moral intuitions, but it also has the potential to seduce us into a materialistic worldview. Similarly, in "The Vampyre," Aubrey's imagination makes him delight in the spirituality that is embodied by the gracefulness of Ianthe, but it also leads him into a fascination with the dead material gaze of Lord Ruthven. This ambiguity, however, is also that of Polidori's class position as a Romantic writer: is his attempt to appeal to the readerly imagination a Wordsworthian exercise in awakening the natural moral intuitions on which middle-class authority is based, or is his writing doomed to succumb to the vampiric corruption of Humean materialism and aristocratic authority? Aubrey's inability at the end of "The Vampyre" to reveal Lord Ruthven's secret suggests that Polidori found no way to resolve his anxiety about the class politics of fiction.

The expressiveness and spontaneity of Ianthe and Miss Aubrey, in their opposition to the studied indifference of Lord Ruthven, represent a secure locus for middle-class values within the narrative, which makes Miss Aubrey's final corruption by the vampire all the more shocking. The character of Aubrey, however, which the narrative so strongly associates with the imagination and which constitutes a focus of identification for the middle-class reader, plays a curiously ambiguous role in the text's class oppositions, in a way that suggests that the vampiric power of Lord Ruthven stems from Aubrey's (and the reader's) unacknowledged affinity with this aristocratic figure.

This potential class ambiguity is present from the beginning of the narrative. Aubrey is introduced as a "gentleman," whose parents have left him "in possession of great wealth" that is held in trust for him by guardians—the rather unspecific nature of the "wealth" implies, though this is nowhere actually stated, that the wealth comes from trade. The narrative characterizes him ironically as possessing "that high romantic feeling of honour and candour, which daily ruins so many milliner's apprentices" (109), a description that juxtaposes the essentially middle-class value of open-hearted "candour" with the notorious aristocratic propensity for debauching women of inferior social status and with aristocratic inscrutability. A similar ambiguity is present later on:

> He hinted to his guardians, that it was time for him to perform the tour, which for many generations has been thought necessary to enable the young to take some rapid steps in the career of vice towards putting themselves upon an equality with the aged, and not allowing them to appear as if fallen from the skies, wherever scandalous intrigues are mentioned as the subjects of pleasantry or of praise, according to the degree of skill shewn in carrying them on [110].

It is not altogether clear whether the cynical tone the narrative assumes here is to be attributed to Aubrey himself, though as this seems incompatible with the previous heavy emphasis on his naïve idealism, it is a possibility the reader tends to discount. The echo, however, of questionings of the value of the grand tour in the literature of Sensibility, does make Aubrey's active desire to undertake the tour seem somewhat dubious.[23]

Aubrey's role in bringing about the vampiric deaths of both of the women that he loves graphically illustrates the ambiguous moral status at which these passages hint. Aubrey rationalistically discounts the Greek peasants' tales of vampires, setting off on an excursion that leads to Ianthe succumbing to the vampire (the story implies that Ianthe, worried by his lateness in returning, has come out to look for him and has met the vampire instead). Aubrey is also indirectly instrumental in promoting the fatal marriage of Lord Ruthven to his sister; his mental collapse on finding Lord Ruthven moving in London polite society after Aubrey has witnessed his death allows the vampire to gain access to his house and court his sister under pretext of inquiring about Aubrey's health.

Lord Ruthven functions, then, as Aubrey's dark alter-ego, a Hyde to his Jekyll, taking his place by the side of the women he loves. This uncannily symbiotic relationship is linked in the narrative to the status Lord Ruthven has taken on within Aubrey's imagination:

> He watched him; and the very impossibility of forming an idea of the character of a man entirely absorbed in himself ... allowing his imagination to picture every thing that flattered its propensity to extravagant ideas, he soon formed this object into the hero of a romance, and determined to observe the offspring of his fancy, rather than the person before him [110].

Lord Ruthven's aristocratic inscrutability, the unavailability of his sub-jectivity, is in league with the imagination that is Aubrey's primary char-acteristic, and it is this that gives him his vampiric power and that renders him the unknowable objectified Other. This connection between Ruthven's vampirism and Aubrey's imagination is reinforced by the fact that until relatively late in the narrative, it remains unclear whether Ruthven really will turn out to be a vampire, or whether the story will end in the demys-tifying mode of Austen's *Northanger Abbey*. The vampiric hints that the narrative throws out may, until a fairly late point, turn out to be the "offspring" of Aubrey's, and the reader's "fancy"; the apparently to-be-debunked tendency to interpret Ruthven as "the hero of a romance" is not only Aubrey's, but, owing to the generic instability of the narrative, ours also.

Aubrey's moral ambiguity within Polidori's narrative is symptomatic of the ambiguous status of the Romantic imagination in relationship to general middle-class values. A similarly ambiguous status is accorded to the Romantic imagination in Walter Scott's *Waverley,* published only a couple of years before Polidori wrote "The Vampyre." Scott's "mediocre" hero was in all likelihood Polidori's model for the character of Aubrey. Like Aubrey, Waverley is strongly associated with the Romantic imagina-tion at an early stage in Scott's narrative; whereas Polidori briefly notes that Aubrey had "cultivated more his imagination than his judgement" (109), Scott gives an extended account of the deficiencies of Waverley's education:

> The instructor had to combat another propensity too often united with brilliancy of fancy and vivacity of talent, — that indolence, namely, of dis-position, which can only be stirred by some strong motive of gratification, and which renounces study so soon as curiosity is gratified, the pleasure of conquering the first difficulties exhausted, and the novelty of pursuit at an end.... Alas! while he was thus permitted to read only for the gratification of his own amusement, he foresaw not that he was losing for ever the opportunity of acquiring habits of firm and incumbent applica-tion, of gaining the art of controlling, directing, and concentrating the powers of his own mind for earnest investigation, — an art far more essen-tial than even that learning which is the primary object of study.[24]

Scott's moralizing commentary on the way Waverley's "brilliancy of fancy" leads him to weaken his mind by reading only for amusement (a common theme in late-eighteenth- and early-nineteenth-century descriptions of the effects of novel reading) stresses the incompatibility of the imagination with middle-class values: Waverley forfeits exactly those "habits of ... applica-tion" that were regarded as indispensable in establishing a professional career.

Yet without Waverley's excessive imagination there would be, of course, no novel, since it is this mental weakness that leads Waverley to throw in his lot with the Jacobite Rebellion. Scott makes this clear in his description of the effect of the crucial meeting with the Pretender at which Waverley is led to declare his allegiance:

> Unaccustomed to the address and manners of a polished court, in which Charles was eminently skilful, his words and his kindness penetrated the heart of our hero, and easily outweighed all prudential motives. To be thus personally solicited for assistance by a prince, whose form and manners, as well as the spirit which he displayed in this singular enterprize, answered his ideas of a hero of romance; to be courted by him in the ancient halls of his paternal palace, recovered by the sword which he was already bending towards other conquests, gave Edward, in his own eyes the dignity and importance which he had ceased to consider as his attributes [Scott 193].

Waverley commits himself to the Jacobite cause because the figure of Charles Stewart appeals to his imagination, corresponding to "his ideas of a hero of romance," an effect of which Scott implies the Pretender and his minions are well aware. The bedazzlement caused by the Pretender's appearance, however, applies just as much to the reader as to Waverley himself: the Pretender is the first non-fictional character to appear in the novel, which up to this point has concentrated on imaginatively appealing descriptions of exotic Highland life, part of whose function is to encourage us to identify with Waverley's viewpoint, in the absence of any other familiar reference point. Scott's reader is, by definition, a novel reader and is, in this, like Waverley himself, so that the ontological discontinuity occasioned by the Pretender's sudden and unprepared appearance as a character in Scott's fictional narrative makes us "encounter" the Pretender in the same way as Waverley does. The whole design of Scott's novel is to make us recognize Waverley's tendency to let his imagination predominate over his judgment as our own tendency as readers of the novel, and so to enable us to experience the political power that the Pretender exerts through his imaginative appeal.[25]

Waverley's encounter with the Pretender is structurally similar to Aubrey's encounter with Lord Ruthven as presented in "The Vampyre." There is the same kind of identification between the reader and the rather ineffectual hero: the reader of Polidori's narrative seeks after imaginative "sensation" in the same way as Aubrey himself does, so that Aubrey's fascination with Lord Ruthven functions as an alibi for readerly desire in a way which recalls Barthes's analysis in *S/Z* of the reader's complicity with narrative mystification. Aubrey could almost exclaim with Baudelaire, "— *Hypocrite lecteur — mon semblable — mon frère!*"[26] The "horror" of Polidori's narrative, which I have been arguing consists in the breakdown of the distinction between middle-class and aristocratic values (or the consuming from within of middle-class "authenticity" by aristocratic superficiality), also has its parallel in Scott's novel, in Waverley's discovery that Jacobitism threatens to replace the bureaucratic rationality, identified with the middle classes, with aristocratic court intrigue, although in Scott the threat posed by the aristocratic Other is averted.

The association of imagination with aristocratic power, which is present in Scott and which I would argue also underlies Lord Ruthven's vampiric fascination, reflects an analysis of the nature of aristocratic dominion presented in Adam Smith's quasi-sociological account of the nature of morality, *The Theory of Moral Sentiments*, which was widely read in the early nineteenth century. Smith explains aristocratic predominance in the society of his day as owing to the natural tendencies of the imagination. For Smith, our capacity for sympathy is due to the imagination, which places us mentally in someone else's situation. But in order for this mental transference successfully to take place, the other's situation has to be *representable* to the mind, and Smith argues that the readiness with which the mind pictures another's situation to itself is affected by the mind's natural tendency to seek pleasure and avoid pain.[27] Smith points out that the situation of the wealthy is especially easy for the imagination to envisage, because they are surrounded by objects that are specially tailored to promote their pleasure and convenience. This ensures that the rich, whom Smith implicitly equates with the aristocratic class, have a ready call on our sympathy that the poor do not. The very fact that aristocrats are the center of attention enables them to exercise a political influence over society that is out of proportion to their means and abilities, since being at the center of attention is the situation above all others that is attractive to the imagination:

> Do the great seem insensible of the easy price at which they may acquire the public admiration; or do they seem to imagine that to them, as to other men, it must be the purchase either of sweat or of blood? By what important accomplishments is the young nobleman instructed to support the dignity of his rank, and to render himself worthy of that superiority over his fellow-citizens, to which the virtue of his ancestors had raised them? Is it by knowledge, by industry, by patience, by self-denial, or by virtue of any kind?
>
> As all his words, as all his motions are attended to, he learns an habitual regard to every circumstance of ordinary behaviour, and studies to perform all those small duties with the most exact propriety. As he is conscious how much he is observed, and how much mankind are disposed to favour all his inclinations, he acts, upon the most indifferent occasions,

with that freedom and elevation which the thought of this naturally inspires. His air, his manner, his deportment, all mark that elegant and graceful sense of his own superiority, which those who are born to inferior status can hardly ever arrive at. These are the arts by which he proposes to make mankind more easily submit to his authority, and to govern their inclinations according to his own pleasure: and in this he is seldom disappointed. These arts, supported by rank and preeminence, are, upon ordinary occasions, sufficient to govern the world [Smith, 181–183; 53–54].

For Smith, then, the chief support of aristocratic authority is the aesthetic quality of gracefulness, because this is a visible indicator of the situation the aristocrat occupies as the habitual center of attention. Aristocratic graces are "sufficient to govern the world" because of the appeal they make to the imagination. The aristocrat learns through his behavior to represent his own social condition, and it is this that ensures that he will always elicit more sympathy, or "public admiration," than those who perhaps have greater merit but do not easily inhabit this dimension of social representation. The ascendency that Charles Stewart, in Scott's novel, obtains over Waverley is a perfect example of this process at work: Waverley acknowledges the Pretender as his sovereign because he looks the part, as Scott's description of his "easy and graceful manners" makes clear (Scott 192).

Aristocratic authority, then, in the views of Scott and Smith, is a product of representation, a connection which suggests that the vampiric fascination Polidori attributes to Lord Ruthven is an expression of middle-class anxiety about the class implications of the imagination, as the faculty that is responsible for representing society. Aubrey succumbs to the evil influence of Lord Ruthven in the same way the reader succumbs to the attractions of Polidori's narrative, and in both cases, Polidori regards this luxuriating in the realm of imagination as a betrayal of middle-class values. Polidori's text thus ends by undoing the middle-class position which its narrative voice articulates, and it is this that constitutes the text's "horror": the reader finds that the text is incapable of policing the distinction between middle-class and aristocratic values, between the middle-class self and the aristocratic Other, which the narrative initially appears to offer. It is the reader, just as much as Aubrey, who is the victim of the aristocratic vampire.

The kind of relationship between aristocratic authority and the nature of representation (that is, the natural tendencies of the imagination) that we have found in Smith, is also present in Hume's philosophy. The Common Sense school's criticisms of Humean philosophy, which I have argued is an important intellectual context for the uncanny fascination that Polidori attributes to Lord Ruthven, can be seen as directed against the equation of social relationships with representation (or the imagination) that is fundamental to Smith's argument: Reid, for example, insists that the primary moral virtue is the essentially unrepresentable one of duty. In the Romantic period, however, this middle-class critique of the aristocratic view of society as constituted by representation remains vulnerable. This vulnerability is expressed by Polidori in "The Vampyre," but can be found in other Romantic writers as well.

One of the closest equivalents to the breakdown of the aristocratic/middle-class distinction found in "The Vampyre" is the account of the imagination offered by Hazlitt. Hazlitt's conception of the social function of the imagination is very close to the one we have found in Smith and Scott. For Hazlitt, the imagination is naturally an "exclusive" and "aggregating" faculty, and this accounts, for example, for Shakespeare's siding with the aristocratic viewpoint in plays such as *Coriolanus*: the poetic imagination cannot help but be attracted to aristocracy. Hazlitt carries this analysis still further when he describes the role the imagination plays in the maintenance of monarchical power. Hazlitt argues that the imagination naturally seeks to extract out of any situation the maximum stimulation for itself, and in the case of politics, this naturally leads to an exaltation of the monarch, and an abasement of his subjects, that is as extreme as possible. The relation of subjects to a monarch, Hazlitt suggests, is essentially sado-masochistic in nature: subjects gain a kind of perverse imaginary enjoyment out of their own humiliation before a monarch, and this leads them to exaggerate the difference between monarch and subjects even further.[28] Hazlitt's theory of the imagination envisages a kind of self-annihilation by the middle-class reader or spectator of their own class position, which, I would suggest, is very similar to what occurs at the end of "The Vampyre." In Hazlitt's view, the imagination cannot tolerate any medium between the despotic monarch and the degraded populace: that is as much to say, it cannot tolerate the middle class. But the imagination, as Smith's *The Theory of Moral Sentiments* makes clear, is also what constitutes the middle-class position itself: the aristocrat does not need to imagine any situation outside his own, whereas middle-class ambition to make one's mark in the world is the product of imagination (Smith 181–183).

This essentially self-destructive character of the Romantic imagination, as presented by Hazlitt, helps to explain the kind of responsibility attributed to Aubrey for his own mental breakdown toward the end of the narrative. Hazlitt's description of the imagination as seeking its own "stimulation" draws on the medical model, known as Brunonianism, put forward by the physician John Brown and his followers toward the end of the eighteenth century. According to Brown, all medical symptoms and treatments could be reduced to the single dimension of under- or overstimulation of the organs. Although this might seem to simplify medical practice radically, the distinction between under- and overstimulation was, in Brown's view, not easy to draw, since both conditions might present exactly the same symptoms: overstimulation weakened the organs, making them unresponsive to milder stimuli, but creating a need for further stimulation, a state known as "irritability."[29]

As a doctor trained in Edinburgh, the center of the Brunonian movement, Polidori would certainly have been familiar with its medical model of "stimulation." The Brunonian model makes an appearance in Polidori's narrative when the "dreadfully vicious" nature of Lord Ruthven's character is revealed:

> It had been discovered, that his contempt for the adultress had not originated in hatred of her character; but that he had required, to enhance his gratification, that his victim, the partner of his guilt, should be hurled from the pinnacle of unsullied virtue, down to the lowest abyss of infamy and degradation: in fine, that all those females whom he had sought, apparently on account of their virtue, had, since his departure, thrown even the mask aside, and had not scrupled to expose the whole deformity of their vices to the public gaze [Polidori 112].

Lord Ruthven is "vicious" not only in the moral sense, but also in his perverse taste for bringing about the moral degradation of others. In a manner that recalls Hazlitt's description of the imagination, Ruthven seeks the maximum effect of contrast between his partner's previously unsullied state and her moral fall, to add some sadistic relish to seduction. The apparently *blasé* attitude by which Ruthven is characterized at the beginning of the narrative accords with the Brunonian model of overstimulation: Ruthven is in a state of moral "irritability," in which he is insensible to normal stimulation, but craves the piquancy of active depravity. But Ruthven's imaginative enjoyment of contrast is also ours, as readers of Polidori's rather melodramatic narrative, and the same Brunonian diagnosis might be applied to our interest in Polidori's supernatural tale: deadened to everyday interests, we seek out the stimulation provided by horror (Polidori 108).

In early-nineteenth-century medical writing, the Brunonian concept of overstimulation was frequently used as an explanation for mental derangement, and, in particular, for monomania. Polidori's description of the process by which Aubrey loses his sanity alludes to the Brunonian model:

He paced the room with hurried steps, and fixed his hands upon his head, as if his thoughts were bursting from his brain. Lord Ruthven again before him —circumstances started up in dreadful array— the dagger— his oath....

Aubrey became almost distracted. If before his mind had been absorbed by one subject, how much more completely was it engrossed, now that the certainty of the monster's living again pressed up his thoughts.... At last, no longer capable of bearing stillness and solitude, he left his house, roamed from street to street, anxious to fly that image which haunted him.... His sister, anxious for his safety, employed people to follow him; but they were soon distanced by him who fled from a pursuer swifter than any—from thought....

They engaged a physician to reside in the house, and take constant care of him. He hardly appeared to notice it, so completely was his mind absorbed by one terrible subject.... He would often lie for days, incapable of being roused [Polidori 121–23].

The thought of Lord Ruthven becomes an obsession that Aubrey is powerless to control, eventually leading to state of complete torpor. This parallels contemporary descriptions of madness as a condition of mental "irritability," brought about by excessive stimulation of particular locations in the brain through too great a preoccupation with a limited range of ideas (a condition to which writers were thought extremely liable). According to the Brunonian model, this mental overstimulation leads to obsession, because it simultaneously makes the brain insensible to normal stimuli (hence Aubrey is finally "incapable of being roused") and leads to a quasi-physical need for more of the same kind of stimulation. The Brunonian description of overstimulation furnishes an early model for the phenomenon of addiction, so that Aubrey's condition can be understood as that of a horror junkie.[30]

Aubrey's final state parallels the kind of mental enervation that was often in the early nineteenth century said to be the result of excessive novel reading. Lord Ruthven's vampiric influence over Aubrey can thus be identified with the vampiric draining of the reader's mental strength by the sensational text. The "horror" of the end of Polidori's narrative represents a collapse of the boundary between reader and text: Aubrey's reduction to a condition of passivity is also that of the reader. But as Hazlitt's account of the imagination makes clear, this passive condition, in which the maximum of sensation is craved, furnishes the chief support for aristocratic authority, and constitutes the self-abnegation of the middle class.[31]

The horror of Polidori's Gothic narrative thus consists ultimately in the revelation of a materiality that, in the dualistic Common Sense philosophical position to which Polidori seems to have subscribed, is conceived of as fundamentally alien to the human mind. This is true at a number of levels within the text. At the thematic level, the "aristocratic inscrutability" of Ruthven derives its Gothic uncanniness from its pure externality: Ruthven's vampiric status as the Gothic Other is shown by the sheer materiality of his gaze, which is not only impenetrable by the perceiving eye but which, uncannily, remains *outside* what it registers and "weighs upon the skin." Ruthven remains wholly unknowable, in the way that matter itself was unknowable within the Common Sense philosophy of Reid and Stewart.[32]

Ruthven seems to pass this materiality on by contagion, and it is in this that his vampiric corruption consists. Not only does he convert the expressive Ianthe into a corpse, but he reveals the fleshy frailty of Aubrey's sister, and, through his appeal to the imagination, ends up by materializing Aubrey's very mind, since the imagination was an essentially material faculty in the Common Sense philosophical position. The final horror of Aubrey's position is that he realizes the materiality of his own mental processes in the condition of madness, which Brunonian mental physiology defined in the material terms of the irritability of mental tissue; the culmination of this materialization of Aubrey's mind is his death from a brain hemorrhage when Ruthven whispers to him the news of his sister's "frailty." In the terms of Common Sense philosophy, which defined the mind as essentially immaterial, this descent into a condition of materiality is a transgression of the boundary not only between middle-class inwardness and aristocratic superficiality, but between self and the ultimate Other, matter itself. But, as I have been arguing, this horrific condition in which consciousness is confronted with its own materiality is also, implicitly, that of the reader of Polidori's text, both in the search for the excessive stimulation of sensational fiction and in the immersion within what Common Sense philosophy regarded as the essentially material nature of textuality.

Notes

1. For example, Ken Gelder, *Reading the Vampire* (London: Routledge, 1994), 31.
2. John Polidori, "The Vampyre," in *Vampyres: Lord Byron to Count Dracula*, ed. Christopher Frayling (London: Faber and Faber, 1991), 108, 111; Charles Nodier, *Lord Ruthven ou les Vampires* (Paris: Ladvocat, 1820, fac. ed. Marseille: Laffitte, 1978), 14–16.
3. Christopher Frayling, ed., *Vampyres: Lord Byron to Count Dracula* (London: Faber and Faber, 1991), 5–6.
4. Eve Kosofsky Sedgwick, *The Coherence of Gothic Conventions* (London and New York: Methuen, 1986), *passim*.
5. William Hughes, "Fictional Vampires in the Nineteenth and Twentieth Cen-

turies," in *A Companion to the Gothic,* ed. David Punter (Oxford: Blackwell, 2000), 148.

6. See Eve Kosofsky Sedgwick, *Epistemology of the Closet* (Harmondsworth: Penguin, 1994), 34 on the complicity of the narratorial voice with the reader; see also Roland Barthes, *S/Z,* trans. Richard Miller (Oxford: Blackwell, 1990), 151. Balzac's *Sarrasine* itself could be read as a parable of class, though this is a perspective which Barthes chooses to underplay.

7. Donald H. Reiman, *The Romantics Reviewed: Contemporary Reviews of British Romantic Writing: Part B, Byron and Regency Society Poets,* vol. 2 (New York and London: Garland, 1972), 759.

8. H.L. Mansel, "Sensation Novels," *Quarterly Review* 113 (1863): 482–483, 485–486; E. S. Turner, *Boys Will Be Boys* (Harmondsworth: Penguin, 1976), 112.

9. Coleridge, *Biographia Literaria* ref.; see John Abercrombie, *Inquiries Concerning the Intellectual Powers,* 7th ed. (Edinburgh, 1833); D. L. Macdonald, *Poor Polidori: A Critical Biography of the Author of "The Vampyre"* (Toronto: University of Toronto Press, 1991), 15–17, 154.

10. For a general account of the Common Sense school, see S. A. Grave, *The Scottish Philosophy of Common Sense* (Oxford: Clarendon Press, 1960); James Boswell, *Boswell's Life of Johnson,* ed. G. B. Hill, rev. L. F. Powell, 6 vols. (Oxford: Clarendon Press, 1934), vol. 1, 471.

11. Thomas Reid, *Works,* ed. William Hamilton, 7th ed., 2 vols. (Edinburgh, 1872), 229, 202, 472.

12. James Beattie, *An Essay on the Nature and Immutability of Truth,* 6th ed. (Edinburgh, 1777), 129–130, 395, see also 307 & 135, 473.

13. W. Forbes, *An Account of the Life and Writings of James Beattie* LLD, 2 vols. (Edinburgh, 1806), vol. 1, 171, 131–132.

14. David Hume, *A Treatise of Human Nature,* eds. L. H. Selby-Bigge and P. H. Nidditch (Oxford: Clarendon Press, 1978), 272; Ernest Campbell Mossner, *The Life of David Hume,* 2nd ed. (Oxford: Clarendon Press, 1980), 205–208; *An Oxford Companion to the Romantic Age,* ed. Iain McCalman (Oxford University Press, 1999), "Beattie," 418, "Reid," 672, 164; Macdonald 43–46, 53.

15. *The Poor Law Report of 1834,* ed. S. G. and E. O. A. Checkland (Harmondsworth: Penguin, 1974), 167–179.

16. David Hume, *Enquiries Concerning Human Understanding and Concerning the Principles of Morals,* eds. L. H. Selby-Bigge and P. H. Nidditch, 3rd ed. (Oxford: Clarendon Press, 1975), 270–271.

17. Reid, 580–586; see Goldsmith's description of the Man in Black in "The Citizen of the World," chaps. 26 & 27, in *Works,* ed. D. Masson (London: Macmillan, 1874), 125–129.

18. *The Mirror,* no. 35, 10th ed. (London, 1794), 257–262.

19. Lord Byron, "The Giaour," in *Complete Poetical Works,* ed. Jerome J. McGann, 7 vols. (Oxford: Clarendon Press, 1980–1993), vol. 3, 55 lines, 473–476.

20. Polidori quoted in Gelder, 33.

21. Theodore Redpath, *The Young Romantics and Critical Opinion, 1807–1824* (London, 1973), 102.

22. Reid, 202, 235, 472–474, 537; Dugald Stewart, *Elements of the Philosophy of the Human Mind,* in *Works,* ed. William Hamilton, 11 vols. (Edinburgh: Constable, 1854), vol. 2, 53–54.

23. Oliver Goldsmith, *The Present State of Polite Learning,* in *Works,* ed. D. Masson (London: Macmillan, 1874), 442–443.

24. Walter Scott, *Waverley; or, 'Tis Sixty Years Since,* ed. Claire Lamont (Oxford: Oxford University Press, 1986), 12.

25. On the exploitation of ontological discontinuity in fiction, see Brian McHale, *Postmodernist Fiction* (London and New York: Routledge, 1987), 7–11.
26. Barthes, 51; Charles Baudelaire, "Au lecteur" in *The Flowers of Evil*, ed. Jonathan Culler, trans. James McGowran (Oxford: Oxford University Press, 1993), 6, line 40; Scott, 250.
27. Adam Smith, *The Theory of Moral Sentiments*, ed. D. L. Raphael and A. L. Macfie (Oxford: Clarendon Press, 1976), 10, 27–29.
28. William Carew Hazlitt, *Works*, ed. P. P. Howe, 21 vols. (London and New York: Dent and Dutton, 1930), vol. 4, 214; vol. 19, 255–256.
29. Christopher Lawrence, "Cullen, Brown and the Poverty of Essentialism," in *Brunonianism in Britain and Europe*, eds. W. F. Bynum and Roy Porter, *Medical History,* Supplement no. 8 (1988): 6; Michael Barfoot, "Brunonianism under the Bed: An Alternative to University Medicine in Edinburgh in the 1780s," ibid., 36–37; Guenter B. Risse, "Brunonian Therapeutics: New Wine in Old Bottles?" ibid., 46, 48.
30. See Alexander Crichton, *An Inquiry into the Nature and Origin of Mental Derangement*, 2 vols. (London: Cadell and Davies, 1798), 29–33; Risse, 46.
31. See B. L. K., "Imagination," *The Monthly Packet* 1 (2nd series), (1866): 472–473.
32. The revisionist Common Sense philosopher Thomas Brown draws attention to the way in which matter remains essentially unknowable and functionless in Reid's adaptation of Berkeley's philosophy, *Inquiry into the Relations of Cause and Effect*, 3rd ed. (Edinburgh: Constable, 1818), 107–125.

Works Cited

Abercrombie, John. *Inquiries Concerning the Intellectual Powers.* 7th ed. Edinburgh, 1833.
B. L. K. "Imagination." *The Monthly Packet* 1 (2nd series) (1866): 469–474.
Barfoot, Michael. "Brunonianism under the Bed: An Alternative to University Medicine in Edinburgh in the 1780s. In *Brunonianism in Britain and Europe*. Edited by W.F. Bynum and Roy Porter. *Medical History*. Supplement no. 8, 1998.
Barthes, Roland. *S/Z.* Translated by Richard Miller. Oxford: Blackwell, 1990.
Baudelaire, Charles. "Au lecteur." In *The Flowers of Evil*. Edited by Jonathan Culler. Translated by James McGowran. Oxford: Oxford University Press 1993.
Beattie, James. *An Essay on the Nature and Immutability of Truth.* 6th ed. Edinburgh, 1777.
Boswell, James. *Boswell's Life of Johnson.* 6 vols. Edited by G. B. Hill. Revised by L. F. Powell. Oxford: Clarendon Press, 1934.
Brown, Thomas. *Inquiry into the Relations of Cause and Effect.* 3rd ed. Edinburgh: Constable, 1818.
Bynum, W. F., and Roy Porter, eds. *Brunonianism in Britain and Europe, Medical History*, Supplement no. 8, 1988.
Byron (George Gordon). "The Giaour." In *Complete Poetical Works.* 7 vols. Edited by Jerome J. McGann. Oxford: Clarendon Press, 1980–1993.
Checkland, S. G. and E. O. A., eds. *The Poor Law Report of 1834.* Harmondsworth: Penguin, 1974.
Coleridge, Samuel Taylor. *Biographia Literaria.*
Crichton, Alexander. *An Inquiry into the Nature and Origin of Mental Derangement.* 2 vols. London: Cadell and Davies, 1798.
Forbes, W. *An Account of the Life and Writings of James Beattie LLD.* 2 vols. Edinburgh, 1806.

Frayling, Christopher, ed. *Vampyres: Lord Byron to Count Dracula.* London: Faber and Faber, 1991.

Gelder, Ken. *Reading the Vampire.* London: Routledge, 1994.

Goldsmith, Oliver. *Works.* Edited by D. Masson. London: Macmillan, 1874.

Grave, S. A. *The Scottish Philosophy of Common Sense.* Oxford: Clarendon Press, 1960.

Hazlitt, William Carew. *Works.* Edited by P. P. Howe. 21 vols. London and New York: Dent and Dutton, 1930.

Hughes, William. "Fictional Vampires in the Nineteenth and Twentieth Centuries." In *A Companion to the Gothic.* Edited by David Punter. Oxford: Blackwell, 2000.

Hume, David. *Enquiries Concerning Human Understanding and Concerning the Principles of Morals.* Edited by L. H. Selby-Bigge and P. H. Nidditch. 3rd ed. Oxford: Clarendon Press, 1975.

____. *A Treatise of Human Nature.* Edited by L. H. Selby-Bigge and P. H. Nidditch. Oxford: Clarendon Press, 1978.

Lawrence, Christopher. "Cullen, Brown and the Poverty of Essentialism." In *Brunonianism in Britain and Europe.* Edited by W.F. Bynum and Roy Porter. *Medical History.* Supplement no. 8, 1988.

Macdonald, D. L. *Poor Polidori: A Critical Biography of the Author of "The Vampyre."* Toronto: University of Toronto Press, 1991.

Mansel, H. L. "Sensation Novels." *Quarterly Review* 113 (1863): 481–514.

McCalman, Iain, ed. *An Oxford Companion to the Romantic Age.* Oxford: Oxford University Press, 1999.

McHale, Brian. *Postmodernist Fiction.* London and New York: Routledge, 1987.

The Mirror. No. 35 10th ed. London, 1794.

Mossner, Ernest Campbell. *The Life of David Hume.* 2nd ed. Oxford: Clarendon Press, 1980.

Nodier, Charles. *Lord Ruthven ou les Vampires.* Paris: L'advocat, 1820. Facsimile edition. Marseille: Laffitte, 1978.

Polidori, John. "The Vampyre." In *Vampyres: Lord Byron to Count Dracula.* Edited by Christopher Frayling. London: Faber and Faber, 1991.

Punter, David, ed. *A Companion to the Gothic.* Oxford: Blackwell, 2000.

Redpath, Theodore. *The Young Romantics and Critical Opinion, 1807–1824.* London, 1973.

Reid, Thomas. *Works.* Edited by William Hamilton. 7th ed. 2 vols. Edinburgh, 1872.

Reiman, Donald H. *The Romantics Reviewed: Contemporary Reviews of British Romantic Writing: Part B, Byron and Regency Society Poets.* 5 vols. New York and London: Garland, 1972.

Risse, Guenther B. "Brunonian Therapeutics: New Wine in Old Bottles?" In *Brunonianism in Britain and Europe.* Edited by W.F. Bynum and Roy Porter. *Medical History.* Supplement no. 8, 1988.

Scott, Walter. *Waverley; or,'Tis Sixty Years Since.* Edited by Claire Lamont. Oxford: Oxford University Press, 1986.

Sedgwick, Eve Kosofsky. *The Coherence of Gothic Conventions.* London and New York: Methuen, 1986.

____. *Epistemology of the Closet.* Harmondsworth: Penguin, 1994.

Smith, Adam. *The Theory of Moral Sentiments.* Edited by D. L. Raphael and A. L. Macfie. Oxford: Clarendon Press, 1976.

Stewart, Dugald. *Works.* Edited by William Hamilton. 11 vols. Edinburgh: Constable, 1854.

Turner, E. S. *Boys Will Be Boys.* Harmondsworth: Penguin, 1976.

12

"Screaming While School Was in Session": The Construction of Monstrosity in Stephen King's Schoolhouse Gothic

SHERRY R. TRUFFIN

The Teacher as Monstrous Other

Malevolent teachers who "would hurt the children in any way they could" are immortalized in Pink Floyd's *The Wall* and in numerous texts that exemplify the trend that I call the "Schoolhouse Gothic." Extraterrestrials attempt to colonize earth by inhabiting the bodies of high school teachers and terrorizing students in *The Faculty*. A demon disguised as a substitute teacher is sent to punish a lapsed satanic cult, that is also a parent-teacher association, by sacrificing cult members and their children/students in *The X-Files*. The "objective" nineteenth-century scientist and the white supremacist are fused in the sinister, slaveholding schoolteacher in Toni Morrison's *Beloved*. These texts suggest that in the popular imagination, schools serve the same social function as prisons and mental institutions—to define, classify, control, and regulate people—as Michel Foucault articulates in *Discipline and Punish*. In response, no area of contemporary culture—music, film, television, fiction, or scholarship—can escape the compulsion to return again and again to schools and teachers to dramatize a central fixation that locates these texts in the Gothic tradtion:

a fixation on mystified power. The work of that most prolific contemporary Gothic writer, Stephen King, is no exception.

David Punter, who notes that the Gothic survives to this day because it continues to offer an "image-language in which to examine social ... fears,"[1] observes that contemporary academic discourse shares with the Gothic a clear set of obsessions: power, alienation, dislocation, otherness (181–214). The Gothic, like the contemporary academy, has its origins in the Age of Reason yet offers what Fred Botting calls "counternarratives displaying the underside of enlightenment and humanist values."[2] Such counternarratives resonate with those of Foucault, whose work is preoccupied with, if not actually haunted by, the legacy of the Enlightenment. According to Anne Williams, Foucault's work reveals the way in which "Enlightenment thought [is] characteristically ordered and organized by creating institutions to enforce distinctions between society and its other, whether it resides in madness, illness, criminality, or sexuality."[3] In specifically Gothic terms, the relationship between the thinking, rational subject and its Other(s) works the same way: "the haunted Gothic castle ... *creates* the haunted, dark, mysterious space even as it attempts to organize and control it" (Williams 248). Thus both the Gothic tradition and poststructuralist discourse interrogate the strategies of classifying and standardizing that is associated with the Enlightenment and question the institutions that reproduce these strategies, including the state, the family, the church, the laboratory, and, yes, the school.

The modern academy is one of the institutions entrusted with the construction of the contemporary subject. It functions as home, prison, and laboratory all at once and is, according to Foucault, a key site where Power and Knowledge intersect and reinforce one another. We do not, however, need Foucault's guidance to see that the modern school has assumed many of the socializing and penalizing functions traditionally associated with the court, the family, and the church. As a result, the teacher becomes a figure of immense power, dictating what children learn, when they work, when they play, and even when they take trips to the lavatory. More importantly, teachers determine which children are prodigies and which ones are problems. And so they wield an inexhaustible and inscrutable authority.

Schools and schoolteachers make frequent appearances in the fiction of Stephen King, whose Schoolhouse Gothic presents teachers as monstrous Others whose teaching breeds monstrous students who, in turn, strike out at the educational system that created them. This fiction equates teaching with crimes that have long prevailed in Gothic texts, even as it reflects shifting configurations and conceptions of power. King's *The Shin-*

ing and *Rage* displace the fears and rivalries that Freud ascribed to parent-child relationships (a pattern evident in earlier Gothic texts) onto educational institutions, portraying the teacher as an abusive surrogate parent and highlighting the power of the teacher to identify and isolate "bad" children and to administer punishment. *Rage* also likens modern education to another Gothic anxiety — rape — locating the male in the position of power over the docile, usually female figure. Images of teachers as abusers and rapists emphasize the way in which the teacher labels and victimizes the student. Other images, however, implicate the teacher and the school in larger systemic processes that *construct* the student as the monstrous Other. Both "Suffer the Little Children" and *Rage* develop the Gothic tradition by exploring the role of the school and schoolteacher in enforcing what Foucault calls the "Power of the Norm"[4] — established and legitimated through strategies of surveillance and consolidated in discourse.

The Shining sets the stage for the constant slippage between the roles of cruel teacher and abusive parent that recurs in King's fiction. Jack Torrence, an alcoholic writer and former English teacher, agrees to be the winter caretaker of what turns out to be a malevolently haunted resort hotel in Colorado, ultimately succumbing to the sinister influences of the hotel and attempting to bludgeon his wife, Wendy, and his son, Danny, to death. Jack takes the job to work on a play about a school headmaster who accuses a "saintly"[5] student of cheating on a final exam, eventually beating him to death; Jack has recently lost his teaching position after assaulting a rich, good-looking student named George Hatfield who slashed Jack's tires after being cut from the debate team because he stuttered. During his time at the Overlook, Jack is increasingly unable to write his play as he comes to see the student-hero of *The Little School* as "a monster masquerading as a boy" (273) and to identify with the schoolmaster who beats him to death.

As Jack becomes increasingly paranoid and violent, he repeatedly confuses his son, Danny — whose imaginative, clairvoyant power to "Shine" draws the envy of his artistically frustrated father — with George Hatfield, whose money, popularity, and good looks Jack had resented. In a trance, Danny imagines his father shaking him and screaming *"Don't Stutter!"* and is bewildered, since he has never stuttered (139). Later, Jack has a vision in which he bludgeons George Hatfield to death with a cane (much like the one his own abusive father had wielded), at which point Hatfield — to Jack's horror — transforms into a crying, pleading Danny (287). Jack then encounters the ghost of Grady, a former caretaker who has murdered his wife and two daughters before killing himself; Grady tells Jack that Danny plans to escape and therefore "needs to be corrected" (366). Ultimately,

Jack roams the labyrinthine hotel,[6] brandishing a mallet, which he uses to break several of his wife's ribs and to threaten his son/student while screaming, "*You cheated! You copied that final exam!*" (444). In Jack, King fuses the cruel father with the sadistic teacher, who is instructed that "education always pays" (368); King thus shows us two monstrous educators who define instruction as violence.

Learning from Monstrous Teachers

King's "Suffer the Little Children" begins to suggest the ways in which monstrous teaching might create monstrous students. Echoing Foucault's argument in *Discipline and Punish: The Birth of the Prison*, a genealogy of Western penal practices, King, in "Suffer the Little Children," indicates parallels between the school and the prison or mental institution, explores the ways in which these institutions define deviance, and inscribes surveillance and forced confession at the heart of the teaching profession.

In *Discipline and Punish*, Foucault argues that the "disappearance of torture as a public spectacle" (7) during the late eighteenth and early nineteenth centuries is an index of the transformation of social power in Western culture. In pre-modern society, power, located in visible authorities, worked to punish physical bodies for specific crimes; in a modern disciplinary society the hidden machinations of power define and regulate deviance through normalizing practices and strategies of surveillance. The aim of this power, in Foucault's formulation, is its own reproduction, which requires the construction of particular forms of subjectivity — the making, in short, of persons. The chief characteristic of these persons is, for Foucault, their homogeneity. Foucault describes the human soul as no more and no less than "the present correlative of a certain technology of power over the body," a thing "not born in sin and subject to punishment, but ... born rather out of methods of punishment, supervision, and constraint" (29). Foucault's rather astonishing claim here is that neither God nor nature nor parents nor mad scientists create people: rather, people are produced by Power, an impersonal force (or, rather, a complex network of related forces) that — despite all ideologies to the contrary — constitutes, legitimates, animates, and reproduces the institutions that, in turn, constitute and help to replicate modern culture. Thus, Foucault argues, power makes people.

Schools — like prisons, asylums, hospitals, factories, and other social institutions — play an important role in constructing these modern subjects and in ensuring that most will be docile and "normal" while others

will be unruly and "deviant." For Foucault, the modern disciplinary society is a "punishable, punishing universality" (178) whose institutions indi-
viduate, distribute, and rank the human multiplicities whose lives they
are charged with improving, rehabilitating, curing, and ordering through
"procedures that constitute the individual as effect and object of power,
as effect and object of knowledge" (192). What unites these different "procedures" is "a relation of surveillance," which Foucault insists is "inscribed
at the heart of the practice of teaching, not as an additional or adjacent
part, but as a mechanism that is inherent to it and which increases its
efficiency" (176). Surveillance is the most important mechanism, according to Foucault, by which Power is obtained, deployed, and transferred in
modern Western culture. Surveillance "automatizes and disindividualizes"
(202) Power, dispersing and mystifying it. It reproduces the specific form
of Power that Foucault calls the Norm, which, he argues, "since the eighteenth century, ... has joined other powers—the Law, the Word (*Parole*)
and the Text" (184). These powers are, in fact, intertwined: the power of
the Norm is both translated into and enforced by discourse, by texts. In
The History of Sexuality, Foucault argues that academic and medical discourses of the Victorian age "transform[ed] sex into discourse"[7] and
implies that modern subjectivity can be understood in the same terms: our
culture believes that the "truth" about a person is found not in intimate
interaction but rather in a confession or, better still, a file. Foucault's Power
of the Norm — established and legitimated through strategies of surveillance and consolidated in discourse — turns out to be a major concern of
King's Schoolhouse Gothic.

The protagonist of "Suffer the Little Children" is Miss Sidley, a rather
severe elementary school teacher who, "like God, ... seemed to know
everything at once."[8] One way that she inspires this fear is by watching
her students in her eyeglasses while writing on the chalkboard: "the whole
class was reflected in [her] thick lenses and she has always been amused
by their guilty, frightened faces when she caught them at their nasty little
games" (82). In fact, she regards control over the students as her crown-
ing professional triumph: "the success of her long teaching career could
be summed and checked and proven by this one everyday action: she could
turn her back on her pupils with confidence" (81). Miss Sidley becomes
convinced that a student named Robert is a monster after she sees his distorted face in her glasses, and then sees him momentarily "chang[e]" (83)
when they are face to face. Assuring herself that "she was not going to be
one of those old-maid schoolmarms dragged kicking and screaming from
their classes at the age of retirement," women who "reminded her of gam-
blers unable to leave the tables while they are losing," she insists that "*she*

was not losing. She had always been a winner" (83). Teaching, for Miss Sidley, is not occasionally punctuated by power struggles: it *is* a power struggle in which nothing less than the prerogative of definition is at stake.

However, Miss Sidley begins to suspect that the power structure has somehow been inverted; she can "feel the weight of their eyes on her like blind crawling ants" (84) when she writes on the board and despairs as her cold, alert, watchful eyes turn into "frightened, watching" (85) eyes. One day, she finds herself watching Robert transform into an ugly monster, and she is terrified. She pulls herself together and concludes that if her students are fiends "hiding behind masks" (85), and if Robert is "a monster, not a little boy," then "she must make him admit it" (87). She longs to grab the children and "shake them until their teeth rattled and their giggles turned to wails ... thump their heads against the tile walls and ... make them *admit* what they knew" (85). Significantly, it never occurs to her to contrive ways of placing the children in the care of colleagues in the hope that they will see what she sees: instead, she plots to make the children confess.

For Foucault, confession is a key component of the exercise of Power. It signals that a subject has internalized the definitions imposed upon him or her. In *The History of Sexuality,* he describes the confession as:

> a ritual ... that unfolds within a power relationship, for one does not confess without the presence [or virtual presence] of a partner who is not simply the interlocutor but the authority who requires the confession, prescribes and appreciates it, and intervenes in order to judge, punish, forgive, console, and reconcile ... [61].

Thus, if Miss Sidley can get the children to confess, then her status as an authority will be unassailable, as will her judgment of the deviance of her students. Miss Sidley marches the class into the mimeograph room one by one for a "Test" ("Suffer" 90) — itself a ritual of definition and classification — and shoots them. Here, as in *The Shining,* King defines education as violence. Miss Sidley executes the children one by one until she is discovered by another teacher, and then she is sent to a mental institution, where the psychiatrist and the orderlies "watc[h] her for the first sign of an aggressive move" (92) just as she once watched her pupils. Eventually, she is allowed to interact with children under carefully controlled circumstances but "see[s] something which disturb[s] her" (92) and eventually commits suicide. Her psychiatrist, in turn, becomes absorbed in contemplation of the children — "hardly able to take his eyes off them" (92) — at which point the story ends. It is not clear from the text whether or not the children *actually* transform into the creatures seen by Miss Sidley (and, presumably, the psychiatrist) or whether these metamorphoses are delusions, brought on, perhaps, by the very power disparities in and through which the teacher has learned to function. That is, to justify and to maintain her power, Miss Sidley needs to regard the children as monsters (at least potential ones), and her visions are depicted as a self-fulfilling prophecy of a most horrific order.

In this story, however, power does not go uncontested: Foucault claims that "where there is power, there is resistance, and yet, or rather consequently, this resistance is never in a position of exteriority in relation to power" (*HS* 95). In "Suffer the Little Children," students who have been subject to the power of "a dominating, overseeing gaze"[9] find a way (at least in Miss Sidley's mind) to resist, to turn that gaze around and thus to reverse the mechanism of surveillance and gain a measure of control — however fleeting and costly — over their tormentor. In this story, the classroom is depicted not as a value-free place in which benevolent teachers facilitate learning but rather as a site of institutional surveillance and control — not unlike the prisons, mental institutions, and hospitals described in *Discipline and Punish*, *Madness and Civilization*, and *The Birth of the Clinic*—institutions designed, according to Foucault, to objectify, classify, and discipline bodies and to construct persons (and, perhaps, monsters).

Monstrous Products of Monstrous Education

Rage, one of King's early novellas, goes much farther than "Suffer the Little Children" in exploring the ways in which the monstrosity of the teacher is reproduced in the student and revisited on the school. In *Rage*, the maladjusted Charlie Decker uses a pipe wrench to mangle a chemistry teacher who has forced him to solve a problem on the board and then mocked him for getting it wrong. When he is expelled, Charlie sets his locker on fire to create a diversion, shoots two teachers, and holds his algebra class hostage. After the initial shock subsides, his classmates join him in a strange form of group therapy that concludes with the ritual humiliation and abuse of the single straight-laced non-participant. As Charlie puts it, school was cancelled for the day, but "in Room 16, education went on."[10]

Rage employs many images to explore the monstrosity of teachers. Like *The Shining*, *Rage* reveals a Freudian subtext that parallels parents with teachers and presents both as monstrous. Charlie's relationship with his father is horrific — rife with unresolved, and irresolvable, Oedipal conflict. He reports that "my dad has hated me for as long as I can remember" (53). After Charlie encounters the primal scene, he begins to regard his father as a monster: he remembers hearing noises and imagining that "something terrible was coming. Coming for me through the darkness ... creaking and creaking and creaking" (50). He realizes that "the Creaking Thing was in Mom and Dad's room," and, shortly thereafter, that "the Creaking Thing was my Father" (51). He "dare[s] to hate him back" (58) at age four, after his father hurls him to the ground in anger and then denies the act. The boy shrieks; his mother temporarily exiles his father, and Charlie admires the "practiced and dreadful ease" with which his mother sends his dad "stomping away like a surly boy" (58). In *Rage*, the Freudian subtext is far from subtle.

Charlie is unable to separate his family trauma from his troubles at school, and so he thinks of his schooling in familial terms, as being "caught for another day in the splendid sticky web of Mother Education" (11). More often, however, he conceives of school as decidedly masculine, as a sophisticated version of his father. As he leads his peers in a group intervention, Charlie is repeatedly distracted and disturbed by Mrs. Underwood's body, admitting to himself that "I wish it was [my father] I'd killed, if I had to kill anyone. This thing on the floor between my feet is a classic case of misplaced aggression" (155). Principal Denver's lecture comes to Charlie as "shark words at deep fathoms, jaws words come to gobble [him]. Words with teeth and eyes" (20). For Charlie, father and teacher are always one, and both are sinister, castrating forces against which he must fight for self-preservation.

Rage also likens modern education to rape, positioning the teacher as the powerful (usually male) subject in contrast to the docile (usually female) other. Anne Williams argues that much male Gothic fiction is about "horror of the female," a horror that is "figure[d]" and "control[led]" in Gothic texts by displays of masculine power, displays ranging from the penetrating male gaze to actual rape and murder.[11] Charlie Decker refuses to be feminized and victimized in this way, to play the docile victim that Williams describes as "an object ... [that] may never be anything else but an object, and a focus of unconscious resentments against the feminine" (109). Charlie taunts the principal about his true role, which Charlie believes to be both sexual and sadistic. Charlie accuses Mr. Denver of "get[ting] a kick out of peddling my flesh" (*Rage* 21) but sarcastically excuses him by conceding that "everybody has to get it on, everybody has to have someone to jack off on" (21). Before leaving the office, Charlie untucks his shirt, unzips his pants, and tells the secretary that Mr. Denver "jumped over his desk and tried to rape me" (22). When the school guidance counselor, Mr. Grace, is asked to take over for the principal,

Charlie refuses to answer his questions, believing that the counselor is "a man with a headful of sharp, prying instruments. A mind-fucker" (67), always trying to "sli[p] it to you" (66). Charlie manipulates and reverses the power dynamic by insisting on being the one who gets answers: he tells Mr. Grace that he will shoot a student if Grace asks him any questions, then tricks him into asking a question, at which point, Charlie shoots into the floor, shocking his peers out of their mesmerized states and terrifying the school officials. Charlie hears Mr. Grace crying over the intercom and congratulates himself on having "made [Grace] fuck himself with his own big tool" (75). Later, as his peers bond, Sandra — one of Charlie's smartest classmates—compares her education to an anonymous, somewhat violent sexual encounter that she has had, musing that teachers "want to stuff things into your head until it's all filled up. It's a different hole, that's all. That's all" (116). Thus *Rage* offers a conception of the school — of its disciplinarians, its counselors, and its teachers— as a power struggle of the sado-masochistic variety, and suggests that students, aware of themselves as sexual as well as pedagogical victims, are able to appropriate power and invert the power structure.

The paranoid vision of high school offered in *Rage* suggests, however, that the power by which the academy operates is more subtle, diffuse, and mysterious than that of either the abusive parent or the serial rapist. Charlie Decker, like Miss Sidley, fears the kind of surveillance that Foucault associates with modern Western culture and its chief normalizing institutions. Charlie suspects that he is even being watched in the restroom: "someone's always got to peek. People like Mr. Denver and Mr. Grace even get paid for it" (11). He remembers bringing his weapon to school "ever since [he] decided that people might ... be following [him] around and checking up" (23). He recalls the day that he assaulted his chemistry teacher and how "everybody was *looking* at [him]. All of them *staring*" (150). He thinks of the aftermath of the attack, "the way people looked at [him] in the halls. The way [he] knew they were talking about [him] in the teachers' rooms" (155). Although Charlie has, in fact, done something to attract the attention of the school officials, the novella suggests that the school, like a prison, is designed not for isolated observation but rather for general, corporate surveillance and control. It is a place that assumes and, in a sense, *creates* deviance.

The physical plant, the daily routine, and the power structure of the school all help to reproduce the Foucauldian Power of the Norm by maximizing conformity. The lockers stand "in silent sentinel rows" (25) like prison guards. The ticking of the clock carves the day into intervals (85, 96, 143, 157), and "the clock buzze[s] away with a vague kind of determination" (52). According to Foucault, segmented time is central to the modern disciplines: "there is not a single moment of life from which one cannot extract forces" (*DP* 165). The school is especially sensitive about time: Foucault reports that "from the seventeenth century to the ... beginning of the nineteenth, ... the complex clockwork was built up cog by cog" so that "in the end, all the time of all the pupils was occupied ... [and] [t]he school became a machine for learning" (165). This machine, Foucault goes on to explain, "requires a precise system of command" and a "technique of training" (166). This training involves "few words, no explanation, a total silence interrupted by signals—bells, clapping of hands, gestures, a mere glance from the teacher.... The pupil will have to have learnt the code of the signals and respond automatically to them" (166). It is not surprising to note, then, that when Charlie shoots the teacher and shuts the classroom door, only one student screams, and even she "stop[s], as if ashamed at screaming while school was in session, no matter how great the provocation" (*Rage* 33). Charlie and his peers tense up each time the schoolbell rings as they resist the automatic response of gathering their things and heading to the next class (85). In *Rage*, the diffuse power relations produced and reproduced in the school expand beyond the single figure of a teacher or a principal; they are, as anticipated by Foucault, ultimately internalized within the psyches of the students.

Constant surveillance — along with its discursive product, the permanent record — ensures that the student will become what Foucault calls "an effect and object of power, ... effect and object of knowledge" (*DP* 192). Foucault claims that modern culture not only makes individuals out of bodies, but also "case[s]" (191) out of individuals. The *case* is "the individual as he may be described, judged, measured, compared with others, in his very individuality ... and the individual who has to be trained or corrected, classified, normalized, excluded, etc" (191). Foucault argues that:

> for a long time ordinary humanity — the everyday individuality of everybody — remained below the threshold of description. To be looked at, observed, described in detail, followed from day to day by an uninterrupted writing was a privilege. The chronicle of man ... formed part of the rituals of his power. The disciplinary methods reversed this relation, lowered the threshold of describable individuality and made of this description a means of control and a method of domination [191].

The *caseness* of the student — or the prisoner or mental patient — is contained in and maintained by his file. During Charlie's visit to the principal's office, Mr. Denver looks at a paper "so he wouldn't have to look at" the boy, and the boy surmises that it is "something from my file, no doubt.

The almighty file. The Great American file" (*Rage* 20). Later, when Mr. Denver is on the intercom, Charlie snarls at him, "I'm out of your filing cabinet now, Tom. Have you got it? I'm not just a record you can lock up at three in the afternoon" ... "before the day's over, we are going to understand the difference between people and pieces of paper in a file" (43). Charlie, in short, recognizes that he has been constructed as a Foucauldian "case" by his teachers and counselors over the years and that in "case" form, he resides in his permanent record. He resists this construction, perhaps because he believes that it is false and perhaps because he fears that it will become true, that its official bureaucratic sanction will *make* it so. Foucault insists that:

> [w]e must cease once and for all to describe the effects of power in negative terms: it "excludes," it "represses," it "censors," it "abstracts," it "masks," it "conceals." In fact, power produces; it produces reality; it produces domains and objects and rituals of truth. The individual and the knowledge that may be gained of him belong to this production [*DP* 194].

Charlie's deepest anxieties come from an awareness that he is, in some sense, the object of such procedures, that he has been carefully observed, monitored, assessed, and classified — and from his suspicion not only that he cannot escape these judgments and classifications but also that they have had some mysterious role in making him the monster that he is.

Significantly, Charlie's drama ends as he leads his classmates in an attempt to force a confession of deviance from all–American boy Ted Jones. Now that he is in a position of power, Charles takes upon himself the prerogatives of Foucauldian power. When Ted refuses, he is accused of a variety of perversions and hypocrisies, then spat upon, punched, kicked, and tortured with the implements of the classroom: ink and notebook paper. He is left in a catatonic state, looking rather monstrous, with "blue black teardrops" all over his face, a bloody nose, and "one eye glar[ing] disjointedly toward no place" (*Rage* 162). King shows that the deviant becomes the Norm, that Power shifts, reproduces itself, endures.

Today, the headline "Horror in the Halls" is likely to announce neither the publication of a Gothic novel nor the release of a teen slasher flick, but rather a real-life school shooting. In light of the Columbine tragedy of 1999, as well as the seemingly ubiquitous school shootings around the U.S., Stephen King's 1971 *Rage*— if not his full inventory of Schoolhouse Gothic tales –appears decidedly prophetic. Ultimately, Charlie Decker may share with the student-gunmen of our time a common nightmare — that they're "another brick in the wall."[12] The same fear appears to plague scholars and teachers, judging from the way in which the contemporary academy has embraced the claustrophobic vision of modern Western culture and its institutions that Foucault offers in *Discipline and Punish*, deploying this vision as a basis for probing its own crimes and complicities. It remains to be seen whether academics will attempt to remake their institutions in such a way as to meaningfully address the sense of dis-ease that gives rise to such disturbing images of schools and teachers— to the horrifying alienation that constructs both teachers and students as the Other — or whether they will simply become bored with those images and develop new, less unsettling self-portraits. Either way, manifestations of the Schoolhouse Gothic will continue to circulate and to enthrall as long the paradigms resonate with the anxieties of the larger culture, as long as they give those anxieties structure and significance.

Notes

1. David Punter, *The Literature of Terror, vol. 2: The Modern Gothic.* 2nd ed. (London: Longman, 1996), 117.
2. Fred Botting, *Gothic* (London: Routledge, 1996), 2.
3. Anne Williams, *Art of Darkness: A Poetics of the Gothic* (Chicago: University of Chicago Press, 1995), 248.
4. Michel Foucault, *Discipline and Punish: The Birth of the Prison*, trans. Alan Sheridan (New York: Vintage, 1977), 184.
5. Stephen King, *The Shining* (New York: Signet, 1978), 271.
6. Evoking the typically labyrinthine Gothic structure.
7. Michel Foucault, *The History of Sexuality: An Introduction, Vol. 1*, trans. Robert Hurley (New York: Random House, 1978), 20.
8. Stephen King, "Suffer the Little Children," in *Nightmares & Dreamscapes* (New York: Signet, 1993), 81.
9. Michel Foucault, *Power/Knowledge: Selected Interviews and Writings: 1972–1977*, ed. Colin Gordon (New York: Pantheon Books, 1990), 152.
10. Stephen King, *Rage*, in *The Bachman Books* (New York: Signet, 1986), 44.
11. Williams, 114.
12. Roger Waters, "Another Brick in the Wall, Part II." *On The Wall* (New York: Columbia Records, 1979).

Works Cited

Botting, Fred. *Gothic*. London: Routledge, 1996.
Foucault, Michel. *Discipline and Punish: The Birth of the Prison*. Translated by Alan Sheridan. New York: Vintage, 1977.
____. *The History of Sexuality: An Introduction, Volume 1*. Translated by Robert Hurley. New York: Random House, 1978.
____. *Power/Knowledge: Selected Interviews and Writings, 1972–1977*. Edited by Colin Gordon. New York: Pantheon Books, 1990.
King, Stephen. *Rage*. In *The Bachman Books*. New York: Signet, 1977.
____. *The Shining*. New York: Signet, 1978.

____. "Suffer the Little Children." In *Nightmares & Dreamscapes*. New York: Signet, 1993.

Punter, David. *The Literature of Terror. Vol. 2: The Modern Gothic*. 2nd ed. London: Longman, 1996.

Waters, Roger. "Another Brick in the Wall, Part II." *The Wall*. 1979. Performed by Pink Floyd. Compact Disk C2K 68519. New York: Columbia Records, 1997.

Williams, Anne. *Art of Darkness: A Poetics of the Gothic*. Chicago: University of Chicago Press, 1995.

PART IV

When the Self Is the Other:
Humanizing the Other,
Demonizing the Oppressor

13

The Cage of Obscene Birds: The Myth of the Southern Garden in Frederick Douglass's *My Bondage and My Freedom*

JOSEPH BODZIOCK

> The monster led her from the door,
> He led her by the hand,
> To be his slave and paramour
> In a strange and distant land!
> — William Craft

> Alas! how wreck'd the promise of her birth!
> In poison'd plants arise the ambrosial seeds.
> She who might be the ornament of Earth,
> A ruined temple overgrown with weeds,
> A golden chamber, where the serpent feeds.
> — William Hayden

> You may believe what I say; for I write only that whereof I know. I was twenty-one years in that cage of obscene birds.
> — Harriet Jacobs

Writing in *My Bondage and My Freedom* (1855), his second antebellum narrative, Frederick Douglass left behind the powerful minimalist rhetorical strategies he had used in the 1845 *Narrative of the Life of Fred-*

erick Douglass. Instead, Douglass frequently indulges in the sort of expansive and effusive language that marks the following description of the Lloyd Plantation on which Douglass was a slave:

> [The] intermediate space [between the carriage entrance and the Great House] was a beautiful lawn, very neatly trimmed, and watched with the greatest care. It was dotted thickly over with delightful trees, shrubbery, and flowers. The road, or lane, from the gate to the great house, was richly paved with white pebbles from the beach, and, in its course, formed a complete circle around the beautiful lawn. Carriages going in and retiring from the great house, made the circuit of the lawn, and their passengers were permitted to behold a scene of almost Eden-like beauty.[1]

This description replicates the verbal expansiveness, and even excess, that marks the whole of *My Bondage and My Freedom.* Significantly, in this expansive excess, Douglass subtly references a potent myth of place that inhabited the culture of a multitude of Americans (though not necessarily the slaves themselves)—that America was a New Land, a place to redeem and be redeemed, a place for revision, the Garden restored.

Douglass, of course, had no interest in writing a travelogue of the antebellum South; readers already familiar with the 1845 narrative or readers simply paying attention to the title of the 1855 work would understand that his text, his language and his descriptions necessarily bore an ideological weight. If we closely read the above passage, we can tease out a certain tension between what the words bear out on the surface and what reverberates beneath. The lawn is "watched with the greatest care," and the enclosure was "select." That passengers "were permitted to behold" suggests a certain, carefully chosen grace has been granted. There is the gentle adumbration, a pinprick of guardedness, here. That guardedness more closely resembles a near-paranoia as Douglass describes a foreboding and insular place where certain, unpleasant secrets may be stored away behind the imposing facade:

> In its isolation, seclusion, and self-reliant independence, Col. Lloyd's plantation resembles what the baronial domains were, during the middle ages in Europe. Grim, cold, and unapproachable by all genial influences from communities without, there it stands.... It is, nevertheless, altogether, to outward seeming, a most strikingly interesting place, full of life, activity, and spirit ... [64–5].

This is quite distant from the warm, inviting Southern garden that marked the homogenized fantasies of sentimentalists and romantic visionaries. Douglass's description seems almost to be lifted from a European Gothic novel or from a rousing Walter Scott adventure. And its suggestion of a self-contained, intimidating place that harbors, in this case, a decadent slaveholding aristocracy strengthens associations of this passage with the populist conceits behind the writings of Scott and the European Gothic.

By referencing the Gothic myth and suppressing the myth of the Southern paradise, Douglass could find common ground with his Northern white readers. This was a significant task, since his readers were not only geographically distant from slavery, but additionally ambivalent about whether a common humanity cut across the bounds of race. Yet Dana Nelson, arguing for a necessary disruption to the white writer/white reader structure common to the discourse on race in early American literature, comments, "in order for there to be a truly constructive confrontation of the issue of 'race,' there must be a direct dialogue [between the white reader and] the heretofore objectified Other."[2] Since cultural myth can seem to be diffused and decentered — that is, shared by all in some amorphous way — such myth works well as a common field upon which black writer and white reader can meet, a place where race may be immobilized as a defining force.

Indeed, if all of America were a potential Eden, the West and the South staked the most trenchant claims for that metaphor in the American imagination. J.V. Ridgeley, in his study of nineteenth-century Southern literature, suggests that "one persistent theme [about the South] was of Eden regained, a paradise into which the new Adam and his Eve could step at once, free of the burden of a failed past."[3] In his study of the sentimental novel in America, Herbert Brown notes that both South and North, including Northern abolitionists, came to share a central mythic vision of the South as "a modern Garden of Eden, perfumed by magnolia blossoms, in which an ignorant and childlike people were being benevolently taught the arts of Christian Civilization."[4] The idea of a Southern garden — a place with Edenic possibilities — flourished as the romantic sensibilities of the eighteenth and nineteenth centuries converted geography into metaphor.

Douglass, as well as many other slave narrators, knew of the benign moonlight-and-magnolias image of the landscape and culture of slavery that thrived in both North and South. But Douglass and other slave narrators, familiar with the "real" underpinnings and inner workings of slavery, knew that this image was exactly that — an image, a grotesque, an "outward seeming," to use Douglass's own words. Harriet Jacobs, who in 1860 published her slave narrative, *Incidents in the Life of a Slave Girl*, complains how easily those who toured the plantations were fooled — intentionally — by their forms, and brought back their skewed visions to the North:

A clergyman who goes to the south, for the first time, has usually some feeling ... that slavery is wrong. The slaveholder suspects this, and plays his game accordingly....[5]

Throughout his descriptions of the Lloyd plantation and the world of slavery, Douglass makes use of a sharply perceptive sense of the grotesque. Douglass is adept at seeing the illusory quality of the world of slavery, and often in his work what appears to be one thing when viewed from what we might call a mythic distance appears to be quite another when viewed up close.

Many of the slave narratives are filled with images of disguise and deceit, of uncertain appearances and transmogrifications. This perceptual difference between the surface and the hidden, between the masked and the unmasked, invites the writers of slave narratives—and Douglass most effectively—to turn to a literary trope that effectively represents the dissonance between appearance and reality, a trope with which Northern white readers would have been intimately familiar: the Gothic.

Although it cannot be empirically stated that Douglas—or other writers of slave narratives who used Gothic modes of expression — were familiar with Gothic forms, we do know that Douglass was a voracious reader. Douglass's evocation of the expansive Gothic tradition is evidenced in the internal rhetoric of *My Bondage and My Freedom*, especially as compared to the more minimalist rhetorical strategies Douglass used in his 1845 narrative. Moreover, something happened in the ten years intervening between the two narratives to compel Douglass to transform a relatively brief document into a near-500-page tome. I believe that "something" was the publication, in 1852, of *Uncle Tom's Cabin*. Harriet Beecher Stowe's own familiarity with Gothic conventions (used most effectively when *Uncle Tom's Cabin* shifts to the Legree plantation) served her well in creating a landmark anti-slavery text. Stowe had demonstrated that literary narrative and conventional forms could be extraordinarily effective devices for converting anti-slavery argument into anti-slavery ideology. Certainly pro-slavery advocates had used myth, shaky biblical exegesis, and racial pseudo-science to envelop the harsh economic and historical realities of slavery with a haze of ideology. Now it was Douglass's turn. I suggest that Douglass, who knew both *Uncle Tom's Cabin* and Stowe herself, could not resist the effectiveness of the Gothic as a literary device with profound sociopolitical implications, and integrated its elements into *My Bondage and My Freedom*.

In *Playing in the Dark*, Toni Morrison comments that the "Africanist presence" in early American literature "is a dark and abiding presence, there for the literary imagination as both a visible and an invisible mediating force."[6] Her rhetorical choices of a "presence" and an "invisible ... force" resonate with elements of the supernatural. As Morrison argues, American writers had used Blackness not only as a means to articulate the definition and value of whiteness, but also to articulate symbolically that dangerous, terrifying region of the hidden self, the region that Poe explores in "The Black Cat" or Hawthorne in "The Birthmark." In the America of Douglass, Poe and Hawthorne, however, Blackness was more than a rhetorical metaphor. In America, Morrison argues, Blackness suggests the physical presence of the slave. Thus while Poe and Hawthorne may not have written explicitly about slavery, both they and their readers lived and worked in a nation intimately formed — and informed — by the existence of slavery and the presence of the African slave. The Africanist presence, in Morrison's formulation, easily assumes the role of the Gothic Other in American literature, not simply because Blackness functions as a convenient metaphor for the unknown, but because Blackness was physically *there*, embodying and encoding that greatest of American *sins* — to use the term frequently used by the writers of slave narratives, including Douglass — slavery, inflicted upon the undifferentiated mass of unknowable others, the slaves.

The Africanist presence that Morrison sees, is, then, the Gothic Other reimagined for a democratic, yet slave-holding, context. To be sure, Southern slaveholders (as Douglass amply indicates in his descriptions of the Lloyd Plantation) worked hard to project the image of a faux aristocracy. But as slaves, abolitionists and even slaveholders tired of Northern moral righteousness pointed out, slavery was sustained by national will, desire and indifference.

It is perhaps this symbolism that lends force to the self-description in *My Bondage*. After fleeing from the slavebreaker Edward Covey, Douglass sets out through the woods to meet with his old master and ask him to intercede for Douglass with Covey. Emerging from the wilderness at his master's place, Douglass presents "an appearance of wretchedness and woe, fitted to move any but a heart of stone." He is spotted with blood "from the crown of my head to the sole of my feet.... My hair was all clotted with dust and blood, and the back of my shirt was literally stiff with the same. Briers and thorns had scarred and torn my feet and legs, leaving blood marks there" (228). In this episode Douglass seems to be embracing the role of the dark Other that would be familiar to his readers. But here the symbolism has a peculiar retributive content to it, occurring as it does in a context in which Douglass presents himself to the man responsible for his re-presentation as the dark Other, his master who had knowingly contracted his services out to Covey, a man with a reputation for excessive brutality. Like Banquo's ghost, Douglass shakes his gory locks at the white man, becoming a signpost of human betrayal and a symbol of the grim substance of slavery itself. He is, to use the terminology of Teresa Goddu, enacting a moment of "haunting back," resisting the tendency of the dominant culture to frame him as Gothic Other and instead locating the source of Gothic horror upon the dominant culture.

A problem in this episode, however, is that the effect of spectacle and symbolic objectivity depends upon the perceptions of his old master, and implicitly, the perceptions of his white readers. Douglass, to use his phrasing from another incident in *My Bondage*, is, as a slave, a text to be read, a text that can only be understood within the ideological framework accepted by his readers: the Black American as the Dark Other, the covert Symbol, the not-quite-human presence haunting the landscape of the American national psyche. At the moment Douglass confronts his master, he also risks nudging this event into the territory of fiction, and risks rendering the brutality of slavery as a Gothic conceit, thereby denaturing it as a real, historical horror. In this instance, Douglass's deployment of the Gothic conventions risks (as Goddu indicates generally about the American slave narratives) giving white readers "a discourse to symbolize and contain their terror" and consequently risks "dematerial[-izing] history"— that is, diminishing the genuine material horror of slavery.[7] Douglass, then, must contend with a "double bind: the difficulty of representing a Gothic history through Gothic conventions without collapsing the distinctions between fact and fiction, event and effect. The slave narrative must rewrite the conventions of Gothic fiction for its own factual ends" (137). Thus, Douglass's Gothic self-representation in this scene, while partly playing into conventional conceptions of Gothic Otherness, overlays that convention with the bloody reality of slavery. The blood may offer spectacle, but Douglass also emphasizes the literalness of his appearance — an emphasis amplified by Douglass's vivid description of the beating that leads to this appearance.

However, reaching those ends through the measured use of the conventions of Gothic *fiction* means that, on some level, Douglass has to regard the whites in his narrative as characters—creations and representations shaped by *his* perceptions and *his* rhetoric. As bell hooks indicates in her essay "Representations of Whiteness in the Black Imagination," this was no ordinary imaginative act. "Some white people," she writes, "may even imagine there is no representation of whiteness in the black imagination.... They think they are seen by black folks only as they want to appear."[8] The potency of the slave narratives lies in their potential to unsettle this comforting assumption on the part of white readers, South and North. While such readers had no problem fixing their gazes upon the Others among them, the slaves, the realization that the Other could and did return that gaze right back (as evidenced by the slave narratives, and in particular Frederick Douglass), reconfiguring the white "character" as a monstrous unknowable Other, was disruptive indeed.

As slaves, the writers of slave narratives frequently had to contend with the slaveholder/tyrant, whose will was singular and inviolable. "One had to keep his black property in check or the entire system might fall apart," Houston Baker points out about slaveholders:

> If the oppressive center would not hold, if white men could not restrain the barbarian within their midst, then not only the plantation economy but also the moral order that had been so laboriously imposed upon the lands of the new world would be destroyed.[9]

If the plantation, the emblem of order in the slaveholding South, was an imaginary structure rigged together with a rope of sand, the master, and sometimes mistresses, were appropriate guardians for this place. Their form also belied their substance. In his 1845 narrative, Douglass describes a "large and fairly cultivated garden" on the Lloyd plantation that seems to resonate, on its own small scale, with the Edenic order just out of reach of the American grasp:

> This garden ... abounded in fruits of almost every description ... [and] was not the least source of trouble on the plantation. Its excellent fruit was quite a temptation to the hungry swarms of boys [and] older slaves, belonging to the colonel, few of whom had the virtue or the vice to resist it. Scarcely a day passed, during the summer, but that some slave had to take the lash for stealing fruit. The colonel had to resort to all kinds of stratagems to keep his slaves out of the garden.[10]

In this brief passage, Douglass creates a richly ironic context. At one and the same time, it is a tongue-in-cheek and bitter inversion of the Edenic myth. If blacks are indeed irresponsible children, as the slaveholding South insists, then the structures of this garden on the Lloyd plantation recapitulate those of the original garden, for here also it is the innocents who are being kept away from the fruit by the master. But something is not quite right here; there is something unpleasant beneath the surface of this Eden. The master, the "demiurge" who owns the garden, whips his innocents and protects his bounty from those who would be nourished by it. Later Douglass mentions that the garden is fenced in, and the fence tarred to keep out the slaves. The slaves, Douglass blandly notes, "seemed to realize the impossibility of touching tar without being defiled" (18).

This garden, then, hardly expresses the bounty of an all-loving God. The relationship between the master and his "children" is rooted in conflict rather than harmony; the master seems possessed by a siege mentality. Unlike the original Eden, innocence is not invited, and, in fact, is repulsed. Furthermore, by insisting that the slaves are defiled by touching the place, Douglass imposes a moral value upon the garden, and, in this instance, a value that indicates a mythic place has been corrupted. The garden, then, in spite of its bounty, is quite unnatural. The normal implications of expansiveness we might assign to the concepts of "garden" and "plenty" are cut off by the paranoia and artificiality that seem to enclose the garden. The garden appears to be ideal, but lacks moral substance and Christian management.

Douglass's choice of an Edenic metaphor is a telling one when considering the Gothic structures that energize his narrative. The "outward seeming" of Douglass's garden and the essential malignance of the master of that garden reference another figure of outward seeming from the original Garden myth: Satan, in the guise of a serpent. Satan is the ultimate dark Other, a relatively frequent and ideal representative for the Gothic Other in the literature, given his unparalleled skill at unsettling the boundaries between appearance and reality, between assurance and uncertainty. Thus in evoking and conflating two complementing traditions, each with its own dark Other, the Gothic and the biblical tradition, Douglass lends even greater power to his enactment of haunting back, to his recasting of the white master as the dark Other.

The brilliance of Douglass's methods illuminates his strategy of turning the concept of the Gothic dark Other on its head. If the dark Other traditionally embodies an unknown and unknowable evil — a concept that, for many in America, was embodied in the figure of the African-turned-slave — Douglass repositions that concept so that the body of the dark Other is, paradoxically, white and calls itself "master." For Douglass, the master may assume the role, the power, and even the identity of God, but that, too, was an illusion, a shape that he assumed. As Douglass reveals, the dark master is, indeed, not God, but Satan. For Douglass, biblical metaphors, Gothic metaphors and the trope of the dark Other generated by both serve as an effective means to lift the debate on slavery out of sociopolitical abstractions, into the realm of dread.

The process of reshaping the demiurgic metaphor of the master is fairly straightforward, given the patriarchal and authoritarian structures of the slave system. But the metaphors turn on the appearances of omnipotence and omniscience, and they become cruelly ironic as the deific mask slips away to reveal a capricious and foolishly arrogant man who plays at a particular role. Douglass at first appeals to the glorious image of the garden myth, but then defuses it by revealing the flawed structures that support it.

Elsewhere in *My Bondage*, Douglass more clearly explores the demonic transformation of the slaveholder. Recalling his childhood with his grandmother, Douglass learnes that "not only [his grandmother's] house and lot, but ... grandmother herself, ... and all the little children around her, belonged to this mysterious personage, called by grandmother, with every mark of reverence, 'Old Master'" (*My Bondage* 38–9). Old Master,[11] like He Who Is Not To Be Named, is absolute in his power, and demands appropriate obeisance:

> I was told that this "old master," whose name seemed ever to be mentioned with fear and shuddering, only allowed the children to live with grandmother for a limited time, and that in fact as soon as they were big enough, they were promptly taken away, to live with the said "old master" [39].

However, when Douglass fixes his gaze upon Old Master, he sees clearly that this is no God. He reduces the godliness of Col. Lloyd to an image of Moloch, eater of children. His conceptions of the Old Master more explicitly resonate with "pagan" values, removing the metaphor from Old Testament monotheism and placing it into a polytheistic world of cruel and unquestioned sacrifice:

> I WAS A SLAVE.... Born for another's benefit, as the firstling of the cabin flock I was soon to be selected as a meet offering to the fearful and inexorable demigod, whose huge image on so many occasions haunted my childhood's imagination [45].

In fact, it was relatively common for many writers of slave narratives to speak about their masters and mistresses in similarly metamorphic terms—thus linking their owners metaphorically to the master of deception and disguise, Satan, and in more particular terms, to the serpent of the garden myth. The masters are often associated with some sort of demonic or animal form, and, at times, even figuratively capable of transforming from human form into another form. Because the trope is fairly common, it seems, at times, little more than rhetoric convention for the writer, a glancing reference that a writer or speaker might easily devise without much thought. The convention, however, becomes more intriguing when the writers more explicitly assign metamorphic powers to the slaveholders. We are then no longer dealing with reflexive terminology, but with authors who consider the full implications of the terminology.

Harriet Jacobs, for example, more fully explores the trope, sketching the tale of her master's seduction in terms reminiscent of Satan's temptation of Eve. Her master, a fascinating character named Dr. Flint (a name that slyly teases the reader with images of fire), has lascivious designs upon Jacobs, which she ultimately thwarts by bearing the illegitimate children of another, seemingly more compassionate white man. As she writes about these children Jacobs speaks of having "sinned against her master" (59), but Dr. Flint is not an anthropomorphism of a Christian deity. He is a deceiver, a shapeshifter: "He sprang upon me like a wolf, and grabbed my arm as if he would have broken it. `Do you love him?' said he, in a hissing tone'" (60). Flint, like the Edenic Satan (his hissing evokes the serpent form), is an insidious tempter, often trying to arouse Jacobs by "whisper[ing] foul words in [her] ear" as he tries to introduce her to his own brand of sexual knowledge (26). Jacobs's fall from grace — the bearing of her illegitimate children — is also not quite what it appears; ironically, her fall leads to her salvation, because that fall leads to the resolve that will eventually save her and her children, though not through any lack of resolve in Flint:

> [Flint] tried his utmost to corrupt the pure principles my grandmother had instilled. He peopled my young mind with unclean images, such as only a vile monster could think of…. [T]here is no shadow of law to protect her from insult, from violence, or even from death; all these are inflicted by fiends who bear the shape of men [26].

Douglass also explores the metaphoric transformations of his master in his descriptions of Edward Covey, a "slavebreaker" and a "farm-renter" with whom Douglass lived for a year and for whom "trickery was natural" (Douglass *My Bondage* 216). Covey's house is in a secluded and fairly wild section of Maryland, and like Col. Lloyd, Covey at first seems to have certain deific powers and capacities that resemble those of God in Eden. "There was no deceiving him [Covey]," Douglass mentions. "He knew just what a man or boy could do, and he held both to strict account" (215). But as with the others, Covey is only a seemingly benign deity; in reality he is a master of shapeshifting, "of quick and wiry motion, of thin and wolfish visage," and, when he speaks, it was "in a sort of light growl, like a dog" (210). His skills as an overseer mark him as an apparent avatar of Lucifer, complete with serpent's guise:

> He had the faculty of making us feel that he was always present…. He would creep and crawl, in ditches and gullies; hide behind stumps and brushes, and practice so much of the cunning of the serpent, that Bill Smith and I … never called him by any other name than "the snake." We fan-

cied that in his eyes and his gait we could see a snakish resemblance....
He was, to us, behind every stump, tree, bush, and fence on the plantation [215–6].

The power of these descriptions is heightened by the fact that they
shortly follow Douglass's self-demonizing described earlier. The two scenes
stand in counterpoint to each other. The key difference is that Douglass's
transformation is a momentary physical event, brutally forced upon him
by another. What is revealed in Douglass's self-demonizing is not some
sort of inner truth about who he is, but (in part) a symbolic representation of a literal and moral truth about slaveholders. Beneath the blood and
the grime it is still Frederick Douglass. Douglass's literary transformations
of Covey and Old Master into the demonic Other are, on the other hand,
not literal, not real, not momentary expressions of unwilled suffering.
They are literary tropes appropriated from the Gothic that signal Douglass's
ability to contain white character within the bounds of his imagination,
and to tease out the "real" nature of those who would be master. Douglass
minimizes the risk of abstracting the genuine brutality of slaveholders
by refusing to mitigate the literal, bloody brutality suffered by himself and other slaves at the hands of the slaveholders. Douglass adds
further power to the literary representations of slaveholders in linking
images appropriated from the Gothic tradition to the Edenic metaphor.
In this web of metaphor, Douglass finds the connection between black
writer/white reader advocated by Nelson, for the Gothic and the Bible are
both encoded into a mythic morality tale of fall and redemption, a tale
central to national self-perception in nineteenth-century America. If the
South were indeed the garden re-discovered, it had fallen under a stew-
ardship far different from that of the original Eden. This metaphor of metamorphosis is especially damaging in the hands of Douglass, since he
persistently holds out Edenic possibilities to the reader for a moment, only
to reveal that the possibilities are mercurial and little more than appari-
tions. The teasing promise exists, but the structures are twisted and perverse.

To the writers of slave narratives, the South was more than a place
where slavery was practiced. They endorsed a metaphor of the South as a
corrupted garden. If it was a place of Edenic promise, that promise had
been shattered by slavery. If it seemed Edenic, it was a place of deceptive
appearances. The slave narrators had invested the Southern landscape and
its cultural icons, such as the plantation and the great house, with moral
values, and so in their own ways recapitulated the efforts of contemporary
Americans and earlier British settlers and visionaries to create a cultural

myth out of the South. But the slave narrators, excluded from the mainstream American mythmaking process, rewrote the Edenic metaphor with which white Americans commonly framed the South. In looking at Eden through a Gothic lens, these writers revealed that beneath the Edenic surface lay moral ruin. The birds that flitted across the Southern landscape were lovely to behold but obscene in their souls.

Notes

1. Frederick Douglass, *My Bondage and My Freedom* (New York: Miller, Orton and Mulligan, 1855. New York: Dover Publications, 1969), 67.
2. Dana D. Nelson, *The Word in Black and White: Reading "Race" in American Literature, 1638–1867* (New York: Oxford University Press, 1993), 132.
3. J.V. Ridgeley, *Nineteenth-Century Southern Literature* (The University Press of Kentucky, 1980), 3.
4. Herbert Ross Brown, *The Sentimental Novel in America, 1789–1860* (New York: Pageant Books, 1959), 243.
5. Harriet Jacobs, *Incidents in the Life of a Slave Girl*, 1861 (New York: Harvest/HBJ, 1973), 76.
6. Toni Morrison, "Playing in the Dark," in *Black on White: Black Writers on What It Means to Be White*, ed. David R. Roediger (New York: Schocken Books, 1998), 156.
7. Teresa A. Goddu, *Gothic America: Narrative, History, and Nation* (New York: Columbia University Press, 1997), 134, 132.
8. bell hooks, "Representations of Whiteness in the Black Imagination," in *Black on White: Black Writers on What It Means to Be White*, ed. David R. Roediger (New York: Schocken Books, 1998), 42.
9. Houston A. Baker, "Black Culture, White Judgment: Patterns of Justice in the Black Narrative," in *Singers of Daybreak: Studies in Black American Literature* (Washington, D.C.: Howard University Press, 1983), 7.
10. Frederick Douglass, *Narrative of the Life of Frederick Douglass, an American Slave, 1845* (New York: Anchor Books, 1973), 18.
11. This designation evokes a number of designations of Satan that begin with the adjective "old": Old Bendy, Old Gooseberry, Old Harry, Old Ned, Old Nick, Old Scratch, the Old Enemy, the Old Gentleman and the Old Serpent, among others [Ed. Note].

Works Cited

Baker, Houston A. "Black Culture, White Judgment: Patterns of Justice in the Black Narrative." In *Singers of Daybreak: Studies in Black American Literature.* Washington, D.C.: Howard University Press, 1983.
Brown, Henry "Box." *Narrative of Henry Box Brown.* Boston, 1849. *Afro-American History Series.* Vol. 7. Edited by Maxwell Whiteman. Wilmington, DE: Scholarly Resources Inc., n.d.
Brown, Herbert Ross. *The Sentimental Novel in America, 1789–1860.* New York: Pageant Books, 1959.

Douglass, Frederick. *My Bondage and My Freedom*. New York: Miller, Orton and Milligan, 1855. New York: Dover Publications, 1969.

____. *Narrative of the Life of Frederick Douglass, an American Slave*. Boston, 1845. New York: Anchor Books, 1973.

Goddu, Teresa A. *Gothic America: Narrative, History, and Nation*. New York: Columbia University Press, 1997.

hooks, bell. "Representations of Whiteness in the Black Imagination." In *Black on White: Black Writers on What It Means to Be White*. Edited by David R. Roediger. New York: Schocken Books, 1998.

Jacobs, Harriet. *Incidents in the Life of a Slave Girl*. 1861. New York: Harvest/HBJ, 1973.

Morrison, Toni. "Playing in the Dark." In *Black on White: Black Writers on What It Means to Be White*. Edited by David R. Roediger. New York: Schocken Books, 1998.

Nelson, Dana D. *The Word in Black and White: Reading "Race" in American Literature, 1638–1867*. New York: Oxford University Press, 1993.

Ridgeley, J.V. *Nineteenth-Century Southern Literature*. The University Press of Kentucky, 1980.

14

Gothic in the Himalayas: Powell and Pressburger's *Black Narcissus*

JOHN STONE

Introduction

It was Terry Castle who, in a richly suggestive essay, first called the attention of critics to a "supernaturalised model of mental experience"[1] operating in the Western consciousness for over two centuries and finding in Ann Radcliffe's *Mysteries of Udolpho* a key early expression. Sidestepping the Gothic core of Radcliffe's narrative, Castle concentrates instead on the language of sentiment in its "supposedly ordinary parts" (233), finding them "tremulous with hidden presences"—the "spectral images of those one loves" (234) to which supernatural ghosts had yielded center stage. Castle reads all manner of material souvenirs—items of clothing, familiar landscapes, personal possessions, furnishings—as restoring the Other to the foreground of Emily St. Aubert's screen of consciousness. It is in identifying the extension of this phenomenon to the living and present—that is, to other people—that Castle's argument takes on particular interest. As in biblical typology, characters are made to make sense as (and are taken for) the ghostly counterparts or mirrors of other characters; they are essentially deindividualized, reducing social relations to an oneiric cast of interchangeable tokens (238–9). Such is the power of "this new cognitive dispensation" (237) with its "obsessional concentration on nostalgic images" (246) that the reality of others is superseded by the haunting mental pictures they generate.

Just such a depersonalization takes place in the "supposedly ordinary sequence" of the 1947 British film *Black Narcissus* (based on Rumer Godden's 1939 novel), directed by Michael Powell and Emeric Pressburger. As in *Udolpho*, the heroine — Clodagh, a daughter of the Irish gentry — is resourceful, though afflicted by loss. Far from home, amid striking mountain scenery, she observes a stranger from the terrace of a crumbling palace. His presence triggers visions of an absent lover, cinematic flashbacks that leave her ecstatic, if disappointed that her reveries should run their course and strand her in the present. The scenario, then, is surprisingly Radcliffean for a text set in the 1930s, bearing out (it would seem) Castle's contention that the Gothic continues to foster "our fixation on the past (or yearnings for an idealized future), our longing for simulacra and nostalgic fantasy," our being "in love with what isn't there" (250) well into the twentieth century. What, though, if a Radcliffean ethos should be deprived of one of the elements making such phantasmatic blurring possible — its portrayal of European characters in a European setting? Emily and Annette, her servant, surmise that an unseen singer must be Valancourt because his song is French: "O! it is a Frenchman that sings."[2] Shared cultural origin makes the imaginings necessary for the occurrence of spectralization all the easier. Contrasting origins should make it all the more difficult, yet Clodagh, who has spent her pined-for youth in Ireland, identifies her lost Irish love with a young Rajput prince, Dilip Rai, the heir to a Himalayan estate where she is an invited guest.[3] "They're not alike" (Godden 159), Clodagh argues to herself: "Con was so white for a man, Dilip was dusky black, yet she had dreamed of them in one" (223).

In Clodagh's vision, then, converge all of the elements that make *Black Narcissus* both Gothic and colonial, elements that manifest themselves elsewhere in the text in patterns that will be discussed in the remainder of this essay. The first pattern is flight from the Gothicism of Europe. (Clodagh claims that she "had to get away" from both nostalgia — with its attendant specters — and her place in a decaying Gothic economy before arriving in the Himalayas.)[4] The second is recourse to Gothic ways of seeing when confronted with the Other. (Clodagh, cast in a colonial role that comes to be gradually compromised, reads Dilip as a spectral Con, and the colonial place as fantastic and disturbing.) Evidently, spectralization is not the only trope of deindividualization to operate in *Black Narcissus*. It overlaps uncomfortably with the typecasting of colonized populations,[5] recasting Castle's formula as "Every Other looks like every other" (Castle 238): Dilip's standing for someone in Clodagh's past, his merging with a cherished memory, serves to question his status as the Other.[6] The third pattern: the objects of a Gothicizing Western vision step aside while Gothic Otherness, displaced onto the Western characters themselves, leads to madness and alienation. (Dilip takes a lover and conveniently drops out of the narrative at just this point.)

Evidently, the Himalayas are not Gothic: their ruined temples are not ruined churches, and their monasteries and fortifications share little with the Gothic in architecture. Moreover, they are free of remnants of a European past with which the European present of the late eighteenth century was thought to have broken[7]; their own history is not an analog of European history; their present, in *Black Narcissus*, exhibits neither tension between aristocrat and bourgeoisie, nor tension between Catholic and Protestant. Yet the Himalayas do contain women and men, property and art, and analogous land forms: for every Western scheme of perception, or social, sexual, and power relationship, an Indian counterpart shows up the former as a cultural construct. Such a setting, in itself a doubling of the scheme of perception European characters bring with them, relativizes the ingredients of the Gothic as it underlines the genre's psychological basis.[8]

The escape attempted by the character who best exemplifies this process, Clodagh, is twofold: she has left for the Empire and taken the habit, arriving in the Himalayas at the head of a small band of nuns charged with bringing Western teaching and medicine to the natives. Like religious hermit crabs, the sisters occupy a purpose-built anti-convent: the Palace of Mopu (formerly a "house of women"), standing in the wind on a high mountain ledge. The palace — something of whose sensual past remains in frescoes, sculptures, and in one painting — has been granted to their order by a Rajput prince, Toda Rai (Esmond Knight), known as the General or old General, whom the nuns never meet. It is through the mediation of his agent, the dissolute but knowledgeable Englishman, Mr. Dean (David Farrar), that they and the viewers gather many of their impressions of the General, the people, and their customs. Isolated and unsettled, the nuns fall prone to illness, fatigue, and an initially intransitive sense of worry. The household grows all the less settled as Clodagh (Deborah Kerr) begins to admit unwanted members to the household: Mr. Dean brings a teenaged coquette, Kanchi (a heavily made up and mute Jean Simmons), who must be cloistered for six months before she can be found a husband; and the young General (Dilip Rai, the Black Narcissus of the title,[9] played by Sabu), a well-spoken and earnest teenager who is nonetheless a perfumed dandy, is admitted as a student against the custom of convents.

At the same time, a number of the nuns are suffering from vocational crises or mental disorders. Sister Philippa (Flora Robson), a middle-aged horticulturist, begins to remember things she had wanted to forget, and to feel overwhelmed by the landscape. Clodagh herself is drawn — only partly against her will, as we have seen — into memories of a failed courtship in Ireland, where she was to have married the son of a local landowner. Her troubles are further exacerbated by a perceived loss of control — for example, she objects to, but dares not remove, a Hindu sunnyasi who lives on the convent grounds. More pressing are the problems of Sister Ruth (Kathleen Byron), the schoolteacher, who feels attracted to Mr. Dean and resentful of Clodagh: her wild moods and constant nervousness soon hold out the promise of danger.

Deserted by the natives after the death of a child that Sister Blanche (Jenny Laird) has treated, the nuns are confined to the convent grounds. One night, while keeping watch, Clodagh finds Ruth in a red dress; she has renounced her vows, is somewhat crazed, and intends to leave. Clodagh tries to keep watch over her but falls asleep. Ruth escapes to the valley floor and, visibly feverish, confesses her love to Mr. Dean. He rejects it; she faints. On regaining consciousness, she is ordered back up the mountain — her eyes now bloodshot and her voice expressionless — by Mr. Dean. Finally, in a dramatically scored scene, a demoniacal Ruth tries to push Clodagh off the cliff as she rings Angelus; they struggle, and Ruth falls to her death. As a defeated and newly humble Clodagh leads the remaining nuns back to Calcutta, Mopu disappears in the mist.

Black Narcissus certainly bears the markings of a Gothic text. The analysis that follows will address the issue of Gothic, as opposed to natural perception, in a colonial setting, the film's invocation of the Gothic family and economy, and the peculiar way in which the nuns are haunted as cultural agents. My analysis will argue that the nuns are doubly disconcerted: first, by ordinary features of Gothic — decaying buildings, veiled statues, and an isolated alpine landscape; and secondly, by the colonial Other in whose midst they live. The nuns are driven to feel that they are haunted by a place that is alien to them, where the past is someone else's past, yet the film deals with these reactions ironically, as though the nuns had brought a predisposition to experience the Gothic with them.[10] For the film's Indian characters, the Gothic is not there to be read: in the same setting, before the same events, their perceptions and reactions display neither uneasiness nor fear. Indeed, the repressed returns not in the guise of local ghosts or mysteries, but as the nuns' own struggles with renounced desires and past disappointments: the haunting, then, is a function of the splitting off of fragments from the self for which the colonial place — and at least one colonial character — are catalysts.

It's Where You Put Your Eyes: Colonial, Gothic, and Natural Perception

On first viewing, it might seem that *Black Narcissus* writes the Gothic into a narrative of waning British colonialism by packing Gothic topoi in the hold of P&O steamer. Sister Clodagh is a mournful but plucky heroine of genteel birth; the names of two of the nuns, Briony and Blanche, have distinctly *Udolphian* rings to them[11]; and the enclosing walls of convents—where wimples and habits obscure identity amidst dark passages, and superstition is allowed to mingle with repressed desire—readily furnish conventional moments of Gothic dread. Yet the House of Saint Faith is only a convent—and only Gothic—inasmuch as the nuns choose to see it as such: they come to perceive (with the camera's collaboration) palace, land, and people in characteristically Gothic ways. Tucked away among the topoi, then, and more powerful than any of them, is a way of seeing—a scheme of Gothic perception that overwhelms the colonial and the natural.

It is chiefly as a colonial text (and a strikingly photographed melodrama) that Black Narcissus has been discussed by academic film critics.[12] Ian Christie, in his book-length study of the filmmakers' output, remarks on the "vertiginous hysteria"[13] of the sequence that is, in fact, the key to the presence of Gothic elements in the film (from Sister Clodagh's discovery of Ruth in red to the latter's death). Yet although these elements are thrilling, Christie does not consider them to be central: "[w]ith hindsight, it is possible to read *Black Narcissus* as a spiritual preparation for the British withdrawal from India" (61). He reads Sister Clodagh's failure as a leader and the decision to abandon the convent in the context of the colonial experience and associates it with contrition and humility. Of course, Clodagh's insecurity and trials in a strange land may be parabolized, though to do so is to minimize the degree to which Clodagh is driven to the brink of suicide (shortly before Ruth pushes her, the thought of jumping appears to cross Clodagh's mind) by her troubled relationship with other (mainly European) women, with the domestic sphere, and with her own sexuality. Moreover, in true Radcliffean fashion, Clodagh ends the film with the prospect of becoming again who she was at its beginning—an underling in a convent—as though the whole story had been a series of doubts that she might be someone else (the younger, Irish Clodagh; an authority figure; Ruth). Moreover, the nuns are not properly invaders: they have been invited to Mopu and are dependent on (and afraid of losing) the General's goodwill.[14]

A related though more theoretically informed approach has recently been provided by Priya Jaikumar, for whom "*Black Narcissus* offers an opportunity to make larger claims about British imperial narratives during decolonisation" inasmuch as it "salvages the breakdown of imperialism's categories of 'self' and 'other.'"[15] What causes *Black Narcissus* to fit "uncomfortably within the colonial canon" (58) is the power of the setting over the nuns: "a colonial place is made central enough to impede the assumptions projected onto it" (59), "[altering] the traveler's identity by revealing him/her to be an outsider" rather than simply functioning "as an element that threatens, tempts, and affirms 'civilisation'" (65):

> [T]he travelers are regenerated by this "othering" as they gain knowledge that redeems them from the collective guilt of their imperial relationship with the colonial land through experiences that are as purifying as they are traumatic [65].

The land itself, then, is resistant to the colonial enterprise, making "its will evident in the colonisers' minds and bodies" (66),[16] generating "the horrors of [the nuns'] visit" (62) while allowing the retreating empire to show its most engaging side as "well-intentioned and fundamentally compassionate women" (63). Though she recognises that Ruth falls into "scarlet passions and cadaverous bestiality" (66), looking "neither alive not human" in the climactic scene, Jaikumar fails to identify the nature of the demon Mopu has conjured, and with it the nature of literary conventions — indeed, of the narrative — that the colonial place throws back at its colonisers. The nuns expect a colonial narrative; they make over the colonial place in their own image and for their efforts are given a Gothic atmosphere, a close fit for Devendra Varma's description of Radcliffean terror: "Sounds unexplained, sights indistinctly caught, dim shadows endowed with motion by the flicker of the firelight or the shimmer of the moonbeam [invoking] superstitious fear."[17] Atmosphere generates plot and, as Jaikumar shrewdly observes, Mopu consequently "ingests [Sister Ruth] and spits out a different person."[18] In *Black Narcissus*, in the absence of a Gothic Other, a colonial place obligingly creates one, remaking the English subject as the unknowable Other, the site and source of Gothic horror.

In an early scene, Sister Clodagh is shown awake in bed, listening anxiously to constantly beating drums in the distance; the camera pans over the dim, sensual painted figures on the wall, the great mountain in the opposite range (seen through the window), a crucifix, and a candle. She is troubled, in Gothic fashion, by a tenebrous confining space: later in the film, when approaching Ruth's cell, she will move gingerly through the dark, as though uneasy about what might lie in wait. The viewer may be expected to react likewise, given the film's overlap with certain Gothic conventions: the Palace of Mopu, like the Castle of Otranto, spreads its ramparts along the brow of a precipice, and the outwardly mouldering and labyrinthine buildings, from whose windows and grounds one might fall to a distant death, are perpetually windswept.[19] The nuns read Mopu as disturbing — Clodagh, when trying to persuade Philippa not to ask to be transferred, blames "this place with its strange atmosphere." Yet neither the caretaker Angu Ayah (May Hallet), the General, nor any other non–Western character finds Mopu in the least spooky or eerie. Before the nuns' arrival, Ayah smiles and dances as she moves through the empty palace, and hopes the "house of women" might be re-established; and the General's thoughts turn on such practicalities as having plumbing installed. Antiquity is not what makes things strange or disconcerting in *Black Narcissus*, for it is doubtful that many Western viewers would know Indian art and architecture well enough to judge the accuracy or the period of the film's art direction. It stands for a different historical scale, a different cultural calculus by which to measure the meaning of the passing of time — or by which to suspend such measurement: at least one character at Mopu, the sunnyasi, is so far removed from temporal concerns that he would not notice whether the fleeing Ruth had passed by or not. The nuns, though religious, are bound to experience time as history, and so fail to understand this.

It is worth noting that even at one of the film's most Gothic moments — that of Sister Ruth's escape, all disembodied cackles and fruitless pursuits in the dark — Ayah is by turns pragmatic and ironic, telling the nuns to stay away from mad people (they can be dangerous!) and imitating their cries of "Sister Ruth! Sister Ruth!" as one would imitate a cranky child.[20] Nor is her experience of the oddly communicated interior spaces in tune with the viewer's. We follow characters through rooms and courtyards, up and down crooked stairwells, without ever being able to map things and so know where the action is going. An oddly luminescent veil flaps; the veil later falls from a statue, and an imposing though serene male form is revealed. (Of course, the nuns had very likely placed the veil over the statue.)[21] Yet in a painting of the palace that Ayah admires, and that Sister Clodagh orders removed, many of these interiors — the pool around which Ayah dances, the grille with the dancing figure — are shown exposed to the open air: the scene is sunny, crowded with figures, and not at all sinister.[22] Powell's and Pressburger's counterpoint to this is to occasionally show the *nuns* in a sinister light, as when Ruth has Joseph Anthony (Eddie Whaley Jr.), the child interpreter, teach a vocabulary lesson consisting of "cannon," "warship," "bayonet," "dagger," and (following Ruth's first murderous glance at Clodagh from the schoolroom window) "gun." The average age of his audience is perhaps six.

The Social and the Sexual

At first, the nuns welcome their assignment: they are part of an order of workers and mean to be self-sufficient. They are to be active, autonomous, and spiritual: passivity and sexuality will be absent from their lives. They attempt to construct a domestic realm that will, in principle, be neither bourgeois nor patriarchal[23]; it is modeled, as we shall see, on their mother house in Sussex, and entails careful imitation of the order's hierarchy, division of labor, and architecture. The nuns are to develop as women and advance toward God through experience and trial: thus, when Philippa confesses to Clodagh that she feels distracted by the landscape and by her own memories, she responds that the problem, once recognized, is to be overcome *in situ* via hard work in the garden. (At this, Philippa displays her blistered and calloused hands.) If they see their lives as barren and so are led to indulge or fall victim to their imaginations—"filling lacks," in Kilgour's words, "with their fantasies which, unrestrained by reason, can lead to madness" (114)—then that barrenness cannot be defined in terms of not striving.

Though destined to fall into the sexualized realm of the Gothic, the nuns are attempting an escape from the Gothic economy and family: they are a kind of family, all sisters, though they have left their mother behind; as they are not concerned with questions of ownership, they are not concerned with rightful or false inheritance. They have received their grant from another economy with different mechanisms: the General, his uncle (the sunnyasi, "General Sir Krishna Rai, KCBO, KCSI, CMG") and nephew (the young General) are aristocrats but not European medieval ones; they travel, mention London shops, speak or are learning various European languages, take an interest in physics, and practice typing. (Curiously, there is no mention of women in the General's family: in fact, with the exception of the flashback scenes, biological families do not have English-speaking parts in *Black Narcissus*—they are parts of the scenery, illustrations for Mr. Dean's opening letter.) Moreover, the Indian aristocrats are able to make choices alien to a European setting: the General is said to be worried that he should follow his uncle's example and become a sunnyasi; the young General takes a concubine. In the film's sexual and cultural division, then, the male and Indian family passes through stages of sensuality, responsibility, and retirement to spiritual ends. The female and

Western family seeks to combine the latter two, rejects the first, and recognizes static vows to which members are beholden rather than stages.

Yet from the arrival of the nuns at Mopu, the life of the body accompanies them: it does not pursue them, but it carries with it a kind of contagion. The body is present in the knowledge that the palace had been a "house of women," and in its abundant frescoes portraying largely unclothed courtesans. Mr. Dean also injects the life of the (male) body into the world of the nuns: he struts through much of the story in various states of undress, showing off his legs and chest, and makes allusions both to the bad reputation that precedes him and to the nuns' sexual inaccessibility. When bringing Kanchi to be "cloistered," he makes it clear that Kanchi had considered him desirable. ("You're sure there's no question you're dying to ask me?" he taunts Clodagh.) Ruth comes to desire Mr. Dean, and rushes down the mountain to confess as much; even Clodagh seems driven to experience often pleasant but involuntary flashbacks of episodes in a failed relationship with a man in part because of Mr. Dean's presence and, in the Christmas scene, voice. Kanchi is another reminder of the (female) sensual life, if only inasmuch as she resembles some of the figures that illustrate the palace. Her disappearance with the young General begins with a kiss, and ends a flirtation that has comprised the lowering of her eyelashes like a theatre curtain, dancing, peeping under screens, and innumerable sidelong glances. That the only consummated sexual relationship in the film should take place between teenagers and bring with it no unpleasant consequences (the young General is contrite but goes unpunished) serves to underline an Indian scheme of stages[24] in life — sexuality is for the young, responsibility for the middle-aged, retirement and contemplation for the old — that the nuns have upset by giving themselves over, at every age, to service and worship.

The Indian acceptance of sexuality is contrasted with an unnatural resumption of sexuality on the part of Sister Ruth. In what should be a haven, removed from conflict, separated from the passions, there develops the story of the mad nun who gets more mysterious as her madness deepens. In treating Ruth's sexuality and her madness, the film offers both Gothic and physiological explanations. Ruth has been ill; she is getting thinner; her field of vision goes blood red as she faints in Mr. Dean's bungalow. It is equally true that Clodagh is severe with her: it is as though friction and rivalry between women in the private sphere trigger the repressed imagination to run amok. Persecuted, Ruth comes to fix her desire and pin her hopes on Mr. Dean. Significantly, Ruth is not very keen on the young General; in a resistance of the tendency to figure the ethnic other as mysterious and unknowable, the film figures the young General as cheerful, steadfastly unmysterious, and unbrooding. Some critics, no doubt, would argue that the film does not permit sexual relationships across the ethnic divide.[25] Once she has dreamt of possessing Mr. Dean and sent away for her red dress and shoes, Ruth spies more insistently on Clodagh and Mr. Dean, grows more jealous, and so more determined to go to him.[26] In contrast to Kanchi's and the young General's kiss (on screen) and sexual possession of one another (off screen), Ruth's play for Mr. Dean is a failure: his attitude, apparently, is to stand aside when the repressed returns. Thus, paradoxically, the white European, unlike the Indian native, becomes the figure of unknowable, unreachable sexuality for the English nun.

And yet, it is the Indian setting that serves to unleash the repressed sexuality of the nuns. Clodagh is compelled to remember at and by Mopu, as are Philippa and Ruth. At Mopu, Clodagh's sexuality also returns to her, albeit in a more benign form: it is arguable whether she ever feels strongly attracted to Mr. Dean or seriously doubts her vocation. Moreover, her flashbacks—especially the second, all foxes, hard riding and ethereal music—have as much to do with lost social status and a failure to fulfill family and community expectations as with sexual desire. In fact, the lack that Clodagh needs to fill with imagined Gothic fantasies is, indeed, the lack of God. The nuns are cloistered in a space that speaks to them of an alien mythology, in which their small figures of consistently female Christian saints pale beside larger and more elaborate dancers and embracing lovers; somewhere across the valley lies a monastery of Buddhist monks; and, perhaps more significantly, as Ruth rushes out of the convent (with Clodagh in pursuit), a veil falls from a large statue, in all likelihood a representation of Shiva. Among the attributes of this god about the house (albeit one kept under wraps) is a vacillation between asceticism and sexual activity—hardly propitious for nuns.

Othered by Art

Hinted at in the film and effectively sketched in the novel is the narrative that Clodagh would have lived had something not driven her to take the veil. She is an escapee from a Big House novel, a daughter of the Anglo-Irish gentry, born a British subject and heiress to England's first colonial venture, only to reach maturity in the Irish Free State amidst the decline of her class.[27] She had meant to marry and stay put in every sense—"I don't want to go away. I want to stay here like this for the rest of my life," as she insists in one flashback—only to be foiled, not by another woman,[28] but by her intended's own escape from the bane of very late Gothic inheritance. Con (Shaun Noble), balking at staging annual dances for the peasants and watching the House decay, immigrates to Michigan and goes into business with his uncle. The pre-plot of *Black Narcissus*, then, echoes Susan Fraiman's analysis of *The Mill on the Floss*: Con's *Bildungsroman* involves a break with his family, flight, and entry into the capitalist economy, as does Tom's, while Clodagh's mission in India is reminiscent of Maggie's relationship with the Gypsies, which Fraiman reads as the undertaking of a mission made "eminently masculine"[29] by its colonial overtones. And while "the colonial version of *Bildungsroman* proves inaccessible to Maggie" (Fraiman 114), Clodagh roves—and becomes a colonial agent. But, like Maggie's, Clodagh's journey is eventually inward. She leaves her home and homeland only to attain greater isolation, continuing confinement, odder and smaller spaces; having abandoned a waxing landed class, she is exposed to a family of aristocratic Indian planters who are plainly doing well (Sisters Blanche and Briony marvel at the cost of the young General's clothes) in the tea business.

Worse still, the nuns are dependent on the General for work. As Jaikumar points out, though work is often depicted in imperial narratives as "a mode of self-realisation," it goes nowhere in the absence of colonial subjects (63). The colonial subjects of *Black Narcissus* do not gladly volunteer to be medical patients, students in a lace school, or pupils. They are paid subjects, put in place to satisfy the nuns' need for a mission by the General. In Jaikumar's reading, these non–English speaking Indian characters are "the most mute of all," "commented on and evaluated," "allowed to be articulate signs of the inexplicable causes that destabilize the nuns" (68), Spivakian subalterns whose "silence is imagined as threatening inscrutability" (Jaikumar 69). Yet it could be argued that the film casts the Himalayan peasants in a number of roles, problematizing the safe assumptions of the audience. The first spoken description of the peasants tends toward universalizing: in Dean's letter, he describes them as being "like mountain peasants everywhere: simple, independent," "no better and no worse than anywhere else," adding later that they are "primitive people" and "like children — unreasonable children" (Dean refers to his groom as "my boy"), apt to consider medicine "a new kind of magic." Even Sister Blanche, nicknamed Sister Honey for her cheerfulness, infantilizes the natives by gushing over their cuteness: when introduced to three young women whom the General has sent to the convent lace school, she tells Clodagh how nice they look, says nothing to them, and remarks that the youngest native children look even nicer. (By way of counterpoint, Ayah invents a system of nicknames for the nuns, few of which are endearing: Briony is "the fat lemini" and Ruth, "the snake-faced lemini.")

The camera tells a different story, challenging the nuns' self-representation as workers by showing natives doing most of the work, and subverting the nuns' gaze by interpolating other gazes. "We are very busy people," Clodagh informs Dean when they first meet; the following daytime sequence is a-bustle with wood-working, lumber-hauling, furniture-winching, and bandage-rolling. Yet the nuns are mainly overseers: one stands motionless in the courtyard, surrounded by workmen; another hands a curtain to a native woman, who hangs it; a third swirls past a girl who is polishing the floor; and only Joseph Anthony is seen teaching the Mopu schoolchildren English words. Such work is often the backdrop for conflict between European characters, contextualizing the melodrama, sapping off some of its importance,[30] as when Dean and Clodagh argue on a path crowded with overladen porters. When Ruth leaves her schoolroom to greet Dean, who has brought Kanchi to the convent, two women are seen scrubbing the landing; they continue to scrub while Dean and Ruth chat, Clodagh challenges Ruth and greets Dean, Kanchi enters, is looked up and down by Clodagh and finally charged to Briony. When the scene dissolves, the scrubbers looking down on the rivalry and sneering provocation played out in the courtyard get up to leave, as though a performance staged for their benefit had drawn to a close. Half-hidden in the passageway along which Briony approaches Clodagh is another onlooker: in one of the film's oddest compositions, the hall is crowded with figures who seem to have frozen in the nun's presence; highlighted by this stillness, by the false impression that no one but Briony and a trailing Ruth are on camera (there may be a dozen people in these shots), a native woman seated on the floor turns her head to follow the action. She is not alone in gazing back: Clodagh complains to Dean that the natives stop and stare at the nuns on their way to see the sunnyasi; Kanchi glares freely at all comers (so long as she is not herself being watched); and the viewer observes Ruth observing Dean and Clodagh from Joseph Anthony's perspective in a relay of gazes, one European and neurotic, the other native and healthy. *Pace* Kaplan, the subaltern in this film, does look,[31] beginning with Clodagh's students in Calcutta, some of whom follow her out of the room with their eyes.

This, then, is the central device by which the nuns' growing tension is triggered; and it can hardly be a coincidence that, in the first sequence showing a nun at Mopu, Ruth scurries nervously past two native women and a male servant after having rung the convent bell. The women have stopped to look at her, while the latter stops his sweeping for a moment to bow reverentially. Ruth makes eye contact with none. The moment is one of avoidance, implicit dread, the wish not to confront (unless as part of a secure group: Ruth is alone) the Other, the population the nuns ostensibly serve. Indeed, this native eye, represented in the actual assertive gaze of the natives and additionally embodied, as we shall see, in native art, will "haunt back" and Other the nuns. Ultimately, the unknowable Other of the film is not the European male or the Indian native but the initial subject, the English nun.

As Robert Sennet argues with regard to Alfred Junge's art direction, it is the central visual conceit of the film "that the nuns are apart from the world at the same time as they are in it"[32]; and the camera's few excursions beyond the convent grounds tend to confirm that the House of Saint Faith is the sisters' chimera or a short-lived caprice of the General's. The very first shot shows a Buddhist religious community on the slope opposite Mopu, whose horns are heard at intervals. Clodagh and Dean later walk past two of these monks, paying them no notice, as they approach the sunnyasi's tree. The monks' chanting, like the conversation of a group of men seated on roadside cushions near the spot where Ayah whips Kanchi, or the work songs of the men and women who repair and fit out the convent, is inaccessible vocally, evidence that the subalterns are speaking, surrounding the nuns with codes of meaning to which they are not privy. It is the multilingual Dilip, Krishna, Toda Rai, Ayah, and Joseph Anthony who are able to participate in both the film's vocalities, hinting to the spectator that the valley is carrying on with its own life, its own discourses, largely indifferent to the ostensibly benevolent but increasingly fantastic invasion at Mopu Palace.

The natives, then, set the scene for the emergence of the Gothic in *Black Narcissus* by withdrawing from the plot, refusing to be changed by the nuns' work. Deserted by their colonial charges, the nuns are warned by Dean that they might be murdered in their sleep in monstrous fashion — a Jekyll-and-Hyde-like metamorphosis of the p[l]easant into the fiendish. There is no attack, except that of stripping the nuns of their status as imperial agents, as powerful subjects; rather than becoming a Gothic Other, the valley-dwellers assert their subjectivity and dodge Gothic dehumanization while the nuns themselves are reduced to the status of unknowable and inhuman Gothic Other. Yet if there is a Godduian "haunting back" in *Black Narcissus*, it is not in terms of "the objects of torture and terror" employing Gothic effects to break free of an "imprisoning plot,"[33] for it is in the choice of nuns rather than soldiers, planters, or traders that "imperial *vulnerability* is articulated."[34] At times, indeed, the contemporary viewer may be lulled into thinking of the Servants of Mary as an NGO *avant-la-lettre*, for by teaching in English only, they further imperial political aims, and they do not proselytize their religious ideology.

Rather, the nuns are haunted back as cultural agents; their imperviousness to the Indian aesthetic and the Indian sensibility; their lack of empathy with Mopu as a cultural site is the key to their eventual madness and displacement. By redecorating Mopu, by Westernizing it — an act of architectural translation if not appropriation — they erase the palace's original aesthetic charge and release a Gothic remainder.

For in Powell and Pressburger's visual text, the haunting back, the key site of resistance, is art-historical. Wherever they go, the Servants of Mary attempt to recreate their mother house in Sussex:

> In [Calcutta] Sister Clodagh had found the same brick buildings, the same green walls and echoing stone stairs; the same figures of saints in coloured plaster.... The reception room floor had even been laid in wood to match the parquet at home and the chapel had been copied exactly from the chapel at Canstead. [Godden 56]

But at Mopu, "The house would not conform" (57). In the film as in the novel, the nuns veil or obstruct Mopu in makeshift fashion, draping proper Christian curtains over immodestly eastern statues and frescoes.[35] They scatter imported Christian images throughout the palace, attempting to obscure the body from which their Western religious ideology has promised escape. Yet neither the building's provenance nor its iconography — clearly centered on the life of the body, celebrated by the religions of India — is ever fully masked. Much of this art comes to unveil itself, as though the house were choosing to manifest both its resistance and its anger at having been muzzled: moments before the giant figure of Shiva is revealed, curtains can be seen slipping away from the frescoes in Ruth's cell, as the Gothic — the realm of the body and of the irrational — is unleashed.

It is, then, through specific aesthetic effects that Clodagh and Ruth are Othered for one another, their aesthetic translation. In moments of kindled or exacerbated passion — usually erotic passion — each is shot from the gaze of the other in ways that invoke the European figurative traditions that have been imported to India nestled in the nuns' cultural baggage and ripe with Gothic potential. The first of these is the mannerist and baroque sculpture of Catholic Europe, especially the painted figures of religious art (of which the "figures of saints in coloured plaster" at Mopu are themselves a naïve variant). As the art historian Marjorie Trusted notes, "glowing pigments" were used in such works to enhance their impact "in the relatively dark interiors of churches and chapels, illuminated perhaps only by candlelight."[36] Trusted charts a Protestant British dislike for such sculpture from the early seventeenth century onwards: its "overdone naturalism" made for "uneasiness," its color imparting, in the words of one nineteenth-century traveller, "an air of life" that seemed "too natural" (1).

Richard Ford, the author of an 1845 guidebook to Spain, described such works in terms reminiscent of the Radcliffean apprehension, verging on terror, created by *Udolpho*'s wax memento mori: "[Spanish works of sculpture] have a startling identity: the stone statues of monks actually seem petrifications of a once living being.... The imitation is so exact in form and colour, that it suggests the painful idea of a dead body."[37] Like Professor Henry Jarrod's "creations" in the film *House of Wax* (1953), their life*like*ness discredits their life*less*ness, suggesting a liminal state. Projected onto living characters, this uncanniness is doubled; and the nuns, whose drapery is always handy, grow statuesque as they grow still. As befits a Gothic text, *Black Narcissus* petrifies Ruth and Clodagh in nearly parallel scenes, emphasizing the former's status as the latter's double. Ruth descends from her classroom to greet Dean in the courtyard, flirts awkwardly and turns to leave; sensing suddenly that she is being watched, she flinches with apprehension and looks back to see Clodagh, utterly motionless on the opposite flight of stairs, an unwanted observer of Ruth's desire. Ruth returns the shudder later in the film: Clodagh walks out of the courtyard with Dean and Dilip Rai after the Christmas service, grows angry with Dean despite her muted attraction to him, turns and begins to climbs the steps. Above her, she sees a still silhouette against a curtain that the camera reveals to be Ruth, almost a columnar figure, rigid, her drapery accentuated, looking both painted and lifelike. The effect in both instances is one of a "growing sense of the ghostliness of other people" (Castle 237). During the sustained haunting of the film's penultimate sequence, Clodagh's near-paralysis from fear renders her all the more statuesque — kneeling in prayer in the chapel, conscious of a malevolent presence that could materialize at any moment, that seems to move past her, unseen. Clodagh's hands especially take on the weird yellowness and odd clenching often found in Spanish *dolorosas*, or grieving virgins.[38] Ruth's climactic emergence from the convent a moment later draws on the second pictorial tradition revealed in the film: the illustrations the Irish artist Harry Clarke, a near-contemporary and follower of Beardsley, created to accompany Poe's short stories. As in so many of Clarke's drawings, Ruth is drained of color, her red dress and hair looking almost black, her eyes set off by dark circles, her figure almost merging with a shadowy background. Yet Ruth's ultimate aestheticization takes place off screen, registering as horror on Clodagh's face; in the novel, it is death by cut bamboo — and by an icon, the most central of her faith and mission: "Her head and veil were flung out curiously sideways. A spike had driven through her chest, holding her up with her head hanging down" (Godden 205).

Conclusion: Truncated Plots of Personal Development, Exaggeration and Association

Gothic doubling may be seen as the logical outcome of a narrative in which Othering is undermined, disrupting a narrative of personal development that depends upon Othering for its ultimate affirmation. Clodagh revises her own master narrative upon her failure to marry into her own class. Her new role is that of a nun and administrator (of a kind) in colonial India. Mopu was to witness the consummation of her narrative, placing her atop a convent hierarchy, as well as inserting her as imperial subject into an imperial narrative.[39] This new identity depends on the pretense of natural authority (thus Dean's reference to her as "a superior being" and the young General's to "the Superior Sister") and is analogous to male myths of discovery and autonomy. Yet Mopu undoes this new Clodagh. In the form of the Generals, young and old, she is outranked by the Other. She is reminded of her origin and, to her consternation, visited by the specter of Con. In the form of Angu Ayah, Joseph Anthony, the sunyassi, and the natives on the path, the native Other ignores her authority, asserting its own Indian subjectivity. Clodagh, then, is given likeness where she had sought defining difference, and is received with indifference where she had expected respect, if not submission. It is Clodagh's project (and projection) of selfhood, then, that plunges down the cliff-face into the fog-shrouded valley in the film's climax: Ruth as Clodagh's Gothic double emblemizes the destruction of Clodagh's self-construction. Mopu is the agent of this destruction, deflecting the label of "disturbing" onto the labeller, the final blow to Clodagh's attempt to define her identity as powerful subject. She is doomed to return to her former status, having exchanged the welcome spectres of her halcyon youth for the less welcome ghosts of India.[40]

The Gothic double is also, of course, an inversion of the phenomenon of spectralization: instead of bestowing a shared identity on two objects of perception, in *Black Narcissus* the subject itself — rational and autonomous in its colonial aspect, community-bound and neo-medieval in its religious one — is twinned and challenged. Clodagh's individual breakdown, then, is mirrored in that of the colonial enterprise, for the entire European community at Mopu suffers from traditionally Gothic irrational alteration in the workings of the rational intellect that ostensibly privileges the heirs of Western modernity. The tendency toward unreason takes two forms: the first is proclivity to speculation, a readiness to jump to conclusions on the basis of meager evidence; the second is a displacement of causal reasoning by association. Just before telling Clodagh that the nuns have to go "before something happens," Mr. Dean looks about anxiously and remarks that "this place has a way of exaggerating things." What "things"? It might be more accurate to say that Dean and the nuns exaggerate their reactions and project their unreason onto the place: Ruth exaggerates a few kind words from Mr Dean; Clodagh exaggerates the significance of Philippa's planting flowers on the front terraces (there are potatoes and beans, in a hidden place) and reads her own very practical decisions with regard to the sunnyasi and the young General in somewhat desperate terms. She loses control over her own train of thought, giving in to association,[41] allowing (to give one instance) mention of the young General's emeralds to transport her to the emeralds she was to have received from her grandmother; significantly, many of Clodagh's flashbacks take place while she is in the chapel. Moreover, in the litany of her failures that she recites to Mr. Dean, Clodagh shows that she has come to experience Mopu not as a problem to be analyzed, but as a series of failures of will: she could not get rid of the holy man; she could not stop the wind from blowing; and she could not hide the mountain. Perhaps it is the peculiarity of *Black Narcissus* that the breakdown of reason and the rise of association and analogy to controlling roles in Clodagh's and the other nuns' minds has to do both with their personal and so foreign pasts, and with the disconcerting effects of a colonial present that, for reasons beyond the nuns' understanding, does not succeed in disconcerting or displacing the subjectivity of the colonized.

Notes

1. Terry Castle, "The Spectralisation of the Other in *The Mysteries of Udolpho*," in *The New Eighteenth Century: Theory, Politics, English Literature*, eds. Felicity Nussbaum and Laura Brown (New York: Methuen, 1987), 248.

2. Ann Radcliffe, *The Mysteries of Udolpho, 1794* (Oxford and New York: Oxford University Press, 1966), 439.

3. In the novel, this confounding of an Indian with an Irishman is itself mirrored by an association of the Himalayas with Ireland: "Why, when it was entirely different? Was it the unaccustomed greenness, or the stillness of the house after the wind outside?" (Rumer Godden, *Black Narcissus, 1939* [London: Pan, 1994], 11).

4. See my discussion below.

5. A reductivist — though perhaps not racist — characterization of the natives forms part of the opening (and in Powell and Pressburger's storyboard, framing) sequence: before setting out for the Himalayas, Clodagh reads of her destination in a letter sent by the British agent, Mr Dean, who later asserts that "these Rajputs are a fighting race." Godden's novel distinguishes between five different ethnic groups living in the valley, each stereotyped, such as the Lepchas, "lazy, lusty, and bawdy" (Godden 76), and "the State men" or Nepalese, "fantastic ... heady and strong with the crude bright clothes and goblin faces" (76).

6. In the novel, the approach of madness and violence is announced by a growing awareness that the Other is not behaving as expected: "Have you noticed," asks one character, "how important these people are? How they've impressed themselves on us, compared with the natives in other places we've been in?" (Godden 123).

7. See Maggie Kilgour, *The Rise of the Gothic Novel* (London: Routledge, 1995),12–13, which conveniently sidesteps the Gothicism of eighteenth-century invocations of the ancient constitution.

8. Though there is nothing in the film to confirm the nuns' awareness of pre-existing Gothic forms, the anonymous narrator of Godden's novel sometimes interprets the Indian present in European terms, as when the nuns' topees, worn "over their veils ... gave them the look of pilgrim women in Gothic tales" (Godden 30) or the young General is said to be "as naïve at charming as the youngest son in a fairy story" (123).

9. "Black Narcissus" is the brand of the London-bought cologne the young General wears to class one day; it is Sister Ruth who calls her student a "fine black peacock" and "black Narcissus." When Sister Blanche objects that "he's not black," Ruth insists that "they all look alike to me." For further uses of "black" in an Indian setting, see E. M. Forster's *A Passage to India*; the protagonist Aziz speaks of "we poor blacks" 1924 ([Harmondsworth: Penguin, 1979], 6). In Godden's novel, Clodagh admits to herself that this nickname echoes her own vision: in a dream, "Dilip and Con had held mirrors in the palm of their hands, and she had tried to attract them but could only echo what they said" (Godden 124).

10. As Oscar Wilde writes in "The Decay of Lying," "a great artist invents a type, and life tries to copy," the experience of Pre-Rapaelite painting giving rise to Pre-Raphaelite-like women in real life, to give one of Wilde's example (*The Works of Oscar Wilde* [London: Collins, 1931], 1089).

11. "Briony," of course, is part of the scenery. See, for example, Chapter XI of Volume III of *Udolpho*, which features a majestic monastic ruin, around whose pointed chapel windows "the ivy and the briony hung in many a fantastic wreath" (Radcliffe 483). The name Blanche recalls Emily's counterpart/double in the second part of *Udolpho*.

12. *Black Narcissus* was notorious in its day for its treatment of Western religion: the original U.S. version had to be cut to avoid offending the Catholic Legion of Decency, which could not stomach the madness-tinged and highly evident sexual desire of a former nun.

13. Ian Christie, *Arrows of Desire: The Films of Michael Powell and Emeric Pressburger* (London: Faber, 1994), 60.

14. In the novel, the entire valley is under lease to the General, who belongs to the extended ruling (though not royal) family of "the State" across the mountains (Godden 15), so remote as to remain unencumbered by British political influence. "The State" is likely Nepal, as Mount Kachenjunga on the present-day Nepal-India border figures prominently in the narrative. The only allusion to Nepalese history — if intended as such — in both novel and film is Ayah's calling the Dilip Rai "General Bahadur" (Godden 15), after Sir Jung Bahadur, the army leader who brought the Rana family to power in 1846. For an account of the Mopu estate's politically ambiguous status in Godden's novel, see Alaknanda Bagchi, "Of Nuns and Palaces: Rumer Godden's *Black Narcissus*," *Christianity and Literature* 45 (1995), 56–57; for the film, see Michael Powell, *A Life in Movies: An Autobiography*, 1986 (London: Faber, 2000), in which Mopu is described as a "remote kingdom" and the General as its "local ruler" (558).

15. Priya Jaikumar, "'Place' and the Modernist Redemption of Empire in *Black Narcissus* (1947)," *Cinema Journal* 20, no. 2 (2001): 58.

16. In a similar vein, Bagchi writes of Godden's Mopu that it "seems to haunt all

those who do not really belong to this site but attempt to appropriate it" (Bagchi: 53–66, 58).

17. Quoted in Christine Ruotolo et. al., ed., "Terror and Horror," *The Gothic: Materials for Study* [home page on-line]; available from <http://www.engl.virginia.edu/~enec98/Group/title.html>; Internet; accessed 30 July 1998.

18. Jaikumar, 66. Note that *all* the sisters are ingested in the novel: "It was as if [the palace] had swallowed them up, they and the restraints they had brought to it: they were gone under the old familiarity, their saints tossed down like beads, the bell on its thread of sound snapped off" (Godden 57). For reasons of their own, Powell and Pressburger excepted Sister Briony from the sway of atmosphere: as Clodagh steps gingerly towards Ruth's cell and their nighttime confrontation, she passes each of the other nuns' doors and stops to listen: the once cheerful Honey is weeping inconsolably, Philippa praying to God for help — and Briony snoring.

19. It lacks only the crypts and catacombs of Lewis's and Radcliffe's Gothic convents, though a number of establishing shots suggest the existence of two or three underground levels.

20. According to Anh Hua, "Aiya" (*sic*) is "physically grotesque, old, short, decaying, resembling a hag. Aiya (sic) is depicted as subhuman, less than human, animal-like.... [She] is degendered" and "desexualised," placing her in a "social and racial hierarchy," "at the bottom of the 'Family of Man,'" "[reinforcing and perpetuating] the genealogies of imperialism" ("Primitive Spectacle in *Black Narcissus*," *J-Spot: A Journal of Social and Political Thought 1*, no. 2 [2000]; [e-journal] http://www.yorku.ca/jspot/2/ahua.htm [accessed 13 October 2001]). Yet Ayah is also bossy and common-sensical; Michael Powell called her "the masterful old guardian" (*A Life in Movies* 578) and intended her to be played as such. In going to such great lengths to find a place for Ayah in a critical framework borrowed from Anne McClintock's *Imperial Leather*, Hua divests this native female character of authority (see especially the scene of the nuns' collective panic after the death of a baby Sister Honey had treated); in ignoring her place in the plot and concentrating on appearance, she reduces the film to a series of stills. Hua likewise reads the sunnyasi as a "typical primitive spectacular body ... embodying the silent and darkened world of mystery and exoticism" while mystifying, romanticizing, and trivializing "native religion and native belief systems." Obviated in this analysis is his status as the most sophisticated, most travelled, and most polyglot character in the film — he has chosen to give up travel, stop talking, and shed his sophistication. Only Hua and Kaplan, among critics, hold the view that *Black Narcissus* is disrespectful in its depiction of Indian religions; see E. Ann Kaplan, *Looking for the Other: Feminism, Film, and the Imperial Gaze* (London: Routledge, 1997), 82: "The rendering of the people's religion is close to mockery."

21. *Black Narcissus* is rich in veils. Transition to the first interior shot of the palace involves the camera approaching and moving past a flutter of black cloth, fleetingly impossible to identify as such, which is blown towards the lens and so nearly fills the screen. Kanchi, who wears blue and burgundy veils in her initial scenes, discards them for the two sequences in which she makes eye contact with the young General. Many of the painted courtesans of the frescoes— present even in the most private spaces, the nuns' cells—are likewise veiled, though gauze can hardly be said to mark "the line between the conscious and unconscious mind" (Eve Kosofsky Sedgwick, "The Character in the Veil: Imagery on the Surface in the Gothic Novel," *PMLA* 96, no. 2 [1981]: 256).

22. I am indebted to Marta Puig, formerly of the Universitat Pompeu Fabra in Barcelona, for her observation that Mopu is located along the routes by which Tantric Buddhism was transmitted from Bengal to Tibet. Though anachronous, the Mopu fres-

coes especially (notice the embracing figures in the Blue Room) may be intended to invoke tantric practice and meditation, an inversion of celibate Christian monasticism.

23. The highest ecclesiastical authority in the film is the Mother Provincial in Calcutta: there are no priests.

24. In such a context, sexuality is not hidden. Thus Joseph Anthony's statement, when asked his age, that he is "six-to-eleven"; he corrects himself, saying, "I can remember that I am six, but my father married my mother eleven years ago, so that I may probably be about ten."

25. "Black Narcissus as a 'magical' scent allows the blurring of class boundaries amongst the primitives (the sexual union of a maid and a prince), yet it denies miscegenation. There is no sexual union between white colonisers and 'black' colonised Indians, particularly between white women and 'black' Indian men" (Hua "Primitive Spectacle"). This invites the question whether Dilip Rai is portrayed as a primitive; Powell, for one, writes that the young General "is friendly and eager, but also has charm and authority" (Powell 580), adding that "I didn't look on Sabu as an exotic" (581).

26. Here Sedgwick's observations on colours and twilight (264) are germane, for the film alternates between day- and nighttime scenes to the exclusion of dawn and dusk until the beginning of Ruth's final crisis: she then plots her escape in a twilight by turns reddish and purplish, tones which return in the moments leading to her attempt to murder Clodagh. By the same token, the prominent blood stains on Ruth's habit in an early sequence dovetail with Sedgwick's reading of Lewis's Bleeding Nun in *The Monk* as bearing "the badge of violence" (257). Of course, Ruth is not bleeding; her stains stem from efforts to stop the bleeding of a worker on the General's estate. Yet the shock and gasps she elicits serve only to reinforce the mechanism producing demonic possession (and spectralization) in *Black Narcissus*: Ruth is the victim of a projection.

27. For Clodagh's class background in the novel, see Godden, 65–66 and 124–27; among her hunting and shooting companions is "young Jerry Caldecott who was the next Lord Toome" (125). My reckoning of the period of Clodagh's birth is based on a rough calculation from internal evidence that the novel is set in 1938–39 (a visiting nun is said to have come to India in the wake of the Japanese bombing of Canton [143], which took place in 1937–38) and Michael Powell's record of conversations with Emeric Pressburger and Deborah Kerr, in both of which Clodagh's age is given as thirty-six (576–77). On Clodagh's Irishness see also Jaikumar, for whom "both the novel and the film fantasize her as willingly subservient to British missionary work in India" (63)— surely not unusual for a woman of Clodagh's class and ethnic background.

28. Both Kaplan (85) and Hua invent such a rival for Clodagh, though there is none in film or novel. Indeed, Kaplan's stimulating discussion of *Black Narcissus* is fairly sprinkled with errors of fact or terminology. The General is not a "Raj" (Kaplan 83) but a raja. One may personify but not be a period in history. Nowhere in the film is it stated or so much as suggested that Clodagh and her colleagues are "Cistercian Nuns" [*sic*] (81); according to both Powell (558) and Pressburger's biographer, his grandson Kevin Macdonald (*Emeric Pressburger: The Life and Death of a Screenwriter* [London: Faber, 1994], 265), they are Anglicans. Prince Sabu was not played by Dilip Rai (Kaplan 82), nor is the young General the General's son: Sabu (1924–63) was an actor; Dilip Rai his part; and the two generals uncle and nephew. The nuns' habits are not "stark white" (Kaplan 85) but oatmeal in colour (see Powell, 584); Mr. Dean rides a pony, not a "tiny donkey" (Kaplan 84); and Clodagh's office is that of Sister Superior rather than "Mother Superior" (84). While none of these oversights may be said to weaken Kaplan's analysis, she over-reads the General as "sensuous" and "despotic," arguing that

these qualities, symbolized by "the Raj's [sic] old harem palace" contribute to the imperial gaze's locating "[Mopu] as the place of the sensuous, the bodily, the sexual in a classic binary of west equals reason, Third World equals the body" (83). Two characters are here confounded, for the harem was the General's father's, as Dean explains to Clodagh at their first meeting. Toda Rai has never used the palace and thinks only of giving it over to other purposes. Ayah recalls this difference in character between father and son when encouraging the young General to whip Kanchi: "You're going to be a great man," she proclaims joyfully, "not like your uncle — oh dear, no — like your grandfather! Ha! Ha! He was a man! Finish the beating and begin to be a man!" The General, Dilip's uncle, is set up as his father's antithesis. He is not "lascivious," as Kaplan suggests (88). Though Kaplan shares with many of today's politically minded critics a sophisticated theoretical framework, I doubt that bracketing off so much textual detail helps to advance her argument.

As for Hua, it should be pointed out that much of the fourth and longest section of her article bears a striking resemblance to passages in Kaplan's book. She too speaks of Cistercian nuns and Prince Sabu. Moreover, at several points, Hua's interpretations are nearly indistinguishable from those articulated previously by Kaplan. Compare, for example, Hua's "Dean's voice-over describing the primitives is accompanied cinematically with close-up shots of smiling Indians, presented as 'noble savages'" with Kaplan's earlier "cinematically, Dean's voice-over describing the people is accompanied by close-up shots of smiling Indians, presented as eighteenth-century 'noble savages....'" (Kaplan 82) — a curious similarity, given that Hua does not here make direct reference to Kaplan. My own examination of Kaplan turned up another ten passages echoed in Hua. At least one other source receives similar treatment: where Hua writes, "However, the temptations which beset the nuns and their young leader Sister Clodagh stem as much from their own unresolved conflicts and repressed desires as from the ghosts of the windswept palace of Mopu." Ian Christie had written, "The temptations that beset the nuns and their insecure young leader, Sister Clodagh (Deborah Kerr) spring as much from their own unresolved conflicts as from ghosts of the windswept Palace of Mopu..." (Christie 60).

29. Susan Fraiman, "*The Mill on the Floss*, the Critics, and the *Bildungsroman*," *PMLA* 108, no.1 (1993): 114.

30. In the novel, the young General mocks Ruth for forgetting her work and brooding over her personal life: "I have written out the whole of the exercise and I have learnt it by rote while I was waiting for you to finish your daydream" (116).

31. "Can the subaltern in [*Black Narcissus* and *Out of Africa*] look? Or is the subaltern merely the object of the gaze?" (Kaplan 81). Kaplan responds that "the gaze structures within the film confirm that their stance is imperialist vis-à-vis the people they have come to educate, convert and help," Joseph Anthony being "allowed to 'look,' but only within certain parameters: the nuns send him away when they don't want his look of curiosity" (82). This seems to me to stretch the case. Joseph Anthony is never explicitly sent away by any of the nuns; he may flee from Ruth in the film's last half hour as her hatred for Clodagh is fanned into madness, but otherwise he looks at whomever he likes and, on one occasion, places limits on Clodagh's scope of action by flatly refusing to ask the sunyassi if he has seen Ruth. If anything, Joseph Anthony is accorded extraordinary agency and vocality for a six-year-old: when the nuns are abandoned by their students and servants, they must ask him the reason; and when they search for Ruth, his status as a linguistic go-between render him indispensable.

32. "[The art director Alfred Junge] decorated their convent at Mopu with dozens of bird cages, symbolizing confinement, and enormous windows, symbolizing freedom" (Robert S. Sennet, *Setting the Scene: The Great Hollywood Art Directors* [New York:

Abrams, 1994], 152). Note that the first, enormous bird cage in the film — large enough for an adult to walk into — is open, its bird flying freely in and out, before the nuns' arrival. For a similar view, see Macdonald, for whom "[*Black Narcissus*'s] central theme is the impossibility of Europeans ever coming to terms with, let alone understanding, the sub-continent" (MacDonald 265).

33. Teresa A. Goddu, *Gothic America: Narrative, History, and Nation* (New York: Columbia University Press, 1997), 143.

34. Jaikumar, 63; my emphasis.

35. Note the limited obstruction of the wall paintings in the dispensary by furniture and shelves.

36. Marjorie Trusted, *Spanish Sculpture: Catalogue of the Post-Medieval Spanish Sculpture in Wood, Terracotta, Alabaster, Marble, Stone, Lead and Jet in the Victoria and Albert Museum* (London: Victoria and Albert Musuem, 1996), 8.

37. Richard Ford, *A Handbook for Travellers in Spain and Readers at Home*, 1845, vol. 1, *Preliminary Remarks, and Andalucia* (London: Centaur Press, 1966), 169. See Sigmund Freud's discussion of waxworks, automata and dolls in the "The Uncanny," in *An Infantile Neurosis and Other Works*, vol. 17 of *The Standard Edition of the Complete Psychological Works of Sigmund Freud*, James Strachey, ed. and trans. (London: Hogarth Press and the Institute of Psychoanalysis, 1955), 226–27, 233.

38. Bony, nearly sketetal, Clodagh's hands seem appropriated from the works of such Spanish sculptors as Alonso Berruguete (c. 1488–1561); see Berruguete's John the Baptist in the Toledo Cathedral choir stalls and the statues of women on either side of the cross in the San Benito retable, Juan Martínez Montañés (1568–1649); see also the statue of Saint Ignatius of Loyola in the University Chapel, Universidad de Sevilla, and the Portuguese Manuel Pereira (1588–1683); see also the statue of Saint Rupert in the collection of the Convent of San Plácido, Madrid.

39. See Kilgour 37–39 and 113–41 on distinct patterns of personal development in male and female Gothic; and 63–68 on *Caleb Williams* as an anti–*Bildungsroman* in which Gothic doubling leads to "the obliteration rather than construction of individual identity" (68). The film's other *Bildungsroman* is resolved in decidedly non–Gothic fashion: the young General, who had shown signs of shirking his role as male heir — "You don't need me as a man," he had informed Clodagh, "I'm only interested in studious things"— later decides that he will be "exactly like my ancestors," who "were modest and brave and polite and … never did anything cheating."

40. The novel uses the Hindi word "bh*u*t" (Godden 214).

41. That Clodagh succumbs to association is more explicitly evident in the novel, where she comes to wonder why she has confounded her Irish boyfriend Con, Mr. Dean, and the young General in her mind (Godden 124, 201).

Works Cited

Bagchi, Alaknanda. "Of Nuns and Palaces: Rumer Godden's *Black Narcissus.*" *Christianity and Literature* 451 (1995) 53–66.

Black Narcissus. Director Michael Powell and Emeric Pressburger. Performers Deborah Kerr, Kathleen Byron, Sabu, Jean Simmons, David Farrar, Judith Furse, Flora Robson. The Archers in association with J. Arthur Rank. 1947.

Castle, Terry. "The Spectralisation of the Other in *The Mysteries of Udolpho.*" In *The New Eighteenth Century: Theory, Politics, English Literature.* Edited by Felicity Nussbaum and Laura Brown. New York: Methuen, 1987.

Christie, Ian. *Arrows of Desire: The Films of Michael Powell and Emeric Pressburger.* London: Faber, 1994.

Ford, Richard. *Preliminary Remarks, and Andalucia.* Vol. 1 of *A Handbook for Travellers in Spain and Readers at Home.* 1845. London: Centaur Press, 1966.

Forster, E. M. *A Passage to India.* 1924. Harmondsworth: Penguin, 1979.

Fraiman, Susan. "*The Mill on the Floss,* the Critics, and the Bildungsroman." PMLA 108:1 (1993): 136–50.

Freud, Sigmund. "The Uncanny." In *The Standard Edition of the Complete Psychological Works of Sigmund Freud.* Vol. 17: *An Infantile Neurosis and Other Works.* Edited and translated by James Strachey. London: Hogarth Press and the Institute of Psychoanalysis, 1955.

Godden, Rumer. *Black Narcissus.* 1939. London: Pan, 1994.

Goddu, Teresa A. *Gothic America: Narrative, History, and Nation.* New York: Columbia University Press, 1997.

Hua, Anh. "Primitive Spectacle in *Black Narcissus.*" In *J-Spot: A Journal of Social and Political Thought* 1:2 (2000). [e-journal]. <http://www.yorku.ca/jspot/2/ahua.htm>. (accessed 13 October 2001).

Kaplan, E. Ann. *Looking for the Other: Feminism, Film, and the Imperial Gaze.* London: Routledge, 1997.

Kilgour, Maggie. *The Rise of the Gothic Novel.* London: Routledge, 1995.

Jaikumar, Priya. "'Place' and the Modernist Redemption of Empire in *Black Narcissus* (1947)." *Cinema Journal* 20:2 (2001): 57–77.

Macdonald, Kevin. *Emeric Pressburger: The Life and Death of a Screenwriter.* London: Faber, 1994.

Powell, Michael. *A Life in Movies: An Autobiography.* 1986. London: Faber, 2000.

Radcliffe, Ann. *The Mysteries of Udolpho.* 1794. Oxford and New York: Oxford University Press, 1966.

Ruotolo, Christine, et al. *The Gothic: Materials for Study.* Home page on-line. <http://www.engl.virginia.edu/~enec98/Group/title.html>; Internet; accessed 30 July 1998.

Sedgwick, Eve Kosofsky. "The Character in the Veil: Imagery on the Surface in the Gothic Novel." *PMLA* 96:2 (1981): 255–70.

Sennet, Robert S. *Setting the Scene: The Great Hollywood Art Directors.* New York: Abrams, 1994.

Trusted, Marjorie. *Spanish Sculpture: Catalogue of the Post-Medieval Spanish Sculpture in Wood, Terracotta, Alabaster, Marble, Stone, Lead and Jet in the Victoria and Albert Museum.* London: Victoria and Albert Museum, 1996.

Wilde, Oscar. "The Decay of Lying: An Observation." In *The Works of Oscar Wilde.* London: Collins, 1931.

PART V

When the Other Is the Self:
Deconstructing the Categories

15

Defanging Dracula: The Disappearing Other in Coppola's *Bram Stoker's Dracula*

ERIK MARSHALL

In Bram Stoker's novel, *Dracula*, the eponymous vampire is the overdetermined figure of cultural, ethnic and racial otherness. The threat that he brings to modern England represents not only a fear of the non–English invader, but also an anxiety over technological and cultural relapse. Since Dracula comes from a premodern area, bringing with him pre-rational, religious and supernatural powers, he threatens the rule of science, progress and order. Because of the myriad dangers associated with Dracula in the novel, he must be destroyed. Francis Ford Coppola's post-modern cinematic version of the novel, *Bram Stoker's Dracula*,[1] revises the figure of Dracula; Coppola's Dracula is a smitten lover, searching for his lost, eternal love. In his revision, Coppola calls into question the very notion of progress, creating a completely supernatural world in which many of the characters in addition to Dracula are supernatural, including a reincarnated Mina and a Van Helsing who is as superstitious as scientific, and who, like Dracula, seems to be immortal. Coppola's film replicates the novel in the minutest visual details, but drastically transforms the narrative so that Dracula no longer represents the invading Other, but rather a more universal and sympathetic character attempting to reunite with his reincarnated wife. Despite the stated intentions of the film's screenwriter to remain faithful to the novel, the film alters the portrayal not only of Dracula, but also of the women, Van Helsing and Renfield, to transform the most basic thematic elements of the novel.[2] Coppola's adherence to the smallest details, his addition of technologies not mentioned in the novel, and his self-reflexive gestures make for more of a postmodern pastiche of narrative elements than a replication or straight adaptation, which ultimately serves to question the nature of the modern anxieties that *Dracula* confronts, to interrogate the figure of Dracula as the primitive, Eastern, sexually disruptive Other that invades the otherwise conservative and orderly West, and to propose a less anxious postmodern model.

Before discussing the film's divergence from the novel, a discussion of the novel and some of the ways in which Stoker's Dracula as Other emblemizes various social anxieties is necessary. Stoker's novel is "concerned with modernity's strengths and weaknesses," its treatment of Dracula reinforcing the ideals of technological modernity as represented by Enlightenment thinking.[3] In late-nineteenth-century Britain, increasing interest in science and technology as guarantors of societal advance led to an environment where more traditional beliefs were left behind, in favor of empirical methods of discovery, increasing reliance on machinery and industrialization, and trust in scientific currents such as Darwinism. Stoker wrote *Dracula* just prior to the rise of literary modernism, which emerged as a way of addressing some of the contradictions within modernity, while ultimately endorsing its goal of progress, and with it, a break with history. While *Dracula* may not fit perfectly into the modernist movement, the novel certainly shares some of its goals, and grapples with issues arising from Enlightenment thought and the conditions of modernity. Stoker's inclusion of modern technologies, such as typewriters, phonographs and trains, signals not only the popular belief in the late nineteenth century that "industrial technology and the power of science appeared to offer a thoroughgoing conquest of nature," but also the fear of relapse to a more primitive state.[4] The figure of Dracula represents the underside of this technological advance, the fear that an as yet unknown, primitive force of nature will be able to enter England (and the West, by extension), and conquer it, causing technological relapse. For example, when Dracula arrives on shore, a wolf escapes from the zoo, signaling a disruption of the order represented by the very institution that seeks to achieve the modern ideal of science, the imposition of order over more chaotic nature.[5] The figure of Dracula acts as a threat to the order established by the practices and ideals of modernity; his ultimate defeat at the end of the novel reinforces and restores these practices and ideals.

Many scholars have noted that Dracula represents a fear of the unknown, or of many unknowns, including that of the social or racial Other. His origin in the East reflects fears of primitive cultures who might enter England and corrupt the social order. His aristocratic pedigree and his immortality make him Other not only in nationality, but also in class and generation. This overdetermined Other comes to represent many of the fears of nineteenth-century England, embodying the multi-faceted anxiety of a nation that is beginning to lose its imperial hold. Much writing about the novel focuses on how the Other, as represented by Dracula, stands in for many of the anxieties of an emerging modern age, including reverse colonization, changing gender roles, and the fear of atavism stemming in part from growing technology.

Dracula's emergence from an obscure, technologically and culturally unadvanced area indicates anxieties in late-nineteenth-century England about reverse colonization and racial purity. According to Stephen Arata, Dracula's penetration into England signals cultural and racial decline. He posits that to historicize Dracula reveals "how the perception [of Britain's non-dominance in the world] is transformed into narrative, into stories which the culture tells itself not only to articulate and account for its troubles, but also to defend against and even to assuage the anxiety attendant upon cultural decay."[6] The appearance and popularity of vampires in the popular culture of the time signals a fear of the Other, of the decay of empire and of reverse colonization. "Vampires are generated by racial enervation and the decline of empire, not vice versa" (88). Arata also establishes that Dracula de-racinates by creating a homogenous group of undead, unfettered by race, class, sexuality, or nationalism, so Dracula's conquerors must reverse this process. Thus, they re-racinate Lucy through blood transfusions, in a specific order: Holmwood, the aristocrat is first choice; then Seward, not an aristocrat, but at least English; followed by Van Helsing, the continental European; and finally, Quincy, the American (90). This order demonstrates anxieties in England about racial purity, illustrating the dominance of concerns about genetics and bloodlines that accompany the rise of Darwinism. In the end, though, little Quincy Harker, whose "bundle of names links all [of Dracula's combatants] together," represents an English appropriation of all foreigners (98), thus stabilizing England's imperial status.

According to David Glover, this preoccupation with relapse signifies modernity's relationship to the past: "In Stoker's work the twin poles of past and present make their appearance through a strangely paradoxical and crucially modern trope, that of the spectator forced to confront a horror whose very existence seems to compromise any possibility of securing the line between the modern and the premodern" (58). As trust in science grows, traditions of the past are left behind as archaic and unneeded, hence Jonathan's observation that the farther East he goes, the less reliable the trains are. Time is different in the uncivilized, non–Western world, where many unknown, forgotten evils dwell. The East represents the past, the premodern, which the West attempts to leave behind through science, as the trains become more and more punctual. And Dracula's emergence in the West threatens this technological hegemony and threatens an effacement of the line between modern and premodern.

In his only direct confrontation with the vampire hunters, Dracula shouts at them: "Your girls that you all love are mine already."[7] The infiltration of the racial and cultural Other into England, then, also poses a threat to established gender roles. Dracula's attentions transform the English women he encounters into sexually desiring creatures. Before transformation, Lucy is a model of a new form of feminism: "Why can't they let a girl marry three men, or as many as want her, and save all this trouble?" she asks. Despite being coquettish and unorthodox, she remains "pure" until her transformation at the fangs of Dracula. At this point she becomes sexually voracious and openly desiring, accepting the blood of four men (each transfusion standing for a ritual of marriage[8]) and wanting more. On the other hand, Mina's references to the New Woman, and her use of modern modes of information technology acknowledge the changing role of women in the home and workplace, without challenging traditional male dominance. She is independent and intelligent, but also fiercely loyal to Jonathan and to the institution of marriage. Mina represents the progressive woman who will work outside of the home, yet keep her place within the traditional patriarchal structure, and it is she who must be saved in the end, lest she become highly sexualized, like Lucy. Despite these characterizations, both women become Dracula's victims, and come under the care of the men in the novel, reinforcing a view of women as hopelessly passive and helpless, and needful of the protection of men.

Thus *Dracula* addresses issues of modernity, such as the increasing faith in science, the mechanization of industry, the advancement of capitalism, and the appearance of early feminism. The self-reflexive techniques of the film, on the other hand, challenge the very concerns underpinning the motivations that inform the original, while questioning the entire act of adaptation and representation in which it participates. Coppola's treatment of the novel revises Dracula's status as Other; this transformation, in turn, distorts or denies many of the anxieties outlined above. In practicing overtly self-reflexive techniques, and paying attention to the minutest detail while ignoring broader thematic concerns, *Bram Stoker's Dracula* becomes an adaptation with an ambivalent relation to its original, resulting in a radically different portrayal of Dracula and the women of the novel, as well as most of the characters. These techniques serve as a postmodern critique of the novel's structure and historical context and attenuate Dracula's status as racial Other and sexual threat.

While the novel represents an endorsement of Enlightenment ideals prevalent in the later stages of modernity, the film takes a decidedly postmodern stance, questioning these ideals. Whether postmodernism represents a break with cultural modernism, or extends its project in different ways, it certainly creates a discourse that contests and complicates the ideals of modernity. "Postmodernism is a critique of scientific rationality; of Enlightenment principles of emancipation; of industrialization, colonization, and authority of all types; and it is a rethinking of the relationship between signifier and signified, texts and contexts, essences and identities."[9] The self-reflexivity of postmodernism differs from that of modernism, lending it a critical stance towards itself and its referent. As Linda Hutcheon observes: "The more complex and more overt discursive contextualizing of postmodernism goes one step beyond this [modernism's] auto-representation and its demystifying intent, for it is fundamentally critical in its ironic relation to the past and the *present*."[10] It is this critically ironic stance that allows Coppola to remain faithful to the details of the novel while questioning its ideological basis. The film, then, participates in at least one of the functions David Harvey outlines for postmodernism: "Eschewing the idea of progress, postmodernism abandons all sense of historical continuity and memory, while simultaneously developing an incredible ability to plunder history and absorb whatever it finds there as some aspect of the present."[11]

While Coppola is painstakingly meticulous about replicating both the general atmosphere and details of the novel, he drastically changes narrative elements. Later, I will point to some of the more obvious narrative inconsistencies, not to disparage the film, but to attempt to discover how the particular narrative devices and themes prevalent in Stoker's work, particularly in his configuration of the overdetermined Other as threat, resist adaptation a century later.[12] Whatever its failings as a faithful narrative adaptation, the film succeeds in visually depicting many of the novel's details. According to Lyndon Joslin, Coppola portrays some of the original novel's details and events cinematically for the first time. For example, in Coppola's film: Dracula can indeed come out in the daylight; horses are four-abreast on Dracula's carriage; Lucy drops the child in the tomb; Quincy dies, or, more remarkably, Quincy appears in the film as a Texan. Some other details that Coppola includes and transforms: the blue flames appear on Jonathan's journey but in the end turn into "New-Age, feminist, witchcraft–Gaia-goddess-nonsense, apparently involving Mina's past-life karma," and Dracula is stabbed by Quincy's Bowie knife, and by Jonathan's kukri, although he is not killed (110). Joslin also points out that Renfield (played by Tom Waits) is explained as preceding Jonathan (Keanu Reeves) to Transylvania as a solicitor; his existence, thus, becomes less mysterious than in the novel. However, as no mention is made of Dracula's need for an invitation, Renfield's presence is superfluous. This transformation of Renfield accompanies other changes in character, all of which revise Dracula's status as the threatening Other.

Coppola's fidelity to detail in *Bram Stoker's Dracula*, then, amounts to an aestheticization of the Gothic elements of the novel, relegating them to atmospherics, superficial postmodern references to the novel, rather than signs of a faithful thematic or narrative adaptation. His unprecedented attention to the small details of the novel masks the complete effacement of the elements that make the novel frighteningly Gothic in the first place. Coppola creates a pastiche of surface details to lend referential authority to his work but, in a major revision of Stoker's text, eliminates any reference to Dracula as cultural Other. Eve Kosofsky Sedgwick lists many of the generic conventions typical of the Gothic novel; many of these conventions are present in *Dracula* and appropriated by Coppola:

> You know something about the novel's form: it is likely to be discontinuous and involuted, perhaps incorporating tales within tales, changes in narrators, and such framing devices as found manuscripts or interpolated histories. You also know that, whether with more or less relevance to the main plot, certain characteristic preoccupations will be aired. These include the priesthood and monastic institutions; sleeplike and deathlike states; subterranean spaces and live burial; doubles; the discovery of obscured family; affinities between narrative and pictorial art; possibilities of incest; unnatural echoes or silences, unintelligible writings, and the unspeakable; garrulous retainers; the poisonous effects of guilt and shame; nocturnal landscapes and dreams; apparitions from the past; Faust- and Wandering Jew-like figures; civil insurrections and fires; the charnal house and the madhouse.[13]

Coppola incorporates many of these elements, originally found in the Stoker text; he uses elaborate sets and costumes, combined with primitive ("naïve," he calls them) camera tricks to evoke an atmosphere of decadence and despair. Slow-lap dissolves suggest Dracula's long existence, while fast-motion simulates his animal-like quickness. However, Coppola's transformation of the narrative weakens the frightening power of the conventional Gothic. Even the scene in which Jonathan is attacked by Dracula's wives is more erotic and stylized than frightening. When Dracula attacks Lucy, the endeavor seems nearly consensual, and the scene revolves not around the attack, but around Dracula seeing Mina. When Dracula finally has the chance to attack Mina, she becomes a willing participant, forcing him to comply, making this a love scene rather than a rape. In these ways, the Gothic elements of the novel become less mysterious than spectacular, serving as beautiful backdrops to an engaging narrative.

Kenneth Jurkiewicz claims that Coppola's failure to adapt Stoker's novel is due to his misunderstanding of the epistolary structure of the novel. Yet Coppola understands this structure all too well, accounting for some of the licenses Coppola takes with the plot. Stoker calls attention to the mediation of the narrative by different points of view, a characteristic inherent to the epistolary novel; in the note at the end, Jonathan remarks:

> We were struck with the fact, that in all the mass of material of which the record is composed, there is hardly one authentic document. Nothing but a mass of typewriting, except the later notebooks of Mina and Seward and myself, and Van Helsing's memorandum. We could hardly ask any one, even did we wish to, to accept these as proofs of so wild a story [Chapter 27, Note].

The epistolary structure, then, leaves convenient holes for the postmodernist to fill, as letters, journal entries, newspaper clippings, and other documents could, hypothetically, be found after the fact, or lost forever. To be sure, the love story between Mina and Dracula does not occur in the novel; it is not even hinted at, except maybe (and this is a stretch) when Mina expresses sympathy for Dracula. Since Mina has gathered and typed most of the material, she is the closest we have to an editor; it would certainly be possible for her to lose, forget or suppress something. In the film version, after Mina writes a letter to Dracula, telling him that she is leaving for Budapest to marry Jonathan, she drops a few leaves of paper into the ocean, suggesting that part of this story (Mina's journal entries?) is lost forever.[14] This visual cue signals the inherent absence of objectivity, the lack created by the epistolary structure, that permits Coppola to fill in the spaces between the letters and journals to create an alternate reading of the novel.

This manipulation of the epistolary structure allows Coppola to question the nature of narrative reliability and to change the characterization of many of the characters in the film, to reduce the difference between the England he depicts and the Dracula who enters it. Collections of correspondence and personal recollections act rhetorically as direct channels into the thoughts and feelings of the characters, and provide multiple viewpoints of the same events, but their arrangement proceeds from editorial choice — in this case, Mina's. Coppola tries to replicate the epistolary structure through voice-over narration, visual depictions of hands writing in journals, newspapers, phonographs, typewriters, and other devices, but the very nature of film precludes this type of interpretation to an extent, as the viewer sees a literal representation of events. As opposed to merely another possibility within the narrative, the literal representation that the film provides acts as a possible reconstruction of the "actual" events that each character in the novel interprets for him or herself, the final document acting as multiple interpretations of an unreachable real event, edited, or censored by Mina herself. In the novel, Jonathan himself is not sure if what he experienced in Transylvania "was real or the dreaming of a madman" (Chapter 9). In the film, he tells Van Helsing that he did not know whether to believe his own eyes. Considering the possibility of an unreliable narrator in the novel, the portrayal of Dracula's "attacks" on Mina at Seward's asylum as a mutual endeavor does not seem absolutely impossible.

Coppola's insertion of contemporary technologies complicates the novel's fear of relapse, and problematizes the film's relation to history. Replacing, or at least problematizing, the modern idea of a teleological history, postmodern thought posits a multiplicity of histories, foregrounding the interests of the historiographer in the telling of history. Whereas Victorian England may have been anxious about relapse from technological advance, the postmodern world eschews the idea of advance altogether, borrowing from the past, reappropriating it while questioning it, re-using old themes, tropes and stories in order to cast new light on them and create new relationships between them. Technological (or any other) innovation is not an advance so much as a new set of relations. Coppola attempts to use and reflect technologies available in the late-nineteenth century, using the past to create a new story. In doing so, he calls attention to historical considerations in the retelling of *Dracula*, and adds accurate historical details (like the cinematograph) that are absent from the novel, positing a revisionist take on the novel and on late nineteenth-century England. Dracula's arrival in England becomes less of a disruption with Coppola's questioning of the relations set forth by new technologies, and disavowal of the idea of progress. Although he looks and acts foreign, Coppola's Dracula is able to mingle in public and function perfectly well in English society.

While Stoker's novel uses fear to deal with the subject of gender roles and female sexuality, the film changes the situation by reinterpreting the gender configurations. Coppola's portrayal of the women in the novel eliminates their status as passive victims, thus changing their relation to Dracula, and his threat as Other. Lucy is lewd, and openly sexual, thus annulling the difference in the novel between the live Lucy and the vampire Lucy. James Hart justifies this by stating that Lucy is punished in the end for the sexual wantonness she displays in life (Jurkiewicz 169–170). In the novel, she does represent a certain type of liberated sexuality, or at least a liberal view of gender roles, but she does not become completely lustful until Dracula transforms her, thus marking Dracula as the transformative agent. This change in her character from novel to film erases her vampiric change, and, consequently, Dracula's role "as sexual liberator and thus transgressive threat to the late Victorian social order" (Jurkiewicz 169–170). This attenuates Dracula's status as Other, as he no longer effects a negative transformation in Lucy; her involvement with Dracula "is as much to fill her sexual appetite as it is for the demon's sanguine nourishment" (Corbin and Campbell). Coppola's portrayal of Lucy, then, gives her a bit more agency than she has in the novel, making her less a passive victim than a "...willing recruit, a breathless follower, a wanton follower," as Coppola's Van Helsing describes her. Her willingness makes her complicit, and since Dracula's original threat is partially sexual, this change in Lucy effects a reduction of Dracula's danger.

Further diminishing the sexual danger Dracula poses, Coppola investigates current assumptions about sexuality and sexual orientation in Victorian England. For example, in three distinct points in the film, Coppola depicts two or more women involved in a potentially erotic situation. The first occurs when Dracula's "wives" attack Jonathan. At one point, they are kissing him, and two of them turn and start to kiss each other. The second occurs when Lucy and Mina are caught in the rain. Lucy is telling Mina about her love for Arthur, when it begins to rain. An eyeline match shows Dracula's face superimposed on the sky, and then it starts to pour. Mina and Lucy run playfully through the labyrinthine bushes, and then, in a quick shot, they begin what seems to be the beginning of a rather passionate kiss. Since this scene occurs before Lucy's transformation, vampirism is not a plausible reason for this implicit lesbianism. The third instance appears in the cinematograph, where the screen behind Mina and Dracula shows a turn-of-the-century film depicting a rather delighted man with two women in his lap, until, through editing, they transform into his wife (presumably), and, disenchanted, he pushes her away. These instances suggest alternatives to traditional monogamous heterosexual coupling in a Victorian setting, and so attempt to historicize *Dracula*, calling into question twentieth-century notions about the nature of sexual relations in late Victorian England, and, thus, our relation to it. This reconfiguration of gender roles and sexual activity lessens the potential impact an invader such as Dracula might have on England's social order, as the women are not steadfastly monogamous or strictly heterosexual, as are Stoker's women.

Coppola's introduction of the supernatural love story between Mina and Dracula, completely absent from the novel, further revises the characterization of Mina, and gives reason for distrust of her narrative. The film posits Mina as Dracula's reincarnated lover, whose suicide Dracula had vowed to avenge four centuries earlier. In Transylvania, when Dracula sees Jonathan's photograph of Mina, he looks at Jonathan and asks: "Do you believe in destiny? That even the powers of time can be altered for a single purpose? The luckiest man on Earth is the one who finds true love." Even the promotional materials for the movie use the tagline "Love Never Dies." In the film, Mina is no longer faithful to Jonathan, as she is destined to love Dracula. Her transformation may be necessary to accommodate the imperatives of the film love story, but it undermines the novel's representation of her as independent, the model of a new type of woman. In fact, her sincerity and honesty are open to question, as she is in love with Dracula, but marries Jonathan anyway. This characterization of Mina suggests that the motivation on the part of the English protagonists for saving her is no longer to destroy evil, or to exterminate the Other, as in the novel, but simple sexual jealousy and revenge. In other words, Dracula no longer presents a threat to all women, or to the perceived social order of England, but only to one woman, and thus, indirectly, to the man who claims her. One suspects that, if successful, Dracula might cease to terrorize England and settle down with Mina. The actions of the vampire hunters, then, do not save all of England from Dracula's menace, but only Jonathan's bride. The social and cultural implications of Stoker's novel are diminished as the narrative is reduced to that of a simple love triangle.

In addition to the obvious perversion of the narrative with the love story between Dracula and Mina, Coppola suggests that Van Helsing (Anthony Hopkins) is a madman awaiting "all [his] life" to destroy Dracula. In the "Prologue," Hopkins plays Chesare, a priest in Dracula's castle. Coppola implies here that in addition to Mina, Van Helsing is reincarnated to chase Dracula down and kill him (perhaps in the name of the Church, which Dracula renounces in the Prologue?). Or perhaps he is not reincarnated, but eternal, like Dracula. Evidence for Van Helsing's continuity from ancient times to modern occurs when he begins to suspect the nature of Lucy's illness. He looks through a book entitled "The

Vampyre," reading aloud in first person what seem to be Dracula's words: "I drank their blood…" then he looks up and whispers, "the blood is the life," as if remembering the Prologue scene where Dracula screams the same words as he impales a cross with his sword. As he reads he gets more excited, and a ferocious wind begins to blow through his room (Dracula has previously summoned winds to display his anger at Mina's leaving for Budapest to marry Jonathan), and he exclaims, "Dracula! I have waited all my life!" This scene suggests Van Helsing's presence in the Prologue scene in which Dracula renounces God, a scene that features a voice-over narration by Anthony Hopkins. This is corroborated by Coppola's statement (in an HBO special on the making of *Bram Stoker's Dracula*) that he believes Van Helsing to be as evil as Dracula (Joslin 109). Indeed, when Van Helsing first meets Mina in this film, he grabs her and begins waltzing with her, mirroring the preceding scene, in which Mina and Dracula dance through a large candlelit room. She is as startled by his behavior as by his enigmatic words: "There are darknesses in life, and there are lights. You are one of the lights, dear Mina. The light of all lights." Van Helsing's apparent affinity with Dracula transforms the battle from that of science versus religion, into two equally alien powers vying for power, and dissipates the fearful force that is, in the novel, centered upon the figure of Dracula.

So why the love story? Why the reincarnation? David Harvey explains that modernism's project is to find a way to express the eternal in art. Postmodernism, however, rejects totalizing notions such as the eternal, creating a world of relations, of fragments. As postmodernism concerns itself with fragmented, or multiply projected identities, the presentation of an identity that transcends not only daily circumstance, but death itself, and spans generations, provides an optimistic, nostalgic model for a unified self. Providing a transcendent, centered ego allows an escapist alternative to relieve late-twentieth-century anxieties about decentered, fragmented identities. While providing this alternative to mortality, Coppola simultaneously deconstructs the notion of an absolute cultural Other, presenting characters who enter into a set of relations based as much on personal desire as on any sense of cultural alienation. The configuration of Van Helsing, thus, challenges the notion of coherent national identities as points from which to establish otherness, as he comes from the same time and place as Dracula.

The minimalization of Dracula's otherness in the film also reduces the fear of reverse colonization that plagues Stoker's novel. Dracula's arrival in England is less a danger for England than a fulfillment of "destiny," as Dracula himself indicates in his castle during Jonathan's visit. In the novel,

Dracula preys on Mina as a direct action against those who try to destroy him; there is no courting, nor mutuality, in the act. Rather than a frightening stranger intent on transforming all of England into a race of vampires, Coppola's Dracula seems more a smitten lover, fulfilling a destiny over which he has no control. In the novel, Dracula's status as Other alienates him, dooming him to isolation, and making him an undesirable, frightening character. In the film, Dracula's mission in London is to find his soul mate, a way out of the lonely existence he has in the novel. This search for love humanizes him in the film; his threat becomes far less tenable. Mina's motivation for killing him in the film, then, comes not from self-preservation or fear, but sympathy. Her betrothal to Jonathan becomes the only reason she does not want to live with Dracula, rather than hatred for what he represents. In this way, Coppola gives his female characters more agency without completely ignoring the Victorian issue of ownership of women.

Coppola's use of self-reflexive techniques throughout this film calls attention, as does his self-conscious title, to the fact that this film is an adaptation. The very appearance of a cinematograph in the film recalls the materiality of this adaptation. Within the cinematograph scene, which acts as the setting for Dracula and Mina's "first date," Coppola uses the image from the film's Prologue of Dracula on the battlefield. As Dracula almost bites Mina, the battle plays in the background, apparently as a shadow-puppet play. In any case, the image is identical to that of the Prologue, which, of course, is an addition to the novel. This self-reflexive gesture brings up the question of fidelity of adaptation, of cross-media translation, in short, the question of this film's relation to its source. Coppola's text, thus, goes beyond the self-reflexivity of modernism, which serves principally to undermine the transparency of representation. The self-reflexive aspects of the film question the film's relation to the past, forcing the viewer to question whether the fears of late nineteenth-century England translate into the fin-de-millenium, and whether *Dracula* still serves as an empty referent to be filled by whatever fears are prevalent at a given time. Coppola's film, then, is a postmodern critique of the modern/premodern dialectic (Corbin and Campbell). The narrative of reincarnated lovers undermines the modernist notion of the triumph of science, and although Van Helsing is a scientist, when he discovers Dracula's identity, he becomes a raving lunatic, abandoning science for superstition.

The infinite play of texts brought about by postmodern practices makes this type of reading possible. When talking of historiographic metafiction, the genre she thinks most represents postmodernism, Linda

Hutcheon states that it "asks both epistemological and ontological questions. How do we know the past (or the present)? What is the ontological status of the past? Of its documents? Of our narratives?" (50). Postmodern film also asks these questions, as it represents itself attempting to represent the past. The question is, then, not only of the past, but of our relationship to the past. Read in this way, Francis Ford Coppola's *Bram Stoker's Dracula* becomes a meditation on how we can enter into a relation with the literature of the past, to render it meaningful while letting it speak for itself. In doing so, the film eliminates the possibility that Dracula represents an invading Other threatening the social order, and makes the viewer ask: what precisely is still frightening about Dracula?

Notes

1. *Bram Stoker's Dracula*. Dir. Francis Ford Coppola, Prod. American Zoetrope, Dist. Columbia Pictures, 1992.
2. Francis Ford Coppola and James V. Hart. *Bram Stoker's Dracula: The Film and the Legend* (New York: Newmarket Press, 1992), 6.
3. David Glover, *Vampires, Mummies and Liberals: Bram Stoker and the Politics of Popular Fiction* (Durham: Duke University Press, 1996), 60.
4. Jonathan Bignell, "A Taste of the Gothic: Film and Television Versions of *Dracula*," in *The Classic Novel from Page to Screen*, eds. Rovert Giddings and Erica Sheen (Manchester and New York: Manchester University Press, 2000), 115.
5. Carol Corbin and Robert A. Campbell, "Postmodern Iconography and Perspective in Coppola's *Bram Stoker's Dracula*," *Journal of Popular Film and Television* 27.2 (1999): 40–48.
6. Stephen D. Arata, "The Occidental Tourist: *Dracula* and the Anxiety of Reverse Colonization," in *The Critical Response to Bram Stoker*, ed. Carol A. Senf (Westport, CT: Greenwood Press, 1993).
7. Bram Stoker, *Dracula*. 1897. Project Gutenberg Edition, <*www.gutenberg.net*>, Chapter 5. Citations to *Dracula* in this text come from the Project Gutenberg e-text, that has no page numbers. Therefore, I will mark each citation with the Chapter number, which should be consistent throughout editions.
8. Nina Auerbach, *Our Vampires, Ourselves* (Chicago: University of Chicago Press, 1995), 78–81.
9. Corbin and Campbell, 41, paraphrasing David Harvey, *The Condition of Postmodernity: An Enquiry into the Origins of Cultural Change* (Cambridge, Mass.: Blackwell, 1990).
10. Linda Hutcheon, *A Poetics of Postmodernism: History, Theory, Fiction* (New York: Routledge, 1988), 41.
11. David Harvey, *The Condition of Postmodernity: An Enquiry into the Origins of Cultural Change* (Cambridge, MA: Blackwell, 1990), 54.
12. The aim of this paper is not to evaluate the film's cinematographic aspects, nor to pass judgement based on whether or to what extent it is faithful to the original. Such debates rarely produce useful insight into film adaptation, and often ignore the necessary inconsistencies between the media, each of which has its particular strengths.

(For an insightful discussion of the pitfalls of evaluating film adaptations using fidelity as the main criterion, see Robert Stam, "Beyond Fidelity: The Dialogics of Adaptation," in *Film Adaptation*, ed. James Naremore (Rutgers University Press, 2000), 54–76.

13. Eve Kosofsky Sedgwick, *The Coherence of Gothic Conventions* (New York: Methuen, 1986), 9–10.

14. This argument is not entirely satisfactory, of course, as the film version not only adds to, but explicitly contradicts the novel, but the suggestion is certainly there, in the film.

Works Cited

Arata, Stephen D. "The Occidental Tourist: *Dracula* and the Anxiety of Reverse Colonization." In *The Critical Response to Bram Stoker*. Edited by Carol A. Senf. Westport, CT: Greenwood Press, 1993.

Auerbach, Nina. *Our Vampires, Ourselves*. Chicago: University of Chicago Press, 1995.

Bignell, Jonathan. "A Taste of the Gothic: Film and Television Versions of *Dracula*." In *The Classic Novel from Page to Screen*. Edited by Rovert Giddings and Erica Sheen. Manchester and New York: Manchester University Press, 2000.

Bram Stoker's Dracula. Dir. Francis Ford Coppola. Perfs. Gary Oldman, Anthony Hopkins, Keanu Reeves, Winona Ryder, Sadie Frost, Tom Waits. American Zoetrope. Laserdisc. Criterion, 1992.

Coppola, Francis Ford and James V. Hart. *Bram Stoker's Dracula: The Film and the Legend*. New York: Newmarket Press. 1992.

Corbin, Carol, and Robert A. Campbell. "Postmodern Iconography and Perspective in Coppola's *Bram Stoker's Dracula*." *Journal of Popular Film and Television* 27.2 (1999): 40–48.

Glover, David. *Vampires, Mummies and Liberals: Bram Stoker and the Politics of Popular Fiction*. Durham: Duke University Press, 1996.

Harvey, David. *The Condition of Postmodernity: An Enquiry into the Origins of Cultural Change*. Cambridge, MA: Blackwell, 1990.

Hutcheon, Linda. *A Poetics of Postmodernism: History, Theory, Fiction*. New York: Routledge, 1988.

Joslyn, Lyndon W. *Count Dracula Goes to the Movies: Stoker's Novel Adapted, 1922–1995*. Jefferson, NC: McFarland and Company, Inc., 1999.

Jurkiewicz, Kenneth. "Francis Coppola's Secret Gardens: *Bram Stoker's Dracula* and the Auteur as Decadent Visionary." In *Visions of the Fantastic: Selected Essays from the Fifteenth International Conference on the Fantastic in the Arts*. Edited by Allienne R. Becker. Westport, CT: Greenwood Press, 1996.

Sedgwick, Eve Kosofsky. *The Coherence of Gothic Conventions*. New York: Methuen, 1986.

Stam, Robert. "Beyond Fidelity: The Dialogics of Adaptation." In *Film Adaptation*. Edited by James Naremore. Rutgers University Press, 2000.

Stoker, Bram. *Dracula*. 1897. Project Gutenberg Edition.<www.gutenberg.net.>

List of Contributors

Ruth Bienstock Anolik received her Ph.D. from Bryn Mawr College and teaches at Villanova University. Most of her work focuses on the Gothic, with a special interest in the interplay between Gothic literature and social and cultural structures. Her publications include: "Appropriating the Golem, Possessing the Dybbuk: Female Retellings of Jewish Folktales" in *Modern Language Studies;* "Horrors of Possession: The Gothic Struggle with the Law" in *Legal Studies Forum*; and "Reviving the Golem: Cultural Negotiations in Ozick's *The Puttermesser Papers* and Piercy's *He, She, and It*" in *Studies in American Jewish Literature.* She is currently at work on a book on the concept of possession in the Gothic mode.

Renée L. Bergland teaches American literature and culture at Simmons College in Boston. She is the author of *The National Uncanny: Indian Ghosts and American Subjects* (Hanover: University Press of New England, 2000).

Joseph Bodziock is an associate professor of English at Clarion University of Pennsylvania.

Gavin Budge has been a lecturer in English literature at the University of Central England in Birmingham since 1995. He has recently published the anthology *Aesthetics and Religion in Nineteenth-Century Britain* (Bristol: Thoemmes Press, 2003) and an article, "Realism and Typology in Charlotte M. Yonge's *The Heir of Redclyffe*," in *Victorian Literature and Culture* (vol. 31, no. 1, spring 2003). He is currently working on a book about Romanticism and nineteenth-century medicine.

Stephanie Burley has a master's degree in women's studies from Ohio State University. Her Ph.D. in English literature is from the University of Maryland; her dissertation is a study of race and popular romance.She is the author of "Shadows and Silhouettes: The Racial Politics of Category Romance" in *Paradoxa: Studies in World Literary Genres* (2000) and is an associate editor of Broadview Press's 2001 edition of Helen Maria Williams's *Letters Written in France.*

Soledad Caballero is an assistant professor of English at Allegheny College in Meadville, Pennsylvania. Her interests include British Romanticism and travel writing. She is currently working on a project on British women's travel writing about the Americas.

Eugenia DeLamotte is an associate professor of English at Arizona State University. Her publications on the Gothic include *Perils of the Night: A Feminist Study of Nineteenth-Century Gothic* (Oxford, 1990) and "'Collusions of the Mystery': Ideology and the Gothic in *Hagar's Daughter,*" forthcoming in *Gothic Studies,* 2005. Her other publications include *Gates of Freedom: Voltairine de Cleyre and the Revolution of the Mind,* forthcoming from the University of Michigan Press, 2004; *Places of Silence, Journeys of Freedom: The Fiction of Paule Marshall* (University of Pennsylvania Press, 1998); and *Women Imagine Change: An Anthology of Women's Resistance, 600 B.C.E. to Present* (Routledge, 1997, co-edited with Natania Meeker and Jean O'Barr).

Katherine Henry received her Ph.D. from Rutgers University and is an assistant professor of English at Temple University, Philadelphia, specializing in nineteenth-century American literature. She has published on Angelina Grimké, and is currently completing *Self-Protection, Self-Exposure: Romantic Eloquence and the Nineteenth Century Rhetoric of Reform,* a study of the rhetoric of antislavery and women's rights, examining the conflicts involved in conceiving citizenship as a zone of protection.

Douglas L. Howard is currently the Writing Center Coordinator and an assistant professor of English at Suffolk County Community College. His publications include articles in *The Chronicle of Higher Education, PopPolitics,* and *Literature and Theology* and *This Thing of Ours: Investigating the Sopranos* (Columbia University Press, 2002).

Karen Kingsbury earned her Ph.D. in comparative literature from Columbia University. She teaches a variety of English language and literature courses in the department of foreign languages and literature at Tunghai University (Taiwan), where she is now an associate professor. She has published articles on Eileen Chang and on plagiarism issues among

Chinese students. Her current projects include a translated collection of Eileen Chang's stories and essays, and studies of Gothicism in both Chinese and English fiction.

Daphne Lamothe, assistant professor in the Afro-American Studies Department at Smith College, is currently at work on a critical study of the ethnographic imagination in African American literature published between 1900 and 1940, titled *The Ethnographic Imagination in the New Negro Renaissance.* She is the author of essays on Black Modernism, Diasporic exchange and memory and myth.

Erik Marshall is currently a Ph.D. candidate at Wayne State University. His interests include film and new media studies, with an emphasis on documentary film and digital culture.

Steven Jay Schneider is a Ph.D. candidate in philosophy at Harvard University, and in cinema studies at New York University's Tisch School of the Arts. He is co-editor of *Underground U.S.A.: Filmmaking Beyond the Hollywood Canon* (Wallflower Press), editor of *Psychoanalysis and the Horror Film: Freud's Worst Nightmares* (Cambridge University Press) and *Fear Without Frontiers: Horror Cinema Across the Globe* (FAB Press), and author of *Designing Fear: An Aesthetics of Cinematic Horror* (Routledge).

John Stone is a Ph.D. candidate at the University of Barcelona, where he also lectures, principally on translation. He has published on a number of topics in seventeenth- and eighteenth-century English literature, as well as interviews with contemporary Canadian authors, an introductory English studies textbook (as co-author), and a Catalan edition of Samuel Johnson's *Preface to Shakespeare* (as editor and co-translator). His dissertation approaches a number of Johnson's writings on linguistics and criticism from a law-and-literature perspective.

Sherry R. Truffin completed her doctorate in English at Loyola University Chicago with a dissertation entitled *Schoolhouse Gothic: Haunted Hallways and Predatory Pedagogues in Late Twentieth-Century American Literature and Scholarship* and recently published an essay exploring Gothic themes in James Baldwin's *Go Tell It on the Mountain.* She currently teaches English at Tiffin University in Northwest Ohio.

Index